Forensic Economics

Frank D. Tinari
Editor

Forensic Economics

Assessing Personal Damages in Civil Litigation

Editor
Frank D. Tinari
Florham Park, New Jersey, USA

ISBN 978-1-137-57109-0   ISBN 978-1-137-56392-7   (eBook)
DOI 10.1057/978-1-137-56392-7

Library of Congress Control Number: 2016958209

Cover image © Image Source / Getty Images

Printed on acid-free paper

This Palgrave Macmillan imprint is published by Springer Nature
The registered company is Nature America Inc. New York
The registered company address is 1 New York Plaza, New York, NY 10004, U.S.A

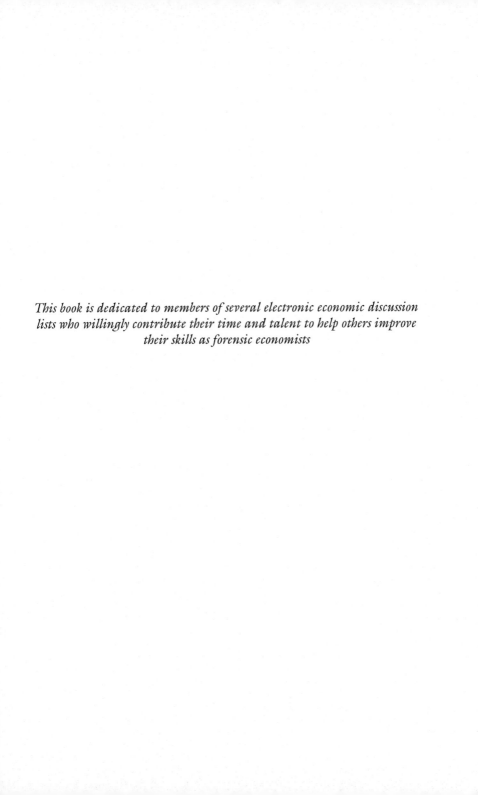

This book is dedicated to members of several electronic economic discussion lists who willingly contribute their time and talent to help others improve their skills as forensic economists

PREFACE

This volume sits, as it were, on the shoulders of numerous other works produced by forensic economists over the past 30 years. This body of knowledge serves as a foundation for anyone who seeks to work as an economic expert or who desires to learn about the standards of measurement that have been tested and developed in books and peer-reviewed articles.

The present volume is an attempt to both look back and look forward over the entire field of personal damage calculations in civil litigation in the USA. Each chapter addresses a major aspect of economic damages calculation, and does so by relaying what forensic economists have learned about that particular topic, and what still needs to be addressed by future research and analysis.

Contributors to this volume, by and large, are among the most published and recognized authorities in the field of forensic economics. I want to take this opportunity publicly to thank each of them for their willingness to participate in this project. I trust that readers will benefit immensely from the content of their contributions.

Frank D. Tinari

CONTENTS

Notes on Contributors

Gary R. Albrecht obtained his master and doctorate degrees in economics from Indiana University and he has a bachelor's degree in economics from Tulane University. His career in economics has covered teaching at the university level, being an academic researcher, and serving as an economic consultant. Since 1988, he has been employed as an economist at Albrecht Economics in Winston-Salem, North Carolina. His current work focuses on forensic economics, economic theory, economic forecasting, and applied econometrics.

Michael L. Brookshire received his Ph.D. in economics from the University of Tennessee. He is a professor emeritus of economics at Marshall University and is in his 41st year of practice as a forensic economist. He has written two books and edited a third book on economic damages and published approximately 50 peer-reviewed journal articles or book chapters on the proper calculation of economic damages, including 15 refereed articles in the *Journal of Forensic Economics*. He was a charter member of the National Association of Forensic Economics in 1986, served from 1990 to 2001 on the Board of Directors, in 1993 and 1994 as the national president, and from 1999 to 2001 as its executive director.

James E. Ciecka is Professor of Economics at DePaul University. He received his Ph.D. in economics from Purdue University. He has published more than 50 papers in journals in the field of forensic economics which include more than 25 papers with Gary R. Skoog, the coauthor of the chapter on worklife expectancy in this volume. He is on the Board of Editors and is the co-executive editor of the *Journal of Forensic Economics*.

Joshua Congdon-Hohman, Ph.D. is Associate Professor of Economics at the College of the Holy Cross in Worcester, Massachusetts. His research focuses on the economic aspects of health insurance markets.

Stephen M. Horner has been a forensic economist practicing in Corpus Christi, Texas, since 1985. He obtained his Ph.D. in economics and master's degree in Public Policy Studies from the University of Michigan and Bachelor of Science in economics from the California Institute of Technology. He previously taught economics at Texas A&M University Corpus Christi, in the School of Public Health at The University of Michigan, and at Wellesley College. Dr. Horner has served on the editorial boards of the *Journal of Forensic Economics* and *Journal of Business Valuation and Economic Loss Analysis*, and was President of the National Association of Forensic Economics in 2003–2004.

Thomas R. Ireland is Professor Emeritus of Economics at the University of Missouri-St. Louis. He received his Ph.D. in economics from the University of Virginia in 1968 and has been a practicing forensic economist since 1974. He has edited or published nine books, more than 150 papers in journals in the field of forensic economics, and contributed chapters to four other books. He is a past president of the American Academy of Economic and Financial Experts, past vice president of the National Association of Forensic Economics, and serves on the editorial board of the *Journal of Legal Economics*.

David D. Jones earned a B.A. in economics from the College of Wooster, Ohio, in 1966, and an M.A. (1968) and Ph.D. (1975) from Indiana University in economics and business. He taught undergraduate and graduate economics at the St. Thomas College (now University) from 1972 to 2000. Since 1980, Dr. Jones has continued to work as a forensic economist.

Kurt V. Krueger obtained his doctorate degree in economics from the University of Missouri-Kansas City and he has master and bachelor degrees in economics from the University of Kansas. Since 1990, he has been employed as an economist at John Ward Economics in Prairie Village, Kansas. Dr. Krueger is a past-President of the National Association of Forensic Economics and currently the Managing Editor of the *Journal of Forensic Economics*. His empirical research is relied upon in the field of forensic economics and used by several US agencies to measure the cost of death, injury, and disease in the USA.

Timothy Lanning received a bachelor's degree from California State University, Fullerton, an M.A. in Economics (2002) from Claremont Graduate University, and completed all the work there toward a doctorate. Mr. Lanning is Managing Associate Economist with the forensic economic consulting firm of Formuzis, Pickersgill & Hunt, Inc., where he has been employed for more than 25 years. In that capacity he provides litigation consulting and expert witness services to law firms in the Southern California area.

Victor A. Matheson, Ph.D. is Professor of Economics at the College of the Holy Cross in Worcester, Massachusetts. He is the author of over 75 refereed journal articles or book chapters, and is a member of the National Association of Forensic Economics. Dr. Matheson has provided expert testimony or assisted in calculating damages in over 200 personal injury, medical malpractice, and wrongful death cases.

James D. Rodgers is Professor Emeritus of Economics at the Pennsylvania State University. He received his Ph.D. in economics from the University of Virginia in 1970 and has been a practicing forensic economist since 1976. He has a number of journal articles and articles in books in the field of forensic economics as well as articles in mainstream economics journals. He also serves as co-editor of a series of articles in the *Journal of Forensic Economics* on assessing economic damages in personal injury and death litigation in the various states and territories of the USA. He is a past president of the National Association of Forensic Economics (2001–2002) and also served as its executive director (2008–2014).

Thomas Roney received a Bachelor of Arts in Economics, *cum laude*, from Washington State University, and completed all the course work toward a doctorate in economics. Mr. Roney offers litigation support to attorneys throughout the country. He has testified as an expert witness in state and federal courts, at depositions and arbitrations, and before the Special Master in Victim Compensation Fund matters. Prior to opening his own firm 13 years ago, Mr. Roney was an economist with several forensic consulting firms and an in-house litigation support consultant to a national law firm. He specializes in the calculation of economic losses in personal injury, wrongful death, and wrongful termination cases.

David Rosenbaum is Professor of Economics at the University of Nebraska-Lincoln. He also has been practicing forensic economics for nearly two decades. Dr. Rosenbaum earned his Ph.D. in economics from the University of Wisconsin-Madison in 1985. He has authored more than 40 articles published in a variety of professional journals. Many of the articles appear in the *Journal of Forensic Economics* and the *Journal of Legal Economics*. He remains active in the American Academy of Economic and Financial Experts and the National Association of Forensic Economics, holding positions on the boards of both organizations.

David Schap is Professor of Economics, College of the Holy Cross. Schap has an M.S. in applied mathematics from The George Washington University and a Ph.D. in economics from Washington University. He has published in outlets of all of the major economics associations (American, Eastern, Midwest, Southern, and Western). Dr. Schap has written scores of forensic economic evaluations and testified as an economics expert in cases in seven states. He has served on the Boards of the National Association of Forensic Economics and the American Academy of Economic and Financial Experts. Schap is currently Editor, *Journal of Legal Economics*.

Gary R. Skoog has been an adjunct faculty member at DePaul University since 1989, and has taught at the Universities of Chicago, Wisconsin, and Minnesota. He received his Ph.D. in economics from the University of Minnesota and has published more than 30 papers in peer-reviewed economics journals, mostly in the field of forensic economics, including more than 25 papers with James R. Ciecka, the coauthor of the chapter on worklife expectancy in this volume. He is a Past President of the National Association of Forensic Economics and the president of Legal Econometrics, Inc., based in Glenview, Illinois.

Frank Slesnick received his B.A. from Oberlin College and Ph.D. in Economics from the University of Minnesota. He taught at Denison University in Granville, Ohio, and for 30 years at Bellarmine University in Louisville, Kentucky. Professor Slesnick has served as a forensic economic consultant since 1979 in the area of personal injury/death cases with a specific focus on medical cost issues. He has published widely in the field of forensic economics and currently serves as an Associate Editor of the *Journal of Forensic Economics*. In 1991–92, he served as the fourth President of the National Association of Forensic Economics.

Lawrence M. Spizman, Ph.D is a Professor Emeritus at State University of New York at Oswego and has been a practicing forensic economist throughout the USA since 1985. He has authored over 35 published peer-reviewed articles and was the 2011 recipient of the State University of New York Chancellor's Award for Excellence in Scholarship for his ground-breaking work in forensic economics. Dr. Spizman was elected president of the National Association of Forensic Economics for the years 2016 and 2017.

Frank D. Tinari, Ph.D (Fordham) is Professor Emeritus of Economics, Seton Hall University, where he taught for 31 years. He is the author of an economics textbook and dozens of peer-reviewed articles in outlets including the *Journal of Forensic Economics, Journal of Legal Economics, Journal of Economic Education,* and the *Eastern Economic Journal.* Dr. Tinari is founder of the Tinari Economics consultancy and has served as Principal Economist of the Sobel Tinari Economics Group. He has written thousands of economic loss appraisals and testified as an expert witness in over 1000 cases in several states. Tinari served on the Board of the National Association of Forensic Economics and was its 2005–2006 President.

John O. Ward is Professor Emeritus of Economics at the University of Missouri–Kansas City and President of John Ward Economics, a litigation support and publishing firm in Prairie Village, Kansas. He has authored or edited seven books, and over 50 papers and book chapters in the field of Forensic Economics. He is a past President of the National Association of Forensic Economics and past editor of the *Journal of Forensic Economics* and the *Journal of Legal Economics.*

LIST OF TABLES

CHAPTER 1

An Introduction to the Field of Forensic Economics

Frank D. Tinari

1.1 ECONOMIC DAMAGES

Like a number of sub-fields of economics, forensic economics is comprised of both theory and application. More precisely, forensic economics applies economic theories, methods, and measurements to economic damages issues in civil litigation. The field of forensic economics in the USA first developed in the 1970s as various courts began allowing expert testimony from an ever-expanding array of specialists in a wide variety of disciplines.[1] The National Association of Forensic Economists [later, Economics] (NAFE) was formed in 1987, bringing together for the first time dozens of individuals from across the country who had been involved separately in calculating economic losses. One of the driving motivations of NAFE's creation was to systematize and improve the quality of forensic economist (FE)'s work. A detailed history of the creation and development of NAFE is presented in Brookshire (2003) with additional history given by Rodgers and Weinstein (2014).

In federal and state courts in the USA, as well as in other nations, when one party sues another based on allegations that harm was done as a result of the actions of the other party, the suing party is required

F.D. Tinari (✉)
Professor Emeritus, Seton Hall University, USA

© The Author(s) 2016
F.D. Tinari (ed.), *Forensic Economics*,
DOI 10.1057/978-1-137-56392-7_1

1

not only to prove that the harm was, indeed, caused by the other party but also to claim and demonstrate that a specified dollar value represents just compensation for the harm. Economic damages or losses are claimed within a wide array of civil law cases. Civil law is subdivided into subfields such as death and injury, breach of contract, lost profits, employment discrimination, and the like. Each of these types of cases is governed both by legislated rules (statutes) and the findings of case law. Further, the rules and cases differ among the states. For example, economic losses in New Jersey civil cases must ultimately be reduced to present value, whereas in New York cases the jury determines the total, undiscounted value which, in turn, is then subject to a Series of post-trial calculations governed by statute. Numerous other differences in methods and scope form the legal landscape from state to state. Chapters 7, 12, and 16 of this volume explore some of the key differences.

In addition, civil cases may be filed in accordance with various federal laws such as those against gender or racial discrimination. Federal courts have their own rules, some of which are completely independent of state statutes, and require experts to provide more disclosure than is expected in a number of state courts.

All civil cases may be viewed as consisting of two parts: proving liability for the egregious act of one or more named parties, and proving the extent of economic damages, if any. The major focus of forensic economics is with respect to economic loss calculations. But such calculations cannot be carried out irrespective of the legal parameters affecting both the scope and methodologies permitted to be used. Thus, effective FEs are those who have familiarized themselves with case law and those statutes dealing with the calculation of economic damages.

Sometimes the harm is non-economic in nature, for example, emotional distress, but in most cases economic damages are claimed.[2] While FEs would not typically be involved in the proof-of-causation stage of a litigated matter, they are often called upon to evaluate, measure, and opine on the degree of economic loss that is alleged to have occurred. According to part of the definition promulgated by NAFE (www.nafe.net), forensic economics deals with the following:

1. The calculation of pecuniary damages in personal and commercial litigation.
2. The analysis of liability, such as the statistical analysis of discrimination, the analysis of market power in antitrust disputes, and fraud detection.

3. Other matters subject to legal review, such as public policy analysis, and business, property, and asset valuation.

It is in these areas that we find economists bringing to bear their knowledge of theory, data sources, and methods of analysis to assess economic damages or losses. This is not to say that all civil claims require or make use of FEs. On the contrary, most claims involve relatively modest dollar amounts, and are satisfied via private insurance companies or government regulations that cover losses due to automobile, residential, and/or employment accidents and injuries. But when the amounts being claimed are substantial, or when the claims are strongly contested, economic damages experts are often called upon to analyze and measure the losses. In contrast, many nations permit neither litigation nor expert testimony to determine the magnitude of economic losses. A detailed examination is provided in Chap. 19 of this volume.

Some caveats are in order at this point regarding the second activity listed above, that is, the analysis of liability (as opposed to damages) in discrimination and personal employment litigation. This is a more limited area for economists, for two reasons. First, the number of such cases is much smaller than damages claims arising from personal injuries and commercial disputes. Second, the laws against wrongful discrimination do not always require proof of discrimination, in the form of statistical analysis, when the facts are such that there is a prima facie presumption of adverse behavior on the part of defendants. Nevertheless, if statistical analysis is needed, economists skilled in the statistical arts, especially analysis of small numbers, may play a role in the proof-of-liability stage of a case.

Turning to antitrust disputes, these are much less common than everyday personal and business litigated claims, and they require a significantly different and specialized set of skills and knowledge, quite different from the methods used in personal and commercial cases. There exist numerous articles and books in the field of antitrust. Given the scope and methodological differences, this volume will eschew inclusion of the topic.

1.2   Role of the Economist

What exactly, then, do FEs do? Experienced experts in the field are sometimes consulted by lawyers for advice on the scope and magnitude of potential damages, well before litigation gets under way. By far and away, however, is what may be described as the typical or standard engagement that consists of review by the economist of the documents and information provided by the retaining attorney, analysis of the facts to determine the scope and types of economic damages, calculation of numerical values, and an opinion offered on the value of all economic losses. The process usually culminates in the issuance of a signed report that becomes part of the documentation in the law suit. When shared with the adversary, it could trigger a response by the opposing side who may engage its own economist to opine on the value of economic damages, or to comment on and critique the other's side report.

Valuation of personal claims involves methods that differ from the methodology used in valuing commercial claims. Due to the higher level of risk in operating a business, the discount rate used to convert future projected values to present value incorporates a number of elements of risk. Not so for personal injury, wrongful death, and employment discrimination torts. In such matters, the analyst will make adjustments to the expected earnings figures, and then apply a "safe and secure" interest rate for discounting to present value. Let us first consider personal litigation.

The process by which the expert arrives at an opinion of loss is not particularly complicated. But it does require careful consideration of various facts and assumptions that touch upon every aspect of the expert's work. For example, had an alleged incident not occurred, the analyst would need to determine what would have been the likely annual earnings in subsequent years. If the plaintiff's earnings history over the past five years were provided, would it be appropriate for the analyst to average the five values to establish a reasonable base earnings as the foundation for projecting future years' earnings? Or would it be better to use the preceding two or three years? If there had been a dip in the earnings rate in the second and third years, but the dip had occurred during a recession, how would the analyst treat these values for purposes of making projections? Alternatively, the earnings history may have exhibited annual increases, year after year, for the past five years. In that case, taking an average of past, lower-earnings years would likely yield an unwarranted lower figure.

Another possible complication would involve projecting earnings for a person with no track record of past earnings, such as a student, who has been injured. In such cases, the analyst must project expected earnings or the earnings capacity of the individual. This generally entails consideration of the individual's potential educational attainment, the person's grade-point average, the educational attainment of the person's parents, and other related factors. Chapter 2 addresses the meaning and measurement of earning capacity, and Chap. 5 deals with earnings estimation in cases of impairment of a child.

Given this brief sketch of the issues involved in determining a reasonable figure for projecting future earnings, it must be reiterated that the forensic economics methodology, though not complicated, requires consideration of numerous elements of each particular case. Choices must be made by the analyst at nearly every turn. Assumptions are unavoidable. And, over time, as knowledge expands, the expert's assumptions may change to reflect current research and statistical sources. Chapter 13 reviews the evolving viewpoints of FEs.

However, all of this rests on a basic, underlying approach used in every analysis. The FE is being asked to create a picture of what would have occurred absent the injury or incident. This is often referred to as the "but for" scenario. In other words, the analyst must examine the available information, consider relevant microeconomic and macroeconomic forces that might have a bearing on the case, make assumptions regarding numerical values needed for projecting future values, undertake research related to the assumptions, and carefully make the calculations necessary to arrive at an opinion of economic loss. The economic loss opinion represents what *most likely would have occurred* but for the incident. It is an alternative universe, but one grounded as best as possible on known facts and known economic and statistical trends.

1.3   OTHER CONSIDERATIONS

We have touched on the determination of a base earnings figure as the starting point in the analyst's calculations. An important and related question involves determining the number of years over which such losses would likely occur. When would the individual have retired? During the entire time period until retirement, would the individual have been in the labor force every month and every year? Chapter 3 examines the concept and measurement of worklife expectancy. Further, even when a person participates in the labor force, would there likely have occurred periods of layoffs or unemployment that would have adversely impacted annual earnings?

These important questions, and others like them, have led to the development of an extensive literature in forensic economics. Several academic journals regularly publish research related to the questions encountered by FEs. Two well-regarded publications, among others,[3] are the *Journal of Forensic Economics* and the *Journal of Legal Economics*, published, respectively, by NAFE and the American Academy of Economic and Financial Experts (AAEFE). In their pages over the past three decades may be found articles about numerous topics including studies of statistical years to retirement and worklife expectancy. Many of the statistical-based articles rely on US government data and, as such, have been accepted by state and federal courts in civil litigation.

Because the research in forensic economics covers a wide variety of topics touching on all aspects of the calculation of economic losses, there is no single "theory" that underpins forensic economics. Rather, FEs use theories and methods based on numerous microeconomic and macroeconomic foundations. Publishers of the *Journal of Economic Literature* classify the sub-field of forensic economics within the broad Law and Economics category. Other sub-fields such as antitrust, environmental, health, sports, and many other economics specialties are assigned separate classification categories. And like these others, forensic economics dips into labor economics, statistics, and welfare analysis, to name a few. In some unusual situations, economists may venture into environmental economics, foreign exchange rate theory, and even international cost-of-living differences.

And, as in other sub-fields in economics, there are several unresolved or disputed findings. What is best source or basis for determining a discount rate? (See the discussion in Chap. 8.) Or, for a person who has lost a job due to discrimination, for how many subsequent years will the losses likely persist (see Chap. 11)? What are the accepted methods for measuring the value of non-cash compensation such as the value of a medical insurance policy? (Chapter 6 discusses fringe benefits earned via employment.) For an injured person who takes twice as long to do household chores, should the additional hours be valued at the person's occupational wage rate, or at the cost of hiring someone to do the chores? (Chapter 10 explores the issues in valuing services.) The list could go on.

In addition to published articles, FEs also make use of data directly available from US government agencies such as the rich data sets on life expectancy, earnings by age, and unemployment statistics. Thus, for example, if the analyst determines that a particular element of damages would extend over the remaining life expectancy of the individual, then the analyst would rely on relevant life expectancy data for that calculation.

Once an earnings base is established, the analyst needs to determine what rate of growth would apply to annual earnings. Would it be a fixed growth rate over the entire remaining period of loss? Would the rate change over time due to specific assumed reasons? Again, research may have to be undertaken to support the analyst's earnings growth rate assumptions. Is there a union contract governing the person's wages? Are local, state, or national economic trends most applicable to the person's likely earnings trajectory?

Then there is consideration of non-cash forms of compensation such as employer-funded retirement plans and medical insurance policies. Employment contracts may have to be reviewed, and knowledge of the employee's contribution, if any, toward these benefits would have to be obtained. What if the medical insurance plan covered the injured party's family members, and would change once the children emancipated—how would the analyst value the changing nature of the medical insurance coverage?

In some state and federal jurisdictions, the loss of earnings must be reduced by likely amounts of federal and state income taxes. Consequently, the FE must determine the tax rates that would likely have been imposed on the person's future earnings. There is some debate within the profession about the scope of taxes to consider. One position is that Social Security taxes ("contributions") should also be incorporated while an opposing position says that they should not be viewed strictly as "income taxes." A discussion of federal and state taxes is provided in Chap. 7.

When analyzing losses in a wrongful death case, there is the added element of the extent to which the decedent devoted part of his or her income for personal use and that, consequently, would not have been available to surviving family members. The analyst would need to determine the magnitude of such personal expenses and subtract them from projected earnings. The literature contains many articles regarding not only the measurement of personal consumption or personal maintenance but also whether or not the subtraction should be made from total household income, or solely from the decedent's own earnings. In this volume, Chap. 4 addresses the issue of personal consumption.

1.4   Loss of Services

Thus far, we have dealt exclusively with the question of lost earnings. But the courts also recognize that impairment or death results in the loss of the individual's ability to perform various services, to the detriment of the injured individual, or the family of a deceased member. As a result, FEs address the valuation of lost services, examined in Chap. 10. The standard analysis focuses on loss of household services, but in some states, economists also measure the value of other lost services such as advice and guidance to other family members, and companionship services that the decedent would have provided. Interestingly, the 911 Victim Compensation Fund (the Fund) did not initially include service losses in its recommended methodology. But, as explained in Chap. 18, the Fund eventually agreed to consider the valuation of lost services as part of the total economic loss calculation.

To calculate the value of lost services, the economist would have to establish the number of hours of such services that the person would have continued to provide, but for the incident in question. For this purpose, many FEs ask the claimant to complete a questionnaire that requests information regarding the types and extent of services that had been provided prior and subsequent to the incident. In addition, data gleaned from the federal American Time Use Survey reveals patterns and statistical averages for a wide array of household structures. *The Dollar Value of a Day*, published by FEs at expectancy data, compiles federal data into easy-to-use tables that are used by many economic damages experts.

In conjunction with the number of hours of services, the analyst needs to apply an hourly wage rate to arrive at a dollar value of lost services. The publication just cited contains average wage rates for various services, while some analysts use local rates. And, of course, once an annual value is established, the analyst must make assumptions about the growth rate per year and the number of years over which such services would have been rendered.

1.5   Communication Skills and Professional Standards

It should be evident that there are many moving parts involved in the content and analysis of economic damages. Our brief review here has merely touched on some of the basic issues. But perhaps as important as proper evaluation of losses is the ability of FEs to effectively communicate their findings to retaining attorneys, to their clients and, if called upon, to explain to a jury at trial the hows and wherefors of determining the expert's opinion of economic loss.

The communication aspect of being a consultant and expert entails an additional set of skills that are partly academic and partly business oriented. As explained in Chap. 17, these additional skills include (1) effective oral and written communication, (2) a reasonable level of familiarity with relevant law, (3) acumen in operating one's practice as a small business, (4) the ability to withstand harsh criticism under oath, and (5) skillful management of interpersonal professional relationships.

Successful forensic economic practitioners must become master of the "art" of applying and communicating knowledge as a paid expert in a legal context. Let us first review, if ever so briefly, the legal aspects.

Litigation is an adversarial process that drives the parties to put the best face on their respective positions. This, in turn, filters down as pressure on experts to make assumptions, select facts, and apply methods that would generate values most favorable to their respective side.[4] Yet, experts, be they engineers, medical professionals, investigators, or economists, are expected to present to the court their professional, objective, and unbiased opinions as an aide to the trier-of-fact (typically, a jury). Considerable writing and discussion has occurred over this inherent tension.[5]

Part of the responsibility of a FE is to establish professional standards not only for one's behavior but also in one's methodology in approaching litigation assignments. If the methods are changed to suit the side that has retained the expert, this practice could be discovered and used to impugn the expert's reputation.

Should an economist falter in this responsibility by offering a biased opinion, the door would then be opened to potential difficulties. Whatever bias was applied could be used against the expert by opposing counsel, either in the given assignment or in potential future cases handled by other attorneys who learn of the bias through communications with their colleagues (via the telephone, meetings, professional chat rooms, and electronic lists). FEs quickly learn that their reputation and credibility in presenting findings that are relatively immune to severe criticism are the most important aspects of their work as experts.[6] If an expert can be easily impeached, his or her usefulness to the client could be seriously impaired, leading to further difficulties in serving as an expert in future assignments.

In fact, the courts have settled on well-developed requirements for accepting or rejecting expert testimony. In federal cases, a motion may be filed requesting a Daubert hearing to challenge the admissibility of an expert's testimony.[7] Similarly, in many state courts, challenges are permitted by means of a motion in limine. After hearing arguments, the judge acts as "gatekeeper" and rules on whether an individual will be permitted to provide expert opinion to the jury.[8]

Irrespective of the practical penalties that could be suffered by experts who have rendered biased opinions, professional associations have developed explicit statements spelling out minimal professional standards of ethical behavior that are expected to be followed by economic damages experts. As explained in Chap. 15, although these ethical statements do not have the same force as legally recognized standards in other professions such as accounting or engineering, they do make explicit what is expected of their members. In the case of NAFE, moreover, members are required to attest to their adherence to the Statement of Ethical Principles and Principles of Professional Practice. (A copy of the Statement is found at the www.nafe.net website.)

It should be noted further that the litigation process occurs in stages and provides opportunities for adversaries to exam the work of experts hired by the opposing side. (See Chap. 15 for a detailed explanation.) In all instances, it is the professional obligation of the expert to answer questions truthfully, irrespective of the implications of one's answers upon the parties' positions.

1.6   TIMING OF EXPERT ENGAGEMENT

In our experience, many attorneys do not retain the services of an economic expert until the latter stages of a case. In some respects, this is a prudent decision, especially if there is doubt by the litigating party regarding the strength of proof of the liability of the opposing side. A case may require substantial efforts by an attorney to gather evidence, garner the testimony of relevant witnesses, and gather the opinions of professionals regarding the cause of the allegedly wrongful event. It is understandable, therefore, that economic experts may be called upon relatively late in a case for their economic damages opinions. Nevertheless, there are at least three disadvantages to this common strategy.

One problem is that the ability of the economic damages expert to gather relevant data and information may be restricted because the window of opportunity to make such requests is fast closing. Attorneys may tell the expert that "discovery has ended" or that "discovery is ending next week." A second disadvantage is that a last minute request for an economic loss opinion may be put on a "rush" basis. This, in turn, exerts unwarranted pressure on the expert to generate a correct and comprehensive report of damages within a very tight time line. A third problem resulting from delaying the retention of a favored expert, albeit a problem for attorneys, occurs when the expert has already been retained by the opposing side, thereby closing the door to the expected use of that expert.

For those attorneys who do engage the services of economic experts early in a case, earlier payment of any required retainer fees is incurred. Yet, timely retention does ensure that sufficient time will be made available to the expert to conduct appropriate research and analysis of the damages aspects of the case, thereby providing the best possible service to the attorney and his or her client.

Sometimes economic experts are retained who then, upon analyzing the case information, realize that calculated economic damages are relatively small. In such cases, the expert may wonder why he or she was hired.

There may be good reasons. For example, there may be substantial non-economic losses being claimed (e.g., pain and suffering) and the attorney simply needs an economic damages report to complete the picture of the claimed components of loss. We note here that economists do not possess the tools for valuing intangible losses such as pain and suffering, or loss of enjoyment, generally referred to as hedonic losses, although a small number of economists have attempted to do just that. Chapter 14 presents a detailed analysis of the reasons why this cannot be accomplished in the litigation setting.[9]

In other instances, attorneys know full well that a case will settle instead of proceed to trial, so they obtain an opinion of economic losses early in a case and serve the expert's report to their opposition. Depending on the attorney's reputation as well as that of his or her expert, this strategy could lead to an early settlement. Because the expert may not be aware of which strategy an attorney is utilizing, all that the expert can do is respond to the request being made for services, do the best job possible, and not worry about the whys or wherefores of being hired in a case.

It is well for the expert to remember that economic analysis services comprise only one part of all of the resources being gathered by the attorney to mount a case. Therefore, there are numerous possible outcomes to a case that could occur due to a variety of reasons. For example, the testimony of the plaintiff or witnesses was not credible; the skills of the attorney were inadequate to the task of mounting the evidence; legal rulings restricted the planned presentation of the arguments in the case; and/or the experts' testimonies were not persuasive or helpful to the jury. So it would be as inappropriate for an economic expert to take too much credit for a successful case award, as it would be to think the trial testimony of the expert "lost the case."

1.7   The Expert's Assignment

An assignment seeking the professional opinion of an economist may take different forms. The most common is asking the economist to calculate the economic losses occurring as a result of a particular event such as an accident, job termination, or breach of contract. Alternatively, an economist may be asked to review and critique the content and quality of an opposing economist's report of economic loss. When this occurs, the expert may be working as a consultant to the attorney as opposed to being named as an expert in the case. If the expert is "named," a legal requirement that must occur well in advance of trial testimony, then the work product of the expert may be discoverable by the other side.

Less common may be a request to calculate the value of one particular type of loss such as the present value of the components of a life care plan, the value of a person's household services, or the loss of a person's pension. It cannot be emphasized enough that the economist should do the job that is requested, nothing less, nothing more.[10]

Once hired by an attorney, the assignment becomes a job that will generate fees for the time spent by the economist. A detailed discussion of billing, setting fees, getting retainer deposits, getting paid by recalcitrant attorneys or clients, and other financial aspects of a forensic economic practice is beyond the scope of this book. Suffice it to say that it is wise to keep things simple and straightforward. As an economist gains more experience doing forensic economics work, he or she will also develop savvy business methods in accordance with his or her preferences as well as market expectations.

During the time one spends on a litigation assignment, it is imperative to keep meticulous records. Experts are often examined, either in deposition or trial, and must be in a position to answer any and (nearly) all questions, such as: When were you first contacted by the attorney? How much did you charge? On what date(s) did you speak with the plaintiff (or defendant) and what did you talk about? What documents did you rely upon? It is better for an expert to retain all notes and documents (some of which could be discarded later) than to suffer criticism that the work is incomplete, sloppy or without adequate basis.

In cases brought in federal court, all communications between the expert and the retaining attorney, as well as all draft reports, notes, and documents relied upon, used to be discoverable, that is, made available to the opposing side. However, federal rules shield communications and draft reports from this requirement, thereby bringing federal discovery requirements in line with those currently operative in many state courts.

All of this presumes that the economist has been provided full and adequate information to enable him or her to conduct a proper valuation of losses. To this end, many economists have developed a questionnaire that they submit to the attorney, stating that the requested information be provided together with backup documentation confirming the critical facts of the case. Frequently, upon review of the documents provided, the economist will determine that information is missing about one or more aspects of the case. Hence, further communication with the retaining attorney would occur, requesting the missing information. Sometimes direct communication will be needed with the attorney's client, that is, the actual party to the law suit. (A discussion of effective communication skills as an expert is presented in Chap. 17 of this volume.) It is not unusual, therefore, to find that an assignment may extend for weeks or months as documents are being gathered. Once the information has been assembled by the economic expert, analysis and calculations may begin.

Regarding numerical calculations, by far and away most economists use computer spreadsheets to make all necessary calculations. Generally speaking, techniques such as regression analysis and matrix calculations are rarely invoked. So it may be said that economic damages calculations are not mathematically sophisticated—but the various calculations, while in and of themselves relatively straightforward, can make for a complex process when all the moving parts are combined. Attention to detail, therefore, is a prerequisite for this type of work.

Once a report has been submitted, a fair amount of time could elapse before hearing again from the retaining attorney. If the case has not settled, there may come a time when the opposing counsel will ask to take the deposition of the expert. This simply means that the economist will, under oath, answer questions regarding his or her involvement in the case and the basis for the opinions rendered in the report.

Trial testimony is an art unto itself. At this stage of an assignment, the expert will be working closely with the attorney to determine how the testimony will be presented. Often, sample questions are developed and reviewed. A decision would need to be made with respect to the method by which calculations and opinions will be presented to the jury. Poster boards replicating the economist's calculations and tables could be made up. Or, the same information could be loaded onto a projector for display in the courtroom. The most appropriate strategy is the one agreed upon by both the attorney and expert so that there are no surprises.[11]

The expert's retaining attorney may also discuss and prepare the expert for potential cross-examination questions or areas of questioning. It is best for the FE to discuss frankly any weak links in his or her analysis, or any problems in his or her background. One should always assume that, if there are any problems or errors or biases, they likely will be discovered by the opposing attorney. It is better for the expert to be prepared for potentially damaging questions than to assume the problems will not be uncovered. Moreover, an experienced attorney will admonish the expert not to answer questions that ask for opinions beyond the economist's expertise, however tempting it might be to offer such opinions.

1.8   CONCLUDING THOUGHTS

Entering the world of forensic economics implies that the economist will be involved in a "practice", that is, an entrepreneurial small business. This implies that good business practices must be learned and applied. Research indicates that the typical FE works alone or independently, and usually on a part-time basis while teaching in academia.[12] Institutional faculty work does not necessarily provide sufficient experience in small business management, although time management and good communications should spill over to running one's practice. Many detailed tasks must be accomplished such as preparing a useful retainer agreement, setting fees (especially if the expert is working in a competitive market), developing reliable methods of fee collection, invoicing for services rendered, maintaining a complete paper trail of communications and work done, discerning when it may be appropriate to decline an assignment, marketing one's practice if so desired, and more.

Many practicing economic damages experts have found that attending the sessions sponsored by NAFE at the conferences it holds six times annually to be enormously helpful not only for building their knowledge and skill base, but also for the advice gained from more experienced practitioners. In addition, members of both NAFE and the AAEFE are eligible to join electronic discussion lists where questions on both the substance and the practice of forensic economics are answered, oftentimes in numerous helpful ways by members.[13] It is the author's experience that such participation yields enormous rewards, not the least of which is becoming acquainted with many other economists who may eventually become good colleagues and even friends.

A beginning FE would benefit greatly from being mentored by a seasoned economist, if at all possible. This is not easy to do inasmuch as competition exists in each local market, thereby warranting against the willingness of economists to teach and train potential competitors. Nevertheless, it has been this author's experience that, with proper and reasonable noncompete and confidentiality agreements, it is possible for newer FEs to learn in this way.

Above all, success as a forensic economic expert depends primarily both on one's character and personality. Establishing and maintaining a credible reputation at the professional and ethical levels is the market test for the practicing consultant. If the expert maintains consistent methods, treats everyone fairly, responds to inquiries on a timely basis, and is cooperative while maintaining one's standards, then it is more likely that repeat assignments will occur.

The contents of the chapters in this volume attest to the fact that the field of forensic economics has come a long way since the early 1970s. Successful FEs can earn substantial income, but practice of this specialty is clearly not for everyone. The role of the expert in litigation is to assist the trier-of-fact in determining the economic impact of some harmful incident. As such, the work of FEs serves the larger socioeconomic purpose of resolving disputes among members of our society.

Those who choose to become an economic expert enter an area of practice that requires gaining knowledge of legal parameters that guide the methods and measurements of economic loss. In addition, the economist must become thoroughly familiar with accepted methods and sources in the field as developed in the forensic economics literature. Perhaps just as important is the ability to apply one's trade in an ethical and professional manner. Finally, the solo practitioner must acquire skills in operating a small business. Those who venture ahead will find that the members of the forensic economics organizations are extremely helpful. Success in the practice of forensic economics yields both professional and personal satisfaction.

NOTES

1. Directories of experts today list specialties such as aviation engineers, computer systems experts, fire and explosion experts, entomologists, food scientists, industrial hygienists, boat and maritime consultants, a wide variety of medical experts, life care planners, psychologists, recreation and safety experts, surveyors, family counselors, zoning and planning experts, audio and video examiners, premises liability experts ad infinitum.
2. A few practitioners have developed methods to measure the pecuniary value of emotional and other subjective losses, termed "hedonic" valuation. But, as explained in Chaps. 13 and 14, the hedonic methodology is not widely accepted by forensic economists, and very few state courts have permitted economic testimony regarding hedonic losses.
3. Other good sources include publications such as Martin and Weinstein (2012); Expectancy Data (2014); Ward and Krueger (1994); Ireland and Depperschmidt (1999); Kaufman et al. (2005); Ireland et al. (1998).
4. See Johnson (1991).
5. See Johnson (1991), Sattler (1991), and Tinari (2014).

6. See, for example, Sattler (1991).
7. Daubert challenges seem to be increasingly used as part of an attorney's strategy to "beat down" the opposing side. The expert whose testimony is being challenged is usually not present at the hearing and may not even be aware that such a hearing is being held.
8. A website managed by Thomas Ireland contains a number of helpful listings of case decisions including 'Legal Decisions Involving Admission of Expert Economic Testimony,' 'Legal Decisions Involving Standards for Damages in Wrongful Death or Survival Actions,' and 'Useful Cases in Forensic Economic Practice.' His website is listed at the University of Missouri-St. Louis as follows: http://www.umsl.edu/divisions/artscience/economics/Forensic Economics/useful.html.
9. While government agencies place a value on a statistical life to help calculate benefits stemming from regulation, that is far removed from figuring loss of life's enjoyment from an accident to, say, a 53-year-old auto worker, or any individual person. In 2012 dollars, the Mining Safety and Health Administration uses a value of $9.1 million for a statistical life, whereas the Food and Drug Administration uses a value of $3.5 million. (See Viscusi 2014.)
10. Very experienced forensic economists will often find themselves advising attorneys on various aspects of economic damages prior to determining the scope of services needed.
11. Analysis of alternative methods of presenting trial testimony of economic damage calculations is given in Tinari (2016).
12. See Tinari and Grivoyannis (2005). The authors found that those experts who specialize in a particular area, such as wrongful death cases, exhibit much higher productivity than those who do a wide variety of cases.
13. Advice received in this manner must be used with caution for two reasons: the information may be different for different court jurisdictions, and the information would not generally be accepted by the courts as authoritative for expert work.

REFERENCES

American Academy of Economic and Financial Experts. www.aaefe.org

Brookshire, M. L. (2003). A history of the National Association of Forensic Economics, 1986–2001. *Litigation Economics Review, 6*(1), 22–32.

Expectancy Data. (2014). *The dollar value of a day: Time diary analysis.* Shawnee Mission, Kansas: Expectancy Data.

Ireland, T. R. University of Missouri-St. Louis web page: http://www.umsl.edu/divisions/artscience/economics/ForensicEconomics/useful.html.

Ireland, T. R., & Depperschmidt, T. O. (1999). *Assessing family loss in wrongful death litigation: The special roles of lost services and personal consumption.* Tucson: Lawyers & Judges Publishing Co.

Ireland, T. R., Horner, S. M., Rodgers, J. D., Gaughan, P. A., Trout, R. R., & Piette, M. J. (1998). *Expert economic testimony: Reference guides for judges and attorneys.* Tucson: Lawyers & Judges Publishing Co..

Johnson, W. D. (1991). Qualifications, ethics and professional responsibility in forensic economics. *Journal of Forensic Economics, 4*(3), 277–285.

Kaufman, R. T., Rodgers, J. D., & Martin, G. D. (Eds.) (2005). *Economic foundations of injury and death damages.* Northampton: Edward Elgar Publishing, Ltd.

Martin, G. D., & Weinstein, M. A. (2012). *Determining economic damages.* Costa Mesa: James Publishing.

National Association of Forensic Economics. www.nafe.net

Rodgers, J. D., & Weinstein, M. A. (2014). An updated history of the National Association of Forensic Economics: 2002–2014. *Journal of Forensic Economics, 25*(2), 175–202.

Sattler, E. L. (1991). Economists, ethics, and the marketplace. *Journal of Forensic Economics, 4*(3), 263–268.

Tinari, F. D. (2016). Demonstrating Lost Earnings: Algebraic vs. Spreadsheet Method. *The Earnings Analyst*, 15, 21–32.

Tinari, F. D. (2014, April). A comment on George DeMartino's "Professional economic ethics: The posnerian and naive perspectives. *Journal of Forensic Economics, 25*(1), 91–97.

Tinari, F. D., & Grivoyannis, E. (2005, Fall). Estimates of labor productivity of economic damages experts. *Journal of Forensic Economics, 18*(2–3), 139–153.

Viscusi, W. K. (2014). The value of individual and societal risks to life and health. In M. J. Machina & W. K. Viscusi (Eds.), *Handbook of the economics of risk and uncertainty* (Vol. 1, pp. 385–452). Oxford: North-Holland.

Ward, J. O., & Krueger, K. V. (1994). *Establishing damages in catastrophic injury litigation.* Tucson: Lawyers & Judges Publishing Co.

CHAPTER 2

The Meaning of Earning Capacity

Stephen Horner and Frank Slesnick

2.1 Introduction

Earning capacity is a legal economic concept. Impairment of earning capacity is the legal standard for loss of earnings in personal injury cases in most jurisdictions, rather than loss of actual or expected earnings. This chapter addresses two questions:

What do we mean when we use the term "earning capacity?"
What guidance does this definition give for measuring earning capacity?

Although case law very commonly uses the term "earning capacity," no clear definition can be found within that case law.[1] "Earning capacity" is seldom found in the labor economics literature and even there, a clear definition is not to be found. The first attempt to develop a clear definition of earning capacity was published by the present authors in Horner and Slesnick (1999). Building on that earlier paper, this chapter reviews

S. Horner (✉)
Senior Economist, Economic Consulting, USA

F. Slesnick
Professor Emeritus, Rubel School of Business, Bellarmine University, Louisville, KY, USA

© The Author(s) 2016
F.D. Tinari (ed.), *Forensic Economics*,
DOI 10.1057/978-1-137-56392-7_2

the theoretical underpinnings of the earning capacity concept and presents a set of principles the forensic economic analyst may employ to simplify some of the complexities of real personal injury analysis.

2.2   Definitions

In our experience, one of the most common sources of error in the analysis of impaired earning capacity is the failure to apply a consistent standard to both pre-injury and post-injury earning capacity. Particularly when measuring a loss of earning capacity, the distinction between what we expect a worker to actually earn and what the worker is capable of earning can be quite subtle. Failure to appreciate these subtle differences can produce or hide error.

A consistent standard is necessary in order to prevent improperly increasing or decreasing economic losses by manipulating the pre-injury and post-injury values. Even in the absence of injury, a false estimate of loss could be produced by comparing pre-event earning capacity with post-event expected earnings. Similarly, an actual loss of earning capacity could magically be made to disappear by comparing pre-injury expected earnings with post-injury capacity. Earning capacity must be defined clearly in order for the forensic professional to maintain a reliable methodology that will produce very similar results when employed by different analysts.

Clear definitions also ease the job of the court and the trier of fact in determining whether an expert has introduced a bias. How could a jury know that an expert witness had improperly increased or decreased economic losses by comparing a pre-injury measurement based on one definition with a post-injury measurement based on another? Indeed, how could the expert determine whether error had not entered the analysis if there were no standards upon which to rely?

This section presents definitions which the authors and others have found useful. While these are not the only possible definitions, decades of thought and practice underlie them.[2] The inexperienced forensic expert should think carefully before departing from the standard established by these definitions.

Actual earnings are the observed earnings of an individual. Thus, actual earnings are a series of outcomes of a stochastic process in which the forces of supply and demand produce labor prices and quantities for that individual. *Future* actual earnings are not observable *in the present*.

Expected earnings are the expected values of actual earnings. Thus, expected earnings is also a series of values that are determined by supply and demand, but the values will be subject to less variance than actual earnings, due to the vagaries of random fluctuations in supply or demand. Expected earnings may be inferred from observation of actual earnings, but are not themselves subject to direct observation.

Earning capacity is the expected earnings of a worker who chooses to maximize the expected present value of future actual earnings. Put simply, this is an individual who "goes for the money." Since earning capacity is the maximum of expected earnings, its present value is always equal to or greater than the present value of expected earnings.

This definition will seem unnecessarily complex compared to "earning capacity is what a worker is able to earn." The simpler alternative leaves open many issues crucial to compensation for personal injury. For example, a worker is theoretically able to earn anything between zero and some theoretical but highly unlikely maximum. The alternative definition gives no direction out of this fog of possibilities. The maximization cannot be exercised at the level of each entry in the stream of expected earnings, because workers clearly accept lower expected earnings in one year in exchange for higher earnings in another year. Maximization must be with respect to present value because discount rates change the tradeoff between current earnings and future earnings. Workers make such choices when they choose optimal levels of education or training. For example, higher discount rates make professional schooling less attractive. This is the motivation for Federal subsidies of student loans. When a worker has chosen the path that maximizes the expected present value of actual earnings, the stream of expected values of actual earnings is also determined.

Latent earning capacity is the difference between earning capacity and expected earnings. Since expected earnings cannot be more than earning capacity, latent capacity cannot be negative.[3] A worker can choose not to exercise his or her full earning capacity such as by working fewer hours, or taking a job that accommodates family interests. Such choices cause the worker's expected earnings to be less than earning capacity. In that case, there would be positive latent capacity.[4]

Vocational experts have generally discussed earning capacity without an explicit definition of the term and have not addressed the distinction between earning capacity and expected earnings. Instead, they have focused on general criteria for the analysis of earning capacity. As a result, much of the discussion of procedure found in the vocational literature lacks sufficient structure to allow another expert[5] to discern whether a specified methodology has been followed in an actual case. The popular and useful RAPEL approach developed by Roger Weed is relatively systematic.[6] RAPEL provides a valuable checklist of many important aspects of valuing earning capacity that must be considered, but RAPEL remains incomplete.[7] RAPEL would be greatly improved by incorporating a clear definition of earning capacity. Any model without such a definition provides room for error or abuse.

Some vocational experts posit that definitions of earning capacity and expected earnings reduce rather than increase clarity. They assert that the process used in measuring earning capacity is a sufficient definition.[8] This approach leaves much to be desired because the measurement of earning capacity depends on the circumstances of the individuals whose losses are being estimated. Because individuals and jobs are so varied, the analysis of earning capacity is necessarily reliant on ad hoc analytic choices. How can one judge if these choices are proper if there are no general principles by which they can be judged? A methodology that rejects explicit definitions is unlikely to be reliable.

Why is earning capacity the standard? We cannot expect to give a complete answer to this question, since the case law evolved separately in different jurisdictions, but we might wonder how it came to be that nearly all jurisdictions agree on the earning capacity standard in personal injury cases.

First, let us consider a standard of loss based on actual earnings. Because actual earnings are the only earnings that can be directly observed, does an actual earnings standard reduce the speculative aspect of estimating losses? The answer is "no." Since actual earnings are only observable after they have happened, actual *future* earnings are necessarily unknown. Actual past earnings both before and after the accident are observable, but the worker's actual earnings that would have occurred in the absence of the accident, between the date of the accident and the time of valuation, are also unobservable.

Furthermore, actual earnings are determined by the worker's preferences as well as the person's abilities. As we shall see below when we discuss expected earnings as the standard of loss, use of any standard where the plaintiff's choices determine earnings results in the injured person choosing the amount of his or her damages.

Second, let us consider expected earnings as the standard of loss. Expected earnings are based on a person's vocational capacity and the wages employers offer for the person's vocational capacity. But expected earnings are also affected by non-binding choices. For example, the individual's choice of how many hours of a given vocational capacity to offer to employers is a crucial determinate of actual earnings. As a result, expected earnings can be anywhere between zero and the person's earning capacity.

Let us suppose that a personal injury case is to be tried in a jurisdiction where expected earnings were the standard of loss. The individual was working prior to the injury and we presume his or her average wages to be indicative of his or her pre-injury expected earnings. Let us now assume the person has not worked since the injury and declared an intention to withdraw permanently from the labor force. Based on this evidence, presumed expected earnings would be zero. Vocational analysis would be unnecessary, because the person's decision to not exercise any capacity and thus not to earn money would result in zero expected earnings. In other words, even if a vocational expert would testify that the person were able to earn money through employing transferable skills, the worker's expected earnings would be zero. The result would be that the person's choice would result in maximization of lost expected earnings and a maximized damage award. This is absurd. No court would force a defendant to pay more merely because a plaintiff chooses not to exercise his or her remaining capacity.

An asymmetric set of standards might be forced on an expert, where the loss is legislated to be the difference between pre-injury expected earnings and post-injury earning capacity. In Longshore and Harbor Workers cases tried under the Longshore and Harbor Workers' Compensation Act (LHWCA), this is the situation. Consider the case of a longshoreman who was offered ten hours per week of overtime but chose to work no overtime prior to an accident. Suppose after the accident the longshoreman is forced to take a lower-paying position in a less strenuous occupation. But suppose that longshoreman was able to work ten hours of overtime in the less strenuous replacement occupation and with the overtime would exactly restore his or her earnings. Under the standard of loss required in LHWCA, there is no loss because the loss is measured as the difference between average pre-injury wages and post-injury earning capacity. The injured person would be forced to work the overtime in order to avoid loss.[9] Under an earning capacity standard, the overtime in the pre-injury occupation would be included in earning capacity if it were included in post-injury capacity, and there would be a loss due to the change in pay rate. Asymmetric rules, such as found under the LHWCA, are the exception, perhaps as a result of a judgment that such asymmetries are unfair.

2.3   Supply and Demand

Actual earnings are determined by supply and demand. Thus, a clearer understanding of earning capacity can be achieved by considering these two sides of the labor market. We turn first to the supply side.

2.3.1   The Supply Side

In the case of injury to an individual, the supply side generally refers to the individual's offer of labor to the market rather than the entire labor supply curve, although the latter is not irrelevant in that most workers are wage takers, and have little or no control over the rate they will be offered. Each worker will possess a unique set of physical, mental, and psychological abilities. We often refer to this set of abilities as the worker's "functional capacity." Physicians and related medical professionals are the primary evaluators of functional capacity. In addition to functional capacity, a worker will possess education, training, and experience. Altogether, these "traits" result in skills that produce vocational capacity.[10] Forensic vocational experts, rather than forensic economists, are the primary evaluators of the vocational capacity of individuals.

An injury may cause any or all of the various factors that comprise vocational capacity to change. A person's physical, mental, or psychological abilities may be impaired. Normally, these impairments would be assessed by physicians or other relevant medical specialists. The vocational expert would determine what vocational capacities remain, based on the person's remaining abilities and skills that might be transferable to new occupations or jobs.

2.3.2   The Role of Preferences

The final ingredient in the labor supply of the individual is the person's preferences or "utility function." In other words, each worker will decide which occupations and jobs within his or her vocational capacity will be offered to employers. Some workers will sacrifice compensation in order to accommodate family or quality-of-life choices. Others may "go for the money" and choose jobs and hours that will maximize the expected value of their lifetime earnings. To some degree, the worker will also choose how many hours of labor to sell to employers, although employers often do not give workers significant control over their hours. For example, with some jobs, overtime and holiday hours will be optional, but with other jobs, the worker will have a take-it-or-leave-it choice. By definition, it is only through the exercise of a choice to sacrifice money earnings for other personal values does latent capacity arise. It should be noted that a person's preferences may change as a result of an injury. A person may still be able to work long hours, but may no longer wish to do so. Worker preferences can play a large role in the evaluation of evidence for loss of earning capacity.

Every worker will possess vocational capacities that will not be used, due to their preferences. Some people may be "earnings maximizers" and always "go for the money." By definition, such a person would not have any latent capacity. Note that this does not imply that their earnings are always at their maximum possible. For example, students may be investing in their human capital in order to raise the expected present value of their lifetime earnings. Thus, we would not say that these students have latent capacity. Some workers may be experiencing temporary cuts in pay due to economic conditions in their industry. Again, this is not evidence of latent capacity. Workers who are not earnings maximizers will exercise their preferences by choosing lower-paying positions that provide a preferred lifestyle. These workers will have latent capacity. This latent capacity is a valuable asset that may be exercised should preferences or needs change. For example, a person who has foregone income in order to "pursue their dreams" may find that family changes, such as illness or divorce, may alter their preferences. The value of this latent capacity might be thought to be the highest and best earnings of the worker times the probability that the latent capacity would be exercised. Quick reflection reveals that such a valuation method would convert the earning capacity standard into an expected earnings standard.[11]

It can be difficult to distinguish between a situation where latent capacity truly exists because the worker has chosen not to exercise a higher-paying vocational capacity and a situation where an unobserved functional or vocational capacity limitation prevents the person from taking a higher-paying position. For example, a person may have demonstrated the ability to work in the petroleum services industry where wage rates are high and much overtime is available, but has found the working conditions too grueling to continue. A person may have a commercial driver's license and experience, but find that the psychological toll of driving a long-haul route renders that occupation infeasible. Evidence that distinguishes the two situations may or may not be convincing and a court may not allow the expert to present loss estimates based on an earning capacity that has never been demonstrated or not been demonstrated in the recent past. These considerations apply to both pre-injury and post-injury situations.

Workers choose when to work as well as which vocational capacities to exercise. For example, a worker may temporarily withdraw from the labor force to care for young children. This person would be viewed as having latent earning capacity. How then do we view retirement? If a worker is forced to retire as a result of functional capacity impairment, then the person has lost earning capacity. If a worker has chosen to retire because he or she finds that opportunity cost of the leisure time to be higher than the wage rates, then the worker has remaining latent capacity. Clearly, such decisions are reflected in worklife statistics, but it is difficult to know to what extent. Thus, while worklife tables do not unambiguously reflect earning capacity, it is difficult to know the degree of bias.[12] For this reason, most forensic economists operate under the working assumption that worklife tables represent earning capacity. Some case law requires this.[13]

To summarize, whether a particular choice is voluntarily chosen or rejected, and hence part of earning capacity, or is unattainable and thus not a part of earning capacity, is often difficult to determine. Thus, a rebuttable presumption that each worker "goes for the money" simplifies the litigation process and reduces speculation without eliminating the opportunity for a litigant to produce evidence to the contrary.

2.3.3   The Demand Side

The demand side is characterized by the wage rate and number of hours of work an employer will offer for a given vocational capacity. The demand side is equally important for both the pre-injury and post-injury earning capacity analysis.

For latent capacity to exist, opportunity for additional income above expected income must be offered by some employer. Consider a coal miner who has worked overtime in the past but has not done so in the last five years. Until a recent accident, he was healthy and physically able to work overtime. Further, his status in his union gave him seniority to work overtime. However, the question still remains whether there was sufficient demand within his firm or another to offer overtime work to him. The economist might have to evaluate firm and industry trends in arriving at an answer. Unfortunately for the analyst, demand for a particular vocational capacity can change, sometimes quickly. Demand for particular vocational capacities can vary considerably over time due to short-term seasonal, or long-term macroeconomic or industry-related changes. Such difficulties are much of the reason past actual earnings history usually serves as a measure of pre-injury earning capacity.

Analysis of past actual pre-injury earnings history does not usually require a reappraisal of the worker's vocational capacity, and thus is often statistical rather than vocational in nature. For this reason, pre-injury analysis of earning capacity is usually undertaken by the economist. In contrast, post-injury analysis of earning capacity requires reappraisal of vocational capacity and thus is usually performed by the vocational expert.

In post-injury analysis, the demand side is characterized by the wage rate and number of hours of work an employer will offer for a given vocational capacity. For the injured worker, it is the task of the forensic vocational expert to do a labor market assessment that will provide such information.

Once the vocational expert has prepared a list of potential job titles within the worker's vocational capacity, the question of evaluating that list remains. If we presume that every position on the list is achievable with 100 % probability with the worker needing merely to choose, then there is only one value that is relevant—the highest value. But if there is some probability that the worker will not be able to secure any particular position on the list, then the evaluation is more complex. The vocational evaluation may not give a clear indication of the probability of the plaintiff actually securing one of these positions. A labor market survey should uncover such problems, but such surveys are not always performed.

2.4 Principles of Measuring Impairment to Earning Capacity

Based on the preceding discussion, we present principles which should guide the analyst in measuring loss of earning capacity.

Principle 1: Symmetry
Pre-injury and post-injury earning capacity should be measured consistently, within the limitations of available evidence. If the information available to the analyst before and after an injury were equally available, the measurement techniques for pre-injury and post-injury capacity would be the same. If the forensic economist uses different techniques for measuring pre-injury and post-injury earning capacity, then losses can be inflated or deflated arbitrarily.

Principle 2: Non-binding Choice
Non-binding choices do not reduce earning capacity. Reductions in remuneration, as a result of choosing a job with lower compensation, or working fewer hours than are available, do not reduce a person's earning capacity. A pre-injury choice of an unimpaired person to be a full-time homemaker does not prove that the worker has no earning capacity. In the light of Principle 1, a choice not to work after an injury, in the absence of physical, mental, or psychological limitations, does not reduce that person's post-injury earning capacity. Some choices are non-binding in the short run, but will reduce earning capacity in the long run. If an attorney chooses not to practice law, a loss of skill is likely to result over time.

Principle 3: History and Maximization
It is a rebuttable presumption that a worker chooses to maximize the expected present value of future actual earnings. It is presumed a person's actual earnings are strong indicators of earning capacity. Thus, in the absence of evidence to the contrary, it is assumed that a worker has no latent capacity. This working assumption is subject to contradicting evidence. If a worker has not worked in an occupation with higher expected earnings, then it is presumed the worker could not secure employment in that occupation, or had physical, mental, or psychological limitations that precluded such employment. If a worker has not worked overtime prior to injury, it is presumed the worker did not have the overtime available or was not able to work the overtime. The strength of the presumption will vary, depending on circumstances. A fully-able 30-year-old full-time homemaker may be presumed with some confidence to have some vocational capacity, and thus the existence of latent capacity might not be that difficult to establish. A 65-year-old full-time homemaker with a history of disabilities is less likely to have latent capacity, and thus stronger evidence would be needed to overcome the presumption.

Principle 4: Existence of Supply and Demand
For earning capacity to exist, there must be vocational capacity and demand for that vocational capacity. If a worker does not possess a given vocational capacity, then earnings associated with that capacity are irrelevant to that person's earning capacity. If there is no demand for that vocational capacity, then earnings associated with that capacity are irrelevant to that person's earning capacity.

These principles require a great deal of judgment in application. For example, consider a former attorney who has quit his job to run a hardware store and is then injured. Is his earning capacity that of an attorney or that of a manager running the hardware store? Based on the second principle, the answer depends upon whether his choice to run the hardware store was "non-binding" or not. That, in turn, depends on a whole host of supply factors such as whether he has kept up his skills as an attorney, and whether he is psychologically prepared to resume his attorney practice. Based on the third principle, it may be a rebuttable presumption that the attorney would not able to resume law practice. On the demand side, whether his earning capacity has been reduced will depend on whether law firms would hire him at his previous wage.

2.5   SUMMARY

Earning capacity is the expected earnings of a person who attempts to maximize the expected present value of actual earnings. For such a person, there would be no latent capacity, because expected earnings would equal earning capacity. More simply stated, there is no latent capacity for people who "go for the money." When people choose an occupation and job, there are many features of that job that may be important—income, job stability, safety, distance from home, colleagues at work, personal satisfaction, etc. A person has achieved his or her earning capacity when the choice of job is based entirely on financial rather than nonfinancial factors.

Although most courts endorse earning capacity as the standard of earnings loss in personal injury cases, they are seldom clear in distinguishing earning capacity from expected earnings. Why is earning capacity the standard and why is it important to make a clear distinction between expected earnings and earning capacity? Expected earnings are clearly determined by choice as well as capacity. An individual who had an accident and still capable of employment could increase economic losses and compensation simply by choosing not to work and reducing expected earnings, perhaps even to zero. Thus, the choice to reduce earnings would increase economic losses. To allow this would require defendants to pay not only for a loss of earning capacity but also for choices made by the plaintiff. To compensate a plaintiff assuming reasonable efforts to mitigate losses is to use an earning capacity standard.

Mitigation of damages implies that the plaintiff take reasonable steps after an injury to minimize the loss by searching for alternative employment within their post-injury vocational capacity. Although the determination of post-injury vocational capacity is the task of the vocational expert, the vocational literature does not clearly differentiate earning capacity from expected earnings. Thus, vocational discussion of the measurement of earning capacity often focuses on the process of measurement with little or no discussion of the objective of that process. As an example, many of the vocational "models" that purport to measure post-injury earning capacity are primarily checklists of items to consider in the evaluation.

If we are to use earning capacity as the post-injury standard for earnings, it should also be the standard for pre-injury earnings. If this principle of symmetry were violated, workers who have the ability to perform high-wage occupations could lose any right to compensation if it could be shown that they could work more hours in reduced wage occupations after an injury than they had actually worked prior to the injury. This was the outcome in the *DeWeert* case footnoted earlier, where the court appeared to recognize the problem but indicated that the LHWCA allowed for no other result.

This chapter has presented basic principles for measuring earning capacity loss: (1) the analyst should consistently use the concept of earning capacity for *both* pre and post-injury earning capacity; (2) any non-binding choice made voluntarily such as leaving the labor force to raise a family should not affect earning capacity (except to the extent it causes a reduction in human capital); (3) it is a rebuttable presumption that the worker has no latent earning capacity; and (4) there must be both the potential supply of and actual demand for the relevant vocational capacity in order for a particular job to be evidence of earning capacity.

Because it is the standard of loss articulated most often in personal injury litigation, it is important to understand the subtleties of the earning capacity concept. The courts themselves have not addressed these subtleties clearly, and substantial uncertainty can remain in actual cases. Thorough knowledge of the potential issues and the exercise of good judgment will allow a skilled forensic analyst to overcome this uncertainty. The result will be valid and reliable economic evidence needed by the trier of fact.

Notes

1. It cannot be overemphasized that the forensic economist must have a working knowledge of the case law that pertains to the evaluation of economic losses in the relevant jurisdiction. The authors have found that many otherwise well-qualified attorneys do not understand how legal limitations direct the economic analysis.

2. The first three definitions were initially presented in Horner and Slesnick (1999). Latent earning capacity is a term of convenience that was developed later, but does not alter the theoretical framework of the 1999 paper.

3. A temporary actual earnings rate above the expected level is not evidence of negative latent capacity, but rather an outcome that is higher than expected.

4. Note that when a non-working adult student pursues an education in order to increase long-term expected earnings, this should not be taken as evidence of latent capacity.

5. The forensic economist should not try to be a vocational expert, but should strive to be an expert consumer of vocational analysis.

6. For a specific reference to the RAPEL model, see Weed (1996).

7. See Robinson (2014). In commenting on the Deutsch/Sawyer Model, the following, according to Robinson, is a statement that could be made of many of the vocational models: "The Deutsch/Sawyer model relies upon sub-methods, and protocols that provide significant flexibility within the model. With this high level of flexibility, the principle (sic) question then becomes, can multiple consultants using the same fact pattern utilize the model to arrive at reasonably consistent opinions? No empirical validation studies were identified in the literature for the Deutsch/Sawyer model... Accordingly, its utility as a model rests upon its face validity alone." (Page 36) Perhaps the most well-known vocational method is the RAPEL method. It has strong face and content validity and incorporates many of the variables considered important in the vocational literature. The method allows for a great deal of flexibility in terms of how the vocational expert uses the framework in a particular case. But again, as stated by Robinson, "This high level of flexibility has the potential to compromise the reliability of the model. The principle (sic) question becomes, can multiple consultants using the same fact patterns utilize the RAPEL to arrive at reasonably consistent opinions? Empirical evidence of the RAPEL model's validity or reliability has not been reported" (p. 42).

8. See Tierney and Missun (2001).

9. See *DeWeert v. Stevedoring Services of America*, 272 F.3d 1241 (9th Cir.) 11/29/2001.

10. Economists often use the term human capital, rather than vocational capacity.

11. Suppose we expect John Smith to earn $50,000 per year running a hardware store but his maximum earnings is becoming a night manager of a large retail store, if he chose to do so, for $100,000 per year. Suppose further that we know that he would choose the higher-income option given a change in family circumstances, which we assume has likelihood of occurring equal to 25%. Thus, the value of the latent capacity would be

25 % of the extra $50,000 or $12,500. Adding this to the expected earnings would give $62,500. The expectation of actual earnings, or expected earnings would be .75(50,000) + .25(100,000) = $62,500. Thus, the option value results in the same value as expected earnings. The authors have found no case law suggesting that this is the way the legal system values latent capacity.

12. Readers are referred to the chapter in this book that addresses worklife expectancy in detail.

13. See, for example the *Madore v. Ingram* decision, 732 F.2d 475 at 478 in the 5th Circuit where the court struck expert testimony that strayed from the worklife statistics without a sound basis for doing so. In other words, the court indicated that it is a rebuttable presumption that worklife tables represent earning capacity. The court repeated this admonition in *Barto v. Shore Construction*, 2015 U.S. App. LEXIS 15810.

REFERENCES

Horner, S., & Slesnick, F. (1999). The valuation of earning capacity: Definition, measurement and evidence. *Journal of Forensic Economics, 13*(1), 13–32.

Robinson, R. H. (2014). Forensic rehabilitation and vocational earning capacity models, chapter 3. In R. Robinson (Ed.), *Foundations of forensic vocational rehabilitation*. New York: Springer Publishing Company.

Tierney, J. P., & Missun, R. E. (2001). Defining earning capacity: A process paradigm. *Journal of Forensic Vocational Analysis, 4*, 3–12.

Weed, R. O. (1996). Life care planning and earnings capacity analysis for brain injured clients involved in personal injury litigation utilizing the RAPEL method. *NeuroRehabilitation, 7*(2), 119–135.

CASES CITED

Barto v. Shore Construction, 2015 U.S. App. LEXIS 15810 (5th Cir.) 9/4/2015

DeWeert v. Stevedoring Services of America, 272 F.3d 1241 (9th Cir.) 11/29/2001

Johnson v. Penrod Drilling Company, 510F.2d 234 (5th Cir.) 1975

Madore v. Ingram, 732 F.2d 475 (5th Cir.) 5/24/1984

CHAPTER 3

Evolution of Worklife Expectancy Measurement

Gary R. Skoog and James E. Ciecka

3.1 Introduction

Some people can live to age 110–120, as reflected in current mortality data and tables used to calculate life expectancy. The US government and other governments publish such information, which is so generally accepted that courts grant it judicial notice. Similarly, people can participate in the labor force at advanced ages—comedian George Burns had a contract to perform on his 100th birthday at the London Palladium. Worklife expectancy is the life expectancy analog—it calculates how long, on average, people will participate in the labor force.

When injured individuals can no longer perform their customary work, the forensic economist needs to measure the loss of human capital. Included in this task is the duration of loss—how long participation would reasonably have persisted. This chapter discusses that issue, worklife expectancy, and related notions.

G.R. Skoog (✉)
Legal Econometrics, Inc., Glenview, IL, USA and
DePaul University, Chicago, IL, USA

J.E. Ciecka
DePaul University, Chicago, IL, USA

© The Author(s) 2016
F.D. Tinari (ed.), *Forensic Economics,*
DOI 10.1057/978-1-137-56392-7_3

3.2   HISTORICAL DEVELOPMENT OF WORKLIFE EXPECTANCY

The earliest treatments of the loss of human capital treated worklife expectancy only implicitly, addressing instead the final result of interest to forensic economists, the money value of a man. A book with that title (Dublin and Lotka 1930) traces the origins of human life valuation to Sir William Petty (1662) and William Farr (1853), who wrote 304 and 127 years before use of the term "forensic economics." The money value of man centered around the ideas of the present value of one's earning power (with the idea of taxing human capital), but other questions interested early writers, such as quantifying society's losses from war deaths, measuring national wealth and power, and, more recently, investigating how life expectancy, found to be increasing over time, would be divided between years in the labor force and years not in the labor force. The latter issue received attention during World War II, when the US Bureau of Labor Statistics (BLS) had an Office of Manpower; an interest in worklife expectancy and labor force participation was a part of the war effort. The Farr and Dublin–Lotka approaches were very similar, and estimated a survival-weighted present value of wage income, net of self-consumption or maintenance, incorporating employment probabilities; they did not apply data to labor force participation.

The BLS calculated worklife expectancies for years beginning with the turn of the twentieth century up to the early 1980s. Garfinkle (1955) estimated a worklife expectancy of 39.4 years for 20-year-old men (whose remaining life expectancy was only 42.2 years) in the year 1900. Also, he projected a worklife expectancy of 45.1 years for 20-year-old men for the year 2000, with a life expectancy of 53.8 years based on a Social Security Administration study. BLS *Bulletin 1001* (1950) contained worklife tables by race and urban–rural residence for men for 1940 and 1947. *Bulletin 1204* (1957) dealt with worklife expectancies for women by marital status in 1940 and 1950. Wolfbein (1949) published worklife estimates independently of the BLS for men for 1940, using methods similar to an earlier study that had produced worklife estimates based on labor market activity for 1890–1900. Fullerton and Byrne (1976) reported worklife expectancies for men and women (by marital status and birth of last child) using 1970 data.

Prior to 1982, worklife tables in the USA could be viewed, as mentioned above, to be the labor force counterpart of life tables. One worked until one stopped, just as one lived until one died. The BLS was the center for much of the work, and the operating assumption was that men entered and left the labor force only once in their lives, while women entered and left the labor force as a result of a change in their marital or parental status.

(BLS Bulletin 2135, 1986) We now refer to this type of theoretical model as the *conventional model* of worklife. The tables of Fullerton and Byrne (1976) concluded this approach to worklife expectancy.

The BLS abandoned the conventional model in two important publications, in 1982 and 1986 (*Bulletins 2135* and *2254*, respectively) when it published worklife tables based on a *Markov process*, or *Increment-Decrement model*. In *Bulletin 2135*, the BLS assumed both men and women to be "entering and leaving the labor market repeatedly during their lifetimes, with nearly all participating for some period during their lives." Tables were based on gender, age, initial labor force status (i.e., initially active in the labor force, inactive, and a blend of the two), and based on either educational attainment or race. *Bulletin 2135*, based on 1977 data, contained the BLS's first Markov worklife table. It also provided a detailed exposition of the conventional model, and computed worklife expectancies based on the conventional model. The 1986 table, based on later 1979–80 data, was the last BLS (or any other) US government-agency prepared set of worklife tables; it contained only Markov process-generated tables. Others [primarily Ciecka and his DePaul University colleagues, including Donley, and Goldman (2000); Skoog and Ciecka (2001a and b); Millimet et al. (2003); Krueger (2004), and Skoog-Ciecka-Krueger (2011)] have produced updated worklife expectancy tables with the same model specification of the BLS. In the case of the Skoog–Ciecka and Skoog–Ciecka–Krueger papers, more advanced theoretical results have led to the tabulation of characteristics of the entire statistical distribution of time in the labor force. Although we are aware of no stated rationale for the BLS' discontinuance of worklife expectancy tables, we have heard several informal suggestions: the transfer of Shirley Smith, who was active in the preparation of the last tables; budget cuts; and some at the BLS felt that they were being hounded by litigation lawyers for opinions and explanations and felt lawyers were misusing their work.

3.3 Current (Markov) Model and Conventional Models

3.3.1 Specification

Transition probabilities and survival probabilities comprise the basic building blocks of the Markov process model. We let $^m p_x^n$ denote the probability that a person in state m at age x will be in state n at age $x+1$, where $m = \{A, I\}$ and $n = \{A, I\}$ and where A stands for active in the labor force and I for inactive. These are estimated directly from data of people in a group, who survive to age $x+1$. We then incorporate mortality, and let $^m p_x^n$ denote the probability that a person in state m at age x will be in state n at age $x+1$ where $m = \{a, i\}$ and $n = \{a, i, d\}$ and where a again stands for active in the labor force, i for inactive, and d for the death state. These entities, with lower case superscripts, incorporate mortality, and are derived from the upper case analogues, which are conditional on survival, as follows: $^m p_x^n = {^M p_x^N} (1 - q_x)$. Here q_x is the probability of death between age x and $x+1$. Clearly $^A p_x^A + {^A p_x^I} = 1$ and $^I p_x^A + {^I p_x^I} = 1$, whether in the population, or as estimates by calculating the relative frequencies of those active at one age who are active a year later, indicated by hats, for example, $(^A \hat{p}_x^A + {^A \hat{p}_x^I} = 1)$, since starting at either state, and assuming survival, we must end up somewhere in the next period. Multiplying the equation $^A p_x^A + {^A p_x^I} = 1$ by $1 - q_x$ results in Eq. (3.1a), and defines the transition to death. Similarly, multiplying $^I p_x^A + {^I p_x^I} = 1$ by $1 - q_x$ gives Eq. (3.1b):

$$^a p_x^a + {^a p_x^i} = 1 - q_x \equiv 1 - {^a p_x^d} \tag{3.1a}$$

$$^i p_x^a + {^i p_x^i} = 1 - q_x \equiv 1 - {^i p_x^d} \tag{3.1b}$$

These equations are often expressed as

$$^a p_x^a + {^a p_x^i} + {^a p_x^d} = 1 \tag{3.1a'}$$

$$^i p_x^a + {^i p_x^i} + {^i p_x^d} = 1 \tag{3.1b'}$$

By construction, the same death probability multiplies the active and inactive state, forcing $^a p_x^d = {^i p_x^d}$. It is not clear which way an inequality would go, if one opened this up to examination: if jobs on average posed a death risk greater than the death risk associated with not participating, we would expect that $^a p_x^d > {^i p_x^d}$. However, in general, healthier people work, arguing for the opposite direction. Over the working years, these death probabilities are small; this point has not been perceived as worrying about, and no one has.

3.3.2   Sample Paths

Let us assume that one starts at age x and active. The probability of surviving one year and remaining active is $^a p_x^a$, and the probability of surviving and being active in two years is $^a p_x^a(^a p_{x+1}^a) + ^a p_x^i(^i p_{x+1}^a)$. The latter expression may be interpreted as saying that there are two sample paths (numbers 1 and 2 in the next chart) starting active at age x in which one is active at age $x+2$, $a \to a \to a$ and $a \to i \to a$. We assume that transitions occur at the midpoints of individual years. There are two more sample paths where one is alive but inactive at age $x+2$, namely $a \to i \to i$ and $a \to a \to i$ (numbers 3 and 5). Finally, one may die immediately, $a \to d$, or after surviving for a period, $a \to i \to d$ and $a \to a \to d$. For each of these $2^3 - 1 = 7$ sample paths or event histories, there is a probability, induced by the basic probabilities, and an associated number of years in the labor force. These are recorded in the following chart:

Path number	Path	Probability	Worklife contribution	Worklife contribution	Path expectation
1	$a \to a \to a$	$^a p_x^a\,^a p_{x+1}^a$	$0.5+0.5+0.5+0.5$	2	$2\,^a p_x^a\,^a p_{x+1}^a$
2	$a \to i \to a$	$^a p_x^i\,^i p_{x+1}^a$	$0.5+0+0+0.5$	1	$^a p_x^i\,^i p_{x+1}^a$
3	$a \to a \to i$	$^a p_x^a\,^a p_{x+1}^i$	$0.5+0.5+0.5+0$	1 1/2	$1.5\,^a p_x^a\,^a p_{x+1}^i$
4	$a \to a \to d$	$^a p_x^a\,^a p_{x+1}^d$	$0.5+0.5+0.5+0$	1 1/2	$1.5\,^a p_x^a\,^a p_{x+1}^d$
5	$a \to i \to i$	$^a p_x^i\,^i p_{x+1}^i$	$0.5+0+0+0$	1/2	$0.5\,^a p_x^i\,^i p_{x+1}^i$
6	$a \to i \to d$	$^a p_x^i\,^i p_{x+1}^d$	$0.5+0+0+0$	1/2	$0.5\,^a p_x^i\,^i p_{x+1}^d$
7	$a \to d$	$^a p_x^d$	$0.5+0+0+0$	1/2	$0.5\,^a p_x^d$

By summing the rightmost column, we compute the truncated worklife expectancy over the age range $[x, x+2]$. We call this $^a e_{[x,x+2]}^a$. The fourth column shows the worklife in each of the half year intervals; the second and third elements in any row of the sum must be equal, from our midpoint transition.

If we consider the next (third) transition, the 4 paths where one ended alive have 3 possible outcomes, while the 3 paths resulting in death remain. We therefore have $2^4 - 1 = 15$ sample paths. The sum of the last column again gives $^a e_{[x,x+3]}^a$. Repeating this process until the table ends in a truncation age, TA, often 110 (when everyone is presumed dead) results in $\lim_{n \to TA} {}^a e_{[x,n]}^a = {}^a e_{[x,110]}^a$ Clearly, the number of sample paths is growing exponentially, essentially doubling each period. There are too many sample paths, and too many multiplications and additions to compute at speeds on current computers. Some other approach is needed, one in which the number of computations grows linearly, rather than exponentially, with the number of ages beyond x.

3.3.3   Computation of WLE by Forward Recursion and Decomposition

It is most useful to divide future ages into one year increments at the transition points rather than at exact ages. Starting at exact age x, from x to $x+0.5$ one is either active or inactive, as they were at exact age x. Let $^a e^a_{[x-0.5+j,x+0.5+j]}, j = 1,2,\cdots,TA-1$ denote the piece of worklife expectancy between $x - 0.5+j$ and $x+0.5+j$. Similarly, $^i e^a_{[x-0.5+j,x+0.5+j]}, j = 1,2,\cdots,TA-1$ denotes the pieces of worklife expectancy starting inactive. We record the expressions for worklife expectancy as

$$^a e^a_x = 0.5 + \sum_{j=1}^{j-TA-x} {}^a e^a_{[x-0.5+j,x+0.5+j]} \tag{3.2a}$$

$$^i e^a_x = \sum_{j=1}^{j-TA-x} {}^i e^a_{[x-0.5+j,x+0.5+j]} \tag{3.2b}$$

Similar expressions (with the upper right superscript now set to i, so that years inactive are being measured:

$$^a e^i_x = 0.5 + \sum_{j=1}^{j-TA-x} {}^a e^i_{[x-0.5+j,x+0.5+j]} \tag{3.2c}$$

$$^i e^i_x = \sum_{j=1}^{j-TA-x} {}^i e^i_{[x-0.5+j,x+0.5+j]} \tag{3.2d}$$

The key forward recursions which, follow from (3.3a, 3.3b, 3.3c and 3.3d) below, solve the computation problem are given here as

$$^a e^a_{[x-0.5+j+1,x+0.5+j+1]} = {}^a p^a_{x+j}\, {}^a e^a_{[x-0.5+j,x+0.5+j]} + {}^i p^a_{x+j}\, {}^a e^i_{[x-0.5+j,x+0.5+j]} \tag{3.3a}$$

$$^a e^i_{[x-0.5+j+1,x+0.5+j+1]} = {}^a p^i_{x+j}\, {}^a e^a_{[x-0.5+j,x+0.5+j]} + {}^i p^i_{x+j}\, {}^a e^i_{[x-0.5+j,x+0.5+j]} \tag{3.3b}$$

$$^i e^a_{[x-0.5+j+1,x+0.5+j+1]} = {}^a p^a_{x+j}\, {}^i e^a_{[x-0.5+j,x+0.5+j]} + {}^i p^a_{x+j}\, {}^i e^i_{[x-0.5+j,x+0.5+j]} \tag{3.3c}$$

$$^i e^i_{[x-0.5+j+1,x+0.5+j+1]} = {}^a p^i_{x+j}\, {}^i e^a_{[x-0.5+j,x+0.5+j]} + {}^i p^i_{x+j}\, {}^i e^i_{[x-0.5+j,x+0.5+j]} \tag{3.3d}$$

The Eqs. (3.3a, 3.3b, 3.3c, and 3.3d) not only permit the calculation of the worklife expectancies $^{a}e_{x}^{a}$ and $^{i}e_{x}^{a}$ and years inactive, $^{a}e_{x}^{i}$ and $^{i}e_{x}^{i}$, but they provide their year by year decomposition, that is, a determination of what fraction of each future year is spent in the labor force, on average. The decomposition above appeared in Skoog (2002); what amounts to a weighted average version, combining those starting active and starting inactive, appeared in *Bulletin 2254*, the second and third equations on p. 33. These versions are consistent with the demographic/actuarial science notions of midpoint transitions and linearity between exact ages. Another version appeared in Alter and Becker (1985); Becker and Alter (1987); and Nieswiadomy and Slottje (1988), with a different timing assumption.

3.3.4   Demographic Exposition of WLE

Let $^{a}l_{x}$ and $^{i}l_{x}$ denote the number of actives and inactives at age x in a specific group (usually defined by gender, education, and initial labor force status). For worklife for initial actives, it is traditional to set $^{a}l_{x} = 100,000$ and $^{i}l_{x} = 0$, although any positive value for $^{a}l_{x}$, known as the radix, would work equally well, and setting $^{a}l_{x} = 1$ would simplify Eq. (3.6a–c). Conversely, for worklife for initial inactives, set $^{a}l_{x} = 0$ and $^{i}l_{x} = 100,000$. The Markov process model utilizes the recursions in (3.2a–d).

$$^{a}l_{x+1} = {}^{a}p_{x}^{a}\,{}^{a}l_{x} + {}^{i}p_{x}^{a}\,{}^{i}l_{x} \tag{3.4a}$$

$$^{i}l_{x+1} = {}^{a}p_{x}^{i}\,{}^{a}l_{x} + {}^{i}p_{x}^{i}\,{}^{i}l_{x} \tag{3.4b}$$

Assuming that transitions occur uniformly throughout the year between age x and $x+1$, then

$$L_{x}^{a} = 0.5\left({}^{a}l_{x} + {}^{a}l_{x+1} \right) \tag{3.5}$$

captures person-years of activity between ages x and $x+1$. Worklife expectancy without regard to initial labor force status at age x becomes

$$^{\cdot}e_{x}^{a} = \sum_{j=x}^{TA-1} L_{j}^{a} / \left({}^{a}l_{x} + {}^{i}l_{x} \right) \tag{3.6a}$$

where TA denotes the youngest age after which everyone in the population has died.

Worklife expectancy, that is, the average years of future labor force activity, for initial actives is given when (3.4a) uses $^a l_x = 100,000$ and (3.4b) sets $^i l_x = 0$.

$$^a e_x^a = \sum_{j=x}^{TA-1} L_j^a / ^a l_x$$

(3.6b)

Worklife for initial inactives is given with (3.4a) set to $^a l_x = 0$ and (3.4b) set to $^i l_x = 100,000$.

$$^i e_x^a = \sum_{j=x}^{TA-1} L_j^a / ^i l_x$$

(3.6c)

3.3.5   Backward Recursion and Probability Mass Functions

The equations above require one to perform a summation over all future ages beginning at, say, age x, and then, when the worklife expectancy at age $x+1$ is desired, another summation is performed. There is a much faster way to compute all of the worklife expectancies: by starting at the highest age where the computation is trivial, one may observe that the worklife expectancies at an age one year less are readily computed; proceeding backwards, with the $x+1$ expectations appearing on the right-hand side of (3.7a) and (3.7b) now known, from the age x transition probabilities the worklife expectancies at age x are readily computed, in one pass through the data.

These recursions were given in Skoog (2002) and Foster and Skoog (2004), as

$$^a e_x^a = \underbrace{0.5 + 0.5\,^a p_x^a}_{\text{First year's contribution } to\, e} + \underbrace{^a p_x^a\,^a e_{x+1}^a + ^a p_x^i\,^i e_{x+1}^a}_{\text{Future years' contribution } to\, e}$$

(3.7a)

$$^i e_x^a = \underbrace{0.0 + 0.5\,^i p_x^a}_{\text{First year's contribution } to\, e} + \underbrace{^i p_x^a\,^a e_{x+1}^a + ^i p_x^i\,^i e_{x+1}^a}_{\text{Future years' contribution } to\, e}$$

(3.7b)

In fact, the insight captured in Eq. (3.7a-b) is that, not only are the means at age x and $x+1$ related by backwards recursion, but the entire probability mass functions (pmfs) of the years of future activity are so related.

Skoog and Ciecka (2001a, b, 2002, 2003 and 2010) were able to capture the Markov model's probabilistic implications by viewing years of activity (YA) and years to final labor force separation (YFS) as random variables. This allowed the determination of the entire pmfs for YA and YFS and move beyond the study of expectations. To explain this approach, let $YA_{x,m}$ denote the years-of-activity random variable with $p_{YA}(x, m, y)$ being the probability that a person who is in state m at exact age x will accumulate $YA_{x,m} = y$ years of labor force activity in the future. In a similar vein, let $YFS_{x,m}$ denote the years-to-final-separation random variable where $p_{YFS}(x, m, y)$ denotes the probability that a person who is in state m at exact age x makes a final separation from the labor force in $YFS_{x,m} = y$ years. YA and YFS differ in that the former only counts time in the labor force, but the latter counts all time, including inactive time, prior to final departure from the labor force.

The YA and YFS pmfs with mid-period transitions for initial actives and inactives are specified below by the combination of global conditions, boundary conditions, and main recursions. With pmfs in hand, measurement of labor market activity was not limited to expected values (like WLE or expected years to final labor force separation in the case of *YFS*), and other measures of central tendency like the median and mode could be computed. Measures of dispersion and shape like standard deviation, skewness, and kurtosis can be computed as well. In addition, probability intervals of various sizes can be calculated. The 50 % probability interval may be of particular importance since it corresponds to the idea of accuracy to within a reasonable degree of economic certainty, a critical concept when providing expert testimony. In short, we know the entire probability distribution implied by the Markov model given gender, age, initial labor force status, and education. Skoog and Ciecka provided 24 tables for YA and another 24 tables for YFS characteristics—for six education groups for two initial labor force states for each gender.

We record these recursions, but indicate that they may be skipped by the reader wishing only an overview of the subject, without mathematical details.

Global conditions for random variables $RV \in \{YA, YFS\}$ with midpoint transitions

$$p_{RV}(x,a,y) = p_{RV}(x,i,y) = 0 \quad \text{if } y \langle 0 \text{ or } y \rangle TA - x - 0.5$$

$$p_{RV}(TA,a,0) = p_{RV}(TA,i,0) = 1$$

$${}^{a}p_{x}^{d} = {}^{i}p_{x}^{d} = 1 \quad \text{for } x \geq TA - 1$$

YA pmfs for $YA_{x,m} = y$ for $m \in \{a,i\}$ with midpoint transitions
Boundary conditions:

$$p_{YA}(x,a,0) = 0$$

$$p_{YA}(x,a,0.5) = {}^{a}p_{x}^{d} + {}^{a}p_{x}^{i} p_{YA}(x+1,i,0)$$

$$p_{YA}(x,i,0) = {}^{i}p_{x}^{d} + {}^{i}p_{x}^{i} p_{YA}(x+1,i,0)$$

$$\text{for } x = BA, \ldots, TA - 1$$

Main recursions:

$$p_{YA}(x,a,y) = {}^{a}p_{x}^{a} p_{YA}(x+1,a,y-1) + {}^{a}p_{x}^{i} p_{YA}(x+1,i,y-0.5),$$

$$y = 1.5, 2.5, 3.5, \ldots, TA - x - 0.5$$

$$p_{YA}(x,i,y) = {}^{i}p_{x}^{a} p_{YA}(x+1,a,y-.5) + {}^{i}p_{x}^{i} p_{YA}(x+1,i,y),$$

$$y = 1, 2, 3, \ldots, TA - x - 0.5$$

$$\text{for } x = BA, \ldots, TA - 1$$

YFS pmfs for $YFS_{x,m} = y$ for $m \in \{a,i\}$ with midpoint transitions
Boundary conditions:

$$p_{\text{YFS}}(x,a,y) = 0, \ y = 0,1,2,3,\dots,TA - 1$$
$$p_{\text{YFS}}(x,i,y) = 0, \ y = 0.5,1,2,3,\dots,TA - 1$$

$$p_{YFS}\left(x,a,0.5\right) = {}^{a}p_{x}^{d} + {}^{a}p_{x}^{i} p_{YFS}\left(x+1,i,0\right)$$

$$p_{YFS}\left(x,i,0\right) = {}^{i}p_{x}^{d} + {}^{i}p_{x}^{i} p_{YFS}\left(x+1,i,0\right)$$

for $x = BA,\dots,TA - 1$
Main recursions:

$$p_{YFS}\left(x,a,y\right) = {}^{a}p_{x}^{a} p_{YFS}\left(x+1,a,y-1\right) + {}^{a}p_{x}^{i} p_{YFS}\left(x+1,i,y-1\right)$$

$$p_{YFS}\left(x,i,y\right) = {}^{i}p_{x}^{a} p_{YFS}\left(x+1,a,y-1\right) + {}^{i}p_{x}^{i} p_{YFS}\left(x+1,i,y-1\right)$$

for $x = BA,\dots,TA - 1$ and $y = 1.5,2.5,3.5,\dots,TA - x - 0.5$

3.3.6 *Bootstrap and Standard Errors*

The underlying data used to estimate transition probabilities which, along with survival probabilities,[1] determine the worklife expectancies by the equations above, come from the Current Population Survey (CPS), and so are subject to (small) estimation error. A glance at Eq. (3.3a-d) or (3.7a-b) shows that worklife expectancy depends non-linearly on the underlying transitions, making closed form expressions for the sample variances impossible to calculate. Fortunately, the use of the bootstrap, a modern statistical technique, permits us to consistently estimate the standard errors of the various population quantities being estimated. Skoog and Ciecka (2004a) provide details. The bootstrap was also used by Millimet et al. (2003).

3.4   SPECIFIC POPULATIONS: MULTIPLE DECREMENTS AND/OR UNIQUE TRANSITION PROBABILITIES

In some cases, it makes economic sense to use the earlier conventional worklife table model, which was built on the assumption that, once out (of the active state), one would remain out of the active state. One such instance is railroad workers. Beyond the few initial years of railroad work (when they may not have enough seniority to hold a steady job), it is the case that railroad workers work continuously until a final exit, which may be due to death, disability, or retirement.[2]

The statistical model of this phenomenon is known in actuarial science as a multiple decrement model; in biometrics, it is the competing risks model. Skoog and Ciecka (2006, 2007 and 2014) have produced abridged (every five years) worklife tables for railroad work based on the 23rd and 25th Actuarial Valuations; unabridged tables may be found on the web site of The Association of American Railroads.

3.5   Variants

3.5.1   Lower Order (LPE)

Some forensic economists have used what is now called the *LPE model*[3] of labor market activity. In this model, one multiplies L (probability of survival) by P (probability of participating in the labor force), and by E (probability of employment). The LP part of this model is, in effect, an alternative to the conventional model, and by the remarks below, a very special case of the Markov model of worklife. It differs from both the conventional and the Markov models by incorporating the E factor, the probability of being employed, conditional on participating. A crude version of the LPE model appears in *The Money Value of a Man* (1930), Table VI, and these authors credit Farr (1853). We discuss relations among the Markov, conventional, and LPE models in this section.

The Markov model places no restrictions of transition probabilities beyond being nonnegative and fulfilling (3.1a-b). However, Skoog and Ciecka (2004b) have shown that both the conventional model and the LP part of the LPE model are in fact Markov models, but with additional restrictions imposed on transition probabilities. To see this, let l_x denote the number of people alive at age x, $L_x = 0.5(l_x + l_{x+1})$ is the average number alive between ages x and $x+1$, and let pp_x denote the labor force participation rate at age x. Then the conventional model requires

$$^a p_x^a = \left(L_{x+1} / L_x \right)$$
$$^a p_x^i = 0$$
$$^i p_x^a = \left(L_{x+1} / L_x \right)\left(\left(pp_{x+1} - pp_x \right) / \left(1 - pp_x \right) \right)$$
$$^i p_x^i = \left(L_{x+1} / L_x \right)\left(1 - \left(pp_{x+1} - pp_x \right) / \left(1 - pp_x \right) \right) \tag{3.8a}$$

before the age of peak labor force participation, and it requites

$$^a p_x^a = \left(L_{x+1} / L_x \right) \left(pp_{x+1} / pp_x \right)$$
$$^a p_x^i = \left(L_{x+1} / L_x \right) \left(1 - \left(pp_{x+1} / pp_x \right) \right)$$
$$^i p_x^a = 0$$
$$^i p_x^a = \left(L_{x+1} / L_x \right) \tag{3.8b}$$

beyond the age of post-peak labor force participation.[4] The LP part of the LPE model requires

$$^a p_x^a = {}^i p_x^a = \left(L_{x+1} / L_x \right) pp_x$$
$$^a p_x^i = {}^i p_x^i = \left(L_{x+1} / L_x \right) \left(1 - pp_x \right) \tag{3.9}$$

We call the LPE a lower order variant, because the Markov model allows the state in one period to affect the probability of the being in the state in the following period; it is a first-order process. The LPE model would be zeroth order, since next period's state probability in (3.9) does not depend on the current state.

These extremely restrictive assumptions do not find empirical support. For example, the conventional model for men requires that nobody leaves the labor force for any reason other than death (i.e., $^a p_x^i = 0$) prior to peak labor force participation which occurs at about age 34, and it completely disallows labor force entry after the age of peak labor force participation (i.e., $^i p_x^a = 0$). The LPE model does not recognize that labor force status at age x tells us anything whatsoever about status at age $x+1$ (since it assumes $^a p_x^a = {}^i p_x^a$ and $^a p_x^i = {}^i p_x^i$). These severe restrictions are dubious and certainly are inconsistent with estimates of transition probabilities. See Krueger (2004) for estimates of transition probabilities which show that these assumptions are wrong.

The BLS therefore properly abandoned the conventional model in *Bulletin 2135* in favor of the more general Markov model, without the restrictive assumptions in (3.9).

3.5.2   Higher Order

Having considered zeroth- and first-order Markov processes, it is natural to consider second- and higher-order models. If the probability of transitioning into the active state next period depends on both today's and last year's states, the model is second order.

Skoog (2002) formulated the model. Skoog and Ciecka (2012) have estimated a second-order model for major league baseball players. Rosenbaum and Cushing (2011) have presented results based on second- and third-order models.

3.5.3   Other Variants: Logit Instead of Relative Frequency Estimates

Millimet et al. (2003) have used data from 1992 to 2000 to estimate worklife expectancies using the traditional (i.e., the relative frequency) approach to transition probabilities discussed and employed in the other papers above. They have also estimated parametric models of transition probabilities, using logit functions. Comparing the two methods, they write "[f]or both males and females the worklife expectancies are extremely close...at all education and age levels" (p. 103). They also estimate a multinomial logit function from which they obtained worklife estimates over three states: initially employed, unemployed, and inactive. They have two main conclusions: (1) for both men and women with less than a high school education, worklife estimates for the unemployed are closer to worklife estimates for inactives than to those employed, and (2) as education increases, worklife estimates for the unemployed approach worklife estimates for employed people.

3.5.4   Other Variants: More or Different States

Krueger et al. (2006) calculated worklife expectancies for full-time and part-time workers based on the Markov model. This research provides estimates of the breakout of worklife spent in full-time activity and part-time activity. It also shows differences in worklife for those initially in full-time activity and part-time work. The underlying Markov theory resembles formulae (3.4a-b). Using ft, pt, and i for full time, part time, and inactive, respectively, we have

$$^{ft}p_x^{ft} + {}^{ft}p_x^{pt} + {}^{ft}p_x^{i} + {}^{ft}p_x^{d} = 1$$
$$^{pt}p_x^{ft} + {}^{pt}p_x^{pt} + {}^{pt}p_x^{i} + {}^{pt}p_x^{d} = 1$$
$$^{i}p_x^{ft} + {}^{i}p_x^{pt} + {}^{i}p_x^{i} + {}^{i}p_x^{d} = 1 \tag{3.10}$$

The left superscript indicates as always the beginning period status at age x, and the right superscript indicates the status at the end of the period. We assume that $^{ft}p_x^{d} = {}^{pt}p_x^{d} = {}^{i}p_x^{d} = {}^{\cdot}p_x^{d}$, that is, the probability of dying is independent of labor force status. If one wishes worklife expectancy conditional upon an initial status, say full time, one sets $^{ft}l_x$ to 100,000, and $^{pt}l_x = 0$ and $^{i}l_x = 0$ to start the recursions in (3.11) and calculate the number of persons in the statuses on the left hand sides of the formulae in (3.11) at age $x+1$.

$$^{ft}l_{x+1} = {}^{ft}p_x^{ft} \, {}^{ft}l_x + {}^{pt}p_x^{ft} \, {}^{pt}l_x + {}^{i}p_x^{ft} \, {}^{i}l_x$$
$$^{pt}l_{x+1} = {}^{ft}p_x^{pt} \, {}^{ft}l_x + {}^{pt}p_x^{pt} \, {}^{pt}l_x + {}^{i}p_x^{pt} \, {}^{i}l_x$$
$$^{i}l_{x+1} = {}^{ft}p_x^{i} \, {}^{ft}l_x + {}^{pt}p_x^{i} \, {}^{pt}l_x + {}^{i}p_x^{i} \, {}^{i}l_x \tag{3.11}$$

Define

$$^{ft}L_x = 0.5\left({}^{ft}l_x + {}^{ft}l_{x+1} \right) \tag{3.12}$$

as the person-years spent in the full-time state, and calculate

$$^{ft}e_x^{ft} = \sum_{j=x}^{j=TA-1} {}^{ft}L_j \, / \, {}^{ft}l_x \tag{3.13}$$

as the worklife expectancy of years in the full-time state (the upper right ft superscript) having started in the ft state (the upper left superscript) for a person exact age x.

To count time in the part-time state, but again starting in the full-time state, we compute

$$^{pt}L_x = 0.5\left({}^{pt}l_x + {}^{pt}l_{x+1} \right) \tag{3.14}$$

as the person-years spent in the part-time activity. We calculate the worklife expectancy of part-time years, starting full time, as

$$^{ft}e_x^{pt} = \sum_{j=x}^{j=TA-1} {}^{pt}L_j \, / \, {}^{ft}l_x$$

$$(3.15)$$

In this way, overall worklife expectancy from the full-time state is defined by the sum of the time in the active states, full time, and part time, as

$$^{ft}e_x^{a} \equiv {}^{ft}e_x^{ft} + {}^{ft}e_x^{pt}.$$

$$(3.16)$$

Had we begun in the part-time state, we would have started formulae (3.11) with $^{ft}l_x=0$, $^{pt}l_x=100,000$, and $^{i}l_x=0$ and calculated $^{pt}e_x^{ft}$ and $^{pt}e_x^{pt}$. If inactivity had been the initial state, we would have assumed $^{ft}l_x=0$, $^{pt}l_x=0$, and $^{i}l_x=100,000$ and had calculated $^{i}e_x^{ft}$ and $^{i}e_x^{pt}$.

Skoog and Ciecka (2009) present estimates of the mean and other distributional characteristics of the present value random variable evaluated at several net discount rates. This research contains the first tabulations of the mean, median, standard deviation, skewness, kurtosis, and probability intervals for present value functions at various values of the net discount rate. Such present value tables, in a related setting, go back to Dublin and Lotka (1930).

3.6   FRONT-LOADING AND UNIFORM LOADING

The years of worklife expectancy computed above in the Markov model give the total additional years in the labor force. These years need not be consecutive and immediate. While theoretically correct decompositions or allocations are embedded in formulae above, for example, the individual terms on the right-hand sides of Eqs. (3.2a) and (3.2b), the underlying transition probabilities would be required for a practitioner to obtain these results. In practice, forensic economists often either front load (assume that the WLE comes immediately) or uniformly load (spread the WLE over a larger number of years, such as to age 65, 66, or 67). It is then natural to ask about the biases or corrections to be associated with these two loading methods of allocation. Skoog and Ciecka (2006) produced charts, or nomograms,[5] which permitted a forensic economist to investigate the bias, if any, associated with front loading or uniform loading. At a net discount rate of 0, there is no bias; only at positive values does bias enter. In practice, the necessary corrections vary with active versus inactive status and the age, sex, and education of an individual. Use of these corrections obviates performing more complex and data-intensive analysis of the exact decomposition, where there is no age-earning profile; if present, such a profile would require further study or the more exact methods.

3.7 Temporal Comparison of WLE Estimates

The following table shows BLS *Bulletin 2254* (1986) worklife estimates for 30-year-old men and women in 1970, 1977, and 1979–80. The table also shows worklife expectancies for initially active and initially inactive men and women regardless of education from Skoog and Ciecka (2001b) based on 1997–98 data. In comparison, we show worklife expectancies for high school graduates from the latest work by Skoog et al. (2011) for the years 2005–09.

Group	BLS 1970	BLS 1977	BLS 1979–80	SC 1997–98	SC 2005–09
All men	30.6 years	29.2 years	28.9 years		
Active men			29.2	29.4 years	29.6 years
Inactive men			27.1	27.5	27.2
All women	16.7	19.9	20.8		
Active women			21.7	25.2	25.5
Inactive women			19.1	22.8	22.7

In the foregoing table, BLS worklife expectancies are not conditioned on educational attainment and are directly comparable to the Skoog and Ciecka worklife estimates based on 1997–98 data, and we also show the Skoog, Ciecka, and Krueger worklife expectancies for high school graduates in 2005–09. The worklife for all men (regardless of initial labor force status) in 2005–09 would be between 27.2 years (for inactives) on the low side and 29.6 years on the high side (for actives). The weighted average would be closer to 29.6 (say about 29 years) because most men are active in the labor force at age 30; similar results are obtained from Skoog and Ciecka based on 1997–98 data. We see that the BLS worklives for 1979–80 and the Skoog and Ciecka worklives for 1997–98 and Skoog, Ciecka, and Krueger worklives for 2005–09 are in close agreement. In 1970, worklife was 30.6 years regardless of initial labor for status. Male worklife has declined slightly (about 1.5 years) for men since 1970. It is a different story for women. The worklife for all women (regardless of initial labor force status) in 2005–09 would be between 22.7 years (for inactives) on the low side and 25.5 years on the high side (for actives). In contrast, worklife expectancy was only 16.7 years for women in 1970—an increase somewhere between 36 % and 53 %.

3.8   DISABILITY

Vocational Econometrics Inc. ("VEI") and Anthony M. Gamboa, Jr., have produced tables going back to 1987 which claim to measure the worklife expectancies for persons with and without disabilities. The three latest versions of these tables have been written with David Gibson, and are known as the Gamboa–Gibson tables (2015). These Tables typically are used only in litigation by plaintiffs to support an opinion about the duration of the remaining length of working life of individuals who have suffered an injury. Frequently, their use is in cases where the plaintiff has returned to some work, or is capable of employment, perhaps in another line of work, which gives rise to an earnings differential. The effect of the Tables is to shorten the post-injury worklife in the new, lower-paying job chosen in mitigation, and to overstate the pre-accident worklife expectancy. Unfortunately, severe methodological and data problems and a variety of biases render these tables invalid for their intended use.

Also, when one is truly severely disabled, the inability to participate in the labor force is evident, and there is no need of tables to state the obvious. It is the classification of "non-severe disability" which has led to widespread abuse. The definition of non-severely disabled involves answering "yes" to one or more of the following three questions posed in the CPS: (1) Do you have a health problem or disability which prevents working or which limits the kind or amount of work? (2) Have you ever retired or left a job for health reasons? (3) Do you receive Veterans' payments for disability? And answering "no" to four other questions which determine the presence of "severe disability." Probabilities of employment are then calculated. Not surprisingly, the probability of employment is lower for those self-reporting a "non severe work disability" and is lower still for those self-reporting a "severe work disability." The partial circularity of the very definition is apparent—people claiming trouble working will not be observed working as much.

The tables go on to multiply the joint probability of employment and participation with survival probabilities taken from the US Life Tables, sum the product over future years to age 90, and report the result as a "worklife expectancy."

Inspection of the questions suggests additional problems. The presence of the word *ever* in (2) and the presence of Veterans' payments in (3), as well as the use of the tables by vocational economics (VE)'s employees and affiliates, makes being "non-severely disabled" a permanent condition. This is obviously absurd—people have been known to recover from disabilities. Equally absurdly, when the tables calculate "worklife expectancy" for those who are not now disabled, they implicitly assume that the individual never will become disabled in the future. Evidently, the ensuing higher worklife from someone magically insured against becoming disabled in the future can logically have no role as a comparator in personal injury and wrongful death litigation. The VE procedure leads to upwardly biased worklife as a base, from which they subtract a downwardly biased disabled worklife to produce a difference which is doubly biased, overstating economic damages.

A reading of the questions defining non-severe "work disability" also reveals their compound nature and ambiguity. Health problems are mixed with disabilities; any connection of the resulting population with those possessing similar impairments to those in the subject lawsuit would be a remarkable coincidence. Further, what does it mean to be "limited"— does this refer to any past job or to one's immediate past job, or to one's current job? It is hard to conjecture what CPS respondents believe they should be answering. Any link between leaving a previous job for health reasons and one's ability to participate in a different present job or a contemplated future job is tenuous.

Another major flaw in the CPS-based tables is *sample selection bias*—if a sample is not random, statistical inference which does not correct for lack of randomness is flawed. Here, a *subset* of the underlying entire CPS sample, those who self-report one of the "non-severe disability" criteria, does not represent a random sample of those with any kind of impairment or condition, since by construction the sample includes those whose impairment presents a work-related problem; systematically missing are those with the same impairment which is *not* work limiting. A second econometric difficulty plagues the construction of the tables—the failure of econometric *exogeneity*. Quite simply, this refers to the lack of clear-cut causation from the presence of the impairment to the purported effect, the inability to participate in the labor market or to be employed. In addition to the desired explanation for the association of impairment and low-ered employment, the presence of a feedback relation or reverse causation is also present: people may first decide that they do not wish to work, and then seek a socially acceptable and remunerative explanation in declaring themselves disabled.

The tables using CPS data have been critically discussed in the foren-sic economics literature, first in a book review by Corcione (1995) and later in full-scale peer-reviewed articles by Skoog and Toppino (1999 and 2002), Ciecka and Skoog (2000), Rodgers (2001), and Ciecka et al. (2002). There has been no serious intellectual defense of these tables, and no defense that has attracted any following of informed PhD economists.

As a result of the criticisms above, VE has followed the US Bureau of the Census, and largely abandoned the use of the CPS-based "work disability" definition in its work. It now uses the American Community Survey (ACS) questions, which lead them to definitions based on six dif-ferent types of disability questions. Those definitions are also inappro-priate, because of the afore-mentioned heterogeneity problem and also because the populations identified in the data indicate that a high percent-age of people who state that they have one of the six ACS disabilities in one period, state that they no longer have that disability a year later; mea-sured ACS disability is transitory.[6] Indeed, when a Markov model is fit to data which allows transition into and out of disability, the effect of being initially disabled results in but a year or two of additional time out of the labor force. An additional and significant problem with these data is that it is known that people claiming to have one of the six disability types in fact have another disability type, so that the individual questions' disability responses should not be used in isolation, but rather in the aggregate, to define the overall disabled population.

Together, research has shown that the Gamboa disability tables are unreliable, invalid, misleading, biased, and so are inappropriate for the purpose of measuring decreases in the worklife expectancies persons with specific impairments.

3.9   FUTURE RESEARCH

Future research regarding worklife expectancy will likely progress along several fronts. (1) Tables will be updated. Updated Skoog–Ciecka–Krueger tables probably will be based on 2010–2015 transition prob-abilities. (2) More parametric functions may be estimated and used to calculate worklife expectancy which incorporates additional labor force variables. The generalization of this concept is LOESS—localized regression. Data on higher-order Markov processes from non-CPS datasets may offer insight into transition probabilities at higher ages.

NOTES

1. These come from a different source, the US Life Tables, and their sampling error is miniscule.
2. The fourth potential reason for exit from the industry, withdrawal (leaving railroad work for other employment), while high in the early years accompanied by little seniority, drops off drastically upon the attainment of sufficient seniority to hold a desirable job.
3. The term is due to Brookshire and Cobb (1983).
4. Monotonicity conditions also must be fulfilled in order to get sensible estimates of transition probabilities. In (5a), $^i p_x^a$ would be negative if $pp_{x+1} < pp_x$ for ages x and $x+1$ prior to peak labor force participation. Similarly, estimated $^a p_x^i$ would be negative in (5b) if $pp_{x+1} > pp_x$ for post-peak participation rates. Since probabilities cannot be negative, the model could not be used if estimated participation rates implied negative transition probabilities.
5. We use the term nomogram to emphasize the use of charts proffered in the paper as graphical calculating devices which approximate exact computations with the belief that often approximate answers will be appropriate and useful to forensic economists in the context in which they are offered. A more exact, but also more time consuming, calculation may be warranted in a particular situation after making an easy and quick bias determination from a nomogram.
6. See Krueger and Skoog (2016).

REFERENCES

Alter, G. C., & Becker, W. E. (1985). Estimating lost future earnings using the new worklife tables. *Monthly Labor Review, 108,* 39–42.

Becker, W. E., & Alter, G. (1987). The probabilities of life and work force status in the calculation of expected earnings. *Journal of Risk and Insurance, 54,* 364–375.

Brookshire, M. L., & Cobb, W. (1983). The life-participation-employment approach to worklife expectancy in personal injury litigation and wrongful death cases. *For the Defense, 25,* 20–25.

Bureau of Labor Statistics. (1950). *Tables of working life, length of working life for men, Bulletin 1001.*

Bureau of Labor Statistics. (1957). *Tables of working life for women, 1950, Bulletin 1204.*

Bureau of Labor Statistics. (1982). *Tables of working life: The increment-decrement model, Bulletin 2135.*

Bureau of Labor Statistics. (1986). *Worklife estimates: Effects of race and education, Bulletin 2254.*

Burr, Chauncey Rea. (1915). Economic value of man, together with rules for determining his economic value in every case of injury or disease. Portland, Maine, presented by Mr. Sutherland in the U.S. Senate, and referred to the Committee of Printing, Washington, DC.

Ciecka, J. E., Donley, T., & Goldman, J. (2000). A Markov process model of work-life expectancies based on labor market activity in 1997–98. *Journal of Legal Economics, 9*(3), 33–66.

Ciecka, J. E., Rodgers, J. D., & Skoog, G. R. (2002). The new Gamboa tables: A critique. *Journal of Legal Economics, 12*(2), 61–85.

Corcione, F. P. (1995). The new worklife expectancy tables: Revised 1985 for persons with and without disability by gender and level of education. *Journal of Forensic Economics, 8*(3), 295–297.

Dublin, J. L. I., & Lotka, A. J. (1930). *The money value of a man.* New York: Ronald Press.

Farr, W. (1853). The income and property tax. *Journal of the Statistical Society of London, 16*(1), 1–44.

Foster, E., & Skoog, G. R. (2004). The Markov assumption for worklife expectancy. *Journal of Forensic Economics, 17*(2), 167–183.

Fullerton, Howard N., & James J. Byrne. (1976). *Length of working life for men and women, 1970, special labor force report 187.* U.S. Department of Labor, Bureau of Labor Statistics.

Gamboa Jr., A. M. (1987). *Worklife expectancy of disabled versus nondisabled persons by sex and level of educational attainment.* Louisville: Vocational Econometrics Press.

Gamboa Jr., A. M., & Gibson, D. S. (2015). *Gamboa Gibson worklife tables.* Louisville: Vocational Economics Inc./VEI Press.

Garfinkle, Stuart H. (1955). Changes in working life for men, 1900–2000. *Monthly Labor Review*, March, 297–300.

Krautmann, A. C., Ciecka, J. E., & Skoog, G. R. (2010). A Markov process model of the number of years spent in major league baseball. *Journal of Quantitative Analysis in Sports, 6*(4), 1–23..

Krueger, K. V. (2004). Tables of inter-year labor force status of the U.S. Population (1998–2004) to operate the Markov model of worklife expectancy. *Journal of Forensic Economics, 17*(3), 313–381.

Krueger, K. V., & Skoog, G. R. (2016). Transitions into and out of disability. *Journal of Forensic Economics, 26*(1), 17–51.

Krueger, K. V., Skoog, G. R., & Ciecka, J. E. (2006). Worklife in a Markov model with full-time and part-time activity. *Journal of Forensic Economics, 19*(1), 61–87.

Millimet, D. L., Nieswiadomy, M., Ryu, H., & Slottje, D. J. (2003). Estimating worklife expectancy: An econometric approach. *Journal of Econometrics, 113*, 83–113.

Nieswiadomy, M. L., & Slottje, D. J. (1988). Estimating lost future earnings using the new worklife tables: A comment. *The Journal of Risk and Insurance, 55*(3), 539–544.

Petty, William. (1662). *A Treatise of Taxes & Contributions, shewing the Nature and Measures of Crown Lands, Assessments, Customs, Poll-Money, Lotteries, Benevolence, Penalties, Monopolies, Offices, Tythes, Raising of Coins, Harth-Money, Excize, etc. With several intersperst Discourses and Digressions concerning Warres, The Church, Universities, Rents & Purchases, Usury & Exchange, Banks & Lombards, Registries for Conveyances, Beggars, Ensurance, Exportation of Money & Wool, Free-ports, Coins, Housing, Liberty of Conscience, etc.,The Same being frequently applied to the present State and Affairs of Ireland,* London, Printed for N. Brooke, at the Angel in Cornhill.

Rodgers, J. D. (2001). Exploring the possibility of worklife expectancies for specific disabilities. *The Earnings Analyst, 4*, 1–37.

Rosenbaum, David I., & Matthew J. Cushing. (2011). Higher order Markov processes in worklife estimates, presented at NAFE session, Western Economics Association meetings, July 1.

Skoog, G. R. (2002). *Worklife expectancy: Theoretical results.* Atlanta: Allied Social Science Association , unpublished.

Skoog, R. G., & Ciecka, J. E. (2001a). The Markov (Increment-Decrement) model of labor force activity: New results beyond worklife expectancies. *Journal of Legal Economics, 11*(1), 1–21.

Skoog, R. G., & Ciecka, J. E. (2001b). The Markov (Increment-Decrement) model of labor force activity: Extended tables of central tendency, variation, and probability intervals. *Journal of Legal Economics, 11*(1), 23–87.

Skoog, R. G., & Ciecka, J. E. (2002). Probability mass functions for labor market activity induced by the Markov (Increment-Decrement) model of labor force activity. *Economics Letters, 77*(3), 425–431.

Skoog, R. G., & Ciecka, J. E. (2003). Probability mass functions for years to final separation from the labor force induced by the Markov model. *Journal of Forensic Economics, 16*(1), 49–84.

Skoog, R. G., & Ciecka, J. E. (2004a). Parameter uncertainty in the estimation of the Markov model of labor force activity: Known error rates satisfying Daubert. *Litigation Economics Review, 6*(2), 1–27.

Skoog, R. G., & J. E. Ciecka. (2004b). Reconsidering and extending the conventional/demographic and *LPE* models: The *LPd* and *LPi* restricted Markov models, Allied Social Science Association, San Diego, CA. NEED THIS? DUPLICATE OF NEXT ITEM?

Skoog, R. G., & Ciecka, J. E. (2006a). Worklife expectancy via competing risks/ multiple decrement theory with an application to railroad workers. *Journal of Forensic Economics, Fall, 19*(3), 243–260 (appeared Sept. 2007).

Skoog, R. G., & Ciecka, J. E. (2006b). Allocation of worklife expectancy and the analysis of front and uniform loading with nomograms. *Journal of Forensic Economics, 19*(3), 261–296.

Skoog, R. G., & Ciecka, J. E. (2007). *Worklife expectancies of railroad workers based on the twenty-third actuarial valuation.* Washington, DC: The Association of American Railroads available at http://www.aar.org/pubcommon/docu-ments/AARMonograph.pdf.

Skoog, R. G., & Ciecka, J. E. (2009). Present value recursions and tables. *Journal of Forensic Economics, 21*(1), 63–98 (appeared January 2010).

Skoog, R. G., & Ciecka, J. E. (2010). Probability mass functions and their charac-teristics for years in retirement, and years to retirement within the Markov model. *Demography, 47*(3), 609–628 and online supplement.

Skoog, R. G., Ciecka J. E. & Krueger, K. V. (2011). The Markov process model of labor force activity: extended tables of central tendency, shape, percentile points, and bootstrap standard errors. *Journal of Forensic Economics, 22*(2), 165–229.

Skoog, R. G., & Ciecka, J. E. (2012a). An autoregressive model of order two for worklife expectancies and other labor force characteristics with an application to major league baseball hitters. *Journal of Legal Economics, 18*(2), 47–78.

Skoog, R. G., & Ciecka, J. E. (2012b). Recursions in forensic economics. *Journal of Legal Economics, 18*(2), 143–160.

Skoog, R. G., & Ciecka, J. E. (2014). Worklife expectancy of railroad workers based on the Twenty-Fifth Actuarial Valuation using both competing risks/ multiple decrement theory and the Markov railroad mode. *Journal of Forensic Economics, 25*(2), 109–127.

Skoog, G. R., & Toppino, D. (1999). Disability and the new worklife expectancy tables from vocational econometrics, 1998: A critical analysis. *Journal of Forensic Economics, 12*(3), 239–254.

Skoog, G. R., & Toppino, D. (2002). The new worklife expectancy tables critique: A rejoinder. *Journal of Forensic Economics, 15*(1), 81–97.

Wolfbein, S. L. (1949). The length of working life. *Population Studies, 3*(3), 286–294.

CHAPTER 4

Personal Consumption and Wrongful Death Damages

Kurt V. Krueger and Gary R. Albrecht

4.1 INTRODUCTION

In most legal jurisdictions, survivors of persons wrongfully killed are allowed to seek their own economic damages caused by the death, and, in a smaller set of jurisdictions, the legal estate of the decedent has a claim for damages. As opposed to injury damages where only productivity losses are relevant, wrongful death damages consider both personal productivity and consumption. While other chapters in this book address productivity factors such as earning capacity, this chapter focuses on the evaluation of consumption in determining wrongful death economic damages.

4.2 NORMATIVE DECISION-MAKING ABOUT WRONGFUL DEATH DAMAGES

The methodologies that forensic economists use to determine wrongful death damages are largely *ad hoc* to some normative goal that they have chosen or have been directed to by case law. If the forensic economist is

K.V. Krueger (✉)
John Ward Economics, Prairie Village, USA

G.R. Albrecht
Albrecht Economics, Inc., USA

© The Author(s) 2016
F.D. Tinari (ed.), *Forensic Economics*,
DOI 10.1057/978-1-137-56392-7_4

able to ascertain the but-for-the-death accumulation of wealth (W) and income (Y) of the decedent and survivors, then a normative goal of *income* restitution to the survivors could be decided as $W+Y$ minus the money cost of the goods and services that the decedent (D) would have personally consumed, P_D. The income-related wrongful death damages to survivors (I_S) would be computed as $I_S = W+Y-P_D$ because I_S equalizes the survivors' (S) pre- and post-death consumption dollars. Conversely, a goal of normative *consumption* attainment would be to determine the amount of money which would ensure the survivors' consumption (C_S) at the pre-death standard-of-living associated with $W+Y$ but without their decedent. As discussed later in the chapter, since the death forces changes in the survivors' make-whole consumption needs, the wrongful death damage amounts I_S and C_S are not equivalents.

Without much examination, forensic economics has focused on variations of the income-related valuation of wrongful death damages and the literature and practice seeks measurement of personal consumption as P_D. In the sections below, the methodologies and controversies surrounding the measurement of P_D are presented. After reviewing the income-related valuations, the chapter turns to the overlooked consumption-related version of damage quantification. If the goal of tort damages is to make the survivors as economically whole as possible, it is argued that the consumption approach is superior to the widely used income approach.

4.3   INCOME-RELATED DAMAGES

This section discusses income-related wrongful death damages determination including the normative decisions required for its implementation. Addressing the components of the formula $I_S = W+Y-P_D$, the section is divided into wealth, income, and consumption measurement issues.

4.3.1   Wealth Effects

At the time of death, the wealth of the decedent and survivors (separate and joint) presumably has a knowable balance (negative or positive) and the would-be lifetime accumulation or depletion of that wealth would have been controlled by the decedent and survivors' but-for-the-death income and consumption (Krueger and Albrecht 2008). Unfortunately, the analysis of wealth as a factor in determining wrongful death damages is largely missing in the forensic economic literature and only partially addressed in a few articles about net estate accumulations. Slesnick and Piette (2009) provide a thorough review of net estate accumulations.

If any portion of the decedent's personal consumption would have been financed through the depletion of the decedent's or survivors' positive wealth held at death, then the inheriting survivors are incrementally financially better-off with the death. Conversely, if any portion of the survivors' consumption would have been financed with the personal debts (or transfers from others) of the decedent, then the survivors are incrementally worse-off with the death. Absent cases involving significant amounts of wealth, the accounting of wealth as a necessary component of wrongful death damages is generally a non-issue, leaving wrongful death damages determined based on consumption from income alone.

An empirical problem with determining personal consumption without consideration of wealth is that the forensic economic methodology to estimate personal consumption is based on household income and not household cash-flow. For example, in the 2013–14 Consumer Expenditure Survey ("CEX") Table 3423,[1] household expenditures exceed household income for all two-person consumer units with annual income up to $40,000. At face value, that result means that those households rely on money from sources other than annual income to fund consumption.[2] Consider Table 3433 of the 2013–14 CEX[3] which shows that the household income for three-person consumer units in the $20,000–$29,999 range averages $24,780 but those units have total average expenditures of $32,433. While error could be a part of the disconnect between income and expenditures, at face value the data show that $7653 in annual expenditures is funded from some source other than annual income.[4] Since personal consumption studies show the percent of household income attributable to the consumption of one of its members, such studies include annual consumption dollars financed by some source other than income. The financial information about the wrongful death family generally available to the forensic economist is contained in the family's pre-death income tax returns. When reviewing low-earner tax returns, wage and salary earnings often comprise nearly all of income. In such cases, matching case wage earnings to empirical household income levels can create an income/consumption/wealth mismatch. Ideally, absent accounting for wrongful death case wealth (positive or negative), the forensic economic determination of personal consumption would require a re-work to include consideration of the empirical household's cash-flows which fund annual consumption.

4.3.2   Income Effects

As evident in other chapters in this book about personal injury damages, the forensic economic literature has settled on the methodologies to forecast personal earnings and/or earning capacity. As opposed to personal lifetime wage earnings, wrongful death damages theoretically require a broader estimate of the loss of the income that the decedent would have produced. If a person is not employed, then his or her income comes from the passive returns on accumulated wealth, pensions and retirement savings, or the person receives transfer payments such as government benefits or charity.

In a typical case, an employed decedent's earnings are forecasted through working life and then sometimes retirement income from defined pensions and Social Security are added through life expectancy to complete the estimate of lifetime personal income. From that stream of income, personal consumption at each stage of life is deducted to compute estimated wrongful death damages to survivors. Often ignored during the decedent's estimated working life are expected intermediate income sources such as unemployment compensation and disability income. The standard worklife expectancy methodology includes time spent away from employment for expected bouts of unemployment and disability. Since all income funds consumption, ignoring the decedent's non-wage income during his or her estimated worklife underestimates survivors' wrongful death losses.

An active forensic economic debate is whether survivors' income should be considered when determining the decedent's personal consumption (Brookshire and Slesnick 2009). Legal directives on whether the survivors' post-death income is relevant to their wrongful death damages are sparse and are usually only related to collateral source issues such as survivor benefits and life insurance. Legally, for financial wrongful death damages to exist, there has to be a reasonable expectation that the decedent would have either given money to his or her survivors or specifically purchased or contributed to the purchase of goods and services for his or her survivors' consumption. Through the normal course of family relationships, it is reasonable to assume that survivors would have reciprocated in similar gifting to their decedent. Whether or not survivor gifting should be factored into creating "net damages" to survivors is a normative decision made by the forensic economist.

Since the wrongful death destroyed the pecuniary benefits that the survivors would have received from their decedent, the damage award seeks to make-whole those benefits to the survivors. Under a rationality assumption, the survivors' gifting to their decedent was at its highest and best use and the death deprives the survivors of that use and personal benefit. If survivor gifting is included in determining wrongful death damages, then the chosen normative make-whole goal is the restoration of the survivors to their financial *status quo ante*. The rationale is that the survivor had spent his or her own money for the benefit of the deceased, and as that expenditure is no longer possible, the survivor does not require that amount to be made financially whole post-death. This normative view voids consideration of the survivors' pre-death utility achieved from using their own money to support their decedent—damages should be based on taking the survivors as they were financially found before the death. While valuing utility with money is contentious, measuring the outcome of utility decisions is an everyday role of economics. To deprive the survivors of the sum of their own money that they gifted to their decedent deprives the survivors of the best use of their own money. If grandma best enjoyed spending much of her own money on grandpa, to keep herself as close as possible to economic whole after grandpa's death, grandma will spend that money on what she perceives as a next best use, say on gifts to her grandchildren. The financial *status quo ante* method of determining personal consumption denies grandma that mitigating capability. So, under the *status quo ante* method of personal consumption determination, grandma is always made less than economically whole after the death.

Absent debilitating grief, a wrongful death does not affect the active income-producing abilities of the survivors. Under the normative assumption of ensuring that the survivors are economically as-well-off as if the death had not occurred, (a) there is no reason to decide how much of the survivors' own income should be a credit to the death, and (b) because the survivors can no longer gift to their decedent, that post-death inability to gift would be a net additional, but likely unmeasurable, economic loss. Including survivors' gifting to their decedent as a part of decedent's personal consumption is a normative, not positive, economic decision.

It is useful to frame the differences between the family income and individual income personal consumption approaches with empirical values. From Table 1502 of the 2013–14 mid-year CEX,[5] consumer units consisting solely of two married persons have average household income of $82,541. Drawing upon the 2013-dollar personal consumption estimates of Krueger (2014), from the $82,541 of household income, a decedent husband likely personally consumed $13,285 leaving the balance of $69,256 for the wife's total consumption. Assume that each spouse equally contributes to household income (i.e., each spouse earns $41,270.50). If the married couple decided to consume from only the husband's earnings of $41,270.50, then from Krueger (2014) the husband would need $11,374 for his own personal consumption. So, if the couple decided to use both of their incomes for consumption, the wife is marginally gifting $1911 of her earnings to her husband for his consumption ($13,285 minus $11,374). Another way of viewing this example is that if in time period t only the husband works and earns $41,270.50, then he personally is expected to consume $11,374. However, if the wife became employed in period $t+1$ and also earned $41,270.50, then the husband's personal consumption would increase only by $1911 out of the newly added $41,270.50 of annual household income created by his wife.

Since there is some minimum cost of personal consumption necessary to produce a given level of own earnings, marginal personal spending associated with additional household income might be mostly the expense of the producer of the incremental income. Returning to the example above, the husband's personal consumption dollars might rise with an employed wife because after a long day at work the wife might decide to take her husband out to eat instead of her fixing dinner more inexpensively at home. Or, because the wife is driving to work, gasoline expenses in the household increase. If the household's total gasoline expenses are split equally to the husband and wife, then the husband's measured personal gasoline expenses increase without him driving more miles. Post death, the employed widow still needs gasoline to drive to work, but under the household income personal consumption estimation methodology, her gasoline budget would fall short. Such examples show that incremental household income can wrongfully elevate individual personal consumption—shedding light on the reliability of determining exclusive personal consumption from household income.

When the decedent and survivors work and have comparable earnings, often the dollar differences between the household and individual income method of determining personal consumption are small. However, for decedents who had a remarkably different income-producing ability or outcome than their survivors, there can be large consumption differences between the methods. Putting aside those cases, unless carefully analyzed, proponents of the household income approach can easily create unreliable personal consumption estimates.

If the household income methodology of computing personal consumption is accepted, then the forensic economist must be able to estimate the lifetime income (or necessary cash-flow) positions of families. Currently, there are no generally accepted methodologies in the forensic economic literature for estimating lifetime household income. Some forensic economists avoid the issue by employing a permanent income assumption while others forecast household income as the sum of the decedent's and survivors' expected wage earnings derived over disjointed working lives. Estimating disjointed lifetime wage earnings is not the same as estimating aggregate household income, and (as noted above) funding the decedent's consumption entirely by expected wage earnings understates the survivors' losses.

4.3.3 Defining Personal Consumption Expenditures

When estimating P_D, there are at least three normative views of what goods and services comprise personal consumption expenditures. The lowest valuation (labeled frugal) is produced by examining only those expenditures required to maintain life and earning capacity. The highest valuation (labeled hedonistic) is produced from considering any expenditure made for personal need or want. The intermediate valuation (labeled standard) examines expenditures reasonably assignable to household individuals at the standard-of-living achieved by a certain income level.

The frugal assumption essentially states that any of the decedent's personal consumption beyond that necessary to maintain his or her life and earning capacity represents monies that could have benefited survivors, if necessary; and, to be made whole, only frugal expenses should comprise the decedent's personal consumption estimation. Frugal expenses are often measured with poverty level data. From the US Department of Health and Human Services ("HHS"), the 2015 poverty guidelines[6] start for one-person households at $11,770 and increase by $4160 for each additional person in the household. A frugal estimate of personal consumption for 2015 could be estimated as $4160 per year. A more realistic method of calculating frugal consumption is to sum minimal expenditures recorded from a variety of sources. For example, the US Department of Agriculture supplies low-cost food plans; the HHS has data on spending for health care in the Medical Expenditure Panel Survey; the Federal Highway Administration provides travel data in the National Household Travel Survey; and so on. Such expenditure and related data can be accumulated at their lowest levels to aggregate to an estimated frugal annual consumption amount. Adding up the most basic and necessary expenses for a decedent earning $\$E$ might amount to $\$0.15E$ even though in reality the decedent had been spending $\$0.25E$ on himself or herself. If survivors ever needed to consume more, it is argued the decedent had the capability of altruistically pulling back his or her own consumption to the frugal level of $\$0.15E$.

The frugal assumption essentially restores the survivors to their maximum consumption budget curve. A common explanation offered by a forensic economist employing the frugal assumption (Thornton and Schwartz 1987, 1989) is that the decedent had the capability of reverting to the frugal level of own consumption if the survivors had become unemployed, ill, disabled, bankrupt, and so on, or if the decedent and survivors had some financial goal to accomplish (e.g., putting children through college). It is not difficult to imagine that most survivors would testify as to having that relationship with their decedent. Wrongful death damages under the frugal personal consumption definition seek to measure the depravation of *any pecuniary benefit* that the survivors might have received but-for-the-death. Because the survivors face a trier of fact only once, the loss of any pecuniary benefit is necessarily argued by the plaintiff as compensable. That argument fits with some jurisdictions which state that the survivors' damage claims are not limited to evidence of the decedent's financial support provided at the time of death.

The hedonistic assumption is *status quo ante* to the decedent's and survivors' pre-death total spending regardless of need. Because of either (a) own or joint preferences, or (b) the absence of need, all households likely have some unnecessary personal expenses. Spouses usually purchase items that their mates do not consume. Tortfeasors often point out that when decedents had habitual personal consumption such as tobacco, alcohol, drugs, or expensive hobbies or tastes, such personal spending would have likely continued throughout the decedent's life. It is likely that most survivors would rebut the permanent hedonistic consumption hypothesis by stating that, if necessary, their decedent would have curtailed such consumption, so the frugal consumption level should determine their damages.

Employing the most commonly found standard assumption of personal consumption, the forensic economist balances the extremes of the frugal and hedonistic approaches by studying the average spending empirically found in households similar to the wrongful death household. The standard approach equates personal consumption to the spending on goods and services which could reasonably by thought as only benefiting or required of individual members in households by household income level.

Under the standard personal consumption assumption, wrongful death damages seek to measure, with population average behavior, the standard-of-living held by the survivors at their pre-death household income level.

4.3.4   Allocating Personal Consumption

Once the lifetime income of the decedent and/or household is deter-mined, the challenge of determining personal consumption becomes allocation. Not only must it be decided what are personal as opposed to household goods and services expenditures, but consumption dollars need to be assigned to individual household members. A common, but often unrealistic method of assigning personal consumption expenditures, is the per-capita approach. Using data such as the CEX, dollars spent on goods and services (GS) are evenly allocated to each individual in the household (I_i), only to the subset of adults in the household (A_a), and jointly to all members of the household (J_j) where $i+a$ is equal to the number of house-hold members and $GS=I+A+J$. Personal consumption for an adult in the household is naïvely estimated as $I\div(i+a) + A\div a$. The approach assumes no economies of scale or the complementarity of certain expenditures.

While surveys such as the CEX provide the forensic economist with estimates of household spending by type of good or service, the chief difficulty in constructing standard personal consumption estimates is the allocation of total household expenditures to individual household mem-bers. Expenditure surveys simply report total household spending by item, not who in the household consumes each item. Some personal consump-tion studies attempt to allocate dollars spent for approximately 20 major expenditure categories such as food, clothing, shelter, medical care, and so on. Other studies use detailed data on hundreds of expenditure items. No matter the expenditure detail, because of expenditure survey design, all personal consumption studies must normatively create a set of allocation rules. Sometimes the rulemaking is strictly naïve to household size and sometimes the researcher will try to weight consumption dollars amongst children alone, adults alone, children and adults together, and the house-hold as a unit. Using the same data set but different normative judgments, two forensic economists will arrive at different conclusions as to what amount of spending is personally allocable to one household member.

Assume that a married couple living by themselves own a convertible and a SUV. Suppose the couple spends an average of $12,000 per year on vehicle expenses: $6000 for purchases, $1000 for repairs and maintenance,

$3000 for fuel, and $2000 for insurance and taxes. The naïve allocation might simply assign $6000 to each spouse for personal consumption transportation expenses. In a wrongful death context, such an allocation would deny the surviving spouse of having a SUV for winter driving and a convertible for the summertime. To ensure that the consumption to the surviving spouse is maintained post-death, an amount such as $1500 of fuel costs and a portion of repairs and maintenance would be allocated to the decedent's personal consumption leaving the surviving spouse with access to the balance. Sometimes allocation rules need to recognize economies of scale. Suppose that the married couple spends $500 per year on wine. The surviving spouse drinking the same amount of glasses post-death as pre-death might spend $300 on wine, not $250, because he/she has to throw out some of the wine that spoiled because it was not consumed fast enough. When creating their own estimates or using personal consumption estimates published by others, forensic economists need to be aware of the amount of consumption dollars influenced by the employed normative allocations.

4.3.5   Other Personal Consumption Measurement Issues

Since family members are the survivors of those wrongfully killed, data regarding the expenditures made by families are crucial in determining an appropriate personal consumption amount of the family's income. The term "family data" has a specific meaning to economists as representing information about the subset of all households that consist solely of related persons living and operating as a family unit. However, some personal consumption estimates originate from statistical "consumer units" including not only families but non-related persons sharing shelter and otherwise making their own spending decisions. From Table 3423 of the 2013–14 CEX, in the USA there are 40.86 million consumer units consisting of exactly two persons and from Table 1502 married couples number 27.01 million of those units. So, 13.85 of the 40.86 million units are populated by two unrelated persons, a single parent with one child, or two persons of some other family relationship. Obviously, substantial measurement error of married spouses' personal consumption could result when one-third of the two-person unit sample includes non-married persons.

Wrongful death damages are computed over the life-cycle of the decedent and survivors. Consumption during the years that the decedent was young, employed, and acquiring assets would be different than expected consumption from middle-aged working persons and persons in retirement. If personal consumption estimates are drawn from households delineated by size and income alone, consumption events are conflated and personal consumption funded by wage earnings across the life cycle is not adequately addressed.

4.3.6   Contingent Wrongful Death Damages

When wrongful death economic loss is measured as the decedent's lifetime income less own personal consumption, that amount represents both actual damages to survivors and potentially other contingent amounts that the survivors could, but not necessarily, have lost due to the death. An actual damage is the amount of financial support that the decedent *would have provided* to his or her survivors. A contingent loss is the amount of financial support that the decedent *could have provided* to his or her survivors. The forensic economist is usually unable to allocate the net lifetime income loss amount between the survivors' actual damages and contingent loss amounts. That is because direct evidence regarding how much financial support decedents would have actually provided to survivors lies outside the general evidentiary scope of forensic economics. Economists encounter great difficulty in translating family particularities and relationships into actual monetary losses which is the sworn duty of the trier of fact to reasonably decide.

In the case of a married decedent, the damage amount of decedent's lifetime income less his or her own personal consumption assumes the continuance of marriage. In most jurisdictions, the probability of the continuance of a marriage is relevant to determining damages. It is not within the expertise of the economist to reliably determine the annual probability of the continuance of a specific marriage. Some jurisdictions do not allow the consideration of the income taxes that the decedent would have likely paid, so those expected tax payments are a contingent loss to society that ends up recovered by the survivors (perhaps for the survivors to benefit some portion of society through their own post-death consumption of those amounts). Or, consider survivors of single decedents who are not expected to personally consume all of their own income. Survivors do not necessarily suffer a financial loss upon the death, though there may be a loss of net estate accumulations. In many cases, at the date of death, parents have greater financial resources than does their child. However, the forensic economist is unable to equivocally state that those parents would have never benefitted from or relied on financial support from their child as their child's and their own life positions might change.

When it is forecasted that a decedent would have not used all of his or her own lifetime income for personal consumption, that residual amount must be described as an economic amount lost due to the death but not necessarily lost to the legal survivors of the death. Forensic economists are unable to measure whether or not the survivors lost the total of the decedent's residual income, only that portions of it *could have* been contingently lost to them. The forensic economist reliably measures contingent losses by considering which of the decedent's expenses *could have* possibly benefited the survivors. It is left to the trier of fact to utilize that information along with other evidence and the legal guidance of the court in determining the wrongful death damages that the survivors are entitled to receive from the contingent economic loss created by the death.

4.3.7   Estimates From the Consumer Expenditure Survey

Within forensic economics, most personal consumption amounts are estimated using the CEX which has the primary governmental use of providing information on the buying habits of American consumers so as to form the appropriate bundles of goods and services to compute the Consumer Price Index. The P_D personal consumption dollar and percentage amounts of household income as computed under the Krueger (2014) methodology updated with 2012–14 CEX data are shown in Table 4.1.

The data in Table 4.1 shows the standard result of a concave-shaped personal consumption rate of household income where the percentage of income devoted to personal consumption declines as household income increases. Retired persons spend more of their income on themselves and the lowest income levels have the greatest differences between the consumption of retired and wage-earning married couples.

4.4   Consumption-Based Estimates of Wrongful Death Damages

As discussed in this chapter, the predominant forensic economic calculation of P_D personal consumption dollars is based on *ad hoc* assumptions and closely tied to the normative viewpoint of *status quo ante*. A major shortfall of damages measured with P_D is that those damages do not reflect the

Table 4.1 Personal consumption rates for married persons, 2012–14

Household income	Employed married couples under age 65, no others in home			
	Husband consumption, $'s and % income		Wife consumption, $'s and % income	
$20,000	$7128	35.6 %	$7354	36.8 %
$30,000	$8572	28.6 %	$8887	29.6 %
$40,000	$9770	24.4 %	$10,165	25.4 %
$50,000	$10,814	21.6 %	$11,281	22.6 %
$60,000	$11,750	19.6 %	$12,284	20.5 %
$70,000	$12,604	18.0 %	$13,201	18.9 %
$80,000	$13,393	16.7 %	$14,050	17.6 %
$90,000	$14,130	15.7 %	$14,845	16.5 %
$100,000	$14,824	14.8 %	$15,593	15.6 %

Household income	Retired married couples 65 & over, no others in home			
	Husband consumption, $'s and % income		Wife consumption, $'s and % income	
$20,000	$8223	41.1 %	$8690	43.5 %
$30,000	$10,051	33.5 %	$10,574	35.2 %
$40,000	$11,589	29.0 %	$12,154	30.4 %
$50,000	$12,943	25.9 %	$13,540	27.1 %
$60,000	$14,165	23.6 %	$14,790	24.6 %
$70,000	$15,288	21.8 %	$15,935	22.8 %
$80,000	$16,333	20.4 %	$16,999	21.2 %
$90,000	$17,314	19.2 %	$17,996	20.0 %
$100,000	$18,241	18.2 %	$18,938	18.9 %

Household income	Retired couples' consumption minus employed couples' consumption			
	Difference in husbands' consumption, $'s and % of income		Difference in wives' consumption, $'s and % of income	
$20,000	$1096	5.5 %	$1336	6.7 %
$30,000	$1480	4.9 %	$1688	5.6 %
$40,000	$1819	4.5 %	$1990	5.0 %
$50,000	$2128	4.3 %	$2259	4.5 %
$60,000	$2415	4.0 %	$2506	4.2 %
$70,000	$2685	3.8 %	$2735	3.9 %
$80,000	$2940	3.7 %	$2949	3.7 %
$90,000	$3183	3.5 %	$3152	3.5 %
$100,000	$3416	3.4 %	$3345	3.3 %

realities of the death wrongfully imposed upon the surviving spouses and minor children. Before the death, such survivors' consumption included a consideration of their decedent. After the death and in mitigating the death, survivors are faced with a new set of consumption preferences and needs. Those forced, altered preferences and needs (Lazear and Michael 1980) have gone unaddressed by forensic economics.

Wrongful death damages based on a normative *consumption* restitution would be measured by the amount of money necessary for the survivors' consumption (C_S) at $W+Y$ but without their decedent. While some extra post-death expenses are due to the loss of the decedent's household services, many expenses are created because of lost economies of scale, complementarity of purchases, or they occur from the mitigating behavior of the survivors. Unless forced, post-death consumption expenses are recognized, the survivors are made less than economically whole after the death.

Ignoring wealth, with the same level of household income both married couples and single persons enjoy a certain standard-of-living. Drawing on microdata from the 2013–14 CEX, Table 4.2 shows that wage-earning married couples and single persons with household income between $50,000 and $69,999 spend roughly the same amount of their household income on housing, entertainment, personal care products and services, reading, cash contributions, and personal insurance and pensions.

The 50-50 consumption items appear to be health care, education, and tobacco (which makes sense because those items are not subject to economies of scale in a married couple household). If the food expenditures in a married couple household are normatively split 50-50, then personal food consumption would be around $3100 each, but the single person spends nearly $5000 on food. Some of that additional $1900 may be the result of economies of scale, but it might also occur because in seeking companionship the single person eats away-from-home more often than do married couples. The single person spends more than half of the married couple's apparel bill—maybe they want to look nice for attracting a mate? The transportation category demonstrates that such expenses may not be completely divisible—single persons might have one newer, more reliable automobile than the married couple's two older vehicles? The single person's entertainment bill is nearly equal to that of the married couple—singles are without a companion to enjoy time at home?

From the data in Table 4.2, the P_D personal consumption dollars for one spouse earning all of the $60,068 married couple's income (computed under the updated Krueger (2014) method) is $12,023 leaving the

Table 4.2 Comparison of spending in married couple and single person households, 2013–14

	Household income—$50,000 to $69,999			
Wage earners under age 65	*Married couple*	*Single person*	*Single minus married*	*Ratio: single to married (%)*
Income before taxes	$60,068	$57,180	($2888)	95
Age of reference person	46.4	41.6	(4.8)	90
Average annual expenditures	$49,413	$44,347	($5066)	90
Food	$6224	$4992	($1231)	80
Alcoholic beverages	$438	$659	$221	150
Housing	$15,477	$16,010	$533	103
Apparel and services	$1539	$1273	($266)	83
Transportation	$9600	$7437	($2162)	77
Health care	$4127	$2306	($1821)	56
Entertainment	$2332	$2288	($44)	98
Personal care products and services	$575	$534	($41)	93
Reading	$72	$90	$17	124
Education	$742	$410	($332)	55
Tobacco products and smoking supplies	$457	$263	($194)	58
Miscellaneous	$425	$629	$203	148
Cash contributions	$1356	$1347	($8)	99
Personal insurance and pensions	$6049	$6109	$60	101

surviving spouse with $48,045 in I_S damages. The single person spends 77.6 % of income on expenditures which would gross up the $44,327 in single person expenditures to $46,587 at a $60,068 household income level. If the normative view is that the surviving spouse should be able to live post-death in relation to their pre-death household income level, they would require $46,587 for consumption expenditures plus the residual $60,068 of income less $49,413 in expenditures as a married couple, or $46,587 + ($60,068 − $49,413) = $57,242. Since the decedent spouse would have likely spent some of the asset accumulation and personal insurance and savings, a wealth haircut to those items might be reasonable. The income-based personal consumption rate is 20 % (i.e., $12,023 ÷ $60,068 = 20 %) which would create a wealth haircut of $3341, or ($60,068 − $49,413 + $6049)×20 %. *Ceteris paribus* to a post-death position as a single person, the consumption-based C_S wrongful death damage amount would be $57,242 minus $3341, or $53,901 leaving net deduction from pre-death income of $6167 which is roughly half of the $12,023 income-based personal consumption deduction. The 50 % reduction in the income-based personal consumption deduction of the decedent is required because the wrongful death forces consumption expenditures on the survivor that he or she would not have had as a married person as determined by pre-death consumption allocation percentages.

4.5   Conclusion

While the personal consumption of the decedent is the key separator between personal injury and wrongful death economic damages, this chapter points out that the personal consumption estimates used in forensic economics are largely normatively determined and contain many empirical challenges. Because of the *ad hoc* nature of the methods that continue to be used to measure decedent personal consumption, this chapter suggests that forensic economists should begin to examine the more direct consumption decisions forced upon the survivors due to the wrongful death. Such a view might cause a change in the determination of the economic losses to survivors caused by wrongful death.

Notes

1. See Table 3423 of the 2013–14 CEX found September 19, 2015 on the Internet at http://www.bls.gov/cex/2014/CrossTabs/sizbyinc/xtwo. PDF.
2. In reality, misreporting and incomplete reporting can cause such problems. See, for example, a BLS article found on September 19, 2015 at http://www.bls.gov/opub/mlr/2015/article/pdf/improving-data-quality-in-ce-with-taxsim.pdf.
3. See Table 3433 of the 2013–14 CEX found September 19, 2015 at http://www.bls.gov/cex/2014/CrossTabs/sizbyinc/xthree.PDF.
4. In the CEX, income consists of wages and salaries before any deductions for taxes, pensions, union dues, and so on; self-employment or farm net income or losses; Social Security and other private and government retirement pensions; interest, dividends, rental income, and other property income; periodic receipts from estates or trust funds; net income or loss from roomers or boarders; unemployment and workers' compensation and veterans' benefits; public assistance, supplemental security income, and food stamps including

educational and job training; regular contributions for support including alimony and child support as well as any regular contributions from persons outside the household; and, other income includes money income from care of foster children, cash scholarships, fellowships, or stipends not based on working, and meals and rent as pay. Omitted from CE income are the proceeds received with the sale of owned assets such as stocks and bonds, homes and automobiles, or other property. See http://www.bls.gov/cex/csxgloss. htm#inc found September 19, 2015.

5. See Table 1502 of the 2013–14 CEX found September 19, 2015 at http://www.bls.gov/cex/22014/midyear/cucomp.pdf.

6. See the Department of HHS found September 19, 2015 at http://aspe.hhs.gov/2015-poverty-guidelines.

REFERENCES

Brookshire, M. L., & Slesnick, F. L. (2009). Self-consumption in wrongful death cases: Decedent or family income? *Journal of Forensic Economics, 21*(1), 35–53.

Krueger, K. V. (2014). Personal consumption by family type and household income. *Journal of Forensic Economics, 25*(2), 203–220.

Krueger, K. V., & Albrecht, G. R. (2008). The present value of lost financial support due to wrongful death. *Journal of Legal Economics, 15*(1), 35–42.

Lazear, E. P., & Michael, R. T. (1980). Family size and the distribution of per capita income. *American Economic Review, 70*(1), 91–107.

Schwartz, E., & Thornton, R. J. (1989). Toward a utility-based theory of loss in wrongful death cases. *Journal of Forensic Economics, 2*(2), 67–74.

Slesnick, F., & Piette, M. J. (2009). Net accumulation to the estate: Meaning and measurement. *Journal of Forensic Economics, 20*(3), 227–250.

Thornton, R. J., & Schwartz, E. (1987). The uneasy case for the personal maintenance deduction. *Journal of Forensic Economics, 1*(1), 11–18.

CHAPTER 5

Estimating Educational Attainment and Earning Capacity of a Minor Child

Lawrence M. Spizman

5.1 INTRODUCTION

Because minor children lack an earnings history, estimating their earning capacity in a personal injury matter is more complicated than determining the lost earnings of an adult. Calculating earning capacity losses for newborns is further complicated because the analysis may entail a life care plan that provides funds for such items as food and shelter which typically would have been paid for out of income, potentially double-compensating the minor.

Estimating the earning capacity of a minor child is a two-step process. First, the likely educational attainment(s) of the child must be established. Second, a determination of the age-earnings profile associated with each level of education is required. The purpose of this chapter is to demonstrate how to estimate the probability of a child obtaining each educational level and the corresponding earning capacity.

The simplest approach is to assume the child will obtain two or more specified educational levels. One level may be a high school degree while the second level may be a Bachelor's degree. Any combinations of education can be utilized. For purposes of simplicity, in this discussion

L.M. Spizman (✉)
State University of New York at Oswego, USA

© The Author(s) 2016
F.D. Tinari (ed.), *Forensic Economics*,
DOI 10.1057/978-1-137-56392-7_5

75

two levels of educations are assumed. Lost earnings are then based on the chosen educational attainments that are assumed. This requires the use of earnings data reported for different educational levels. Two sources for earnings by age and education are available: the US Bureau of the Census (2015) and Expectancy Data (2014).

Parental education is sometimes used to justify selection of a child's assumed educational level (usually a higher level) by asserting a connection between family education and a child's higher educational attainment. Vocational experts may discuss not only the parents' educational level but also that of grandparents, uncles, aunts, and siblings. Unfortunately, this simple approach ignores demographic and familial characteristics that may influence the probability of a child achieving each educational level.

Use of educational scenarios implicitly recognizes that there is a 100 percent probability of obtaining a specific degree but ignores the statistical probability of obtaining that degree. If the earnings associated with the two degrees are averaged, then the forensic economist is assuming that there is a 50 percent probability of obtaining each of the two degrees.

If both parents are highly educated, the jury might be convinced that the child would have obtained a Bachelor's degree or higher with 100 percent certainty. This could occur despite the fact that there is no combination of family characteristics that shows any statistical outcome for educational attainment with 100 percent certainty.

This either/or approach, while simpler from a computational perspective, is nevertheless flawed. It requires the economic expert to assume a specific educational attainment when, statistically, the level of educational attainment is based on many family background factors, parents' education being just one.

5.2   Educational Attainment Model History

Estimating the earning capacity of a minor child can be accomplished by determining the probability of a child attaining different educational levels based on family demographic variables. Once these probabilities are determined, they can then be associated with the earning capacity calculated for each educational outcome. The methodology used to estimate the probability of a child's attaining various educational levels is called an ordered probit econometric technique, which is a version of regression analysis. The idea behind an ordered probit model is that an individual's choice of different alternatives can be ranked from lowest to highest in an ordinal fashion. Different levels of education provide such an ordinal ranking. The probabilities that a minor child will not complete high school, will complete high school, will receive a general educational development (GED), will receive an Associate's degree, will receive a Bachelor's degree, will receive a Master's degree, will receive a PhD or will receive a professional degree are calculated. These probabilities depend on parents' years of education, child's sex and race, as well as such other factors as whether the child has siblings, lives with both parents, the age of mother at first birth, income to poverty ratio and other family background characteristics.

Spizman and Kane (1992) developed the first economic model that provides a methodology for estimating the educational attainment of a minor child based on family demographic variables. The variables used to determine the educational levels in the Spizman/Kane (SK92) model are specifically, whether the child was Hispanic, Black or Asian, whether they lived in a rural or urban area and if the parents had less than a high school education, a high school education some college a Bachelor's degree or a graduate degree. Willis (1987), Becker (1983), Schultz (1974), Leibowitz (1974) and Manski and Wise (1983) show the importance of family background in educational achievement as well as adult achievement or failure.

The SK92 paper used a two-stage procedure to estimate the child's expected lifetime earnings. "In the first stage, the probability distribution over alternative levels of the child's expected educational attainment is estimated from observable family background information using an ordered probit model." "In the second stage, the child's expected lifetime earnings' stream is generated using the estimated probit equation" (Spizman and Kane 1992, p. 160).

The second stage requires more effort on the part of the forensic economist compared to estimating the earnings of a child under the two-case scenario. The ordered probit model uses the same process to estimate earnings but requires earnings to be estimated for all educational levels. In this chapter, we do not discuss how the age-earnings profiles and growth rates are established. Every economist has his or her own procedure for accomplishing these.

Other studies using the SK92 model have demonstrated the robustness of the SK92 model's results. Gill and Foley (1996) expanded SK92 by adding variables such as parents' occupation, family composition, number of siblings and religion. They also introduced proxies for the amount of reading that took place in the household. Gill and Foley (GF96) utilized data from the National Longitudinal Survey of Youth (NLSY) rather than The National Longitudinal Study of the High School Class of 1972 as used by SK92.

Kane and Spizman (2001) updated both SK92 and GF96. Kane and Spizman (KS01) took advantage of six additional years of data from the NLSY which made it possible to obtain better estimates of educational attainment for the sample population. Jepsen and Jepsen (2001) introduced a human capital variable into the model. Specifically, they examined the effects of household income and private schooling on educational attainment. Bruce and Anderson (2006) used the Canadian General Social Survey data on the KS01 and Jepsen models. Their study is of particular importance because it demonstrates the robustness and supports the original conclusions of the SK model using international data. Kane et al. (2010) utilized the SK92 and KS01 model approach and examined how the absence of a biological parent affects the future earnings of a minor child. The results suggest that the death of a parent has a relatively small effect on a child's lifetime earnings.

Kane et al. (2013) most recent reiteration of the original SK92 paper took advantage of the current round of interviews from the National Longitudinal Survey of Youth-1997 (NLSY97) to reestimate their educational attainment model. The Kane, Spizman, Donelson (KSD13) study introduced a direct measure of household income to capture the human capital stock of the head(s) of the household. That measure used the ratio of gross household income to the regional poverty level which can be estimated by the forensic economist.[1] The NLSY97 provides data on the age of the biological mother at the birth of her first child, a factor that was found to be an important determinant of educational outcomes. The results of KSD13 are consistent with the findings of all the previous studies using the ordered probit technique, further demonstrating the robustness of the original SK92 model.[2]

5.3   THE EDUCATIONAL ATTAINMENT MODEL

KSD (2013) shows the ordered probit specification modeled as:

$$Z_i = X_i \beta + \mu_i$$

where Z_i is the unobservable variable that shows the benefits and/or costs of different levels of educational attainment. The vector X_i represents the family background and demographic variables that are correlated with Z_i. Z_i is unobservable so an indicator variable is used to represent the actual educational level for each individual. It is assumed that individual i acquires

- Less than a high school degree if $Z_i \leq \theta_1$
- GED if $\theta_1 < Z_i \leq \theta_2$
- High school diploma if $\theta_2 < Z_i \leq \theta_3$
- Associate's degree if $\theta_3 < Z_i \leq \theta_4$
- Bachelor's degree if $\theta_4 < Z_i \leq \theta_5$
- Master's degree if $\theta_5 < Z_i \leq \theta_6$
- PhD degree if $\theta_6 < Z_i \leq \theta_7$
- Medical Doctor (MD), Juris Doctor (JD) or Doctor of Dental Surgery (DDS) degree if $Z_i > \theta_7$

The coefficients from the ordered probit estimates are then used to determine the probability of obtaining each educational level as the highest level of education. Table 5.1 lists the probability designations associated with educational attainment.

The Journal of Forensic Economics' supplemental material provides a spreadsheet associated with Table 5.1 allowing users of the KSD13 model to insert the demographic variables appropriate to their case in order to calculate the probability of obtaining educational outcomes which, in

Table 5.1 Probabilities of alternative levels of educational attainment

Outcome	*Probability
Less than high school degree	$\Phi(\hat{\theta}_1 - \hat{Z})$
GED	$\Phi(\hat{\theta}_2 - \hat{Z}) - \Phi(\hat{\theta}_1 - \hat{Z})$
High school	$\Phi(\hat{\theta}_3 - \hat{Z}) - \Phi(\hat{\theta}_2 - \hat{Z})$
Associate's degree	$\Phi(\hat{\theta}_4 - \hat{Z}) - \Phi(\hat{\theta}_3 - \hat{Z})$
BA or BS degree	$\Phi(\hat{\theta}_5 - \hat{Z}) - \Phi(\hat{\theta}_4 - \hat{Z})$
Master's degree	$\Phi(\hat{\theta}_6 - \hat{Z}) - \Phi(\hat{\theta}_5 - \hat{Z})$
PhD degree	$\Phi(\hat{\theta}_7 - \hat{Z}) - \Phi(\hat{\theta}_6 - \hat{Z})$
Professional degree (DDS, JD, MD)	$1 - \Phi(\hat{\theta}_7 - \hat{Z})$

*$\Phi(\cdot)$ is the cumulative density function for a standard normal random variable

turn, are used to estimate the earnings of the minor child.[3] The medical malpractice traumatic brain injury section of this chapter provides an example of the demographic variables and how they are used.

5.4   USING THE EDUCATIONAL ATTAINMENT MODEL

5.4.1   Age-Earnings Base Year Profiles

As part of the projection of future losses to an impaired child, earnings profiles by educational attainment must be established. The methodology used for this purpose varies among economists. The methodology used by an economist to estimate earnings for a child with a high school degree and a college degree, in the two-case scenario, would also be used to estimate earnings for the other educational levels.

One excellent source of earnings data that is updated annually is Expectancy Data (2014). Expectancy Data constructs summary earnings regarding year-round, full-time workers using data in the 2011, 2012 and 2013 Census' American Community Survey (ACS). This expands the ACS data by publishing percentile views of year-round full-time earnings. Data for different educational levels by age are found on pages 13–17. Age-earnings profiles typically use median earnings for ages 18–24, 25–34, 35–44, 45–54 and 55–64. A more detailed breakdown of age levels is also

Table 5.2   Earnings of males by age and educational level, 2013

*Earnings by age and educational level**

Male 2013

	18–24	25–34	35–44	45–54	55–64
Less than high school diploma	$20,038	$25,622	$30,747	$34,802	$35,871
GED	$21,092	$30,747	$38,287	$41,130	$41,108
High School	$21,662	$31,638	$40,302	$45,095	$45,095
Associate's degree	$25,622	$40,995	$52,731	$59,058	$56,423
Bachelor's degree	$35,264	$52,393	$75,566	$84,369	$78,916
Master's degree	$40,302	$63,543	$90,679	$100,755	$92,240
Ph.D. degree	$29,529	$63,277	$94,915	$110,830	$108,625
	$36,911	$71,714	$128,111	$143,484	$143,484

Source: Expectancy Data (2014), 13–17

available. Table 5.2 shows the age-earnings profile by educational level for males based on the latest available data (Expectancy Data 2014).

Since these data give earnings by age and education as they exist at present, it is necessary to project what the earnings would be in future years extending over several decades. Growth of earnings is determined by the expert. The simplest method is to choose one growth rate for all educational levels. A more detailed method would be to choose a specific earnings growth rate for each educational level. Fringe benefit losses are also to be determined. Statistical data from US Bureau of Labor Statistics (2014), such as Employer Costs for Employee Compensation, may be used.[4]

5.4.2 Worklife Expectancy

Unique to a child case is the need to determine the worklife expectancy for each educational level and corresponding age of the child for that educational level.[5] One source for worklife expectancy is Skoog et al. (2011). Table 5.3 shows if a newborn (born in 2015) male attained a high school diploma at age 19, his worklife would be 38 years. He would have entered the labor market in 2031.7. Alternatively, assuming he were to attain a Bachelor's degree at age 23, his worklife expectancy would be 38.06 years. He would have entered the labor market in the year 2035.7. This process

Table 5.3 Michael Boon

A. Date of Birth	Year and fractional equivalent				
September 11, 2012	2012.70				
B. Date of Trial	2016.33				
May 1, 2016					
Age as of trial	3.64				
C. Work-life expectancy (WLE) by educational levels	Age entering labor force	Year entering labor force	Year of WLE	Age of WLE	Years of WLE
Less than high school diploma	18	2030.70	2064.40	51.70	33.7
GED	18	2030.70	2065.24	52.54	34.54
High school	19	2031.70	2069.70	57.00	38
Associate's degree	21	2033.70	2072.16	59.46	38.46
Bachelor's degree	23	2035.70	2073.76	61.06	38.06
Master's degree	25	2037.70	2076.33	63.63	38.63
Doctorate degree	27	2039.70	2079.04	66.34	39.34
Professional degree	26	2038.70	2078.78	66.08	40.08

is repeated for each educational level. The year the degree would have likely been obtained is to be determined by the expert.

Example: Medical Malpractice Traumatic Brain Injury
The purpose of this section is to demonstrate an application of the model in litigation. Case facts: Michael Boon was born with a traumatic brain injury on September 11, 2012. His mother graduated college (16 years of education) and earns $47,000 annually. His father graduated high school (12 years of education) and earns $43,500. Michael's biological parents are both black and live in an urban area. His mother was 29 years old when she had her first child. The household is Catholic with two other siblings for a total of five family members.

5.4.2.1   Earnings Estimates
An age-earnings profile for each educational level must be computed. Table 5.2 shows abbreviated-form earnings for males by age and educational attainment. The age that Michael will enter the labor force upon completing each educational level and his worklife expectancy for each level of education must be determined. Table 5.3 shows this information.[6] Essentially, Michael's earnings for each of the eight educational levels must be established. If the calculation of earnings for each educational level is not done, then this model should not be used. Table 5.4 shows our calculated lifetime earnings for males at each educational level.

5.4.2.2   Education Probability
To determine the probability of each educational level for a particular individual, a 1 is entered in the model for each appropriate variable and the model will automatically generate the probabilities. Although econo-

Table 5.4 Lifetime earnings of males for each educational attainment

Less than high school diploma	$1,759,640
GED	$2,600,064
High school	$3,292,468
Associate's degree	$4,553,498
Bachelor's degree	$6,823,029
Master's degree	$8,297,874
Ph.D. degree	$10,019,827
Professional degree	$13,821,623

Table 5.5 Model 1 male

Variable (Yes =1&No = 0)		Demographic coefficients	Data input	$\acute{Z}_i =$
Hispanic		−0.1542	0	0.0000
Black		−0.0829	1	−0.0829
MSA		−0.0438	1	−0.0438
Rural		−0.0094	0	0.0000
Mother's years of schooling		0.0190	16	0.3040
Father's years of schooling		0.0199	12	0.2388
Both biological parents present		0.4269	1	0.4269
Mother's age at first birth		0.0345	29	1.0005
Baptist		−0.0775	0	0.0000
Catholic		−0.0163	1	−0.0163
Jewish		0.3472	0	0.0000
Other		0.3812	0	0.0000
No religion		−0.3259	0	0.0000
Number of siblings		−0.0119	2	−0.0238
Income to poverty ratio		0.0563	3.351	0.1886
Model output	θ_1 _	0.1982	$\check{Z}_i =$	1.9920
	θ_2 _	0.7211		
	θ_3 _	2.2012		
	θ_4 _	2.4518		
	θ_5 _	3.6178		
	θ_6 _	4.3556		
	θ_7 _	4.4295		

mists may create their own spreadsheet to generate the probabilities, the Supplemental section on the KSD (2013) provides the spreadsheet.[7] The Supplemental section can be used to verify any economist's calculations.

Table 5.5 shows the coefficient and Z score for KSD (2013) Model I male given the demographic characteristics of Michael.[8]

Each demographic variable receives a 1 where applicable, zero otherwise. The Z column shows the Z scores. These Z scores and thetas from the model are used to generate the probability of obtaining each level of education from the model as shown in Table 5.5.

Table 5.6 shows the results after combining the probabilities generated from the ordered probit model shown in Table 5.5 with the lifetime earnings capacity for Michael from Table 5.4.[9]

Column A (based on family background characteristics) shows the probability of Michael's getting a high school diploma is about 48 percent while the probability of his getting a Bachelor's degree is about 27 percent and the probability of his getting a Master's degree is a bit

Table 5.6   Probability of earnings of males by educational attainment

Probability of earnings for each level of education

Educational attainment

Model—Male

Michael Boon

	Probability of attaining this level of education	Cumulative probability	Lifetime earnings by educational levels	Earnings adjusted for probability
	(A)	(B)	(C)	(D)
Less than high school diploma	3.6419%	3.64%	$1,759,640	$64,085
GED	6.5456%	10.19%	$2,600,064	$170,189
High school	48.0963%	58.28%	$3,292,468	$1,583,557
Associate's degree	9.4317%	67.72%	$4,553,498	$429,474
Bachelor's degree	27.0844%	94.80%	$6,823,029	$1,847,975
Master's degree	4.2950%	99.09%	$8,297,874	$356,395
PhD. degree	0.1655%	99.26%	$10,019,827	$16,580
Professional degree	0.7395%	100.00%	$13,821,623	$102,217
Total earning capacity				$4,570,471

more than 4 percent. Column B shows the cumulative effect of the probabilities to be 100 percent. Column C shows the earnings capacity of Michael for each educational level (from Table 5.4). For example, a male's earning capacity with a Bachelor's degree is shown as $6,823,029. However, since there is only a 27.0844 percent probability that Michael would obtain a Bachelor's degree, the earnings capacity (column C) must be multiplied by the probability of attaining that degree (column A). Michael's earnings, adjusted for the probability of attaining a BA degree, are $1,847,975 (column D). This process is repeated for each educational level and summed to give the total earnings capacity of $4,570,471. If the demographic variables were to change, the total earning capacity calculated in the model would adjust correspondingly.

Some economists may aggregate probabilities and then use those aggregated probabilities to justify using only one educational level. But aggregating either probabilities or educational levels would be a misuse of the model.

5.5   SELF-CONSUMPTION IN PERSONAL INJURY WITH A LIFE CARE PLAN

Child cases can often originate at birth due to alleged medical malpractice. The child in these circumstances may be born with multiple medical issues that require life-long care. In these situations, a life care planner will provide requirements and costs for the remainder of the child's life. The economist will project the costs of the life care plan.

However, the lost earnings estimates can be further complicated if the life care plan is very extensive and requires care for shelter, food, home health, etc. For example, during their adult working life, a percent of future income would have been used for their own benefit for such things as shelter, food and health care. But since the life care plan provides funds for those items, expenditures on them do not have to be made out of income. Thus, a percent of the child's future earnings that would have been allocated for these expenses would therefore be deducted from the loss estimate of his earnings capacity. In other words, it is necessary to determine the appropriate percent deduction for the self-consumption component for the child when he or she is projected to be cared for in a residential care facility.

The child's personal consumption amounts must be derived using the expert's usual methodology. One method is to make use of the percentage for incremental consumption for a one-person male family unit. As noted in Chap. 4 of this book, self-consumption varies by income levels. The process of removing self-consumption for the child avoids double-compensating the child since the extensive life care plan already provides for the loss (see Tinari 1995).

5.6   CONCLUSION

We have explained a methodology for estimating the earnings capacity of a minor child who was injured. A two-stage process is required. One is to estimate the probability of a child obtaining different educational levels based on family background characteristics. An ordered probit model is used for this purpose. The second stage is to use those probabilities to determine earnings capacity associated with each level of education.

Notes

1. KSD13 footnote 29 uses family income, as defined by the Census Bureau's measures of poverty, that includes earnings, unemployment compensation, workers' compensation, Social Security, Supplemental Security Income, public assistance, veterans' payments, survivors benefits, pension or retirement income, interest, dividends, rents, royalties, income from estates, trusts, educational assistance, alimony, child support, assistance from outside the household, and other miscellaneous sources. It is before taxes and does not include noncash benefits such as food stamps and housing subsidies, as well as excluding capital gains or losses, US Census.
2. Although the variables and data sources are different in the different ordered probit models, all the results of the different models are very consistent thus leading to the conclusion that the model itself is robust.
3. See http://www.journalofforensiceconomics.com/loi/foen
4. For more details, see the chapter that follows for a discussion of the calculation of fringe benefits.
5. For a detailed examination of worklife, see Chap. 3 of this volume.
6. For any given educational level, a complete age-earnings profile shows estimated earnings for each projected year, including the effects of assumed wage increases due to inflation and productivity.
7. The supplement to the Kane et al. (2013) article provides the excel spreadsheet to make the necessary calculations and can be found at the following. jfe-360r1 supplement.xls (713 KB)
8. The KSD (2013) paper presents two versions of the model. Model I U.S. Census Bureau (2016) includes the income to poverty ratio while Model II excludes this variable. In actual legal cases, parents may not provide or are not required to provide information about their income to the defense. When that is the case, Model II is to be used.
9. Table 5.5 provides the coefficients used to obtain the probabilities of attaining each level of education. The probabilities are obtained by entering the Z value from Table 5.5 into Table 5.1 using the NORMDIST function in Excel. Endnote 8 provides the source for the excel spreadsheet that generates the calculations.

References

Becker, G. S. (1983). *A treatise on the family*. Cambridge, MA: Harvard University Press.

Bruce, C., & Anderson, C. (2006). The impact of family background on educational attainment in Canada. *Journal of Forensic Economics, 18*(2–3), 125–137.

Expectancy Data (2014). *Full-time earnings in the United States: 2013 edition*. Shawnee: Shawnee Mission.

Gill, A. M., & Foley, J. (1996). Predicting educational attainment for a minor child: Some further evidence. *Journal of Forensic Economics, 9*(2), 101–112.

Jepsen, C., & Jepsen, L. (2001). Re-examining the effects of parental characteristics on educational attainment for a minor child. *Journal of Forensic Economics, 14*(2), 141–154.

Kane, J., & Spizman, L. M. (2001). An update of the educational attainment model for a minor child. *Journal of Forensic Economics, 14*(2), 155–166.

Kane, J., Spizman, L. M., Rodgers, J., & Gaskins, R.. (2010). The effect of the loss of a parent on the future earnings of a minor child, Symposium Paper. *Eastern Economic Journal, 36*(x), 370–390.

Kane, J., Spizman, L. M., & Donelson, D. (2013). Educational attainment model for a minor child: The next generation. *Journal of Forensic Economics, 24*(2), 175–190.

Leibowitz, A. (1974). Home investment in children. In T. W. Schultz (Ed.), *Economics of the family* (pp. 432–452). Chicago: Chicago University Press (for the N.B.E.R.).

Manski, C. F., & Wise, D. A. (1983). *College choice in America.* Cambridge, MA: Harvard University Press.

Schultz, T. W. (1974). *Economics of the family.* Chicago: NBER, University of Chicago Press.

Skoog, G. R., Ciecka, J. E., & Krueger, K. V. (2011). The Markov model of labor force activity: Extended tables of central tendency, shape, percentile points, and bootstrap standard errors. *Journal of Forensic Economics, 22*(2), 165–229.

Spizman, L. M., & Kane, J. (1992). Loss of future income in the case of personal injury of a child: Parental influence on a child's future earnings. *Journal of Forensic Economics, 5*(2), 159–168.

Tinari, F. D. (1995). Do we double-count damages in severe personal injury cases? *Journal of Legal Economics, 5*(2), 23–32.

U.S. Bureau of Labor Statistics. (2014). Office of Compensation and Working Conditions, Employer Costs for Employee Compensation, Table 1. Civilian workers, by major occupational and industry group, all workers. Last modified September 2014. http://stats.bls.gov/news.release/ecec.t01.htm

U.S. Bureau of the Census. (2015). *American Community Survey.* http://www.census.gov/programs-survey/acs/

U.S. Bureau of the Census. (2015). *Educational attaiment people 18 years old and over, by total money* earnings in 2015, work experience in 2015, age, race, hispanic origin and sex. (PINC-04). http://www.census.gov/data/tables/time-series/demo/income-poverty/cps-pinc/pinc-04.html

U.S. Bureau of the Census. (2016). *How the Census Bureau measures poverty.* http://www.census.gov/hhes/www/poverty/about/overview/measure.html

Willis, R. J. (1987, May). What have we learned from the economics of the family. *American Economic Review, 77*(2), 68–81.

CHAPTER 6

Incorporating Fringe Benefits in Loss Calculations

James D. Rodgers

6.1 INTRODUCTION

When a personal injury, wrongful death or wrongful termination causes an employee to suffer a loss of money earnings, this monetary loss is frequently accompanied by a loss of employer-provided fringe benefits. The purpose of this chapter is to provide an overview of the way such fringe benefits can be valued.[1] In presenting the analysis, significant controversies are noted, along with some of the most commonly observed errors in fringe benefits valuation.

Some of the fringe benefit costs employers incur on behalf of employees are legally required; some, such as health insurance, a pension plan, paid leave, a company car, a cell phone and employee discounts, are provided voluntarily.[2] Section 6.2 discusses why employers choose to offer voluntary benefits at all. The answers to this question have implications for the measurement of fringe benefit losses. Section 6.3 discusses the major types of fringe benefits measured by the costs employers incur to provide them, the two most significant being health insurance and retirement plans. Section 6.4 discusses the kind of information needed to value fringe benefits. Section 6.5 discusses general issues in valuing insurance

J.D. Rodgers (✉)
Professor Emeritus, Penn State University, USA

© The Author(s) 2016
F.D. Tinari (ed.), *Forensic Economics*,
DOI 10.1057/978-1-137-56392-7_6

89

and pension benefits, while Sect. 6.6 discusses valuation issues that arise in situations of limited information. Section 6.7 deals with workers with an established employment history, and Sect. 6.8 addresses valuing the loss of benefits to those who were dependent on a deceased worker. Finally, Sect. 6.9 concludes.

At this point, we note that the Patient Protection and Affordable Care Act (PPACA) is in process of being fully implemented, and this act has the potential to change the way the most valuable employer-provided fringe benefit—health insurance—is provided. The National Compensation Survey (NCS) program at the US Bureau of Labor Statistics (BLS) is conducting a study of how the implementation of the PPACA may impact the collection of data on employer-provided health insurance coverage.[3] Because the PPACA is not fully implemented, its impact has not yet fully been manifested, but significant changes may be in the offing, including a major shift in the manner in which the working-age population in the USA obtains health insurance coverage. However, for employers who continue to provide health insurance to workers or pay a portion of the cost of the insurance the worker obtains from whatever source, the methods of fringe-benefit valuation described in this chapter will continue to apply.

6.2   Why Do Firms Offer Voluntary Fringe Benefits to Employees?

In the USA, the costs employers incur on behalf of employees for Social Security and Medicare, federal and state unemployment insurance, and workers compensation are legally required. For voluntarily provided benefits, why do employers incur such costs? A recent paper (Eriksson and Kristensen 2014) offers a succinct explanation:

> The inclusion of nonmonetary benefits and job amenities as important parts of employees' compensation packages have [sic] proliferated across many countries in recent years (see, e.g., the annual reports of the Society for Human Resource Management). From an economic perspective, providing nonmonetary benefits can be rational behavior on the part of both the employer and the employees for three reasons. First, by exploiting scale economies employers can sometimes acquire these goods at a lower cost than single employees. Occasionally the fringe benefits may also be taxed less heavily than income from work. Second, including nonpecuniary benefits in

> compensation packages can also act as a sorting device to attract and retain
> key employees (Oyer and Schaefer 2005; Oyer 2008). Still a third way
> of thinking about nonmonetary compensation, one common in industrial
> psychology studies, is to consider nonmonetary rewards as status and iden-
> tity aspects of a job or position as complements rather than substitutes for
> monetary rewards. (Milkovich and Newman 2010, p. 900)

Health insurance is an example of a benefit for which there are scale economies and tax advantages. Obtaining a group rate for all its employees,
a firm may be able to insure workers for an average cost of $10,000 per
employee, whereas the employee would need to spend $12,000 to pur-
chase the same health insurance as an individual.[4] In addition, the health
insurance offered to the employee is not considered part of the employee's
taxable income.[5] If the firm did not offer health insurance and instead paid
its employees $10,000 more per year, the employees would pay income
and payroll taxes on the additional $10,000, netting, say, only $7,500,
which would be insufficient to purchase equivalent private health insurance coverage priced at $12,000. When the employer provides health
insurance coverage for its employees, the same overall employment cost
is incurred while workers receive a service with a private market price of
$12,000 at a cost of only $7,500 in after-tax dollars. The cost differential and the tax effects raise the effective overall compensation from the
perspective of employees, perhaps making them willing to accept a lower
wage rate and thereby lowering the employer's cost of labor.

   Thus, one reason a firm offers voluntary benefits is that they serve to
assist a firm in attracting the type of workers it desires—the non-wage benefits serve as a sorting device. This is one of the central themes in the field
of personnel economics.[6] Another example of the use of fringe benefits as
a sorting device is a firm that wants to hire highly motivated college graduates who want to work a few years and then return to school for an MBA
degree. The firm may offer a pay package consisting of a reduced salary
and a promise to pay tuition in an MBA program.

   The basic motivation for a firm to provide voluntary benefits is to
attract and keep more suitable employees than the firm could attract and
keep by offering an equivalent amount of money pay. To the extent that
the firm succeeds in this effort, the employees who work for the firm will
be those that value the nonmonetary benefits that are being provided at
least as much as the cash equivalent cost to the employer. In the health
insurance example above, the employee receives health insurance coverage
that would cost $12,000 on the private market at a net-of-tax cost of

only $7500. All of this "gain" might not be kept by the employee. For example, if the employee was required to pay, say, 30 % of the overall health insurance cost as an employee contribution, the employee would pay $3000 and the gain of $4500 ($12,000–$7500) in the previous example gain would drop to $1500. The portion of the cost of health insurance paid by the employer ($7000 = $10,000–$3000) would still represent an underestimate of the value of the health insurance to the employee: $9000 = $12,000–$3000.

6.3   Types and Cost of Employer-Provided Fringe Benefits

The number of different kinds of employer-provided fringe benefits is almost endless,[7] and these benefits may vary considerably among workers. By definition, the employer-provided fringe benefits of self-employed workers are self-financed and do not qualify as an additional element of compensation in loss calculations. Indeed, to count both the money income from self-employment and the value of benefits bought with that money income would be an example of double counting—an error the economic expert should diligently avoid.[8] For workers who are employees, the most important benefits that employers voluntarily provide, as measured by employer cost of provision, are (a) health insurance and (b) a pension and/or retirement savings plan. Data showing the costs employers incur for providing the major categories of fringe benefits are published four times per year by the US Department of Labor's BLS *Employer Cost for Employee Compensation* (ECEC).[9] The data are presented in dollars per hour worked by employees.[10]

Table 6.1 is for all civilian workers and major occupational and industry groups. The categories of benefits shown in Table 6.1 are: paid leave, supplemental pay, insurance, retirement and savings, and legally required benefits. The first two categories of benefits, paid leave and supplemental pay, are included as part of money pay and appear as such in administrative records, for example, employer W-2 forms. The remaining categories are non-wage benefits.

As shown in the "All workers" column in Table 6.1, in September 2015, total compensation per hour worked for all civilian workers averaged $33.37. This total was divided between $22.88 for wages and salaries and $10.48 for benefits. However, $2.32 of the $10.48 was for paid leave, and $0.94 was for supplemental pay, so $3.26 worth of "benefits" was actually money earnings that would show up on employer W-2 forms, for total hourly pay of $26.14. Non-wage fringe benefits amount to $7.22 per

Table 6.1 Employer costs per hour worked for employee compensation and costs as a percent of total compensation: civilian workers, by major occupational and industry group, September 2015

Compensation component	Occupational group						
	All workers[a]		Management, professional, and related		Sales and office		Service	
	Cost	Percent	Cost	Percent	Cost	Percent	Cost	Percent
Total compensation	$33.37	100.0	$55.26	100.0	$24.59	100.0	$17.24	100.0
Wages and salaries	22.88	68.6	37.86	68.5	17.28	70.3	12.25	71.0
Total benefits	10.48	31.4	17.40	31.5	7.31	29.7	4.99	29.0
Paid leave	2.32	7.0	4.41	8.0	1.60	6.5	0.89	5.2
Vacation	1.14	3.4	2.15	3.9	0.80	3.2	0.43	2.5
Holiday	0.70	2.1	1.28	2.3	0.49	2.0	0.28	1.6
Sick	0.34	1.0	0.71	1.3	0.21	0.9	0.14	0.8
Personal	0.13	0.4	0.27	0.5	0.10	0.4	0.05	0.3
Supplemental pay	0.94	2.8	1.73	3.1	0.55	2.2	0.29	1.7
Overtime and premium[d]	0.26	0.8	0.16	0.3	0.15	0.6	0.15	0.9
Shift differentials	0.06	0.2	0.08	0.1	0.02	0.1	0.05	0.3
Nonproduction bonuses	0.63	1.9	1.49	2.7	0.37	1.5	0.09	0.5
Insurance	2.97	8.9	4.46	8.1	2.42	9.8	1.43	8.3
Life.	0.05	0.1	0.08	0.1	0.03	0.1	0.02	0.1
Health	2.83	8.5	4.21	7.6	2.32	9.4	1.39	8.1
Short-term disability	0.06	0.2	0.09	0.2	0.04	0.2	0.02	0.1
Long-term disability	0.05	0.1	0.08	0.1	0.03	0.1	(c)	(f)
Retirement and savings	1.72	5.2	3.30	6.0	0.86	3.5	0.76	4.4
Defined benefit	1.07	3.2	2.02	3.7	0.42	1.7	0.61	3.5
Defined contribution	0.65	2.0	1.27	2.3	0.45	1.8	0.15	0.9

(continued)

Table 6.1 (continued)

Compensation component	Occupational group							
	All workers[a]		Management, professional, and related		Sales and office		Service	
	Cost	Percent	Cost	Percent	Cost	Percent	Cost	Percent
Legally required benefits.	2.52	7.6	3.51	6.3	1.89	7.7	1.62	9.4
Social Security and Medicare	1.84	5.5	2.93	5.3	1.43	5.8	1.01	5.8
Social Security[g]	1.46	4.4	2.30	4.2	1.15	4.7	0.81	4.7
Medicare	0.38	1.1	0.63	1.1	0.28	1.1	0.20	1.2
Federal unemployment insurance	0.03	0.1	0.03	(f)	0.04	0.2	0.04	0.2
State unemployment insurance	0.19	0.6	0.17	0.3	0.18	0.7	0.16	0.9
Workers' compensation	0.46	1.4	0.38	0.7	0.24	1.0	0.41	2.4

Compensation component	Occupational group				Industry group			
	Natural resources, construction, and maintenance		Natural resources, construction, and maintenance		Goods producing[b]		Service providing[f]	
	Cost	Percent	Cost	Percent	Cost	Percent	Cost	Percent
Total compensation	$34.76	100.0	$27.48	100.0	$37.71	100.0	$32.60	100.0
Wages and salaries	23.07	66.4	18.00	65.5	24.99	66.3	22.51	69.1
Total benefits	11.69	33.6	9.48	34.5	12.72	33.7	10.09	30.9
Paid leave	1.94	5.6	1.68	6.1	2.48	6.6	2.29	7.0
Vacation	0.98	2.8	0.86	3.1	1.29	3.4	1.12	3.4
Holiday	0.64	1.8	0.56	2.0	0.86	2.3	0.67	2.1
Sick	0.21	0.6	0.20	0.7	0.23	0.6	0.36	1.1
Personal	0.12	0.3	0.07	0.2	0.09	0.2	0.14	0.4
Supplemental pay	0.99	2.8	0.97	3.5	1.41	3.7	0.86	2.6

Overtime and premium[d]	0.70	2.0	0.56	2.0	0.58	1.5	0.20	0.6
Shift differentials	0.05	0.1	0.09	0.3	0.08	0.2	0.05	0.2
Nonproduction bonuses	0.24	0.7	0.32	1.2	0.75	2.0	0.60	1.9
Insurance	3.31	9.5	3.04	11.1	3.56	9.4	2.87	8.8
Life	0.04	0.1	0.04	0.1	0.07	0.2	0.04	0.1
Health	3.14	9.0	2.88	10.5	3.36	8.9	2.73	8.4
Short-term disability	0.09	0.3	0.06	0.2	0.08	0.2	0.05	0.2
Long-term disability	0.03	0.1	0.07	0.2	0.06	0.2	0.04	0.1
Retirement and savings	2.16	6.2	1.22	4.4	2.07	5.5	1.66	5.1
Defined benefit	1.54	4.4	0.70	2.6	1.18	3.1	1.05	3.2
Defined contribution	0.62	1.8	0.51	1.9	0.89	2.4	0.61	1.9
Legally required benefits	3.29	9.5	2.57	9.3	3.20	8.5	2.40	7.4
Social Security and Medicare	1.95	5.6	1.53	5.6	2.12	5.6	1.79	5.5
Social Security[g]	1.57	4.5	1.23	4.5	1.70	4.5	1.42	4.4
Medicare	0.37	1.1	0.30	1.1	0.41	1.1	0.37	1.1
Federal unemployment insurance	0.03	0.1	0.04	0.1	0.04	0.1	0.03	0.1
State unemployment insurance	0.26	0.8	0.21	0.8	0.25	0.7	0.17	0.5
Workers' compensation	1.05	3.0	0.80	2.9	0.79	2.1	0.41	1.2

(continued)

Table 6.1 (continued)

Note: The sum of individual items may not equal totals due to rounding

[a]Includes workers in the private nonfarm economy excluding households and the public sector excluding the Federal government

[b]Includes mining, construction, and manufacturing. The agriculture, forestry, farming, and hunting sector is excluded

[c]Includes utilities; wholesale trade; retail trade; transportation and warehousing; information; finance and insurance; real estate and rental and leasing; professional and technical services; management of companies and enterprises; administrative and waste services; educational services; health care and social assistance; arts, entertainment and recreation; accommodation and food services; other services, except public administration; and public administration

[d]Includes premium pay (such as overtime, weekends, and holidays) for work in addition to the regular work schedule

[e]Cost per hour worked is $0.01 or less

[f]Less than .05 percent

[g]Social Security refers to the Old-Age, Survivors, and Disability Insurance (OASDI) program

hour, of which insurance benefits amounted to $2.97 per hour worked, and retirement and savings benefits amounted to $1.72 per hour. Hence, slightly under two-thirds of non-wage benefits are accounted for by insurance and retirement plans.

Of the $2.97 for insurance benefits, $2.83 was for health insurance, which is about 95 % of all voluntary insurance costs employers incur. The employee is likely to pay a portion of the cost of health insurance as a deduction from pay but it is only the employer's portion of the cost that represents a fringe benefit loss. Coverage under the plan may include the employee and the employee's immediate family. Some firms offer employees additional money pay if they choose to refuse health insurance coverage under the plan.

Retirement and savings plans provided by employers are virtually always "qualified" retirement plans, meaning the plan provides for income that is deferred to the time of retirement and the plan is given special tax treatment for meeting requirements under the Internal Revenue Code. Income taxes on any employee contributions to the plan are deferred, as well as any income earned by investing such contributions. Retirement and savings plans come in two forms: defined contribution (DC) plans and defined benefit (DB) plans.

DC plans allow the worker to set aside savings for retirement. Each worker has an account showing the contributions (the worker's and the employer's) made to that account. Employers may make contributions to the worker's account whether the worker contributes or not (e.g., 1 % of pay), and the employer may make additional matching contributions (e.g., $0.50 for each $1.00 contributed by the worker) up to some maximum allowed percentage (e.g., 4 % of pay) the worker is allowed to contribute. There is a direct relationship between the firm's contributions on behalf of an employee and the value of the benefit the employee receives. The percentage of pay the employer contributes can be multiplied by the employee's earnings loss to determine the loss of DC benefits.[11]

DB plans promise a specific monthly benefit at retirement. The benefit is payable at a specified time of retirement and may be a fixed dollar amount, for example, $100.00 per month, or it may be an amount based on a formula that depends on the worker's average earnings (e.g., the highest three years) and years of service with the firm. The plan usually specifies the normal retirement age, whether early retirement is permitted and, if so, the amount by which the pension payment is reduced for retiring before the normal retirement age. Workers as well as the firm may make contributions to the plan. The appropriate method of computing a loss of pension benefits as a result of an injury is to compute the present value of the future pension benefits (less any worker contributions) but for an earnings-reducing event, and deducting the present value of the future pension benefits (less any worker contributions), given the earnings-reducing event (Rodgers, 2000; 2002).

Some analysts may be tempted to simplify calculation of the loss of DB plan benefits by computing this loss as a percentage of the worker's lost earnings. This method does not provide an accurate estimate of the lost benefit. The employer contribution to the plan each year is determined by a variety of factors, including: the age distribution of employees and their mortality; employee turnover, which affects the percentage of employees who are vested; the level of interest rates; and the rate of return on other assets in which the plan's funds are invested. The firm's pension contribution in a given year or over recent years, expressed as a percentage of payroll, and multiplied by the worker's lost earnings, would be expected to bear only a very loose and uncertain relationship to the true loss of pension benefits.

There has been a marked shift away from DB plans and toward DC plans over the past 30 years.[12] Many of the DB plans that remain have been modified in some way so as to reduce the future cost of the plan to the employer. Changes include plan terminations, plan "freezes" for new and/or current employees, and changes to the formula by which pension benefits are calculated to make the pension benefits less generous.[13] The changes are designed to reduce the cost exposure of the companies to their DB plans. Hence, when projecting losses of pension benefits for a DB plan, the forensic economist would be wise to assess the likelihood that the worker's employer would have continued offering the plan in the form that existed at the time of the worker's injury or termination.

6.4   INFORMATION NEEDED TO VALUE EMPLOYER-PROVIDED FRINGE BENEFITS

To compute the value of lost fringe benefits for an employed person, information is needed about the following: (a) the type of fringe benefits that was provided by the person's employer at the time of the accident or termination, (b) whether the employed individual chose to receive that benefit or not, if a choice was given, (c) the cost to the employer of providing the fringe benefits, or the cost to the person of replacing the lost benefits.

Whether benefits not chosen at the time of accident should be valued as part of the loss depends on the specifics of the situation. Examples: the availability of company-provided childcare not ever chosen prior to the accident might be used in the future after the employee's pregnant spouse has a baby; a "couch potato" employee might decide to become active and use the company gym. This change in behavior might be the result of a new company policy of reducing the employee's share of health insurance costs if the employee participates in the company "wellness" program. Any valuation of a fringe benefit must adjust for the fact that the benefit was unused, relative to the valuation of that benefit if it was being used by the employee, but making such an adjustment will often prove difficult.

Other useful documents include union contracts[14] and booklets or other documents the employer distributes to employees giving details about the various benefits available and the employee's cost of participating. A "Benefits Statement," may also contain information about the costs the employer bears for providing some or all benefits. Many firms like to tout the costs they incur to provide benefits to employees. For employees who have had to terminate employment due to an injury, most employers are required to offer the employee the opportunity to purchase health insurance benefits for 18 months after ending employment under the Consolidated Omnibus Reconciliation Act (COBRA) of 1985. A document showing the cost the employee must pay for COBRA coverage is provided to the employee.

For adult individuals who were not employed at the time of the incident, it may be possible to make a reasonable projection of the likely occupation that the person would have pursued, based either on the past employment history or plans at the time of the accident. If the injured person was planning to obtain a unionized job, then the relevant union contract should be supplied. Even if a specific job cannot be identified, the occupation and/or industry where the person is likely to have sought employment may be known, allowing the economic expert to use employer cost information for a particular industry or occupational grouping, as shown in Table 6.1.

6.5   VALUING FRINGE BENEFITS

When a dollar of wage income is lost, a dollar can be provided in compensation and that compensation is considered adequate, fair and reasonable. When a particular fringe benefit is lost, such as medical insurance coverage or access to the company's exercise facilities, the appropriate dollar compensation for that loss is less obvious. The benefit lost is not wage dollars but rather an "in-kind" benefit.

What is the ideal measurement of the loss of a fringe benefit? One might first think that the ideal is to measure the value that the worker places on this benefit. However, measuring the value the worker puts on a benefit may be difficult because the worker may not have acquired the fringe benefit in a direct way like the purchase of a good or service in the market. Hence, the familiar revealed preference approach may not be applicable in any direct sense.[15] However, if the worker can be offered the replacement cost of the benefit, then the worker is "made whole" because the worker has the opportunity to replace the fringe benefit that has been lost. Knowing how much the worker values the benefit is unnecessary. Thus, the ideal measurement is the replacement cost of the benefit because being paid the replacement cost puts the worker back in the same situation as if the benefit had not been lost.

For some types of fringe benefit losses, such lost employer contributions to a worker's 401(k) plan, the computation of the replacement cost is easy. The replacement cost is the amount that the employer would have contributed to the plan in the past and in the future but did not because of the worker's injury, similar to the computation of the dollar value of past and future wage losses. However, as Ireland (2014) has emphasized, for lost insurance fringe benefits, it is necessary to make a distinction between past and future losses. Past lost insurance benefits are different from future lost insurance benefits in that while the latter can be both compensated and replaced, the former can only be compensated but not replaced because we cannot turn back the clock to provide insurance for a period of time that is already in the past. Ireland reviews a number of court cases[16] that have compensated for past lost insurance in three alternative ways:

1. The out-of-pocket approach: Allows plaintiffs to recover for their own out-of-pocket cost for replacement insurance and/or amounts paid by plaintiffs that would have been covered by lost past insurance;
2. The employer cost approach: Allows plaintiffs to recover an amount equal to what employers would have paid for insurance if the injury, death or termination had not occurred;
3. The market-replacement cost approach: Allows plaintiffs to recover an amount equal to what it would have cost plaintiffs to purchase replacement insurance (even if they did not so so) equivalent to the insurance that employers would have provided if the injury, death or termination had not occurred.

In a personal injury or wrongful termination case, it is the replacement cost of the lost benefit to the injured or terminated worker that needs to be measured. In a wrongful death case, it is the replacement cost of the lost benefit to the worker's dependents who are named in the wrongful death suit. Because the replacement cost of a fringe benefit to a worker or a worker's dependents may not be directly observable or readily available, forensic economists may rely for better or worse on the employer cost of the benefit to estimate its replacement cost. Replacement costs for some types of benefits, such as medical insurance, are more difficult to determine and substantiate than the employer cost because medical insurance is complex with different types of coverage and different deductibles and co-payments. Hence, without the advice of a medical insurance specialist, matching products in the private insurance market to what was offered by the employer may be difficult and outside the expertise of the forensic economic expert.

Let us examine several situations and indicate the way in which the forensic economic expert would go about placing a value on lost fringe benefits.

6.6 Valuing Fringe Benefits When There Is Limited Information

Estimates of fringe benefits must be made in some legal cases where there is limited information about the person's future-specific employer and/or type of job. For example, the case may involve a young person who has not yet completed his or her education and entered the labor force. Another example is a case that involves a wrongfully terminated worker who has yet to choose another job, and benefits from that future employment must be estimated to compute mitigation benefits. Finally, the case may involve a worker for whom the job and type of benefits is known but the cost of benefits is unknown.

In these situations, the forensic economic expert may choose to estimate statistically the value of benefits using several types of data. The US Bureau of Labor Statistics' NCS collects data from firms on fringe benefits that are reported in two publications: (a) "Employer Cost of Employee Compensation" (ECEC), as presented in Table 6.1; and (b) "Employee Benefits Report" (EBS). For health insurance benefits, another useful source of data showing employer costs is the Kaiser Family Foundation Employer Health Benefits Survey.

The data in Table 6.1 can be used to estimate the fringe benefits for a young person, John Smith, who has not completed his education and entered the labor force. Based on family background and school records, the economic expert projects that Smith, but for a severe brain injury, would likely have graduated from high school and continued his education until he received an associate's degree. Further, he would have earned the median 2014 US earnings for males with this level of educational attainment, namely, $51,202.[17] Adjusting for the average unemployment rate over the past 15 years among males age 25 and over with an associate's degree of 4.72 % and cutting this rate in half to reflect the receipt of unemployment compensation benefits, the unemployment-adjusted annual earnings become $(1 - 0.0236) \times \$51,202 = \$49,994$.[18] Let us also assume that Smith's lifetime earnings but for his injury are projected using a worklife expectancy of 38.9 years from age 20 (taken from Table 36 of Skoog et al. (2011)).

The assumptions in the previous paragraph imply that the estimate of Smith's lifetime earnings but for his injury have incorporated allowances for the negative contingencies of death, disability and unemployment. As Frasca (1992) has noted, in regard to disability, a distinction must be drawn between short-term disability and long-term disability. During periods of short-term disability, the worker is highly likely to be classified as active in the labor force because during the period of short-term disability the worker is likely to be classified as still technically employed. Hence, the time spent in short-term disability would be included in worklife expectancy.

On the other hand, a worker on long-term disability is likely to be regarded as not active in the labor force and the time in the long-term disability status would be excluded from worklife expectancy. Hence, if fringe benefits for short-term disability are excluded and long-term disability insurance are included as a loss, there will be no double counting. On the other hand, if the forensic economic expert does not use a statistical worklife expectancy to set the duration of the working life but rather uses the assumption of continuous employment to some fixed age, such as age 67 or age 70, then the cost of both short-term and long-term disability must be excluded from the estimate of lost fringe benefits because the estimate of lifetime earnings has excluded the possibility of becoming disabled. In the same vein, because of the aforementioned unemployment adjustment that takes unemployment compensation into account, it would be double counting to include in the measure of lost fringe benefits any employer-paid costs for unemployment insurance.

The fringe benefit percentage can be computed using the average wage and benefit cost data shown in Table 6.1. As mentioned in Sect. 6.3, in September of 2015, for all civilian workers in the US economy, money earnings were $22.88 per hour for wages and salaries, $2.32 for paid leave and $0.94 for supplemental pay, for a total of $26.14 per hour.

The next step is to determine the cost of benefits. This cost will normally be the employer cost incurred for health, life and disability insurance, plus the amount for retirement and savings. Using the data in Table 6.1, the fringe benefit cost per hour worked would be $2.97 for insurance, $1.72 for retirement and savings. For the reason discussed, I ignore the $0.03 for federal unemployment insurance and the $0.19 for state unemployment insurance. The $0.46 for Workers Compensation is included because the probability of disability is incorporated into the estimate of Mr. Smith's lifetime money earnings, but for his head injury.

Social Security costs are excluded from the fringe benefit calculation because the use of the employer cost of $1.46 per hour worked to measure this benefit is highly unlikely to bear any resemblance to any potential loss of Social Security benefits. Taylor and Ireland (1996) review cases involving Social Security and Railroad Retirement benefits. A key finding of their review of several US Supreme Court cases[19] involving Social Security is that Social Security benefits (a) are not well-measured by employer taxes paid, (b) are non-contractual and (c) should not be treated as a compensable fringe benefit.[20]

Social Security retirement benefits constitute a type of DB plan (Rodgers 2002). As explained in Sect. 6.3, losses of a DB pension should be computed by estimating the present value of retirement benefits provided by the plan less the present value of any costs the employee pays out of wages to fund the plan during the employee's remaining working years, but for the incident.[21] Hence, if Social Security benefit losses are computed at all and if the correct method of valuing the Social Security pension losses is used, it would be double counting to include the employer cost as shown in Table 6.1 when computing a fringe benefit percentage. Regarding Medicare, the tax the employer pays bears no relationship to the worker's future Medicare benefits after reaching age 65. The employer-paid benefit costs included in lost fringe benefits are therefore $2.91 + $1.72 + 0.46 = $5.09. The fringe benefit percentage is therefore computed as $100 \times \$5.09/\$26.14 = 19.47\,\%$.

However, a major issue must be confronted about the accuracy of the $2.83 component of the $2.91 per hour figure for insurance. The employer cost of $2.83 for health insurance is a weighted average of the employer cost of employers who provide (a) no coverage, and (b) individual coverage and (c) family coverage. If the young person is single, there is a presumption that the courts would hold that "you take the person as you find them" and would not consider it appropriate for the expert to speculate that the young person will form a future family of wife and children. Hence, the assumption is made that the young person remains single. With such an assumption, use of the $2.83 figure to compute the value of health insurance will overstate the value of health insurance because the figure is enlarged by the higher cost of health insurance plans providing family coverage.

A solution to this overstatement problem has been suggested by Foster (2014). He proposes using the BLS EBS survey's average premium for single **medical** insurance coverage for full-time civilian workers, $4,918 (= $409.81 × 12 months) in March 2015,[22] weighted by the proportion of these employees who participate in the employer **medical** insurance plans (67 %),[23] producing an employer cost of $3,295 (= 0.67 × $4,918). By contrast, the implied annual employer cost of **health** insurance using the figure of $2.83 for an employee working 1982 hours per year (2080 hours per year but experiencing average unemployment of 4.72 %) is $5,609, and only a few hundred dollars of this $2,314 difference is accounted for by the fact that the latter figure is for **health** insurance and the former figure is for **medical** insurance. The difference between **health** insurance and **medical** insurance is that the former includes dental and vision insurance. A rough estimate of employer costs for dental and vision coverage combined is in the range of $500 to $600 per employee per year.[24] However, the participation rate for dental and vision is likely to be lower than for medical insurance,[25] meaning that just adding the cost of dental and vision coverage to $4,918 before multiplying by 67 % may produce something of an overestimate of the expected cost. Given the lack of comparable data for dental and vision, the employer costs incurred for dental and vision and participation by employees in such plans, and given the relatively small cost of such plans compared to the cost of medical insurance, it would be prudent for the forensic economist not to attempt to add such costs to the cost of medical insurance.

Given the overstatement involved is using the figure of $2.83 for the cost of health insurance and, therefore, the overstatement involved in computing the overall value of fringe benefits as 19.47 % of money earnings, what should be done? One solution would be to remove the $2.83 from the computation, leaving the fringe benefit percentage as 8.65 % (= 100 × ($0.08 + $1.72 + $0.46)/$26.14)), and adding a fixed dollar amount equal to $3,295 for medical insurance. Then the total dollar value of fringe benefits would be computed as $3,295 + 8.65 % × E, where E is money earnings.

An alternative approach would not remove the cost of health insurance from the fringe benefit percentage; rather, the figure of $2.83 is adjusted downward to a figure consistent with the more accurate cost of health insurance for a single individual. The figure of $2.83 could be replaced by $1.66 (= $3,295/$5,609 × $2.83). Then the fringe benefit percentage of earnings would be computed as 15.0 % (= 100 × [$0.08 + $1.66 + $1.72 + $0.46]/$26.14]). Which of these two approaches to take is not obvious. As Foster (2014) points out, within health insurance plans themselves there is no evidence that benefits are greater for employees with higher earnings, suggesting that the computation of fringe benefits should use 8.65 % × E + $3,295.

But Foster calls attention to evidence in the ECEC itself that occupational and industry groups with higher earnings have more expensive health benefits and these higher benefit costs are approximately proportional to different levels of earnings of these groups. This evidence argues for computing earnings as 15.0 % × E. The approach chosen by a given forensic economist may be based on which approach is easier to defend. Jurors are probably more familiar with health insurance that is the same for everyone in the firm in which they work regardless of pay grade. On the other hand, the PPACA is getting the public familiar with medical insurance plans of different quality sold at prices reflecting those quality differences. So the association between having higher earnings and having better, more expensive health insurance may be becoming more obvious with the use of private insurance exchanges.

6.7   VALUING FRINGE BENEFITS WHEN AN EMPLOYED PERSON IS INJURED

When an employed person is injured, the task of valuing loss fringe benefits begins by determining the nature of the benefits provided by the employer, and using one or more information sources described above in Part IV to assess the cost the employer incurs to provide those benefits. Every situation must be evaluated for its own special circumstances and peculiarities. For highly paid managers and CEOs, there may be stock options and bonuses that depend on the profitability of the firm. For the valuation of stock options, see Carpenter (1998), and Shapiro and O'Connor (2001).

After determining the specific fringe benefits made available to the worker, the utilization of these benefits by the worker needs to be assessed. For example, some workers are offered but reject the opportunity to participate in the employer's 401(k) retirement plan, or choose not to be covered under the employer's health insurance plan. A benefit that is not chosen by the worker arguably has less value to the worker than would be the case if the worker did choose to participate in the benefit coverage. Adjustment for non-use must be made on a case-by-case basis. The percentage of payroll that the employer paid for such benefits for all employees might, in some instances, be a reasonable estimate of the expected value of this benefit. Benefits not chosen have some "option value" in that the worker's circumstances may change (e.g., getting a divorce) in such a way as to make the worker want to participate in the benefit plan (e.g., the employer's health insurance plan once such coverage under the former spouse's plan is no longer available).

Before discussing the valuation of lost health insurance and pension benefits, a couple of general points need to be made. First, there may be a period after the injury but prior to termination from the employer, when certain benefits, such as health insurance coverage, continue even though the worker has stopped receiving a paycheck for time worked. Care must be taken not to count a loss before it begins to occur. Subsequent to this time, employer cost data can be used to project the loss of benefits, taking care to count as a loss only what the employer would have paid, excluding any costs paid by the employee. Second, if an employee is injured but retains a residual ability to work, the fringe benefits provided by the jobs where the injured person is still able to work must be valued and deducted from the value of benefits in the pre-injury job in order to estimate the net loss of fringe benefits, in a manner analogous to the kind of analysis that is done to compute a loss of money earnings.

Health Insurance When the injured worker's employer is known, one good approach to valuing lost health insurance is to determine from the firm's own records the dollar cost of the insurance that is paid by the firm as an estimate of the value of lost health insurance. The cost of a comparable policy priced in the open market is also a good measure. Using the ECEC, EBS or Kaiser EHBS data is only advisable when data on the worker's own firm are unavailable. As noted above, the ECEC will provide a poor estimate because it includes firms that provide no coverage blended with the cost of individual and family coverage. When, for example, the worker is known to have had family coverage, and data regarding the cost incurred by the firm to provide that coverage is unavailable, either the EBS or the Kaiser EHBS should be consulted for the average cost of family coverage. For married workers with working spouses, health coverage may be selected by one of the spouses to cover the entire family, with coverage not being selected at the place of employment of the plaintiff. In such a situation, there is an obvious option value even if insurance coverage is not selected. The evidence may suggest that at some point in the future, the spouse providing the coverage may become unable to do so.

Retirement Benefits The method used to place a value on lost retirement benefits depends on the type of retirement plan offered, that is, DC and DB plans. Within each of these broad categories, there is a very wide variety of retirement and savings plans offered by employers.[26] The forensic economic expert must collect information about the particulars of the plan or plans available to the injured person and the person's participation. The valuation of one type of DC plan and one type of DB plan is discussed for purposes of illustration.

For DC plans, the loss can be readily computed as the percentage of earnings that the employer was contributing to the plan. For example, an injured worker was contributing 4 % of his/her money earnings to a 401(k) plan, with an employer match of 50 cents for each dollar the worker contributed, then the value of the 401(k) benefits lost would be computed as 2 % of the earnings lost from not being able to work for this employer after the accident.

An injury that causes future earnings to be diminished causes a loss of future retirement benefits under DB plan whose formula makes future retirement benefits depend on the worker's average earnings. There may also be a reduction in future pension benefits because of a reduction in the number of years of service due to the need to cease working at the firm because of the injury. The size of the loss depends on the details of the plan.

6.8   VALUING FRINGE BENEFITS WHEN AN EMPLOYED PERSON IS KILLED

Valuing fringe benefits arising from the death of a worker follows the same principles as the valuation when a worker is injured. The major difference in the estimation of lost fringe benefits is the change of focus, under most wrongful death statutes, from what the injured party has lost to what survivors have lost. From the loss of earnings and fringe benefits there will be a deduction for the decedent's personal consumption (or personal maintenance in some states).

When a person dies who was covered at work by health insurance and by a pension plan, the relevant question is how does that death change the value of the fringe benefits that accrue to survivors? For health insurance, death of a covered worker is a qualifying event under COBRA that triggers the requirement that the employer offer continuation coverage to the decedent's spouse and dependent children (Berger, *et al.*, 2002). The premium for COBRA coverage provides a good estimate of the value of the benefit the family has lost. The premium for continuation coverage will be lower than the insurance cost for the entire family because the coverage is for one less person than was being provided before the employee's death. After the end of the 18-month continuation period, the dependents have to go into the private market place for health insurance coverage. Prior to the PPACA, this posed a problem for some survivors who had pre-existing conditions and could not purchase replacement health insurance at any cost. But now replacement coverage can be found on one of the exchanges.

With respect to the effect of a death on pension plan losses, the loss depends on the type of plan. For a DC plan, the loss is the employer's contributions that would have been made to the plan computed as a percentage of lost earnings, just as in an injury case. With a DB plan, a lot depends on the details of the plan. Some plans provide for a death benefit if the employee dies before the age of retirement. For example, the Pennsylvania State Employees Retirement System has a provision for a death benefit. The amount of the death benefit is essentially the present value of future retirement benefits. The death of an employee in state service "activates" this death benefit. Some forensic economists regard such an activation of benefits as a reason to ignore a loss computation because the activated benefit is as large as the benefit that the surviving spouse would have received if the employee had not died. However, "activated" benefits may be considered by the court as a collateral source and ignored, meaning that the economic expert could include the loss of future pension benefits as an element of damages in spite of the death benefit. The expert will need to consult the retaining attorney for a legal opinion before proceeding.

The effect of the death on the level of pension benefits will depend on the plan features. If the death occurs prior to retirement, the number of years of service may be reduced below what this number would otherwise have been. There may also be a reduction in the average earnings used in the benefit formula. For older workers nearing retirement, the likely retirement benefits they would have received from a DB private pension plan and from Social Security soon to be paid are very predictable. For the DB plan, a key issue is the provisions elected for continuation of benefits to the spouse at the time of death. Some decedents may have elected to have the pension benefit payments terminate at the decedent's death. In such a circumstance, there will be a 100 % loss of pension due to the death. At the other extreme, the decedent may have elected a smaller monthly pension that continues being paid to the spouse in the same amount after the decedent's death. In that case there would be no loss of pension benefits.[27] Under the Employee Retirement Income Security Act of 1974, or ERISA, DB plans must provide a spouse benefit that is at least 50 % of the decedent's benefit during their joint lives, unless the plan participant and spouse choose otherwise.[28] Accurate present value computations of pension losses in death cases require the use of joint life expectancy.[29] Furthermore, pension loss calculations using an annuity certain for a term equal to life expectancy are not correct.[30]

6.9   CONCLUSION

This chapter has reviewed the forensic economics literature dealing with the valuation of non-cash (fringe) benefits associated with workers' employment. Employers voluntarily provide fringe benefits to attract desired workers, and such benefits can take many forms. The two major forms are medical insurance and retirement benefits. We have reviewed the statistical sources that are helpful in calculating the value of fringe benefits, cited case opinions, and identified the information needed by the analyst in order to accurately assess their value. The chapter discusses the valuation of fringe benefits in injury cases and notes how it is somewhat different than their valuation in death cases.

NOTES

1. The author wishes to thank David Tucek and Frank Tinari for their helpful suggestions.
2. Since the implementation of the PPACA, the "voluntary" nature of medical insurance has altered in important ways. Firms with 50 or more full-time equivalent employees are required by the "employer mandate" to provide affordable health insurance coverage to their employees, or pay a

fine. For such firms, health insurance is no longer quite the "voluntarily provided benefit" that it was prior to the passage and implementation of the PPACA.

3. http://www.bls.gov/opub/mlr/2015/article/the-national-compensation-survey-and-the-affordable-care-act-preserving-quality-health-care-data-3. htm.

4. PPACA, otherwise known as Obamacare, http://tinyurl.com/h4trsok, has caused a need to reconsider the idea that group health insurance rates are lower than individual health insurance premiums for policies purchased on one of the health insurance exchanges set up under the PPACA. The link at http://tinyurl.com/phgbpam provides examples of the 2015 monthly insurance premium for the two lowest cost silver plans for a 40-year-old male, and the subsidized premium if his income is $30,000 per year. The range of unsubsidized monthly premiums in major cities in 11 rating areas was from $171 to $436. The range of subsidized premiums was from $171 to $208 per month. The average monthly cost of insuring an individual employee under all employer plans was $521 in the 2015 Employer Health Benefits Survey conducted by the Kaiser Family Foundation (Kaiser) and the Health Research & Educational Trust (HRET) at http://tinyurl.com/oj7dhwp. This may cause some employers, especially with relatively small numbers of employees to encourage employees to get health insurance on the health insurance exchanges.

5. https://www.irs.gov/Businesses/Small-Businesses-&-Self-Employed/ Employee-Benefits.

6. See Lazear and Shaw (2007) and Lazear and Oyer (2013).

7. Some examples include the following: Google offers the surviving spouse or partner of a deceased employee 50 % of the decedent's salary for 10 years; Zillow pays employees who are traveling to ship their breast milk back home; Epic Systems offers employees a paid 4-week sabbatical to pursue their creative talents after 5 years with the company; Facebook provides $4000 in "baby cash" to employees with a newborn; Walt Disney offers free admission to its parks for employees, their family and friends and discounts on hotels and merchandise; Accenture covers the cost of gender reassignment for their employees. See http://tinyurl.com/jew8l4j.

8. However, if a self-employed person is injured in an accident and can no longer pursue self-employment, the after-tax cost of items formerly deducted as a business expense (e.g., health insurance, cell phone and internet expenses) would increase. In states that permit consideration of income taxes in the computation of economic damages, such increases in after-tax costs should be taken into account.

9. See http://www.bls.gov/news.release/pdf/ecec.pdf.

10. These data have been presented in an alternative format by Kurt Krueger as benefit costs as a percentage of total money wages, rather than as a per-

centage of total compensation. See Expectancy Data, *Employer Paid Benefits: Ending March, 2015*, Shawnee Mission, Kansas, 2015. Foster (2014) points out that it is possible to convert the ECEC figures showing costs **per hour worked** to costs **per hour paid** under certain assumptions (no overtime, no bonuses) using the data from the ECEC on paid leave to determine the number of hours worked for each hour paid. Using the data in Table 6.1, every hour paid represents about 0.9079 hours worked (assuming no overtime and no bonuses). However, there is overtime and bonuses, so this relationship cannot be computed exactly.

11. Some employer 401(k) contributions are made only on straight-time pay and not on overtime or shift differential pay.

12. For a discussion of the reasons for this trend see http://tinyurl.com/hymorbf. Also see Costo (2006) and US Bureau of Labor Statistics (2012).

13. For a list of companies that have modified their DB plans, see http://tinyurl.com/h9m63az.

14. See Tinari and Betz (2013) for a discussion about valuing non-wage compensation of labor union workers.

15. Because workers do not purchase the benefits directly, but rather get the benefit through their employment, it is not obvious that they value the benefits as much as the employer's cost for providing that benefit. If all fringe benefits were voluntarily provided, such that each worker could accept the benefit or decline it and receive an increase in money wages equal to the employer's cost of the benefit, then those taking the benefit would reveal by that choice that they value the benefit at least as much as the employer cost. However, some benefits, such as medical insurance or a retirement plan, may be provided by an employer to all workers whether they want them or not, and the option of accepting higher wages instead of the benefit may not be available. In this situation, how do we know that any given worker values a benefit at least as much as the employer's cost of providing it? The answer is, we don't. However, because group rates are lower than individual rates for insurance and because most fringe benefits are not taxed as income to the worker, it is reasonable to conclude in many situations that workers value the benefits as least as much as the employer cost of provision. Also, as discussed in Sect. 6.2, employers use fringe benefits to attract the type of workers they prefer. Hence, employers have a strong incentive to provide benefits that will succeed in that goal, and if they do succeed, the workers attracted and retained by the firm will value the benefits provided. Also, note that employers who offer benefits set wages below what they would have been in the absence of the benefits. If the benefits an employer offers are not worth at least the employer cost to its workers, other firms have an incentive to compete the workers away by offering higher wages or different benefits, instead of offering benefits on

which workers place a low value. By this competitive process, it is likely that the benefits being offered by firms are benefits that the workers value as least as much as the employers' cost of provision.

16. The cases are *EEOC v. Dial Corporation*, 469 3d 735 (8th Cir. 2006); *EEOC v. Wilson Casket Co.*, 24 F.3d 836 (6th Cir. 1994); *Fariss v. Lynchberg Foundation*, 769 F.2d 958, 965 (4th Cir 1985); *Galindo v. Stoody Co.*, 793 F.2d 1502 (9th Cir. 1986); *Hance v. Norfolk Southern*, 571 F.3d 511 (6th Cir. 2009); *Jacobson v. Pitman Moore, Inc.*, 582 F. Supp. 169, 179 (D. Minn. 1984); *Kossman v. Calumet County*, 800 F.2d 697 (7th Cir. 1986); *Lubke v. City of Arlington*, 455 F.3d 489 (5th Cir. 2006); *McMillan v. Mass. Society for the Prevention of Cruelty to Animals*, 140 F.3d 288 (1st Cir. 1988); *Moore, et al. v. The Health Care Authority et al.*, 2014 Wash. LEXIS 641 (WA 2014); *Talan v. Levi Strauss & Co.*, 867 F2.d 467 (8th Cir. 1989).

17. These earnings are the median earnings of males of all ages working full-time, year-round, and are taken from Expectancy Data (2016, p. 15). For simplicity, I ignore the age-earnings cycle through which the worker's earnings would likely move as the worker ages through his working life. I also ignore the fact that some portion of the average working life will be spent working part-time rather than full-time. See Rodgers (2013) for empirical findings on the prevalence of part-time work by sex and level of educational attainment.

18. 2001–2008 data on unemployment are taken from US Bureau of Labor Statistics (2003–08) and (2009–2015), Table A16. See Rodgers (2012) for a discussion of the approach of adjusting downward the unemployment rate to allow for the payment of unemployment compensation benefits.

19. *Fleming v. Nestor*, 363 US 603 (1980); *Richardson v. Belcher*, 404 US 78 (1971); and *Weinberger v. Wiesenfeld*, 420 US 636 (1975).

20. In Pennsylvania, on the other hand, both retirement and Social Security income are admissible to establish loss in wrongful death and survival actions. *Thompson v. City of Philadelphia*, 294 A.2d 826 (Pa. Super. 1972).

21. Responses to Question 19 of the 2009 NAFE members survey (Brookshire et al. 2009) indicates that 41 % of the respondents use a percentage of earnings to estimate the loss of Social Security benefits. Erroneous but simple short-cut methods die hard.

22. http://www.bls.gov/ncs/ebs/benefits/2015/ownership/civilian/table11a.pdf.

23. http://www.bls.gov/ncs/ebs/benefits/2015/ownership/civilian/table09a.pdf.

24. https://www.deltadentalins.com/documents/market-report-dental-benefits.pdf.
In 2001, employer cost of dental plans amounted to 0.5 % of employee payroll at $279 per employee per year. The dental services price index

increased 52.6 % from 2001 to 2015 (see: http://data.bls.gov/pdq/
SurveyOutputServlet). The $279 cost per employee is assumed to have
increased in tandem with the increase in the dental services price index,
which would produce a value of $469 in 2015. Added to this is the cost of
a vision plan of $100 per year per employee, producing a total cost of
$569. An alternative source indicates an employer cost for a dental and
vision plan of $40 to $50 per month per employee, or $480 to $600 per
year.   https://www.quora.com/How-much-does-employee-insurance-
(health-vision-dental)-cost-per-employee-for-a-young-startup.

25. https://www.shrm.org/publications/hrmagazine/editorialcon-
tent/2014/0914/publishingimages/0914infographic.pdf.

26. For a discussion of the various kinds of plans, see Rodgers (2002).

27. It might be argued that the lessor pension during the joint lives is a kind of
insurance premium that is paid in order to provide payments to the spouse
after the participant's death. Hence, the payments to the widow should be
treated as a collateral source, just like insurance policy proceeds. However,
I do not know of any case law that addresses this matter.

28. A basic description of how ERISA regulates employer retirement plans is
found at http://www.dol.gov/ebsa/faqs/faq_consumer_pension.html.

29. For a treatment of joint life expectancy and its application to pensions, see
Foster (2010).

30. See Fjeldsted (1993) and Ben-Zion (2001–2002) for a discussion of this
error. Tucek (2009), Foster (2010) and Jones (2010) discuss how to perform the correct calculations.

REFERENCES

Ben-Zion, B. (2001–2002). The valuation of the loss of future pension income.
Journal of Legal Economics, 11(3), 1–24.

Berger, M. C., Black, D. A., Messer, J., & Scott, F. A. (2002). COBRA, spouse
coverage, and health insurance decisions of older households. *Journal of
Forensic Economics, 15*(2), 147–164.

Brookshire, M., Luthy, M. R., & Slesnick, F. L. (2009). 2009 survey of forensic
economists: Their methods, estimates and perspectives. *Journal of Forensic
Economics, 21*(1), 1–31.

Carpenter, J. N. (1998). The exercise and valuation of executive stock options.
Journal of Financial Economics, 48, 127–158.

Costo, S. L. (2006, February). Trends in retirement plan coverage over the last
decade. *Monthly Labor Review*, pp. 58–64, http://www.bls.gov/opub/
mlr/2006/02/art5full.pdf

Eriksson, T., & Kristensen, N. (2014). Wages or fringes: Some evidence on tradeoffs and sorting. *Journal of Labor Economics, 32*(4), 899–928.

Expectancy Data (2015). *Employer paid benefits: Ending March, 2015.* Kansas: Shawnee Mission.

Expectancy Data (2016). *Full-time earnings in the United States: 2014 edition.* Kansas: Shawnee Mission.

Fjeldsted, B. (1993). The significance of the distinction between a life annuity and an annuity certain for a term equal to life expectancy. *Journal of Forensic Economics, 7*(1), 125–127.

Foster, E. (2010). Life expectancies, joint life expectancies, life annuities, and joint life annuities. *Journal of Legal Economics, 16*(2), 111–122.

Foster, E. (2014). Measuring lost health insurance benefits with limited information. *Journal of Legal Economics, 20*(1–2), 125–139.

Frasca, R. (1992). The inclusion of fringe benefits in estimates of earnings loss: A comparative analysis. *Journal of Forensic Economics, 5*(2), 127–136.

Ireland, T. R.. (2014). Determining the value of past lost insurance. Unpublished Manuscript, March 16.

Jones, D. D. (2010). A note on life expectancy and mortality adjustment. *Journal of Legal Economics, 17*(1), 101–111.

Kaiser Family Foundation and Health Educational Trust. (2015). Employer health benefits survey. http://kff.org/health-costs/report/2015-employer-health-benefits-survey/

Lazear, E. P., & Shaw, K. L. (2007). Personnel economics: The economist's view of human resources. *Journal of Economic Perspectives, 21*(4), 91–114.

Lazear, E. P., & Oyer, P. (2013). Personnel economics. In R. Gibbons & D. J. Roberts (Eds.), *Handbook of organizational economics* (pp. 479–519). Princeton: Princeton University Press.

Milkovich, George and Jerry Newman (2010).*Compensation.* New York: McGraw Hill.

Oyer, Paul. (2008). Salary or benefits? *Research in Labor Economics, 28*, 429–67.

Oyer, Paul, & Scott Schaefer. (2005). Why do some firms give stock options to all employees? An empirical examination of alternative theories. *Journal of Financial Economics, 76* (1), 99–133.

Patient Protection and Affordable Care Act (PPACA). Public Law 111–148 (enacted 3/23/2010), and Health Care and Education Reconciliation Act (Reconciliation Act), Public Law 111–152 (enacted 3/30/2010), collectively referred to as the Affordable Care Act or "ACA."

Rodgers, J. D. (2000). Estimating the loss of social security benefits. *The Earnings Analyst, 3*, 1–28.

Rodgers, J. D. (2002). Valuing losses of pension benefits. *Journal of Forensic Economics, 15*(2), 205–231.

Rodgers, J. D. (2012). Handling unemployment. Unpublished manuscript, http://tinyurl.com/gt8qwff

Rodgers, J. D. (2013). Should the earnings of full-time year-round workers be used to estimate the lifetime earnings of children? Unpublished manuscript. http://tinyurl.com/h7ctfwt

Shapiro, S. J., & O'Connor, M. L. (2001). Employee stock options as a source of compensation. *Litigation Economics Review, 5*(1), 11–18.

Skoog, G. R., Ciecka, J. E., & Krueger, K. V. (2011). The Markov process model of labor force activity: Extended tables of central tendency, shape, percentile points and bootstrap standard errors. *Journal of Forensic Economics, 22*(2), 165–229.

Social Security and Medicare Boards of Trustees. (2015). Status of the social security and medicare programs: A summary of the 2015 annual reports. https://www.ssa.gov/oact/TRSUM/tr15summary.pdf

Taylor, P. C., & Ireland, T. R. (1996). Accounting for medicare, social security benefits and payroll taxes in federal cases: Federal case law and errors by many forensic economists. *Litigation Economics Digest, 2*(1), 79–88.

Tinari, F., & Betz, K. T. (2013). Valuing non-wage compensation of private sector labor union workers in the construction trades. *Journal of Forensic Economics, 24*(2), 205–220.

Tucek, D. G. (2009). Calculating survival probabilities. *Journal of Legal Economics, 16*(1), 111–126.

U.S. Bureau of Labor Statistics. (2003–08). *Employment and earnings,* 2003–08, Table A16 for the months of January, April, July and October. For 2009–2015. http://www.bls.gov/opub/ee/2011/cps/annavg7_2010.pdf

U.S. Bureau of Labor Statistics. (2012, December). Retirement costs for defined benefit plans higher than for defined contribution plans. *Beyond the Numbers: Pay and Benefits, 1*(21), pp. 1–4.

U.S. Bureau of Labor Statistics. (2015a). National compensation survey: Employee benefits in the United States, 2015. http://www.bls.gov/ncs/ebs/2015/benefits_health.htm

U.S. Bureau of Labor Statistics. (2015b, December 9). Employer costs for employee compensation—September, 2015. *News Release* USDL-15-2329. http://www.bls.gov/news.release/pdf/ecec.pdf

U.S. Department of Labor. FAQs about retirement plans and ERISA. http://www.dol.gov/ebsa/faqs/faq_consumer_pension.html

CHAPTER 7

Federal and State Income Tax Aspects in Forensic Economics

David Schap

7.1 Introduction

Forensic economists are retained to perform expert assessments of damages in a variety of contexts. The types of cases considered here are (1) personal injury and wrongful death and (2) employment discrimination and wrongful termination. The bifurcation is apt for the purpose of addressing the consequences of income tax law on forensic economic damages assessments inasmuch as, broadly (and so somewhat inaccurately) speaking, income taxes do not apply to awards made in the first category but do apply to awards in the second category.

In a personal injury-type case, if taxes are not to be owed on an award of money damages (or settlement payment, if one is to be negotiated), yet taxes would have been owed on the "but for" injury (i.e., injury-absent) earnings stream, it may seem that forensic economists would need to account for tax differences in calculating the appropriate amount of money damages. Actually, and rather paradoxically, such is not the case in most legal jurisdictions in the USA. Despite the apparent need to account for differences in income taxes between the award scenario and the "but for" injury scenario

D. Schap (✉)
Department of Economics and Accounting, College of the Holy Cross, USA

© The Author(s) 2016
F.D. Tinari (ed.), *Forensic Economics*,
DOI 10.1057/978-1-137-56392-7_7

to arrive at an appropriate award level, the majority of state jurisdictions preclude by law any accounting for income tax liabilities. The states adopting that position are identified herein, with the rationales applied in case law in those states summarized. Likewise, the several states that require taking account of income tax differences (between a money damages award for personal physical injury and the earnings over time that it is designed to replace) are also identified, along with the rationales offered for doing so in the case law in those states. Not all states fall into one of the two camps, as not all state courts have ruled definitively on the income tax treatment issue in personal injury-type cases. Tax treatment in wrongful death-type cases also differ across state jurisdictional lines, as will be explained.

Consider next cases of employment discrimination (or wrongful termination) leading to lost earnings over time. Here the federal tax code provides no exemption of an award from federal income taxes. Since the award and the earnings it is designed to replace are both fully taxable, it may seem there is no need to address income taxes in the calculation of a suitable compensatory award. Income taxes, however, need to be addressed in the context of discrimination (or wrongful termination), if the victim is to be made "whole," owing to the timing of when and how much taxes are owed under the award scenario versus the "but for" discrimination (or "but for" termination) scenario—if permitted by law. The laws of the various states are not uniform in allowing tax adjustments, no matter how meritorious the economic argument for making such adjustments may be. Indeed, even the federal courts differ across venues as to whether tax adjustments are permissible in discrimination cases. Unlike the law governing treatment of income taxes in personal injury and wrongful death-type cases, where extensive summaries of jurisdictional differences already appear in the literature, analysis of case law controlling the treatment of taxes in discrimination (or wrongful termination) type cases across jurisdictional lines is in a nascent stage.

In situations in which tax adjustments are warranted and in jurisdictions where such adjustments are permitted, a forensic economist must know how to go about making the appropriate adjustment. Here the literature provides methodological guidelines and specific stylized examples of how to take appropriate account of federal and state income taxes in performing a forensic economic assessment. The relevant forensic economic literature is reviewed in this chapter to provide a sense of what is legal, methodologically sound, and practical. Armed with an overview of the law, dispatched with knowledge of the issues and methods involved, and guided by specific citations to the literature that may be called upon to hone one's skill in any particular application, forensic economist readers will be capable of addressing the multifaceted aspects of income taxes in their applied work. For any engagement involving an unfamiliar type of case or one to be adjudicated in a jurisdiction new to the forensic economist, prudence strongly suggests consulting with the retaining counsel concerning the legal particulars prior to commencing analysis.

7.2   PERSONAL INJURY AND WRONGFUL DEATH

7.2.1   *Legal and Jurisdictional Concerns*

The material in this section draws heavily from Guest and Schap (2014a, b). Internal Revenue Service code, namely 26 U.S.C. § 104(a)(2), exempts awards of compensatory damages from federal personal income tax for "the amount of any damages (other than punitive damages) received (whether by suit or agreement and whether as lump sums or as periodic payments) on account of personal physical injuries or physical sickness." Physical injury or physical sickness leading to death makes the exemption also applicable to wrongful death-type cases. Although the award or negotiated settlement is not itself subject to federal income tax, any interest accruals on the settlement or court-awarded amount are *not* similarly exempt, as made clear by 26 U.S.C. § 61(a).

Guest and Schap (2014a, p. 85, 2014b, p. 87) limit their findings to the treatment of federal personal income taxes and not other forms of taxes, like possible state and local taxes, or required payments, such as those for Medicare or Social Security; for more on these other tax and payment types, see Taylor and Ireland (1996). Among the large majority of states that levy state personal income taxes, however, Guest and Schap (2014a, p. 86) concede no knowledge of an example of a state code that differs from the federal code with respect to award exemption or award earnings non-exemption from personal income taxes, nor knowledge after careful review of state-level case law where state and federal taxes are substantively differentiated relative to personal income tax treatment of awards or award earnings.

Instituted by the US Congress in 1954, the income tax exemption on the specified awards created a concern for the various state courts and federal courts. The courts searched for ways to give the law its due despite the tension it created between the ostensible Congress-intended tax benefit for any plaintiff receiving an award and the court's mission to award damages according to a well-established "make whole" principle intended to leave the plaintiff no better or worse off than had an injury not occurred. It seemed that only a downwardly adjusted award that took account of its tax-exempt nature might be capable of leaving the plaintiff net "whole." A related issue concerned whether and how to make juries aware of the tax code implications, since by law it is juries who typically specify award amounts.

The response to the tax exemption with respect to award calculation was far from uniform across the various jurisdictions. At the federal level, the matter was resolved in *Jones & Laughlin Steel Corp. v. Pfeifer*, 103 S. Ct. 2541 (1983). In federal courts, personal income taxes must be taken into account in fashioning a suitable award, with the courts adhering strictly to the "make whole" principle. Moreover, tax aspects also must be accounted for in the investment earnings on the award residual (i.e., the diminishing award remainder over time, as a portion only of the lump-sum award may be thought of as being consumed annually, reflective of the after-tax annual earnings that would have been available for consumption absent the injury event). As mentioned previously, although the award itself may be tax exempt, earnings on the award residual over time are not exempt from taxes (unless maintained in a tax-free instrument, like municipal bonds). The court in *Jones & Laughlin Steel Corp. v. Pfeifer* (1983) further mandated use of an after-tax interest rate for discounting.

In contrast to the uniform treatment of personal income taxes adopted in federal courts, state courts differ in their respective treatments—and may differ in their reasoning even when agreeing on the particular treatment! Table 7.1 presents a listing of those jurisdictions (including DC)

Table 7.1   Treatment of personal income tax exemption in setting compensatory damage awards in personal injury cases, by jurisdiction (states plus District of Columbia)

Treatment	State
Adjust damage award to account for income tax exemption (10 jurisdictions)	CT, DC, FL, HI, MS, NJ, NM, NC, OR, TX, (but see NY and WA below)
Do not adjust damage award to account for income tax exemption (31 jurisdictions)	AK, AZ, AR, CA, CO, DE, GA, ID, IL, KS, KY, LA, ME, MI, MN, MT, NE, NH, NY[a], ND, OK, PA, RI, SD, TN, UT, VA, WA[b], WI, WY, WV [a]NY calls for adjustment in dental/medical malpractice cases [b]WA case law leaves open the possibility of adjustment in high-income cases, but the exception actually may have never been applied

Sources: Guest and Schap (2014b) and Schap (2015)

that require adjustment of awards to reflect their tax-exempt status and those that do not permit award adjustment. The number of states presented plus DC does not sum to 51, owing to the fact that not all jurisdictions have ruled definitively one way or another on the matter of taking account of taxes—a small minority neither require nor preclude consideration of personal income taxes in setting the amount of a compensatory damage award for personal physical injury/sickness.

Forensic economists should have a sense of why it is that some state courts mandate an adjustment for taxes, whereas others do not, and still others preclude adjustment. Five distinct **rationales** have been identified in various state court cases **for adjusting awards** to account for income taxes. Among the five main rationales exist more nuanced variations in court-offered rationales (Guest and Schap 2014b), but here attention remains focused on the five main rationales, arranged (as in the original source) in descending order according to the number of different state courts offering the particular rationale.

First, most prominently, is strict adherence to the "make whole" principle: since the earnings the award is designed to replace would have been taxable, but the award is nontaxable, the award requires downward adjustment to make the plaintiff "whole," no more and no less. Second, failure to adjust the award for tax concerns is thought to result in an excessive payment by the defendant, hence punitive and unjust. Third, the court will not give priority to simplicity over accuracy. Fourth, future income taxes may be too significant to ignore. Fifth, and finally, estimation of future tax liabilities is no more complex/speculative/conjectural than the many other components that require estimation in assessing money damages.

Twelve distinct **rationales** are offered in Guest and Schap (2014b) **for not adjusting awards** for taxes, again presented in decreasing order of popularity of appearance across state jurisdictions. First and foremost, consideration of taxes, because they may change in the future or because they are an extraneous subject or because of insufficient information, results in speculation and conjecture, which is impermissible. Second, taxes on estimated future earnings are irrelevant to the court proceeding, being a matter between the plaintiff and the taxing authority only. Third, adjusting an award for its tax status erodes the tax code's intended benefit to plaintiff. Fourth, consideration of taxes would be complicated and confusing for a jury (and so may distract it from basic consideration of liability). Fifth, the courts in the majority of states ignore taxes. Sixth, adjusting the award results in an unintended windfall to the defendant. Seventh, no statute specifies adjustment of awards for taxes. Eighth, the collateral source rule (which limits the focus of the finders of fact to pecuniary aspects arising between the litigants only and not third parties) implies ignoring taxes. Ninth, taxes are immaterial to the court proceeding. Tenth, taxes should be ignored when defendant has failed to provide expert testimony on the subject of taxes. Eleventh, use of gross income in calculating a loss is more equitable. Twelfth and lastly, adjustment for taxes for a plaintiff in a middle- or lower-income position results in under-compensation.

There are six distinct rationales arising from case law in various states for instructing juries on the matter of taxes and an additional dozen rationales for not instructing, and the interested reader is referred to the original source material for details (Guest and Schap 2014b). A well-informed forensic economist is one who knows the case law that bears on the treatment of taxes in the venue(s) in which the forensic economist practices. The information is found in Guest and Schap (2014a). Practitioners in Arizona should consult as well Guest and Schap (2014b). Those practicing in West Virginia, or contemplating doing so, should take note of Schap (2015).

Some special consideration needs to be given to wrongful death cases in regard to award adjustment for taxes, as the tax issue is not quite the same as in the personal injury context. The fundamental argument for adjusting for taxes in the personal injury context is that the "but for" injury earnings stream would have been taxed, whereas the award is not. Under wrongful death, the typical (but not universal across state jurisdictions) basis for recovery is the amount that would have flowed to a statutory beneficiary or estate had the decedent not died as a consequence of the injurious act alleged in the legal action at hand. The entirety of gross earnings is thus typically not relevant (but exceptions appear in the wrongful death discussion in Chap. 12 of this volume). Rather, the portion only that would have been received by the estate or statutory beneficiary is relevant, after suitable reduction of gross decedent earnings for (depending on the state law) personal consumption or personal maintenance of the decedent absent the death event and, if permitted by law, reduction for income taxes, other payroll taxes and payments for Social Security and Medicare. Not all states that preclude consideration of taxes in personal injury-type cases also preclude their consideration in wrongful death-type cases—two documented states are Nebraska and Rhode Island (Guest and Schap 2014b, p. 115). Although Georgia law is not definitive on mandating or precluding adjustment for taxes in personal injury-type cases, in wrongful death-type cases the award is based on decedent gross income without adjustment for taxes (or adjustment for decedent consumption absent the death event for that matter, as noted in Guest and Schap 2014b, p. 104). Arizona precludes consideration of taxes in personal injury cases, but in wrongful death cases the judiciary is divided, with some judges following the case law related to personal injury-type cases while other judges follow a nonbinding (on the state court) federal case ruling interpreting Arizona law as permitting consideration of personal income taxes in a wrongful death proceeding (Guest and Schap 2014b, p. 114). An experienced forensic economist who practices in Arizona offered the advice that two sets of estimates of damages should be developed for any wrongful death case, one set ignoring taxes and the other set adjusting for them, most especially if the judge for the case is yet to be determined or if his or her disposition toward the matter of taxes is yet unknown.

Thus far, the discussion has focused on possible adjustment for *federal* personal income taxes. Research concerning jurisdictional differences in the treatment of other forms of taxation or payroll reductions such as FICA taxes awaits further development. The interested researcher of this topic will be somewhat frustrated by the lack of clarity in statutory and case law on the subject. Exceptions include the appeal of a New York State medical malpractice case, for which tax adjustment to awards are mandated by state statutory law (as noted in Table 7.1), in which the court ruled that FICA contributions are not taxes in the same manner as federal, state, and local income taxes, so awards in medical malpractice cases in New York are not to be adjusted for FICA contributions (*Boyer v. Kamthan*, 978 N.Y.S.2d 633, 2013). In a rare finding that addresses a wide variety of payroll deductions in a sweeping and consistent way, *Hicks ex rel. Saus v. Jones*, 217 W.Va. 107 (2005) contains the following language (pp. 114–15):

> a plaintiff's income taxes, Social Security and Medicare payments, vacation fund payments, health and life insurance premiums, Christmas club deductions, union dues, and so forth should not be accounted for when assessing a plaintiff's loss of earnings or earning capacity.... [T]he award of damages should be based upon the plaintiff's gross earnings or earning capacity and should not be reduced because of any income tax or other paycheck-type deduction.

Seldom does one find such detail offered in state case law concerning the gamut of possible payroll reductions. As mentioned previously, forensic economists, especially novice ones, would be wise to seek guidance from retaining counsel when encountering unknown ramifications of taxes and other legal aspects.

7.2.2   Tax Implications in the Practice of Forensic Economics

Articles in the forensic economics literature addressing implications of federal income tax policy date back decades. Articles appearing as early as in the 1980s are not explicitly reviewed here, for a dual reason: the lessons taught in the articles are mentioned or carefully addressed in subsequent publications (as in, e.g., Aalberts et al. 1994; Brush and Breeden 1994a, b, and Markowski and Cross 1991), while the detailed presentations in the original articles are by now of mere historical interest given reform of the tax code. The Tax Reform Act of 1986, in an effort at tax simplification, reduced the number of marginal tax rates to just three (15, 28, and 31 %). By 1993, there were five different marginal tax rates specified in the revised code, and by 2003 the number had risen to six. Thus, many details presented in articles dating to the 1980s and even some from the 1990s have been rendered obsolete, even though many of the principles articulated remain valid.

By the 1990s, it was widely understood by forensic economists that there were two divergent tax influences. First, failure to account for taxes on the "but for" future earnings, relative to the nontaxable award proceeds, results in an element of overcompensation to plaintiff. Second, failure to account for taxes on future investment earnings on the residual award amount results in an element of under-compensation to plaintiff. Albrecht (1994, p. 239) points out (without endorsing the position) that some at the time reckoned the tax effects were offsetting on balance and could be ignored. An overall overcompensation to plaintiff by ignoring taxes became termed the "ordinary" effect, whereas an overall under-compensation was termed the "reverse" effect (Aalberts et al. 1994, esp. p. 245).

As a matter of fact, ignoring taxes can result in, depending on the particular circumstances, a very large ordinary tax effect or a very large reverse tax effect. Aalberts et al. (1994) illustrate overcompensation errors of as much as 47 % and under-compensation errors as high as 74 % of the award in stylized examples; see also Harris (1994, 1995, 1997) and Brush (1997); Brush and Breeden (1994a) reports error swings of about 20 % in either direction for the range of examples considered. The direction of the error can be tied to the duration of the payment stream at an intuitive level: an award designed to compensate for just a few years of lost earnings has scant time to accumulate investment earnings on its unspent residual, so the ordinary effect tends to occur, whereas a protracted loss or an unusual case with a delayed start to the loss period tends to favor the reverse effect (Aalberts et al. 1994; Lewis and Bowles 1996; Benich 1996). Modeling enhancements appear in Anderson and Barber (2010), which explores the switchover point from ordinary to reverse effect in the duration of the payment stream, a topic explored via a formal theory in Gilbert (2014). Furthermore, Gilbert (2014) studies the effects of varying wage growth rates and discount rates on the switchover point, given a fixed and "sufficiently small" tax rate, thus refining results concerning growth and discount factors that appear in Aalberts et al. (1994). Albrecht (1994, p. 239) notes *inter alia* that awards to compensate for losses of fringe benefits, household services and future medical expenses have no associated up-front tax-advantaged treatment, so the reverse effect would dominate these types of losses. There are also articles specifically address-ing tax effects relative to valuation of lost retirement benefits (Bowles and Lewis 1996) and personal consumption in wrongful death (Jennings and Mercurio 1991). Forensic economists looking for specific ways to model federal income tax effects can consult the articles already cited, as well as Bell and Taub (1994); Brush and Breeden (1996), and Schieren (1994). Formal models of income tax effects in the forensic economics literature often assume a fixed tax rate for analytical tractability, but Lewis and Bowles (1999) cautions that a tax function (taking account of such factors as income and family size over time and the graduated personal income tax) is more appropriate in actual forensic economic case analysis.

In federal courts, and in those states that adhere to the guidance set forth in *Jones & Laughlin Steel Corp. v. Pfeifer* (1983), not only must taxes be addressed, but the choice of a discount rate is also affected. Many forensic economists follow the court admonition specifying an after-tax discount rate by simply making use of tax-free municipal bonds as the basis for formulating a rate for discounting future losses to present value. Another approach is to use a taxable rate, which is then reduced by the plaintiff's own tax rate. Marlin (2007) is critical of both approaches and presents a third option in which a taxable interest rate is initially used, after which the award is "grossed up" (i.e., increased) by enough to cover tax liability. Marlin (2007) suggests two favorable attributes of the proposed method (apart from computational feasibility, given "optimizer" proto-cols in ordinary spreadsheet applications): variability of the tax rate need be addressed only once (namely when calculating net-of-tax income); and the discount rate underpinning the method can be a low-risk instrument (satisfying another *Pfeifer* requirement, namely that of "safest" invest-ment instrument), indeed one actually available to plaintiff as a bona fide investment option. The notion of "grossing up" for taxes appears again as a prominent feature in the next section concerning employment discrimination and wrongful termination losses.

7.3   EMPLOYMENT DISCRIMINATION AND WRONGFUL TERMINATION

7.3.1   Legal Background

A variety of federal laws prohibit discrimination in the American workplace. According to the US Equal Employment Opportunity Commission website (accessed 2015), a variety of federal statutory laws offer protection and recourse against discrimination (with various forms of illegal discrimination specifically noted): the Equal Pay Act of 1963 (sex-based pay differences); Title VII of the Civil Rights Act of 1964 (employment discrimination based on race, color, religion, sex, or national origin); Age Discrimination in Employment Act of 1967 (age-based for those 40 and older); Sections 501 and 505 of the Rehabilitation Act of 1973 (discrimination against qualified individuals with disabilities working in the federal government); Title I and Title V of the Americans with Disability Act of 1990 (against qualified individuals with disabilities working in the private sector or in state or local government); the Civil Rights Act of 1991 (intentional employment discrimination); and Title II of the Genetic Information Nondiscrimination Act of 2008 (discrimination based on genetic information about an applicant, employee, or former employee). Numerous employer actions and activities involving employees and prospective employees are covered, including hiring/firing; compensation/assignment/classification; transfer/promotion/layoff/recall; employment advertising/recruitment/testing; use of company facilities; training/apprenticeship; pay, fringe benefits, retirement plan, and disability leave; and miscellaneous other aspects related to employment conditions or terms. Discriminatory actions include harassment, retaliation, stereotyping, or uneven treatment on account of marital status, ethnicity, religious identification/practice, and the like. Greater detail is available at: www.eeoc.gov/facts/quanda.html

With respect to how tax law handles awards in discrimination cases, prior to 1996 the federal income tax code was seen as permitting tax-exempt recovery on a wide range of types of awards, including those for mental distress as a consequence of employment discrimination. The Small Business Job Protection Act of 1996 (Public Law No. 104-88, Sec. 1605) changed the status of certain awards, as reflected in the portion of the tax code cited previously to the effect that only awards for "personal *physical* injuries or *physical* sickness" are tax-exempt (26 U.S.C. § 104(a)(2), emphasis added here). Presently, awards in discrimination cases (including wrongful termination) and the income loss they are designed to replace are both taxable income sources. Thus, unlike in personal injury and death cases, there is no award adjustment needed on grounds of tax-advantaged status of the award itself. Nevertheless, a tax adjustment is called for on other grounds in following the "make whole" standard, as explained in the next section.

7.3.2   Tax Implications in the Practice of Forensic Economics

A lump-sum award and a stream of earnings over time it is to replace have far differing tax implications, given the discounting of future losses to present value and the progressivity in the tax code: the lump-sum award will face stiffer and sooner tax consequences. If a plaintiff is to be made whole, the award itself must be increased to account for the larger tax burden, which results in a still higher tax burden, necessitating a second-round increase in the estimated damages, then a third round increase for the same reason, then a fourth, fifth, and so forth. Each incremental increase is smaller than the previous one, so the process dampens to a finite outcome reflective of an accurate make-whole award, if all of the many possible factors influencing taxes are taken into account. That is a mighty big "if."

Bowles and Lewis (1996) describe the tax issue involved in discrimination cases and the iterative process needed to adjust money damages accordingly. The article illustrates in detail how "grossing up" of an award works, at least in a highly simplified context involving only future losses. Still, the contribution to the literature was an apropos first step. Ben-Zion (2000) examines the damages adjustment in a context that includes past and future losses (in employment cases termed "back pay" and "front pay" losses), also highlighting additional layers of complexity by noting the simplification achieved using "single" for marital status, discussing Social Security taxes and tax-deferred 401K contributions, and specifically illustrating the ramifications of foregone fringe benefits.

Rodgers (2003) presents an illustration that actually incorporates a married person with dependent children, and brings to the fore the aspect of attorney fees in the example. Indeed, the treatment of attorney fees was likely a chief motivation for the article because, at the time, as explained in the article, it was possible for a plaintiff to win a court case in which attorney fees were made part of the award (and hence part of plaintiff gross income at the time) and actually be made worse off (relative to losing the case) due to tax consequences. The reason for the anomaly has to do with running afoul of the Alternative Minimum Tax (AMT), which could wipe out attorney fees as a miscellaneous deduction in the income tax computation at the time.

No mere theoretical construct, Rodgers (2003) recounts a tale of woe, originally presented in Liptak (2002), involving Cynthia Spina, who found herself $99,000 worse off after being awarded $1.25 million, of which $950 thousand was for attorney fees and costs that were later deemed ineligible for deduction due to the AMT. Given that the AMT has not been indexed for inflation, there are likely far more people affected today by the AMT than at the time Cynthia Spina suffered her particular version of winner's curse, but thankfully revision of the tax treatment of attorney fees now works to prevent similar anomalous occurrence of a plaintiff losing by winning. In recognition of Section 703 of the American Jobs Creation Act of 2004, attorney fees and costs have become so-called "above the line" deductions (up to the extent of the associated award anyway), so no longer part of adjusted gross income subject to the AMT, for any award or settlement of a discrimination claim post October 22, 2004. The protections afforded by the Act are imperfect, however, as the Act leaves unaltered the treatment of attorney fees and costs related to a claim of emotional distress within a discrimination lawsuit (Hulley 2012, p. 187); the Act makes no provision for attorney fees and costs not explicitly made part of an award, thus relegating them, if more than 2 % of income, to the status of miscellaneous itemized deductions and so still possibly subject to the AMT (Johnson and Roney 2015, p. 10); and the Act does not address the "bunching" problem, which refers to the adverse tax consequences of receiving a lump-sum award with a related tax spike rather than a stream of annual payments with a lower total tax liability given graduated marginal tax rates (Polsky 2004).

7.3.3   Award Gross Up and Jurisdictional Legal Concerns

Articles in the forensic economic literature cited previously herein are sufficient to guide a forensic economist through the challenge of most discrimination case assignments provided the governing law is understood. Where grossing up of an award is economically appropriate and legally permissible, the gross up can be accomplished in one of two ways. If the foray into discrimination casework is a one-time event for the forensic economist, the iterative adjustment process as described and summarized by Bowles and Lewis (1996) in a single equation could be used. The procedure would permit the expert to testify "to a reasonable degree of economic certainty." Alternatively, the forensic economist can invest in gaining expertise and confidence using the Solver protocol, available as an Add-In software item from the Excel Tools menu, which will mimic the iterative process described previously in mere moments to a solution of great precision.

Before grossing up any award, the forensic economist needs to know whether a gross up is permissible in the jurisdiction in which the suit has been brought. According to legal research contained in an as-yet unpublished paper, it appears at the federal level that the First, Third, and Tenth Circuits have explicitly recognized tax gross ups as appropriate in discrimination cases, whereas the Sixth, Seventh, and DC (in a reversal of itself) Circuits prohibit award tax gross ups, while within the Second, Fourth, Fifth, Eighth, Ninth, and Eleventh Circuits certain trial courts have permitted gross ups on an evidentiary basis, meaning when the evidence is available and sufficient to calculate competently a suitable tax adjustment (Johnson and Roney 2015, pp. 18–19, 20–21).

Often, differing treatment by the federal courts across jurisdictional lines becomes an impetus for action by the US Supreme Court or Congress. Barca (2011) addresses whether victims of discrimination, in seeking an equitable resolution of their related tax issues, would be better served by gross ups in the court award or by statutory tax relief (e.g., restoring a taxpayer's ability to income average across years), concluding that a hybrid combination would work best. After reviewing the diverse legal rationales applied both for and against gross ups, Cheverud (2011/2012) calls on the courts to expand the application of gross ups (termed an "increased tax liability award" or ITLA therein) to other areas of law besides discrimination cases, such as employer retaliation and violations of maximum hours or minimum wage under the Fair Labor Standards Act, to name but one of the many laws considered. Stay tuned awaiting further developments concerning gross ups under federal law.

Where state anti-discrimination laws exist alongside of the federal statutes, state courts in such states as New Jersey, Ohio, and Washington have permitted award gross ups for taxes (Johnson and Roney 2015, pp. 19–20). As with other legal matters, the forensic economist is admonished to check with retaining counsel for the current legal status of award gross ups for taxes in the venue(s) of practice.

Although the focus of this chapter is limited primarily to consideration of federal and state income taxes, there are other types of payroll taxes that, in conjunction with factors affecting a plaintiff's base income, may cause any gross up calculation to become highly complex indeed. Ireland (2010) is devoted to these aspects, and the contents therein are presented here in a four-point summary.

First, it may appear that the Medicare payroll tax would have no bearing on the gross up calculation inasmuch as the Medicare tax rate is fixed and has no associated income cap. If lost fringe benefits that would have been insulated from Medicare payroll taxes are instead compensated by a back pay award, however, the payroll tax becomes applicable to the award amount, thus necessitating another type of tax adjustment in the year of the award.

Second, there is an argument for a "gross down" adjustment based on the Social Security payroll tax in cases in which the "but for" discrimination (or termination) annual earnings would have existed at a level below the annual Social Security payroll tax cap, whereas the award-year income far exceeds the cap, resulting in a net gain to the award recipient in the absence of a gross down adjustment. Unlike the ordinary gross up adjustment, which has been described as an iterative process, the gross down adjustment for the Social Security payroll tax is but a single, one-time downward adjustment calculation assuming the award-year income net of the adjustment still exceeds the Social Security payroll tax annual cap.

A third consideration has to do with the amount and timing of tax payments as related to fringe benefits. Consider a worker's ordinary 401(k) plan with an employer matching contribution. Amounts contributed by the employee and employer do not escape income taxation, but instead postpone income taxation, leading to added complexity in an award gross up calculation. Further complicating the matter are two additional aspects: Social Security and Medicare payroll taxes are neither avoided nor postponed on the employee contribution to a 401(k), whereas the employer contribution on behalf of the employee does avoid those particular forms of payroll taxation.

Fourth and finally, there are miscellaneous other tax-related complications, such as lost medical coverage and the 2 % of adjusted gross income threshold applicable to deduction of medical expenses. Of considerable importance is spousal income (mentioned previously by Ben-Zion 2000), as it affects base income and thus potentially shifts the applicable marginal tax rates in the years leading up to the award year and in the award year. One particularly vexing consideration has to do with punitive damages, which if awarded obviously shift up the income base in the award year and thus potentially the applicable marginal tax rate. Consideration of punitive damages necessarily confounds an economic determination of appropriate pecuniary damages to be presented to a jury because no economist can know in advance the amount a jury will recommend for punitive damages. Ireland (2010, p. 54) mentions the general suitability of a post-trial hearing in which the many factors could be sorted out in assessing damages that require gross ups, gross downs, and related concerns. Jurisdictions (such as New York), which commonly make use of post-trial hearings to set damage awards, would appear to provide greater opportunity for precision in arriving at proper make-whole compensation.

7.4 CONCLUSION

An economic case can be made for adjusting court awards to reflect their tax-exempt status in cases of physical personal injury/sickness or death, but whether the law permits such award adjustment is another matter. Although not tax advantaged, a similarly economic-type case can be made for adjusting awards in discrimination cases to reflect the earlier and steeper taxes assessed on a lump-sum payment as opposed to a more even flow of income over time. The permissibility of such an adjustment, however, also rests in the law and not necessarily in economic judgment. The law on these matters lacks uniformity across jurisdictions, except for cases involving personal physical injury or sickness adjudicated under federal law, so forensic economists would do well to inform themselves concerning the legal particulars in the jurisdictions in which they practice. Moreover, it cannot be assumed, just because a case is tried in a federal court, that federal law is applicable, as "diversity cases" (involving, e.g., parties with differing citizenship by state) in federal court are bound by the laws of the state in which the court sits, under what is known as the *Erie* Doctrine (*Erie R.R. v. Tompkins* 1938). Much tax-relevant information sits in the pages of this chapter, but a good deal more detail rests in the forensic economics literature cited herein. Retaining counsel is the best source for legal advice in preparing a forensic economic evaluation when unusual legal aspects arise, and the judge is without question the ultimate authority concerning the controlling law (including related tax aspects) affecting the assessment of money damages.

REFERENCES

Aalberts, R. J., Clauretie, T. M., & Jameson, M. (1994). Ordinary and reverse tax effect in personal injury and wrongful death cases. *Journal of Forensic Economics, 7*(3), 245–266.

Albrecht, G. A. (1994). Modeling taxes in personal injury and wrongful death award calculations. *Journal of Forensic Economics, 7*(3), 239–243.

Anderson, G. A., & Barber, J. R. (2010). Taxes and the present value assessment of economic losses in personal injury litigation. *Journal of Legal Economics, 17*(1), 1–28.

Barca, R. (2011). Taxing discrimination victims: How the current tax regime is unjust and why a hybrid income averaging and gross up remedy provides the most equitable solution. *Rutgers Journal of Law & Public Policy*, 8(Spring), 673–708.

Bell, E. B., & Taub, A. J. (1994). An analysis of alternative methods of calculating tax-adjusted awards. *Journal of Forensic Economics*, 7(3), 267–274.

Benich, J. J. (1996). Alternative approaches to tax adjustments in appraising economic loss: Comment. *Journal of Legal Economics*, 6(2), 91–93.

Ben-Zion, B. (2000). Neutralizing the adverse tax consequences of a lump-sum award in employment cases. *Journal of Forensic Economics*, 13(3), 233–244.

Bowles, T. J., & Chris Lewis, W. (1996). Taxation of damage awards: Current law and implications. *Litigation Economic Digest*, 2(1), 73–78.

Brush, B. C. (1997). The distributional effects of using a before-tax standard: A comment. *Journal of Forensic Economics* 10(1), 65–68.

Brush, B. C., & Breeden, C. H. (1994a). Income taxes and economic damages. *Journal of Legal Economics*, 4(2), 51–63.

Brush, B. C., & Breeden, C. H. (1994b). The measurement of economic damages: Do taxes really matter? *Journal of Forensic Economics*, 7(2), 227–228.

Brush, B. C., & Breeden, C. H. (1996). A taxonomy for the treatment of taxes in cases involving lost earnings. *Journal of Legal Economics*, 6(2), 1–16.

Cheverud, E. (2011/2012). Increased tax liabilities after Eshelman: A call for expanded acceptance beyond the realm of anti-discrimination statutes. *New York Law School Law Review*, 56, 711–747.

Gilbert, S. (2014). A theory of tax effects on economic damages. *Journal of Legal Economics*, 20(1–2), 1–13.

Guest, L., & Schap, D. (2014a). Case law concerning the treatment of federal income taxes in personal injury and wrongful death litigation in the state courts. *Journal of Legal Economics*, 20(1–2), 85–123.

Guest, L., & Schap, D. (2014b). Rationales concerning the treatment of federal income taxes in personal injury and wrongful death litigation in the state courts. *Journal of Legal Economics*, 21(1), 85–117.

Harris, W. G. (1994). The distributional effects of using a before-tax standard in damage awards. *Journal of Forensic Economics*, 7(3), 275–291.

Harris, W. G. (1995). Tax-induced errors in the calculation of lump-sum awards. *Journal of Forensic Economics*, 8(1), 37–47.

Harris, W. G. (1997). The distributional effects of using a before-tax standard: A reply. *Journal of Forensic Economics*, 10(2), 217–219.

Hulley, Jr., M. K. (2012). Taking your lump sum or just taking your lumps? The negative tax consequences in employment dispute recoveries and Congress's role in fashioning a remedy. *Michigan State Law Review*, 2012(1), 171–210.

Ireland, T. R. (2010). Tax consequences of lump sum awards in wrongful termination cases. *Journal of Legal Economics*, 17(1), 51–73.

Harris, W. G. (1997). The distributional effects of using a before-tax standard: A reply. *Journal of Forensic Economics, 10(2), 217–219.*

Jennings, W., & Mercurio, P. (1991). Accounting for taxes in the determination of the reduction for personal consumption. *Journal of Forensic Economics, 5(1),* 85–86.

Johnson, S., & Roney, T. (2015). "Make whole": The need for gross ups in employment discrimination cases, unpublished paper dated 5/28/15.

Lewis, W. C., & Bowles, T. (1996). Alternative approaches to tax adjustments in appraising economic loss. *Journal of Legal Economics, 6(1), 27–38.*

Lewis, W. C., & Bowles, T. (1999). A statistical analysis of federal income tax rate stability over time and implications for valuing lifetime earnings. *Journal of Forensic Economics, 12(3), 201–213.*

Liptak, A. (2002, August 11). Tax bill exceeds award to officer in sex bias suit, *New York Times.*

Markowski, E. P., & Cross, E. M. (1991). Determination of tax adjusted lost income awards. *Journal of Legal Economics, 1(2), 11–18.*

Marlin, M. (2007). The problem of discounting with an after-tax rate of return in cases of personal injury or wrongful death. *Journal of Legal Economics, 14(1),* 33–48.

Polsky, G. D. (2004). Employment discrimination remedies and tax gross ups. *Iowa Law Review, 90, 67–120.*

Rodgers, J. D. (2003). Handling taxes in employment case law. *Journal of Forensic Economics, 16(2), 225–256.*

Schap, D. (2015). Correction concerning the treatment of federal income taxes in personal injury and wrongful death litigation in the state courts. *Journal of Legal Economics, 21(2), 129–130.*

Schieren, G. A. (1994). Taxes and present value awards for wrongful death. *Journal of Forensic Economics, 7(3), 293–304.*

Taylor, P. C., & Ireland, T. R. (1996). Accounting for medicare, social security benefits and payroll taxes in federal cases: Federal case law and errors by many forensic economists. *Litigation Economic Digest, 2(1), 79–88.*

U.S. Equal Employment Opportunity Commission website. (Accessed 2015). Federal laws prohibiting job discrimination questions and answers. http://www.eeoc.gov/facts/qanda.html

CASES CITED

Boyer v. Kamthan, 978 N.Y.S.2d 633 (2013).
Erie R.R. v. Tompkins, 304 U.S. 64 (1938).
Hicks ex rel. Saus v. Jones, 217 W.Va. 107 (2005).
Jones & Laughlin Steel Corp. v. Pfeifer, 103 S. Ct. 2541 (1983).

CHAPTER 8

Issues in Applying Discount Rates

David D. Jones

8.1 INTRODUCTION

The guy was a plumber making $40,000 a year. After his injury he earns $30,000 a year working the plumbing desk at a hardware store. It is agreed that he has a 10-year worklife expectancy. Loss due to injury: $10,000 × 10 = $100,000. Except that...

After a few years, his earnings were expected to grow 10%, from $40,000 to $44,000, now from $30,000 to $33,000. Thus, his annual loss will also have grown 10% to $11,000. We must allow for future inflation of the loss.

On the other hand, if he is given funds to cover his loss today, a few years from now, when he has an $11,000 loss, he will have the funds awarded plus interest that they have earned to cover the loss. We must allow for earnable interest.

The joint adjustment, allowing for future inflationary growth and earnable interest, are combined in the process of discounting future values to present value. The process is the same for any future value, be it lost income due to injury or termination, care costs due to injury, or loss of the value of routine household services. In some cases, other service losses (e.g., for guidance and support) are also discounted to present value.

D.D. Jones (✉)
Economic Consulting Services LLC, USA

© The Author(s) 2016
F.D. Tinari (ed.), *Forensic Economics*,
DOI 10.1057/978-1-137-56392-7_8

The process is conceptually simple. Let g be an assumed constant rate of growth of future values and R be the annual rate of earnable interest. Future values increase yearly at the rate $(1 + g)$ and are reduced to present value by the rate $(1 + R)$. The gross loss divisor is

$$1+d = \frac{1+R}{1+g} \tag{8.1}$$

where d is the net discount rate (NDR).

A simplistic expression of the NDR is the spread between R and g, that is,

$$d \approx R - g \tag{8.2}$$

For R positive and greater than g, the relatively minor error introduced by this approximation grows with the size of R and the spread between the two.

The choice involved in discounting boils down to nothing more than the choice of R, g, and/or d.

There are 58 articles in the *Journal of Forensic Economics* with 'discount' or 'discounting' relating to reducing future values to present value in their title; 34 in the *Journal of Legal Economics*; 17 in the *Journal of Risk and Insurance* (most by members of the National Association of Forensic Economics [NAFE]). This is not an exhaustive list. Not all articles dealing with discounting use the term in their title (see, e.g., Nieswiadomy 2012). There are 331 articles in the *Journal of Forensic Economics* with 'discount' in the title and/or text. There is no lack of input and opinion on the matter.

This chapter reviews the literature on discounting. There is no 'right choice' about R, g, and/or d. There are advocates and critics of each choice. But, in most cases, there is no objective method for claiming that one is the single best approach.

There is a triennial survey of the membership of the NAFE (the latest: Luthy *et al.* 2015) that is sometimes cited as foundation for one or another of the basic assumptions underlying economic loss calculations, including questions about discounting. In every edition the authors include a caveat that the survey is not scientifically valid. An earlier edition (Brookshire and Slesnick 1999) included "the use of this survey in court, deposition, or

other litigation settings to buttress or criticize the use of particular parameter values or particular techniques should not be undertaken...". Nothing
has changed about the survey since then. That respondents favored one
discounting procedure or level over another is no indication of superiority
of that approach. We are left to summarize the various choices among R,
g, and/or d.

8.2 Interest (R)

There are myriad investment instruments that someone awarded funds to
cover future losses and costs might be expected to use to generate earnings to help cover those losses, including US Treasury debt instruments
or agency bonds, state and local bonds (munis), private sector corporate
bonds, and equity, domestic or international.

It is not the job of the forensic economist to do legal research or cite
legal opinions. But *Jones & Laughlin* (1983) is central to discounting
questions. It limits the choice of investment instruments that we can use
in calculating the present value of losses and costs. In the opinion, Justice
Stevens wrote:

> Once it is assumed that the injured worker would definitely have worked for
> a specific term of years, he is entitled to a risk-free stream of future income
> to replace his lost wages; therefore, the discount rate should not reflect
> the market's premium for investors who are willing to accept some risk of
> default. (Section 1, ¶ 9)

Thus, only Treasury debt instruments and guaranteed agency bonds are
acceptable as basis for R in our present value calculations. All of the others
(municipal bonds, private sector debt, and equities) have default risk. It is
not unheard of to see reference to present values based on these other debt
instruments in the literature or expert reports (Brush 2011; Albrecht 2012).
There is no presumption that plaintiff will invest only in federal government debt if she is granted an award. In fact, people receiving damage
awards would be expected to diversify their investments into a range of
instruments of varying risk. But, we are not approximating plaintiff's
investment behavior. We are undertaking calculations given the constraints
imposed by the Court. Present value calculations done to determine the
size of those awards based on anything but default-free government debt
are unacceptable.

Treasury debt instruments are comprised of bills (maturity of one year or less), notes (maturity of two to ten years), and bonds (maturity of 20 or 30 years). All are equally free of default risk. I know of no forensic economics articles citing guaranteed federal agency bonds as a source of R data. But, being free of default risk, those would certainly be acceptable.

There is forensic economics literature reporting research based on all maturities of government debt, from bills through bonds. Bills are counted as cash by private businesses. It can be argued that accepting the low rate on bills (effectively 0% for several years) and a continual rolling over of an award of perhaps several million dollars is not reasonable foundation for present value calculations. Longer-term notes and bonds include a greater inflation risk. They may rise or fall in value. But they satisfy the *Jones & Laughlin* criteria of being free of default risk.

Treasury Inflation Protected Securities (TIPS) are issued in maturities varying from 5 to 30 years. Their maturity value is adjusted monthly to account for (offset) interim inflation. Because their face value increases, their nominal yield is lower. It includes an inflation adjustment. There are arguments for (Ireland 1999–2000; Weckstein 2001) and against (Jayne 1998) using TIPS in present value loss calculations. Fourteen articles in the *Journal of Forensic Economics* reference TIPS.

The yield on awarded funds is often assumed to be a single interest rate (e.g., that on 10-year Treasury notes). But earnings on large awards are typically greater than the assumed initial draw down on funds. This creates a conceptual problem of reinvestment of the excess. With a single interest rate, implicitly that is assumed to be at the same rate as the initial discount. But there is no inherent reason to expect yields to be unchanging over time.

One approach to this problem is to use a ladder of interest rates of varying maturities (Rosenberg and Gaskins 2012). There are only a few articles in the literature suggesting this approach. Laddering may lessen the problem, but it does not resolve it. An added step is to use a ladder of STRIPS, zero-coupon debt instruments offering no interest, only principal payment (Rosenberg 2010). Conceptually this resolves the problem. Principal payments are scheduled to come due at precisely the time funds are needed in the future. *Jones & Laughlin* (1983) warned against 'delusive exactness'. Although discounting with interest rates based on a laddered array of STRIPS would yield more precise results, precision should not be conflated with accuracy. It is not clear that those results would be significantly 'better'. For the most part, the question of reinvested funds is not addressed in the literature or in practice. Discounting is done by most analysts using a single interest rate or by some with a ladder of rates.

The Court requires a risk-free discount rate. But, not all potential losses are risk-free. In the case of lost business profits, there may be significant uncertainty about likely future profits. To account for this, a risk premium can be added to the risk-free discount rate. That can be based on a capitalization rate (the inverse of the price-earnings ratio), using a Capital Asset Pricing Model (CAPM), or a combination of market and subjective risk factors to build up a discount rate (Trevino 1997/98).

8.3 GROWTH FACTOR (g)

The second element in determining an NDR is g, the loss or cost growth factor. Those future dollar values may be earnings and fringe benefits, the cost of goods and/or services in a life care plan, the value of household services, or business profits. Each may have its own potential growth rate.

In the case of earnings losses for someone not previously active in the labor force, US Bureau of the Census, Current Population Reports, http://www.census.gov/hhes/www/cpstables/032014/perinc/toc.htm (Foster 2014) or American Community Survey data, compiled at https://marketplace.mimeo.com/ExpectancyData, are the most common source of earnings by age, education, gender, and race. If there is opinion about plaintiff having pursued one particular occupation or another, Occupational Employment Statistics, found at http://www.bls.gov/oes/tables.htm, provide hourly earnings for nearly 1400 occupations and groups of occupations.

Potential growth rates of annual earnings can be derived from a longitudinal review of earnings from these sources, or from broader measures of national earnings growth as reported in Table B-15: "Hours and Earnings in Private Nonagricultural Industries" of the *Economic Report of the President*: http://tinyurl.com/2015ERP. Growth in weekly wages is preferred to hourly, as weekly reflect both change in hourly compensation and changes in hours.

Another, forward-looking source of potential earnings growth figures is found in the long-run projections published by the Social Security Administration www.ssa.gov/oact/tr/2014/tr2014.pdf, Table V.B1, "Principal Economic Assumptions". A comparison of historic SSA wage forecasts with actual national average wage growth since the projections were made shows that they leave much to be desired (See also Kashin *et al.* 2015).

In addition to expected earnings growth, the inflation of costs in life care plans is the most common concern in determining NDRs. The plan may include medical as well as non-medical costs. These have and are expected to increase more rapidly than prices in general. The medical component of the Consumer Price Index (CPI), http://data.bls.gov/pdq/querytool. jsp?survey=cu, includes nearly a score of goods and services. But, not all of them demonstrate extraordinary inflation. Some (e.g., medical equipment and supply) have lagged overall inflation significantly. The largest cost element in life care plans is often for attendant care. Although Home Care was added to the medical CPI in 2006, its inflation rate has clearly not been like that for direct medical intervention. Occupational Employment Statistics show that the inflation rate of home health aide wages has failed to keep up with inflation in virtually all parts of the country since the turn of the century.

The choice of cost inflation rates must be reasoned and linked to specific care plan costs. But, there may be 100 or more items in the plan. One could have 100 different inflation projections. *Jones & Laughlin* (1983) also acknowledges that future loss calculations are 'rough and ready'. It is common to have only a few inflation rates be a part of discount rate calculations.

8.4   NET DISCOUNT RATE

Having chosen an interest rate (R) and growth rate (g) or array of Rs and gs, the analyst has effectively chosen an NDR (Eq. (8.1)) or array of NDRs. Although some object to using an NDR, it is equivalent to using specific R & g figures. Most of the literature on discount rates cites NDRs. An advantage of this approach is that there is no need to make explicit R and g forecasts. One NDR is consistent with myriad R and g forecasts (Payne et al. 1999).

8.5   BASIS FOR SELECTING RATES

With either explicit R and g or an NDR, you are saying that the present values of losses and/or costs next year or 10 or 30 years from now depends upon some relationship between earnable interest (R) and the growth in dollar values under consideration (g). From whence do R and g come? They may be based on historic averages of some length, or on contemporary measures and forecasts. The line between the two has been clearly drawn among forensic economists. There is no sign of compromise on either side.

Those favoring the use of some measure of contemporary rates (e.g., the current yield on some single maturity of Treasury debt instruments or a ladder of rates of varying maturities) argue that historic rates are irrelevant. You cannot expect a bank to pay you the interest rate available ten years ago. A logical inconsistency with this argument is that the other half of the NDR, the growth rate g, is either some historical average or a forecast based on historical averages. The mix of forward-looking contemporary interest rates and historically based growth rates may be problematic as may be long-term calculations based on contemporary rates far out of line with historic rates (e.g., 15% yields in 1980 or 0% in 2012).

In the face of current R and g different from historic averages, those relying on past rates are implicitly arguing for a reversion to the mean (Pelaez 1996). That leaves open the question of which mean. How long should the historic average baseline be (Haydon and Webb 1992)?

Ibbotson SBBI average-yield data start in 1926 (Morningstar 2015). Some forensic economists (apparently with a straight face) rely on the average of interest rates from the Coolidge administration to date. Others cite those since WWII or the 1950s. Times have changed. The relationship between interest and inflation in the 1920s or the Eisenhower administration is unlikely to be relevant to that in the next few decades (Johnson and Gelles 1996). If historic averages are to be used, both R and g should be of the same period, and that should be limited to a few decades at most. The precise period is not certain and may be variable (Rosenbaum and Guthman 2007).

Occasionally an expert may use the 'mirror image' approach for choosing the period for historic averaging: future losses for five years use a five-year historic average; losses for 40 years use a 40-year average. *Determining Economic Damages*, a digest of forensic economic information about what damages experts do, includes discussions about household services, personal consumption, and discount rates. Jerry Martin, the author for three decades, aimed at reporting, not judging. The mirror image is the only technique that he said was *wrong* (Martin and Weinstein 2012, §313).

Some argue forcefully against relying upon historic averages as foundation for discounting future values (Havrilesky 1990). Others find no problem with the approach (Sen et al. 2000). The results are mixed.

This paper attempts to identify and analyze many of the theoretical and practical issues surrounding the choice of discount rate methods to valuing damage awards, in particular, the usage of current interest rates vs. historical interest rates.... The results found in this study were... that neither the current or historical interest rate methods have proven to be very accurate, nor does either method show a dispositive forecast superiority. (Rosenberg and Gaskins 2012, p. 25)

Most of the literature on discounting cites averages of historic rates.

8.6   Conclusion

In cases involving future damages most courts require either explicit discounting to present value or allow testimony about the subject. Discounting is no more than taking into account the potential growth in value of future damages due to expected inflation or anticipated real wage growth (the g factor) and the time value of money (the R factor) which reduces the estimated losses to present value. This may be done with separate, individual consideration of g and R, or with their being combined into a NDR. There may be a single value for g and R (and NDR), or an array of values. The choice of values for those discounting factors may be based on a historic average of some length, or on projections of future value.

There is no consensus in among forensic economist which is the 'best' approach. Each has its strengths and weaknesses. The discounting process is the same in all cases. Any difference comes down to assumptions about g and R.

References

Albrecht, G. (2012). A review of the three arguments used to justify including a risk- premium in the discount factor. *Journal of Legal Economics, 18*(2), 1–15.

Brookshire, M. L., & Slesnick, F. L. (1999, Fall). A 1999 survey study of forensic economists—Their methods and their estimates of forecast variables. *Litigation Economics Digest, IV*(2), 65–96.

Brush, B. C. (2011). On the relative accuracy of discounting based on risk-free and risky portfolios. *Journal of Forensic Economics, 22*(1), 59–73.

Council of Economic Advisors. (2015). *Economic report of the President.* Washington, DC: U.S. Government Printing Office. https://www.white-house.gov/administration/eop/cea/economic-report-of-the-President/2015

Foster, E. (2014). Real earnings of full-time workers by education, age group, and sex, 1974–2012. *Journal of Forensic Economics, 24*(2), 221–241.

Expectancy Data. (2014). *Full-time earnings in the United States, 2013.* KS: Shawnee Mission.

Gamber, E. N., & Sorensen, R. L. (1993). On testing for the stability of the net discount rate. *Journal of Forensic Economics, 7*(1), 69–79.

Havrilesky, T. (1990). Those who only remember the past may be doomed to repeat its mistakes. *Journal of Forensic Economics, 3*(1), 23–28.

Haydon, R. B., & Webb, S. C. (1992). Selecting the time period over which the net discount rate is determined for economic loss analysis. *Journal of Forensic Economics, 5*(2), 261–271.

Ireland, T. R. (1999-2000). Comment: Is the rate on TIPS bonds an adequate measure of the real interest rate?: Correction and elaboration. *Journal of Legal Economics, 9*(3), 105–108.

Jayne, K. A. (1998, January). Why inflation-indexed treasury securities are not well suited for discounting a future earning stream. *Journal of Forensic Economics, 11*(1), 1–2.

Johnson, W. D., & Gelles, G. M. (1996). Calculating net discount rates: It's time to recognize structural changes. *Journal of Forensic Economics, 9*(2), 119–129.

Kashin, K., King, G., & Soneji, S. (2015). Systematic bias and nontransparency in US social security administration forecasts. *Journal of Economic Perspectives, 29*(2), 239–258.

Luthy, M. R., Brookshire, M. L., Rosenbaum, D., Schap, D., & Slesnick, F. L. (2015). A 2015 survey of forensic economists: Their methods, estimates, and perspectives. *Journal of Forensic Economics, 26*(1), 53–83.

Martin, G. D., & Weinstein, M. A. (2012). *Determining economic damages*. Costa Mesa: James Publishing.

Nieswiadomy, M. L. (2012). The risk and reward of investing a lost earnings award: A comparison of stocks, bonds, and bills. *Journal of Forensic Economics, 23*(2), 199–207.

Payne, J. E., Ewing, B. T., & Piette, M. J. (1999). Mean reversion in net discount rates. *Journal of Legal Economics, 9*(1), 69–80.

Pelaez, R. F. (1996). Mean-reversion in the net discount rate: The evidence from the manufacturing sector. *Journal of Legal Economics, 6*(2), 29–40.

Rosenbaum, D. I., & Guthman, M. (2007). Net discount rates: Does duration matter? *Journal of Legal Economics, 14*(2), 1–24.

Rosenberg, J. I. (2010). Discounting damage awards using the zero coupon treasury curve: Satisfying legal and economic theory while matching future cash flow projections. *Journal of Forensic Economics, 21*(2), 173–194.

Rosenberg, J. I., & Gaskins, R. R. (2012, March). Damage awards using intermediate term government bond funds vs. U.S. treasuries ladder: Tradeoffs in theory and practice. *Journal of Forensic Economics, 23*(1), 1–31.

Schap, D., Baumann, R., & Guest, L. (2014). Wage net discount rates: 1981–2012. *Journal of Forensic Economics, 25*(2), 153–174.

Sen, A., Gelles, G. M., & Johnson, W. D. (2000). A further examination regarding the stability of the net discount rate. *Journal of Forensic Economics, 13*(1), 23–28.

The Ibbotson SBBI. (2015). *Classic yearbook*. Chicago: Morningstar.

Trevino, G. A. (1997/98, Winter). A note on formulating and corroborating discount rates for small firms. *Journal of Legal Economics, 7*(3), 45–54.

U.S. Bureau of the Census. (2015). Income, poverty, and health insurance coverage in the United States: 2014. *Current Population Reports: Consumer Income, P-60*(252).

U.S. Department of Labor, Bureau of Labor Statistics. (various years). *Consumer price index*. http://www.bls.gov/cpi/home.htm

U.S. Social Security Administration. (2015, July). *The 2015 annual report of the board of trustees of the federal old-age and survivors insurance and federal disability insurance trust funds*. Washington, DC: Government Printing Office.

Weckstein, R. S. (2001). Real discounting and inflation in indexed treasury securities. *Journal of Forensic Economics, 14*(3), 261–270.

CASES CITED

Jones & Laughlin Steel Corp. v. Pfeifer, 103 S. Ct 2541, or 462 U.S. 523 (1983). http://www.admiraltylawguide.com/supct/Jones&Laughlin.htm

CHAPTER 9

Potential Effects of the Affordable Care Act on Loss Calculations

Joshua Congdon-Hohman and Victor A. Matheson

9.1 INTRODUCTION AND BACKGROUND ON THE AFFORDABLE CARE ACT

In tort cases involving a personal injury resulting from medical malpractice, workplace accidents, and traffic incidents, the cost of future medical care is often the single largest component of a settlement or award for the plaintiff. When a defendant is ruled liable for injuries to a plaintiff, the cost of future medical care should be paid by the injuring party in order to make the injured individual "whole." At the time the award is made, no one can know with certainty what those future costs will be, and therefore a jury or trial judge must rely on expert witnesses to inform them of the best estimate of those costs. First, a life care planner must identify what care they would expect the injury to necessitate over the course of the injured party's lifetime. Next, a forensic economist (FE) will take the life care plan and determine what the cost of that future care will be in present value terms. In determining this amount, the FE will consider the amount that the injured party will expect to pay for each treatment or

JEL Classification Codes: I13, I18, K41

J. Congdon-Hohman • V.A. Matheson (✉)
Department of Economics and Accounting, College of the Holy Cross,
USA

F.D. Tinari (ed.), *Forensic Economics*,
DOI 10.1057/978-1-137-56392-7_9

145

device needed and account for medical care inflation and expected returns on safe investments.

In 2010, the federal government of the USA passed the Affordable Care Act (commonly referred to as the "ACA" or "Obamacare") which will certainly impact the cost of future care paid by the injured party. (The ACA is an abbreviation for the policy changes initiated by two laws, the "Patient Protection and Affordable Care Act" and the "Health Care and Education Reconciliation Act of 2010.") Specifically, the law guarantees access to insurance and prohibits insurance companies from using pre-existing medical conditions to determine who to insure or what premiums to charge. These provisions of the law went into effect on January 1, 2014. Furthermore, the ACA puts restriction on the amount of cost-sharing by insured individuals for medical expenses beyond the premium charged and contains a number of measures that are hoped to slow the rate of medical care inflation. The question then becomes how FEs should go about estimating future medical costs in light of these dramatic changes and what other legal doctrines, if any, need to be considered when deciding how to move forward. This topic was first addressed in the forensic economics literature by Congdon-Hohman and Matheson (2013), and this chapter draws upon and extends our previous work.[1]

In the next section, we provide more details regarding how the ACA has changed the acquisition costs of medical care for patients. Next, we briefly examine the initiatives in the ACA that are designed to rein in the high growth rate in the cost of medical care. We then focus on the implications for FEs when estimating the costs of a life care plan and provide an example of how this might be done in practice. Finally, we examine the issues yet to be resolved by the courts in regard to this application of the ACA and discuss the initial rulings that have been made to date.

9.2   HEALTH INSURANCE FOR THOSE WITH PREEXISTING CONDITIONS BEFORE AND AFTER THE ACA

Prior to the implementation of the Affordable Care Act, a FE would not consider the possibility that health insurance may defray the cost of the medical care included in a life care plan. He or she had no reason to believe that an injured party would be insured for a number of reasons. First, the primary source of health insurance was and still is through employers. That said, only about 55 percent of employers offered coverage to their employees in 2014 (Kaiser Family Foundation and Health Research & Educational Trust 2014). Further, an injured individual may no longer be able to work at all or in the type of jobs that commonly offer insurance as a fringe benefit. Even if he or she were still able to work in some capacity, the individual should not be locked into such jobs for the remainder of his or her life due to the tortuous act of the defendant simply in order to not jeopardize health benefits.

Other than insurance offered by employers, the injured party's options were significantly limited. There are other government programs such as Medicaid, Veteran's Administration health care, and Medicare eligibility for those with a disability, but all of these require specific qualifications or means testing which could make it unlikely for the injured party to qualify. In the cases where the individual was covered by a "workers compensation" insurance plan or was within two years of eligibility of federal Medicare insurance program, these insurance programs may have covered some medical costs but were also statutorily granted subrogation rights from the injured party. Finally, the availability of insurance in the non-group, private market was heavily restricted prior to the ACA. Insurance companies had great leeway to determine who they would insure, what rate they would charge for premiums and co-payments, and what care would be covered. Insurance companies would often deny policies to those with costly pre-existing conditions like those of an injured party in a tort case. In cases where companies were willing to issue policies for those with preexisting conditions, the policy would most likely include explicit exclusions of coverage for care related to that condition.

The ACA dramatically changed the market for health insurance by imposing two key limitations on the insurance market: guaranteed issue and standardized insurance offerings. Guaranteed issue insures that all legal citizens in the USA can purchase an insurance policy from a government-established marketplace without restrictions based on pre-existing conditions. Insurance companies cannot consider expected costs of anyone who enrolls in their insurance programs when determining eligibility or costs. In fact, insurers can only adjust premiums for a specific plan based on age, tobacco use, and geographic location (US Centers for Medicare & Medicaid Services 2015a). Therefore, a 30-year-old, non-tobacco-using resident of New York City is able to attain health insurance with the same premium on a health insurance exchange regardless of whether he or she is perfectly health, recently diagnosed with cancer, or a victim of a tortious act that will require a lifetime of expensive medical care.

Though access to insurance for everyone is an important tenet of the Affordable Care Act, the law's establishment of standardized coverage in those plans insures that insurance companies cannot sort customers based on expected medical care by designing plans that are more desirable for "healthy" individuals. Specifically, the plans that are available on the health insurance exchanges established by the ACA are required to cover ten broad categories of "essential health benefits." Essential health benefits include (1) ambulatory patient services (outpatient care), (2) emergency services (trips to the emergency room), (3) hospitalization (treatment in the hospital for inpatient care), (4) maternity and newborn care, (5) mental health services and addiction treatment, (6) prescription drugs, (7) rehabilitative services and devices, (8) laboratory services, (9) preventive services, wellness services, and chronic disease treatment, and (10) pediatric services (US Centers for Medicare & Medicaid Services 2015b).

Not all services within these broad categories must be covered, but the law requires general coverage within each of these service areas. Individual states are responsible for approving plans subject to federal guidelines. The Center for Consumer Information and Insurance Oversight at the Centers for Medicare and Medicaid Services provides benchmark plans for each state and the District of Columbia as well as lists of individual state-required benefits. For each benefit listed in a state's benchmark plan, the state provides a description of the benefit, whether the benefit is covered, a designation as to whether the benefit is considered an essential health benefit subject to out-of-pocket yearly maximums, any quantitative limits on the service, and if any exclusions or additional limitations or restrictions on coverage of the benefits exist (see https://www.cms.gov/CCIIO/Resources/Data-Resources/ehb.html).

In addition to coverage standards, the ACA also limits the amount of cost sharing that can be part of the standard insurance policy. Though insurers are still allowed to pass along some costs in the form of co-payments and deductibles, the US Department of Health and Human Services sets annual limits for the total amount of out-of-pocket medical expenses paid by an insured individual. The limit in 2015 was set at $6600 for an individual and $13,200 for a family; it increases to $6850 and $13,700, respectively, for 2016, and increases annually thereafter by an amount determined by the US Department of Health and Human Services based on the rate of growth of the average per capita premium for health insurance coverage (US Department of Health and Human Services 2015). Additionally, the ACA prohibits insurance providers from setting annual and lifetime maximum benefits for covered expenses.

9.3   The ACA and Medical Inflation

The ACA also has provisions designed to curb the explosive growth of health care in the USA. In the 35 years prior to the passage of the ACA, health care costs increased at an average annual growth rate of around 6 percent while the consumer price index (CPI) increased by only 3.7 percent. Though medical care costs have consistently grown more quickly than the costs of all goods and services more broadly between 1980 and 2009, Table 9.1 shows that the gap between the CPI and two medical care cost indexes calculated by the US Bureau of Labor Statistics has been narrowing in the last 15 years, even before the ACA. That said, the ACA was designed to further narrow that gap by restricting both the premiums that insurance companies can charge and creating programs to stem the growth of medical care payments. In an attempt to limit the growth of premiums, the ACA instituted a 20 percent cap on the share of premium revenue that can be allocated to non-medical care items such as advertising, administrative costs, and profits. The law also requires insurance companies to receive approval for any premium increases over 10 percent.

In regard to the cost of medical care itself, the ACA includes a number of initiatives and experiments to attempt to limit the price of care and

Table 9.1   Consumer Price Index (CPI) and medical components

	CPI	Medical care CPI		Medical care services CPI	
Range of years	Average annual percent change (%)	Average annual percent change (%)	Difference with CPI (%)	Average annual percent change (%)	Difference with CPI (%)
Average 1980–2009	3.71%	5.92%	2.21%	6.13%	2.42%
Average 1990–2009	2.78%	4.73%	1.95%	5.04%	2.26%
Average 2000–2009	2.57%	4.13%	1.56%	4.53%	1.96%
Average 2005–2009	2.59%	3.91%	1.32%	4.34%	1.75%
Average 2010–2014	1.99%	2.99%	1.00%	3.19%	1.20%

Source: Authors' calculations based on data from the US Department of Labor (2015)

amount needed. First, by increasing the pool of insured individuals, the rate of unpaid care should decrease significantly and health care providers will not pass along those costs through higher prices for those who do pay. A 2014 Kaiser Family Foundation report estimates that $21.1 billion of medical care was uncompensated in 2013, the last year before the health care mandate took effect (another $63.8 billion in medical care to uninsured individuals was compensated by other entities—such as federal and state government-funded programs—or was explicitly identified as charity). Assuming the cost of uncompensated care resulted in higher prices for those who were insured, this total makes up 2.3 % of the total private health insurance expenditures of $925.2 billion that year (Coughlin et al. 2014).

Additionally, the law provides funding for pilot programs to advance health outcomes while reducing the cost of care. Examples of programs that have been funded to date include new payment models that increase efficiency through linking payments to the quality of care provided, penalties for patient readmissions, and bundled payments for services related to a procedure or condition rather than payment on a per service basis (Blumenthal et al. 2015). Early results appear to support the effectiveness of the ACA on this front. The gap between the growth of medical costs and overall CPI has narrowed by 25 percent in the five years since the passage of the ACA when compared to the average growth rates between 2005 and 2009. Though the recent economic downturn may have had a different impact on medical costs than the costs of all goods, it should be noted that 2013 and 2014 had the two lowest medical cost growth rates since 1960 (US Department of Labor 2015).

9.4   IMPLICATIONS OF THE ACA WHEN ESTIMATING THE COST OF A LIFE CARE PLAN

The changing landscape of the health insurance marketplace and health care provision may have important implications for FEs. Suppose a FE were to consider the ACA when calculating life care costs. Rather than identifying the costs of each item in a life care plan, the expert would start by identifying which services and devices are covered by all insurance policies under the essential benefit mandate and which are not. The annual cost of covered expenses for the injured party would be limited to the insurance premium in the area where the individual lives plus the out-of-pocket maximum. For items in the life care plan that are unlikely to be covered, the FE would calculate the likely cost of such treatment or devices in accordance with the requirements spelled out in a life care plan, as they did prior to the ACA. The FE would then calculate the present value of the expected lifetime of insurance premiums, out-of-pocket maximum payments, and the cost of uncovered care while taking into consideration the effectiveness of the ACA to control medical costs and insurance premiums.

It is reasonable to argue that the determination about which items would be covered by insurance should be left to life care planners who have specific expertise regarding medical care needs and health care costs. Certainly, as this area of litigation expertise develops, it may become more common to find life care planners addressing this issue. Many life care planners already are prepared to exclude items such as speech therapy from life care plans for injured children on the basis that these services are frequently provided by public school systems, so it would not be unreasonable to presume that some life care planners would begin to address insurance coverage in a similar way. However, just because this is an area that could, and perhaps should, be handled by life care planners does not preclude its examination by FEs. The determination of whether a service, device, or procedure is covered by insurance does not require medical expertise but instead simply requires comparing the state's benchmark insurance plan to the items in the life care plan. FEs already routinely engage in a similar activity of sorting life care components into various categories when determining which inflation rate to apply to various components of a life care plan. It should be noted that a strong argument could be made that the insurance premium should not be included in any award. The ACA includes an individual mandate which requires all individuals to acquire health insurance or pay a significant financial penalty. Therefore, the plaintiff would have been required to purchase insurance whether they had been injured or not. At the very least, the FE would include the cost of the penalty associated the individual mandate as an offset to the cost of insurance. Anecdotally, an offer from the defendant to cover the cost of an ACA-compliant insurance plan along with expected out-of-pocket costs has been reported to be an effective negotiating tool in settlement negotiations in cases involving large future medical costs.

9.5   APPLYING THE ACA TO A LIFE CARE PLAN: AN EXAMPLE

Suppose an accident to a single, 35-year-old adult male results in annual expected future life care costs of $100,000 for home health care, $10,000 for transportation, $20,000 in prescription drugs, $20,000 in routine medical evaluations and diagnostics, and $10,000 in durable medical equipment such as wheelchairs and/or prosthetic devices.

Prior to the ACA, assuming liability on the part of the defendant, this plaintiff has an identifiable increase in life care costs of $160,000 per year, all of which could reasonably be expected to be paid for out-of-pocket by the plaintiff. Thus, to make the victim whole, $160,000 should be paid annually until life expectancy (appropriately grown and discounted to present value terms).

Applying the ACA to this case, the first step is to identify which items are typically covered by an ACA-compliant insurance plan. Prescription drugs, routine medical care, diagnostic tests, and durable medical equipment are all generally deemed as "essential health benefits," and would therefore be covered by insurance. Home health aides as well as modifications to vehicles and housing are generally not covered by health insurance plans. Thus, the FE is left with $110,000 in uncovered expenses and $50,000 in covered expenses.

Using either the federal government's health exchange or an individual state's insurance exchange website, one can quickly determine a price for a basic health care plan. For example, in 2015 in San Francisco, one could purchase the "Kaiser Bronze 60 HMO" for $332.59/month or $3,991.08 per year. Due to the guaranteed issue provision of the ACA, Kaiser could not refuse the sale of this insurance product to the plaintiff nor could it charge him a higher price than any other purchaser, nor could it subrogate any portion of a tort award.

This insurance would cover the plaintiff's $50,000 per year in medical costs while passing on a maximum of $6600 per year in co-payment in 2015 (indexed to health insurance premium adjustment percentage) for a total of $10,591 per year. Combined with the uncovered life care expenses, the new total life care costs have fallen from $160,000 per year to $120,591 per year.

Furthermore, since the ACA mandate requires purchase of insurance whether or not the plaintiff had been the victim of negligence, the $3991 per year of insurance costs arguably should be removed from damages leaving total medical care costs of $6600 per year and total life care costs of $116,600 per year. Furthermore, most cases involving large medical awards generally include a claim for lost compensation as well. Lost compensation claims typically include both a wage and benefits component. If the plaintiff is awarded lost benefits, a large portion of which is usually employer-paid health care, also awarding the plaintiff the cost of insurance under the life care plan results in a double award.

It should be noted that even this amount might represent a conservative estimate of the differences between the expenses in the life care plan and the expected out of pocket costs to the plaintiff for several reasons. First, this methodology assumes that, but for the accident, the plaintiff would have incurred no out-of-pocket expenditures for health care. Second, it is assumed that at no time would the plaintiff qualify for the subsidies to purchase health insurance available to low income households under the ACA. Third, it is possible that a portion of home health care, especially for services requiring skilled nursing, would be deemed an essential health benefit and therefore eligible for reimbursement under a typical health insurance plan. As home nursing care is a large component of the life care plan, even partial coverage of this item could result in a significant additional reduction in out-of-pocket expenses for the plaintiff. Finally, it is assumed that the plaintiff would pay the maximum allowable amount in out-of-pocket payments each year. Depending on the type of insurance and the co-payment regulations for the insurance product he purchases, he may face total out-of-pocket expenditures below the allowable maximum.

Of course, this is just one possible way to address the ACA in an economic analysis of a life care plan. Alternatively, the FE could assume that 60 percent of medical costs would be paid by the insurer with the rest covered by the plaintiff up to the statutory maximum. The least generous ACA-compliant plans, "Bronze plans," are designed to cover 60 percent of the customer's covered health expenditures on average. Silver, gold, and platinum plans which are designed to cover 70, 80, and 90 percent of costs on average are also available in the health insurance marketplace. Yet another approach is for the life care planner or economist to examine the potential coverage of an actual plan available for sale on the exchanges in the defendant's state.

Finally, it is worth noting that the negotiated prices that insurance companies face is quite often lower than the billed prices that individuals might face when paying for medical goods and services out-of-pocket. Thus, not only might insured plaintiffs find a portion of medical care covered by their ACA policy, but the prices they face for this care may be lower in the first place. The issue of "bill vs. pay" and its connection to the ACA is beyond the scope of this chapter and perhaps outside the domain of forensic economic analysis, but it may become an important factor as the applicability of the ACA to life care awards develops.

9.6   Issues Still to Be Resolved

The previous interpretation of the impact of the ACA is not undisputed as there are several arguments that could be made to ignore the ACA in estimating damages. The first question is whether the ACA will remain in existence with a reasonable degree of economic certainty. This is clearly open to opinion, but with each passing year the law becomes more entrenched. The law was passed by Congress, signed by the president, and has survived two challenges at the Supreme Court. It is true that public opinion on the ACA remains deeply divided and that some in Congress urge repeal of the ACA, but national polling on the ACA shows that only slightly more respondents have a negative opinion on the law than a positive opinion, and full repeal of the law is deeply unpopular (Knowles and Brody 2015). Furthermore, most proposed alternatives to the law would preserve the most popular aspects of the ACA which include the guaranteed issue provision which is at the heart of this analysis. Finally, while it is a simple task to campaign against a law before it takes effect, it is quite another to repeal one once it has taken hold. An estimated 28 million Americans have received health insurance coverage through provisions of the ACA since the law was passed (Gaba 2015), many for the first time in their adult lives, and the American un-insurance rate has fallen from 18 percent to 11.4 percent (Marken 2015). It is true that no FE can state with absolute certainty that the ACA will remain in place in its current form for the indefinite future, but if absolute certainty is the bar that must be met, there is indeed little to which a FE, or most expert witnesses, could testify.

Perhaps a larger hurdle is the issue of collateral source. In states where collateral source payments to compensate an injured party are not allowed to be considered by a jury or trial judge in determining an award, insurance payouts are often excluded from the court record. There are at least two economic rationales for excluding collateral source payments from consideration in damage awards. The first is to ensure that people have the proper incentives to make wise investments in insurance products. If insurance benefits serve to reduce tort awards dollar for dollar, why would individuals ever purchase insurance in the first place? This reasoning for excluding collateral source health insurance benefits disappears under the ACA. The individual mandate serves to ensure that people have strong incentives to purchase health insurance as confirmed by the rapidly falling un-insurance rates following the enactment of the ACA. Furthermore, most of the insurance payments that will be used to cover the costs of future medical treatment will be from policies that were initiated after the injury takes place. If the exclusion of collateral source payments is motivated by the principle of encouraging the public to take prudent precautions against financial shocks, post-event insurance policies would not be precautionary, but instead a reasonable measure to mitigate the expense of the necessary medical care. Assuming the injured party has a "duty to mitigate," the assumption that an injured party will enroll in an available insurance program would seem to be an appropriate measure, especially when one considers the fact that the individual is legally mandated to buy that insurance under the ACA.

The second idea is the rationale that defendants shouldn't benefit from the forethought of plaintiffs or beneficence of other income sources in order to avoid responsibility for payment of damages. This rationale remains in place even under the ACA. In the previous example, the tortfeasor has still caused $50,000 in annual medical costs whose responsibility for payment has shifted from the party who caused the damage to the insurance company. If the goal of an award in a tort case is to make the injured party "whole," clearly we would want to focus on the costs that will be incurred by the plaintiff due to the tortuous act. On the other hand, this amount does not reflect the true financial burden caused by the act in that much of the medical costs have been passed on to the injured individual's future health insurers (and thus all policyholders). If awards are instead motivated to punish injurers and force them to pay the full cost of their act, an award should consider the costs incurred by all entities, not just the plaintiff. With either philosophy, the expenses borne by the insurance companies are not being repaid and are instead either being retained by the injurer or being awarded as a windfall to the plaintiff even though he or she will not bear the full costs of the medical care.

Although this is likely an unsatisfactory choice set, there is not an obvious solution or a statutory basis for a more encompassing solution under current law. Subrogation would normally be the appropriate tool to transfer the plaintiff's windfall to the company forced to pay for the increased coverage expenses of the victim, but health insurers in the individual policy market have no right of subrogation for future medical expenses under the ACA. Under the guaranteed issue provision customers have the right to purchase insurance at a uniform price regardless of pre-existing conditions, but subrogation, in effect, would charge customers who have received a tort award a higher price for health insurance by collecting both an insurance premium and a subrogation payment. Allowing subrogation for future care costs would also be exceedingly difficult administratively. Unlike cases where all future medical care for the injured party is likely to be covered by a single program like Medicare or workers compensation insurance, there is no reason to believe the injured party will have his or her current insurance provider for any longer than the current annual contract. Without long-term insurance contracts, it would be inappropriate to award the current insurer the expected cost of all future medical care and impractical to set up an alternative way to compensate future insurers under current law.

9.7   COURT TREATMENT OF THE AFFORDABLE CARE ACT

Given the recent passage and implementation of the ACA, state and federal courts' treatment of the ACA with respect to medical losses is still rapidly evolving, but several court rulings have addressed the issue arriving at conflicting conclusions. In *Deeds v. University of Pennsylvania Medical Center* (2015), the Superior Court of Pennsylvania ordered a new trial after a defense verdict in a medical malpractice case because defense counsel's comments suggesting that the minor-plaintiff's medical costs were being covered by Medicaid and the ACA were a "patent violation of the collateral source rule." Similarly, in *Vasquez-Sierra v. Hennepin Faculty Associates* (2012), Minnesota state courts rejected the defense's argument that annual medical damages for Ms. Vasquez-Sierra be capped at approximately $7000 per year, the sum of out-of-pocket medical and insurance premium costs, stating, "[The court]... is not inclined to speculate that the recent and controversial federal health care legislation upends Minnesota's collateral source doctrine. Until the Minnesota legislature passes new legislation regarding collateral sources in light of the Affordable Care Act, this court will not re-write long-standing law regarding collateral sources." Persuaded by the reasoning of *Vasquez-Sierra*, the US District Court, Minnesota District in *Halsne v. Avera Health* (2014) found that any benefits received through the Affordable Care Act do not provide a basis for reducing the potential award to plaintiff. Similarly, in *Caronia v. Philip Morris USA* (2013), a New York state case, the plaintiffs sought compensation to cover the cost of monitoring for future smoking-related diseases. The defendant unsuccessfully argued that the ACA would allow the plaintiffs to obtain free access to the monitoring services that they were seeking.

Other courts have appealed to the uncertain future of the ACA as a reason to omit consideration of the current law from damage awards. A California state court in *Aidan Ming-Ho Leung v. Verdugo Hills Hospital* (2013) determined that despite defense arguments that the ACA provided guaranteed access to insurance, future health insurance would not be taken into account when calculating the expected future medical costs stating, "the mere possibility that private insurance coverage will continue, and the availability of government programs for the purchase of insurance, do not, in themselves, constitute relevant, admissible evidence of the future insurance benefits that a plaintiff is reasonably certain to receive." In *CSC v US* (2013), a US District Court judge ruled that, "the viability of the Affordable Care Act is far too speculative to give [an ACA] plan any credence." Finally, in *Brewster v. Southern Home Rentals* (2012), an Alabama court found that references to "the possibility of future insurance coverage would be too speculative to be relevant, or if relevant at all, any probative value of this evidence is substantially outweighed by the danger of confusion of the issues and misleading the jury."

In contrast, other courts have taken a much more favorable view of considering the ACA, especially in more recent rulings. In Michigan, the court in *Donaldson v. Advantage Health Physicians* (2015) ruled in a pre-trial motion that "health insurance provided under the Affordable Care Act is reasonably likely to continue into the future and that its discussion before the jury is not precluded by [Michigan law]. Accordingly, what medical care and therapies would be provided by insurance through the ACA can be discussed/argued at trial." Two cases in Ohio, *Jones v. MetroHealth Medical Care* (2015) and *Christy v. Humility of Mary Health Partners* (2015) both allowed the application of the ACA to medical malpractice damage awards. In the case of Alijah Jones, the court limited his damages to $116,000, comprising eight years' worth of $8000 premiums and $6500 maximum out-of-pocket expenses. Finally, in *Brewington v. United States* (2015), tried in the US District Court for the Central District of California, the judge wrote that the "ACA ensures that Mr. Brewington will have access to insurance covering his future medical care needs .... Thus, this Court finds it appropriate to take insurance benefits available under the ACA into consideration in calculating reasonable future life care plan needs."

Two other courts have found that it is permissible to address the discounted prices that plaintiffs may receive as a result of being able to purchase their health care through an insurance plan. In a pre-trial motion, the court in *First Bankers Trust v. Memorial Medical Center* (2015) ruled that the defendants could not refer to the ACA and its effect on out-of-pocket medical costs but could produce evidence "as to its effect on the actual reasonable costs of medical services." Similarly, in *Stayton v. DE Health Corp. et al.* (2015) the Delaware Supreme Court affirmed a lower court ruling that "the collateral source rule does not apply to [insurance] write-offs. Stayton's heathcare provider expenses are limited to the amount paid by [insurance] for her medical care." Thus, the ability to purchase health insurance due to the ACA may reduce the cost of life care plans not by eliminating the defense's responsibility to pay for future medical care but instead by lowering the price of that care.

9.8   CONCLUSION

Based on the mixed early rulings regarding the application of the ACA to medical awards, it remains unclear how courts will treat the availability of health insurance when assessing tort awards for future medical costs and whether courts around the country will coalesce around a single interpretation. From an economic standpoint, however, it is clear that the full implementation of the ACA in January 2014 marked a serious change in the way plaintiffs will finance their future medical care. Prior to the ACA, it was reasonable to presume that a great deal of a victim's future health care costs would be paid for out-of-pocket as there was little guarantee that the plaintiff would have access to affordable insurance. Requiring defendants to bear the full cost for any damages that they imposed on plaintiffs was generally economically efficient because it resulted in a windfall for a plaintiff only in the rare cases where the plaintiff could obtain health insurance and subrogation was not possible.

Conversely, under current health care law, victims will typically obtain insurance that will cover a significant portion of any medical costs up to the maximum annual limit and pay for all covered costs beyond that point. In this post-ACA world, making defendants pay the full cost of their actions nearly always results in a plaintiff windfall. Any analysis of future life care costs that seeks to "make the victim whole" rather than simply "make the tortfeasor pay" must at least be aware of the ramifications of the ACA, and it is likely that FEs will increasingly encounter this argument from defense lawyers and experts.

NOTE

1. The authors would like to thank Coan Calabrese for excellent research assistance.

REFERENCES

Blumenthal, D., Abrams, M., & Nuzum, R. (2015). The Affordable Care Act at 5 years. *The New England Journal of Medicine, 372*(25), 2451–2458.

Congdon-Hohman, J., & Matheson, V. A. (2013). Potential Effects of the Patient Protection and Affordable Care Act on the award of life care expense. *Journal of Forensic Economics, 24*(2), 153–160.

Coughlin, T. A., Holahan, J., Caswell, K., & McGrath, M. (2014). Uncompensated care for the uninsured in 2013: A detailed examination, report for the Henry J. Kaiser Family Foundation, May.

Gaba, C. (2015). ACA exchange qualified health policy enrollments. http://aca-signups.net/graphs. Accessed 3 Sept

Kaiser Family Foundation and Health Research & Educational Trust. (2014). *Employer health benefits: 2014 annual survey*, September.

Knowles, D., & Brody, B. (2015). Bloomberg Politics Poll: Majority of Americans say Obamacare should get time to work, Bloomberg Politics. http://www.bloomberg.com/politics/articles/2015-04-17/bloomberg-politics-poll-majority-of-americans-say-obamacare-should-get-time-to-work, posted April 17

Marken, S. (2015). U.S. Uninsured rate at 11.4% in second quarter, gallup poll. http://www.gallup.com/poll/184064/uninsured-rate-second-quarter.aspx, posted July 10

U.S. Centers for Medicare & Medicaid Services. (2015a). How marketplace plans set your health insurance premiums. https://www.healthcare.gov/lower-costs/how-plans-set-your-premiums/. Accessed 1 Sept.

U.S. Centers for Medicare & Medicaid Services. (2015b). What marketplace health plans cover. https://www.healthcare.gov/coverage/what-marketplace-plans-cover/. Accessed 1 Sept.

U.S. Department of Health and Human Services. (2015, February 27). HHS notice of benefit and payment parameters for 2016. *Federal Register, 80*(39), 10750–10871.

U.S. Department of Labor, Bureau of Labor Statistics. (2015). Consumer Price Index. http://www.bls.gov/cpi/. Accessed 3 Sept 2015.

CASES CITED

Brewington v. U.S., Case No. CV 13-07672-DMG (CWX) (U.S. Dist. CD Cal.) 2015.

Brewster v. Southern Home Rentals, Civil Action No. 3:11CV872-WHA (U.S. Dist. M.D. Alabama, Eastern Division) 2012.

Caronia v. Philip Morris USA, NY Slip Op 08372, 22 NY3d 439, (NY Court of Appeals) 2013.

Christy v. Humility of Mary Health Partners, Pre-trial ruling, (Trumball County Court of Common Pleas in Ohio) 2015.

CSC v. US, Civil No. 10-910-DRH (Dist. Court. SD Illinois) 2013.

Deeds v. University of Pennsylvania Medical Center, 2015 PA Super 21, J-A33035-14, No. 755 EDA 2014 (PA Super) 2015.

Donaldson v. Advantage Health Physicians, File No. 11-09181-NH,(Michigan Circuit Court County of Kent) 2015.

First Bankers Trust v. Memorial Medical Center (Illinois Circuit Court for 7th Judicial Circuit).

Halsne v. Avera Health, Case No. 0:12-cv-02409-SRN-JJG, (U.S. Dist Minn.) 2014.

Jones v. MetroHealth Medical Care Center, No. CV 11-75713, (Court of Common Pleas of Cuyahoga County, Ohio) 2015.

Leung v. Verdugo Hills Hospital, Los Angeles County Super. Ct. No. B251366/ BC343985, (Court of Appeal, State of California 2nd Appellate District Division 4) 2014.

Stayton v. DE Health Corp. et al. No. 601 2014, Court below C.A. No.: K12C-04-026 RBY (Delaware Supreme Court) June 12, 2015.

Vasquez-Sierra v. Hennepin Faculty Assocs., No. 27-cv-12-1611, 2012 WL 7150829 (Minn. Dist. Ct.) Dec. 14, 2012.

CHAPTER 10

Challenges in Valuing Loss of Services

Frank D. Tinari

10.1 INTRODUCTION

In addition to a loss of cash and non-cash income, a personal injury (or, of course, death) causes surviving family members to lose the services that the impaired/deceased individual would have continued to provide but for the incident. Thus, it would seem reasonable that a claim for such a loss be made along with other damages claims. Since at least 1913, courts have recognized this reality (*Michigan Central Railroad Company v. Vreeland*). But there are at least five analytical challenges to the expert who undertakes a valuation of lost services:

(1) establishing what types of services have been lost;
(2) identifying which of these services are permitted by the courts to be valued;
(3) determining the magnitude or extent of each service that would have continued to be provided;
(4) determining a proper valuation method to apply to the identified services; and
(5) specifying the monetary value of each service being measured.

F.D. Tinari (✉)
Professor Emeritus, Seton Hall University, USA

© The Author(s) 2016   161
F.D. Tinari (ed.), *Forensic Economics*,
DOI 10.1057/978-1-137-56392-7_10

Because family services are typically provided gratis, there are no receipts or records of payments as there are for lost earnings. Economists label them *non-market services* since prices are not paid for them when provided within the household. One economist has labeled these services "unpaid (but still productive) household work." (Greenwood 1996, p. 89.) In this author's experience, attorneys typically view the valuation of services as "soft" losses. The analytical challenges facing the expert in valuing services appear to lend credence to this view. Lawyers sometimes describe claimed losses as "economic" (by which they mean lost earnings and benefits) and "non-economic" (by which they mean services and everything else). This is in stark contrast to the economic view which treats all productive time use on the same basis, that is, having real value irrespective of whether or not monetary payments are made. In other words, if a human activity generates benefits or utility, it has economic value. For example, there is real value to Johnny when his mom helps him with his homework. If the mom were to die wrongfully, a claim could legitimately be made for the value of her lost services even though no financial payment by Johnny to mom had ever been made.[1] Nearly all state and federal courts recognize this reality and permit claims for the value of lost services. Dulaney et al. (1992, p. 124) cite at least four court opinions in support.

But general recognition by the courts does not go very far in addressing the analytical challenges we have listed. This task has fallen to forensic economists who have written extensively about the valuation of services. This chapter relies heavily on that literature found primarily but not exclusively in the *Journal of Forensic Economics* and the *Journal of Legal Economics*. The following sections address each of the challenges identified above, followed by concluding observations regarding future consideration of service loss valuation in the courts.

10.2   Types of Services

Given that economists recognize that any and all human activity has real economic value, one might think that an overall measure of time spent producing "all services" would be sufficient for litigation purposes. For example, given 24 hours in a day, one might want to subtract sleep time, personal grooming, leisure and meal time, and time spent in compensated labor, in order to arrive at a residual amount of time that could have been devoted to providing "services." But that approach is too broad and general to have legitimacy. What kinds of services, if any, were undertaken?

How much of each? Obviously, some types of service are valued more highly than others by family members. And some services may have been provided mostly for the benefit of the provider, not other family members.[2] So what is needed is more specification regarding the types of services that could be provided.

Nearly all courts recognize claims for a loss of "household services" as compensable. Further, a majority of court systems permit claims for a loss of "parental guidance, care and nurturing." But these categories do not exhaust the range of possible services. New Jersey courts allow economic experts to calculate the value of loss of "companionship" services and loss of "advice, guidance and counsel." Further, one federal court in New Jersey has permitted calculation of the value of lost "overnight, protective sleep-time services" resulting from the death of a husband. We might also conceive of other services such as "on-call services" provided by parents by telephone to their children.

Most case opinions and state statutes governing economic damages claims refer to the *pecuniary value* of lost services. The opinion in *Michigan Central Railroad Company* (1913, p. 71) states: *"A pecuniary loss or damage must be one which can be measured by some standard."* Ireland (1999a, p. 242) states that the term typically implies some sense of a market equivalent value. This is meant to distinguish proper claims for lost services from the loss of intangibles such as love, affection and other personal impacts resulting from the death of a family member. Ireland (p. 237) concludes that there are two primary criteria for determining lost services. "First, the value of that service to the recipient must not be based on the lost love and affection for the decedent. Second, that the service must be shown to have reasonable market equivalents in the commercial marketplace." His analysis is based primarily on his reading of *Michigan Central Railroad Company* (1913), from which he quotes extensively.

A bimodal characterization of services has been presented by Olson and Rodgers (1999). They posit a distinction between *household services* and *emotional services* based on two characteristics:

> First, emotional services are something that a person is always providing. Unlike the lawn mowing which occurs periodically, counsel, instruction and advice exist to a considerable degree through example set by the person (now deceased), in addition to direct time spent in talking to and doing things with the family. ... [I]t is therefore the availability of the services, rather than mere direct provision, which has value.

...

> Second, emotional services are in some considerable measure jointly consumed, taking on the characteristics of a public good .... In other words, consumption of at least some aspects of these services by one family member does not preclude the consumption of these services by another family member. (pp. 256–57)

The distinction is interesting, but isn't airtight by any means. For example, many household services provide jointly consumed benefits as well (explained later in this chapter). And, using their example, being available "when your child has an unsuspected crisis at 2 a.m." requires physical presence, as does the provision of household services as they define them.

It is evident that in measuring a loss of services, it is necessary to identify and define each type of service. We do so here, as follows:

a) *Household services:* these services are "individuals' contribution of their time and energy to the maintenance of the household and services performed for the benefit of family members" (Ward and Krueger 1994, p. 95). Or, succinctly put, the chores necessary to maintain a household. Some non-exhaustive examples are mowing the lawn, taking out the trash, fixing broken household items, cooking, house cleaning, running errands, automobile care and gardening.

b) *Advice, guidance and counsel services:* these services refer specifically to oral, telephonic and written advice given by one member of the household to another. Consider the wording in a Kansas Supreme Court case: "There can be no doubt plaintiff and his two small sons suffered a pecuniary loss when deprived of the services, care and guidance of (the mother) ..." (*Wentling v. Medical Anesthesia Services* 1985, p. 945). Examples of her guidance might have included helping with homework, giving advice on medical, financial, familial and other concerns, and so forth. Olson and Rodgers (1999, p. 258) point out that, in *Garza v. Berlanga,* an economist "gave values for services in the area of moral guidance and housework. In arriving at the economic value for the loss of moral guidance, he equated the loss as being equal to the annual salary of a school teacher ...." Ireland (1997) argues that economists should be cautious in valuing advice and counsel services without foundation from a "family expert."

Unlike household services that typically involve physical activity and often occur without other members of the household being present, advice-type services are person-to-person.[3]

c) *Companionship services*: these services include the time, again, in person, one spends as a companion with one or more members of the household. This time does not include giving advice but simply accompanying another household member. Examples include having dinner together, watching television or a movie together, playing board games, going shopping or sightseeing together and so on.

New Jersey courts distinguish between service and familial feelings or love by stating that it is that portion of companionship that is represented in the marketplace by those hired to provide companionship, for example, an aide who accompanies grandma on her errands or going to church.[4] That such services have value is not in contention. Rather, most courts and many economists view such services as too difficult to dis-entwine from emotional feelings of household members toward one another and, therefore, believe that they cannot be valued separately.

Ireland (2011a) has argued that calculation of lost companionship services is liable to be too speculative to be accepted by the courts and, further, should be defined in a narrower way than given above. Tinari (2011a) rebutted those arguments, explaining that, at least in New Jersey courts, the *Green v. Bittner* (1980) opinion emphasized how to assign a pecuniary value for companionship services by reference to the marketplace.

d) *Overnight protective services*: the loss of the security, safety and protection provided by a spouse due to his death may be felt by the surviving spouse each night she goes to sleep. These services are akin to those provided by doormen overnight in large city buildings, or guards at public and private facilities when they are closed. Time together during the night is not counted as part of companionship services as defined above and may be viewed as time during which a different set of services is being provided.

It is instructive that, in Ireland and Depperschmidt (1999), the two readings authored by life care planners contain reference to overnight protective services. In particular, one such expert opined in detail, as follow:

Mr. Doe was a military man who survived combat, so Mrs. Doe felt especially safe when he was around. She knew he would and could protect her, their children and grandchildren.

I always felt safe, especially at night. Many times, I'd hear something. I'd wake him up and he would get up and investigate. Or when I was afraid of a bad storm, he would comfort me. .... Mrs. Doe is now afraid of being at home alone at night, driving at night, and being alone in storms. Outside resources should and can be provided to approximate the services of protection and security that Mr. [Doe] provided for his wife in these circumstances. (Boss 1999, pp. 295–96) [correction made by editor]

e) *On-call services*: when a family member says to other members, "you can call me anytime if you have a problem, have a question, or need my help," a real service is being provided, even if no phone call occurs that day. Boss (1999, p. 295) describes these services of a husband to his wife this way: "Even when he was working, he carried a cell phone, so that in an emergency, she could call him."

In their discussion of emotional services that have economic value, Olson and Rodgers (1999, p. 256) allude to this type of service:

it is therefore the availability of the services, rather than mere direct provision, which has value. Being there when your child has an unsuspected crisis at 2 a.m. is very valuable, but so is the peace of mind to other family members that an individual will be there if needed, even if not used. The evaluation of emotional services, then, spans every hour of every day. It is much as the fireman or policeman provides services. We don't pay them for fires put out or arrests made, but rather for being there.

Like computer companies who offer consumer assistance via telephone call-in services, parents and spouses who make themselves available to answer the questions of family members by telephone, no matter the location or time of day, are providing on-call services.

Except for generally recognized household services, claimed losses of the value of the other services we have defined above are often lumped into what are often called "general damages" or "pain and suffering." When treated in this manner, the determination of the value of the loss of such services is left entirely to the jury without assistance from an economic expert. As Fischer (1999) notes: "The tradeoff is between scope and subjectivity /softness. A more narrow approach is more easily quantifiable, but it may not be more realistic in delineating the contribution of the homemaker." (p. 181)

The inclusion of each specific type of service is generally guided by the specific statutes and case law in a particular state, and by the advice of the retaining attorney. Attorneys may choose to broaden their claims by requesting their economic expert to include several types of service loss, or may choose to keep the focus narrow by requesting the expert to ignore any claims for lost services. It sometimes happens that several types of services may be valued in an expert's report, but then, in preparing for trial testimony, the attorney may instruct the expert to drop consideration of some if not all of the services. There are some, but not many, attorneys who prefer to "push the envelope" in their damages claims while the majority sticks closely to traditional case law. In one federal case, this author was asked to value overnight protective services in his report, and eventually was permitted to testify at trial as to their valuation.

Among practicing forensic economists, a small minority have had the experience (or willingness) to include valuation of the other services listed here beyond standard household services. In a survey administered to members of the National Association of Forensic Economics (NAFE), only 11 % of the respondents said they have included a measure of companionship services, and 19 % said they have included valuation of guidance, counsel and/or advice services (Slesnick et al. 2013, p. 90).

10.3   THE QUANTITY OF SERVICES PROVIDED

The loss of services to surviving family members may be viewed in two ways. The most common method is to determine and value the *hours* devoted to various services by the injured or deceased party. A second way is to consider the *output* that the services produce, that is, the mowed lawn, the cooked meal, the cleaned home and so on. Dulaney et al. (1992) argue that the output approach is the preferred method for measuring the loss of services:

> Because household production entails the combination of labor with other inputs, and because labor productivity may differ between households and business firms, the conceptually correct way to assess the value of household production is to measure the market value of the output itself (the direct output approach). (p. 124)

One of their criticisms of the labor hour approach, borrowed from the macroeconomic literature that they cite, is that the value of labor inputs fails to consider the value added by inputs other than labor, such as vacuum cleaners and clothes dryers. The criticism unfortunately is misplaced for litigation purposes. After all, persons paid to vacuum the rugs or cook meals in the home would be using the same or comparable non-labor inputs. Nevertheless, labor input measurements of services serve as an imperfect "proxy for measuring the lost dollar value of an individual's household services output." (Ireland 2011b, p. 63)

Dulaney et al. (1992) state that micro-data on household production became available from a study of 480 households in Missoula, Montana. These data enabled the authors to create a number of output categories such as interior cleaning, meal preparation, clothing care, and child care, among others. Although they argue that the data can be updated for inflation and applied to any location in the country, their methodology is rarely seen in practice. One of its shortcomings is the thin data base on which they rely, a fact that would be revealed were an analyst to examine and use any subset of relevance to a particular case such as a single female-headed household with three children. Nevertheless, it is interesting to note that when they compared the output approach to the labor-hour input approach, they found that the labor value method always gives lower market values to various services than the direct output method. Cushing and Rosenbaum (2012, p. 49) come to a similar conclusion:

> Results show that the Direct Output estimates are at least twice as large as the labor value estimates. This divergence suggests that in forensic applications, the more commonly used Labor Value Approach may produce a fairly conservative estimate of the loss related to provision of household services.

These findings imply that economic valuation of services that makes use of hours of input, rather than output, tends to understate the true value of the services. The remainder of this discussion focuses upon the labor hours input to provide services.

Had mom not wrongfully died, how much would she have continued to provide in terms of household services? Ten hours per week? Twenty? While it may seem that one need only ask how many hours of services she was providing to the household prior to the injury, complications quickly arise. The most important is that she provided many services without any other household members being present. Or, if they were present, they may have been attending to their own activities, thereby not keeping track of mom's time usage. A second problem is that in a litigious setting, there is the temptation faced by plaintiffs to exaggerate some of the facts they are being asked to provide. "Mom spent twenty-five hours maintaining the household, not twenty." The temptation exists even in injury cases where mom herself is asked to provide facts about what she had been doing prior to the injury. Further, many of us do not consciously keep track of the time we spend on various activities including service provision.

One way to help ascertain the magnitude of services that would have continued to be provided is to request that a detailed questionnaire be completed by the plaintiffs or their legal representatives. It is this author's experience that the process of answering a series of questions focuses the attention of the plaintiff. To be useful, a questionnaire should include multiple questions that serve as a cross-check of the answers. Nevertheless, given the measurement problems noted above, it is wise to corroborate a plaintiff's responses by reference to more comprehensive and statistically sound data. Thankfully, since 2003, the US Department of Labor has been gathering annually information from thousands of households, called the *American Time Use Survey* (ATUS), and compiles the data for access by researchers. In particular, the data that are collected include the hours of services performed by household members.

ATUS data allow experts to study households possessing various characteristics in which they are interested. For example, for an injured male head of household with a wife and two children, it is possible to identify the average number of household services hours reported in the Study for all comparable households. Despite the fact that courts generally want experts to analyze the specific hours of services of the specific individual in the case, it is very helpful to cite as a benchmark the average number of hours reported by thousands of comparable households. For this purpose, a convenient source used by many forensic economists is *The Dollar Value of a Day* (2014). The volume arranges ATUS data in convenient table format cross-tabulated by a number of important variables regarding household structure, size and so forth, and is widely used by forensic economists to help establish reasonable values for the number of hours of household services.

Data on the other services identified and defined above are not readily available from national time use studies. Thus, the analyst must rely on questionnaires as well as other sources of factual evidence in each case in order to establish a basis for including each specific type of service in the assessment of damages, and a reasonable number of hours of provision of each type of service. Further, it is known that the quantity of services provided by various household members changes as individuals age and take on changing roles (e.g., mom no longer needs to drive Mary to school after Mary obtains a driver's license, or Johnny leaves the household to attend college). Therefore, it is often necessary for the analyst to make assumptions about the future quantity of services that likely would have been provided but for the impairment. For this purpose, questionnaires are of no use since they describe past relationships. It is the responsibility of the forensic economist to state and explain assumptions about future expected household relationships, assumptions that must be logical and reasonable to the average jury member.

For example, what number of hours of services should be assigned in litigated cases in which the injured persons are retired from active employment? On the one hand, they likely have more time to perform household services. On the other, as people age they tend to slow down and perform fewer physical activities. Ireland (2011b) addresses these and other aspects of retired individuals, observing that "hours listed in a time-use survey as being spent on activities identified as household services have become an even more imperfect proxy for the household service output values that we cannot directly measure" (p. 72). The problem occurs because, among other things, national data regarding the elderly reveal an increased number of hours of services. But, at a slower pace, the output of services may be comparable to those performed by younger, more active persons who devote fewer hours to those same tasks. Since the objective of the economic loss calculation is to estimate a pecuniary amount sufficient to replace the lost services, it is this author's practice to use the number of hours of services provided by those who are younger and not retired. This serves as an approximate measure of the cost of replacing the lost services in the marketplace, a market that is populated by younger individuals who could be hired to perform the services.

An alternative approach is to project future losses of services up to a specified age, and not beyond. This approach incorporates an assumption that elderly individuals are more prone to one or more physical impairments that would reduce their ability to perform household services. One way of determining the end date is to use what is termed *healthy life expectancy*. Expectancy Data (various) has combined data from the US Department of Health and Human Services (DHHS) into a format the economist can use to determine how many years of "healthy life function" a person has remaining, given his or her sex, age and race, that is, "when a living person perceives that his or her health is excellent and his or her activities are not limited in any way." As conveyed by Martin and Weinstein (2012):

> Rarely does a person go from a healthy life one day to an unhealthy life the next, absent some catastrophic event. But the actual onset and rate of decline is difficult to measure. The authors of Healthy Life Expectancy have analyzed the data from DHHS and have developed a table similar to a life

expectancy table, except that it measures the years of healthy life and full function life remaining rather than years to end of life expectancy. ...

Expectancy Data offers an alternative measure called Full Function Life Expectancy (FFLE). These expectancies fall somewhere between Life Expectancy and Healthy Life Expectancy (HLE). The reasoning is that it is not always necessary for a person to curtail activities due to a medical problem that places him or her in the less than healthy category. For instance, a diabetic may live to a normal life expectancy and remain fully functional for many years. For this reason, some economists will prefer to use FFLE rather than HLE to determine the end of the ability of a person to perform household services. (Section 620)

Another problem deals with the question of who benefits from the provision of household services. In wrongful death litigation, the expert attempts to value the loss of services to surviving family members who have legal standing to make a claim. The presumption in such analyses is that services that the decedent provided for himself or herself are not included in the expert's opinion of losses. But the matter is not so clear-cut. Some experts attempt to make an adjustment to the amount of services assigned to an injured or a deceased member of a household to account for the *personal consumption* of the specified services. Martin and Weinstein (2012, Section 631) define the term as "the amount of household services performed by the decedent that were for his/her benefit only and were not a loss to the family. This is analogous to the deduction of personal maintenance (consumption) from the income lost due to the death of a family member."[5] Yet the analogy is quite weak, given the nature of services that are akin to public goods in that provision of many services provides benefits to all household members. This aspect of the nature of services is discussed next.

One of the most perplexing aspects of the quantification of services has two parts. On the one hand, the production of some services benefits more than one household member simultaneously. Activities such as washing clothes, preparing meals and mowing the lawn are, in the economist's lingo, *jointly consumed*. Olson and Rodgers (1999, p. 260) refer to this phenomenon as the *public goods* aspect of the provision of services. In contrast, other activities such as helping Natasha with her homework are individually consumed. But for jointly consumed services, each household member receives the benefit at the same time. Hence, if mom dies, each has lost her services. In the litigation context, the expert may be put on the defensive in attempting to explain that the three hours mom spent in companionship with her two daughters yields a loss of six hours of such services (three for each daughter). Of course, in the case of a married couple with no children, the losses would be individually consumed services.

It may be helpful to examine each of the different types of services outlined above with respect to the nature of their consumption, as follows:

Type of service	Could be Individually consumed	Could be Jointly consumed
Household	Yes	Yes
Advice and counsel	Yes	No
Companionship	Yes	Yes
Overnight protective	Yes	Yes
On-call	Yes	Yes

How the forensic economist handles this complication has not yet been resolved in the literature.

The other quantification dilemma is that there may be *joint production* of services in any given hour. When damages experts attempt to measure more than one type of service, they may have to address the *multi-tasking problem*.[6] Here are some examples: (a) While dad is fixing the family model train set with young Bill, he is also chatting with Bill about his school work and dealing with a bully at school. If dad were wrongfully killed, Bill would lose both the household services of his dad as well as dad's advice, guidance and counsel. (b) While mom is preparing a meal, she is also helping Sally decide on the color and style of her prom dress and shoes. If mom were wrongfully killed, Sally would lose both the household services of her mom as well as mom's advice, guidance and counsel. (c) Having a restaurant meal together, Mr. and Mrs. Cromwell are providing companionship services to one another. During the meal, Mrs. Cromwell explains the problems she is having with their bank and suggests to Mr. Cromwell how they can be resolved. If she were wrongfully killed, her husband would lose both her companionship services and her advice and counsel services.

In these examples, as in many others within households, separate and different services are being provided contemporaneously. Multitasking is common both in employment and home environments. So, should the forensic economist value the loss of each type of service separately, given that they are distinct services that provide real yet different benefits, or should an hour of multitasking time be split up in some way? To address this problem, we need to explore how the analyst approaches the pecuniary valuation aspect of measuring a loss of services, discussed in the next section.

10.4   THE MONETARY VALUE OF SERVICES

There are two methods that could be used to determine the monetary equivalent value of services that are not paid for within the household.[7] One is the *opportunity cost method* that assumes that the value of *any* service is best represented by the market wage that would have been earned in that same time period. Using this method, if dad were earning $25.00 per hour at his employment, then any and all services he would have continued to provide to family members would be valued at that wage rate. This standard, classic approach used in economic analysis to value time usage relies on the market wage of the individual who devotes time to non-market activities. The opportunity cost method takes the perspective of the provider, not the recipient of the services, and has the singular benefit of using one wage rate to measure any and all services. However, valuation of services based on this method would vary from case to case, reflecting the wage rate of each individual. For example, a doctor who earns at a rate of $200.00 per hour would be assigned that wage rate for mowing the lawn or doing other chores, whereas the services provided by a minimum wage worker would be valued at under $10.00 per hour.

An alternative measure of service value that does not rely on the particular wage rate of an injured or a deceased individual is the *replacement cost method* that relies on the market wage of persons who provide comparable services in the labor market. It does not matter what wage is earned by the injured party because the wage earned by people who provide the specified services in the marketplace becomes the basis for the monetary value of the services.[8] The beneficial characteristic of this method is that it uses the same wage rate to value any particular service, no matter who the injured party may be. However, it does require that the expert analyst establish a separate market wage rate for each different service being assessed. For example, the labor market sets a higher wage for advice and counsel services (teachers, financial advisors, marriage counselors) than it does for manual chores.

According to respondents to periodic surveys administered to NAFE members (Luthy et al. 2015), in figuring the value of lost household services, a preponderance of respondents prefer to use the "cost of hiring one or more individuals to replace the particular services that were lost." (p. 66) This 50 % response matched the response in 2003, leading the authors to conclude: "Clearly, this is one area where there is not necessarily agreement among all forensic economists, but opinions are remarkably stable over time." (p. 82)

Ireland (1999b) argues that neither the opportunity cost nor replacement cost approach is superior to the other: "In some circumstances, only the replacement cost approach would work. In others, only the opportunity cost approach would work. In many other valuation circumstances, estimates can be made using either method." (p. 56)

10.5   Concluding Observations

Readers may surmise correctly that valuation of lost services in personal litigation matters can range from the simple to the complex. Valuing lost household services of so many hours at such-and-such wage rate may be straightforward, but the expert very soon encounters complicating factors among which are what number of future years should be incorporated in the value of loss, and whether or not the number of hours of services may reasonably be expected to change over time as the household continues through its normal evolution. Other challenges include consideration of the joint provision of services and their joint consumption, as well as consideration of how much personal consumption, if any, should be taken into account. In addition, the expert needs to consult carefully with retaining counsel to establish what types of services are to be considered for valuation.

The topics covered in this chapter should give readers a good sense of the issues that need to be addressed in valuing services. These are not insurmountable challenges, but care needs to be applied to the process the expert chooses to use.

Notes

1. Wyrick (1993) argues that children who lose a parent suffer an additional, long-term loss: "the death of a parent can negatively affect the child's ability to establish and sustain relationships with others and lower the child's lifetime earning potential" (p. 82). However, the study by Kane et al. (2010) finds that "the death of a parent appears to have a relatively small effect on a child's lifetime earnings ...." The authors conclude that "the common practice of not estimating the loss of lifetime earnings of any minor children in cases involving the death of a parent appears to be sensible and defensible." (p. 388)

2. If an expert considers an individual's services from a whole time perspective, then it would be necessary to determine the extent of self-consumption of that individual's services.

3. For a description and analysis of advice services as well as companionship services, see Tinari and Kucsma (2012).
4. For an in-depth discussion of the basis for inclusion of companionship and other forms of services, see Tinari (1998) and (2005).
5. Readers are referred to Chap. 4 of this volume that addresses in detail the calculation of personal consumption as applied to lost earnings.
6. Dulaney et al. (1992, p. 117) refer to this problem as production involving joint outputs of services, or engaging in multiple household production activities. Ireland and Ward (1999, p. 134) refer to the problem as "decoupling concurrently performed homemaker services."
7. More detailed treatment of these methods is found in Ireland (1999b) and Ireland and Ward (1999).
8. There is the possibility that the quality, reliability and intensity of the services provided by someone in the marketplace who is paid to provide services may be lower than that which had been provided by a deceased family member. "A replacement worker will not be as concerned with the welfare of the family as the decedent was before his or her death" (Ireland 1999b, p. 60). Hence, this is yet another argument that the replacement cost method provides a lower bound to the time value of lost services.

References

Boss, P. (1999). A qualitative assessment of loss in the family system. Reading 24 in Ireland and Depperschmidt (1999), 289–301.

Cushing, M. J., & Rosenbaum, D. I. (2012). Valuing household services: A new look at the replacement cost approach. *Journal of Legal Economics, 19*(1), 37–60.

Dulaney, R. A., Fitzgerald, J. H., Swenson, M. S., & Wicks, J. H. (1992). Market valuation of household production. *Journal of Forensic Economics, 5*(2), 115–126.

Expectancy Data (2014). *The bollar value of a day: 2013 dollar valuation.* Shawnee: Shawnee Mission.

Expectancy Data. (various). Healthy life expectancy. Shawnee: Shawnee Mission.

Fischer, C. C. (1999). Measuring household production: Methodological considerations and current practice. Reading 15 in Ireland and Depperschmidt (1999), 171–190.

Greenwood, D. T. (1996). Estimating hours of lost household production using time-use data: A caution. *Litigation Economics Digest, 2*(1), 89–91 [Editor's Note: this journal is no longer published].

Ireland, T. R. (1997). Compensable nonmarket services in wrongful death litigation: Legal definitions and measurement standards. *Journal of Legal Economics, 7*(2), 15–34.

Ireland, T. R. (1999a). Compensable nonmarket services in wrongful death litigation: A conceptual evaluation based on legal standards. Reading 20 in Ireland and Depperschmidt (1999), 237–252.

Ireland, T. R. (1999b). Opportunity cost versus replacement cost in a lost service analysis for a wrongful death action. Reading 6 in Ireland and Depperschmidt (1999), 55–64.

Ireland, T. R. (2011a). Green v. Bittner and Progeny: Projecting dollar values for advice, counsel and companionship in New Jersey. *Forensic Rehabilitation & Economics*, 4(1), 99–106.

Ireland, T. R. (2011b). Uses of the American Time Use Survey to measure household services: What works and does not work. *Journal of Legal Economics*, 18(1), 61–77.

Ireland, T. R., & Depperschmidt, T. O. (Eds.) (1999). *Assessing family loss in wrongful death litigation: The special roles of lost services and personal consumption*. Tucson: Lawyers & Judges Publishing Co., Inc.

Ireland, T. R., & Ward, J. O. (Eds.). (1999). Replacement cost valuation of production by homemakers: Conceptual questions and measurement problems. Reading 12 in Ireland and Depperschmidt (1999), 131–142.

Kane, J., Spizman, L. M., Rodgers, J., & Gaskins, R. R. (2010). The effect of the loss of a parent on the future earnings of a minor child. *Eastern Economic Journal*, 36(3), 370–390.

Luthy, M. R., Brookshire, M. L., Rosenbaum, D., Schap, D., & Slesnick, F. L. (2015). A 2015 survey of forensic economists: Their methods, estimates, and perspectives. *Journal of Forensic Economics*, 26(1), 53–83.

Martin, G. D., & Weinstein, M. A. (2012). *Determining economic damages*. Costa Mesa: James Publishing, Inc.

Olson, G. W., & Rodgers, J. D. (1999). The problem of valuing emotional services: An analysis of legal and economic criteria. Reading 21 in Ireland and Depperschmidt (1999), 253–262.

Slesnick, F. L., Luthy, M. R., & Brookshire, M. L. (2013). A 2012 survey of forensic economists: Their methods, estimates, and perspectives. *Journal of Forensic Economics*, 24(1), 67–99.

Tinari, F. D. (1998). Household services: Toward a more comprehensive measure. *Journal of Forensic Economics*, 11(3), 253–265.

Tinari, F. D. (2005). A note on household services: Toward a more comprehensive measurement. *Journal of Forensic Economics*, Fall 2004 (published December 2005), 17(3), 383–385.

Tinari, F. D. (2011a). Comment on "Green v. Bittner and Progeny". *Forensic Rehabilitation and Economics*, 4(2), 109–112.

Tinari, F. D. (2011b). Comment on Smith, Smith & Uhl, "Estimating the value of family household management services: Approaches and markups". *Forensic Rehabilitation and Economics*, 4(1), 33–36.

Tinari, F. D., & Kucsma, K. K. (2012). Section 640: Companionship, advice, and counsel services, in Martin and Weinstein (2012).

U.S. Department of Labor. (various years). *American Time Use Survey.* Washington, DC: Department of Labor, Bureau of Labor Statistics.

Ward, J. O., & Krueger, K. V. (1994). *Establishing damages in catastrophic injury litigation.* Tucson: Lawyers & Judges Publishing Co., Inc.

Wyrick, T. L. (1993). The economic value of parental guidance. *Journal of Legal Economics, 3*(2), 81–94.

CASES

Garza v. Berlanga, 598 S.W. 2d 377 (Tex. Civ. App.).

Green v. Bittner, 81 N.J. 1; 424 A.2d 210, 1980.

Michigan Central Railroad Company v. Vreeland, 227 U.S. 59, 1913.

Wentling v. Medical Anesthesia Services, P.A., 701 P2d 939, Kan., 1985.

CHAPTER 11

Issues in Employment Litigation Analysis

Thomas Roney and Timothy Lanning

11.1 INTRODUCTION

A wrongfully terminated employee experiencing a reduced level of compensation (or a total loss) is made whole through a damage award that makes up the difference in compensation for the shorter of the time periods that (1) the employee could reasonably have expected to remain employed with the defendant employer, absent the incident, or (2) the employee can reasonably expect to experience a reduced level of compensation.

The economic loss analysis can be broken down into nine components. These are: (1) The relevant past loss period, which may extend to some time prior to the actual termination; (2) The time period over which any future losses are assumed to exist; (3) The time period over which the plaintiff reasonably would have remained employed by the defendant; (4) The duration of unemployment, both past and future, in conjunction with whether plaintiff's mitigation experience was reasonable; (5) The relevant compensation base with the defendant employer; (6) What income qualifies as mitigating income; (7) Discounting any future losses to present value; (8) Any adverse

T. Roney (✉)
Thomas Roney LLC, USA

T. Lanning
Formuzis, Pickersgill & Hunt, Inc., USA

© The Author(s) 2016
F.D. Tinari (ed.), *Forensic Economics*,
DOI 10.1057/978-1-137-56392-7_11

179

income tax consequences resulting from the receipt of a lump- sum award compared to earning the income over time; and (9) Specific worker characteristics, such as age.

These nine components are common elements the forensic economist faces in preparing an economic loss analysis in an employment matter. However, they should not be considered as exhaustive. Case-specific factors may create additional considerations or eliminate others.

11.2   TIME PERIODS

11.2.1   Past Loss Period

The projected loss of compensation in an employment case is divided into back pay (past loss) and front pay (future loss). Because economic damages in employment litigation result from alleged behavior that may span a period of time, back pay damages sometimes begin prior to the date of actual or constructive termination. It may be alleged, for example, that the plaintiff's earnings were adversely affected by unfairly limited pay increases or promotional opportunities, or by inhospitable conditions or workplace environment affecting hours worked. The past loss of compensation is calculated through the anticipated trial date, unless the plaintiff has fully mitigated or other circumstances point to an earlier loss cutoff date.

11.2.2   Future Loss Period

Because an employment case generally does not involve a permanent disability resulting from the wrongful behavior of the defendant, projected earnings in an employment case are often limited to the anticipated earnings with the defendant employer,[1] rather than the plaintiff's earning capacity throughout worklife. The future loss, if any, is also limited to the period in which the plaintiff will now earn less than his projected pre-termination earnings.

Numerous case-specific factors will inform the trier-of-fact's determination of the future loss period. It is unlikely that the economist would have either the qualifications or the expertise to provide expert opinions regarding when the loss is likely to end. Accordingly, retaining counsel may provide the economist with working assumptions regarding the future period of loss based on anticipated testimony from witnesses and other evidence to be presented at trial. Economists may present alternative loss hypotheticals with the objective of providing the trier-of-fact with loss magnitudes that cover a range of periods.

Some economists look to economic statistics to estimate the loss period. The US Bureau of Labor Statistics (BLS), for example, reports data from both the National Longitudinal Survey (NLS) and the Current Population Survey (CPS) on duration of employment and unemployment statistics. The BLS also conducts the Displaced Worker Survey (DWS), a biennial supplement to the CPS, collecting data on the number and characteristics of persons who had been displaced from their jobs over the prior three calendar years.

Caution should be used when relying on economic statistics for duration of employment or unemployment of displaced workers to determine the loss period. While these statistics provide measures of central tendency, limitations in the data make them ill-suited for application to a particular employment case for a variety of reasons. Data on job tenure, for example, include individuals still actively employed with a company, whose years of employment at the time the data are collected understate their ultimate job tenure. While some statistics on job duration and unemployment account for the effects of age, sex, education, and earnings level, many other case-specific variables are excluded. Importantly, the effect of being singled out for termination and pursuing litigation against a former employer cannot be isolated within the data on displaced workers. The BLS defines displaced workers as "persons 20 years of age and older who lost or left jobs because their plant or company closed or moved, there was insufficient work for them to do, or their position or shift was abolished."[2] Workers who have been terminated for cause or for whom it is alleged that continued employment should have been available would not be identified as such in the data.

When separation is involuntary (even if constructively terminated), the plaintiff may be subject to the stigma of being singled out for termination.[3] Prospective employers may view a worker's termination as a signal of poor work quality[4] or inability to work well with others. Relying on general unemployment rate or duration statistics doesn't account for these and other potential difficulties terminated workers face in finding replacement employment. The cumulative impact of these issues is likely to fall outside the scope of the assignment and the expertise of the forensic economist. Accordingly, it may be helpful for the economist to provide alternative loss period calculations, whether multiple fixed periods or for a range of cumulative time periods. Under either approach the future loss period will be constrained by the shorter of the duration of employment with the defendant employer, absent the incident, or the time period required for plaintiffs to fully mitigate their loss of earnings.

Roney (2012) surveyed 20 years of studies related to the loss of earnings after a mass layoff, job dismissal, or separation and found that many of the studies utilized the Displaced Workers Survey, therefore limiting the use and application of past research in an employment case. However, research studies do document dramatic and long lasting economic losses from job loss, with significant variation in loss depending on the prevailing business cycle and worker demographic. Several of the studies cited found that displaced workers with longer tenure experienced greater reduction in earnings due to the loss of firm-specific capital.

Baum (2013), using longitudinal survey data, found that "longer tenures are associated with higher probabilities of remaining with an employer." Because early years with an employer are associated with higher rates of job losses, a long-tenured terminated worker's replacement earnings may be both lower and less certain to continue (see Coleman 2015, p.88). Some job separations occur when an employee leaves for a higher-paying job. A termination or subsequent unemployment spell resulting in reputational harm may reduce a worker's opportunities to advance in this way or to keep subsequent jobs. In those circumstances, damages could extend beyond the projected period of employment with the terminating employer (Baum 2015).

Ireland (2012) notes that extended damages resulting from reputational effects are essentially a lost earning capacity. The 7th Circuit in *Williams v. Pharmacia* (1998) recognized that:

> Damages for lost future earnings, in contrast [to front pay] are not limited in duration in the same way. The reputational or other injury that causes the diminution in expected earnings can stay with the employee indefinitely. Thus, the calculation of front pay differs significantly from the calculation of lost future earnings. Whereas front pay compensates the plaintiff for the lost earnings from her old job as long as she may have been expected to hold it, a lost future earnings award compensates the plaintiff for the diminution of expected earnings in all of her future jobs for as long as the reputational or other injury may be expected to affect her prospects. (p. 954)

If at the time of trial, the plaintiff has not obtained mitigation employment, plaintiff's counsel may argue that, due to wrongful termination and litigation with the former employer, it is uncertain whether the plaintiff will ever be employed in the future or for some finite period of time. If the plaintiff has obtained alternative employment, but at a lower earnings level, the economist may be instructed to project that the earnings gap will remain constant or gradually decline over the loss period.

11.3   ASSUMED DURATIONS

11.3.1   Duration of Employment with Defendant

Almost by definition in employment litigation, opposing parties will have differing views on whether or not ongoing employment would have been available to the plaintiff. In order to successfully claim lost earnings over a period of time, the plaintiff will need to convince the trier-of-fact that his employment would have continued over that time period, absent the employer's alleged wrongful behavior. For an older worker nearing retirement age, or for one who had accrued many years of firm-specific experience or seniority, the time period may extend to retirement. The defendant will attempt to show that the action against the plaintiff was justified and legal, and/or that the plaintiff's employment would have ended anyway, for reasons unrelated to the plaintiff's allegations.

A review of the plaintiff's employment history may be informative. A record of relatively short job durations for a number of previous jobs may weaken the argument that the employee would be expected to have a long work history with the defendant employer.

11.3.2   Duration of Unemployment

In addition to the duration of employment with the defendant, the trier-of-fact will consider the period of time the terminated worker can expect to remain unemployed (if the plaintiff has yet to find qualifying post-termination work). Evidence of the plaintiff's reasonable efforts, or lack thereof, to find suitable replacement employment will be presented. In a number of cases, other professionals such as employability experts may be engaged to evaluate the job prospects of the plaintiff. If the fact-finder determines the plaintiff has met his obligation to look for mitigating employment and yet remains unemployed, it will have to decide on a reasonable future period of time for the plaintiff to find a job and eliminate any anticipated earnings differential.

11.4   COMPENSATION

11.4.1   Projected Compensation with Defendant Employer

The starting point for projected compensation in an employment case is often the plaintiff's final pay rate at defendant employer. Pay increases following the date losses begin may be provided by the employer or calculated using average compensation growth data. Sometimes, the plaintiff's actual earnings may not be used for projected compensation if it is alleged that those earnings were adversely affected by factors related to the litigation at hand. In a case where the plaintiff was "wooed away" from a previous employer and then wrongfully terminated by the new employer, the projected earnings may include an alternative based on the earnings and benefits at the previous employer.

11.4.2   Qualifying Mitigation Income

Counsel can instruct the economist to consider all post-termination earnings as mitigation earnings or to exclude some portion or all for determining the economic loss. In this area, the attorney will be guided by case law. For instance, in the 2013 California Fourth Appellate District decision in the *Villacorta* (2013) case, the court ruled as follows:

> The general rule is that the measure of recovery by a wrongfully discharged employee is the amount of salary agreed upon for the period of service, less the amount which the employer affirmatively proves the employee has earned or with reasonable effort might have earned from other employment. However, in order for the employee's earnings to be applied in mitigation, the employer must show that the other employment was comparable, or substantially similar, to that of which the employee has been deprived. Thus, if the new job is different or inferior, then the wages from that job may not be used to mitigate damages. Wages actually earned from an inferior job may not be used to mitigate damages because if they were used then it would result in senselessly penalizing an employee who, either because of an honest desire to work or a lack of financial resources, is willing to take whatever employment he or she can find. The location of the new job is one of the factors to consider in determining whether the new job is inferior. (p. 9)

Counsel will provide direction regarding what will be asserted as qualifying mitigation income, which may include severance pay and disability or unemployment benefits. If the income is received from a source independent of the defendant employer, it may not qualify as mitigation income under the collateral source rule (Fleming 1983). If defendant employer contributed toward the funding of such benefits, then they may be included as an offset. Paid accrued vacation or sick time may not be an offset to the economic loss if the plaintiff would have ultimately been entitled to this income anyway.

11.5 DISCOUNTING FUTURE LOSSES TO PRESENT VALUE

An important role of the economist in any case is to discount the future income stream to present value to account for the fact that money awarded today can be invested, and the interest income earned on that award will assist in the replacement of the lost income. While a net discount rate is utilized by many economists in personal injury loss calculations, the future loss period is often relatively short in employment litigation. In this circumstance, more consideration may be given to the current yield curve. A future wage growth rate will then need to be estimated, if information regarding likely or actual pay increases is not available from the defendant employer. When the loss period is limited to a few years or less, the discount rate is not likely to be a significant determinant of future losses.

11.6 ADVERSE TAX CONSEQUENCES

An anomaly of the US tax code as it applies to awards in litigation is that lost wages are not subject to income and employment taxes in personal injury litigation but are subject to taxes in employment litigation. Given the *Small Business Job Protection Act of 1996*[5] enacted after the Supreme Court ruling in *Commissioner of Internal Revenue Service v. Schleier* (1995), a lump-sum award for damages in a wrongful termination and age or sex discrimination case is subject to income taxes in the year in which it is received. Given the progressive nature of the income tax system in the USA, this ruling may result in the plaintiff paying higher taxes on the replacement of lost compensation than if the income had been taxed as it was earned.

The adverse tax consequence or increased tax paid on the replacement of lost compensation includes (1) the difference between the taxes paid on the lump-sum award and the taxes on both the projected and mitigation income earned on an annual basis, and (2) the marginal tax paid on that difference. For the lump-sum award to be "tax neutral," it should be "grossed up" to reflect both of these additional taxes. The tax adjusted award can be estimated in various ways, but requires iterative techniques to be accurate. This is because adding an adjustment to an award will also incur taxes on the adjustment, and so on. In particular, three papers in the literature of forensic economics specifically deal with the calculation issues: Bowles and Lewis (1996), Ben-Zion (2000), and Rodgers (2003).

The adverse tax consequence includes federal and state taxes. Because of the taxable earnings limit for Social Security, there may be tax savings if the lump-sum award includes multiple years of lost earnings that would have been subject to additional Social Security taxes in subsequent calendar years. However, the plaintiff loses the employer contributions equivalent to such tax savings (See Ireland 2010).

While some economists and courts ignore the tax issue by not adjusting the damages for taxes and making no adjustment for higher taxes on the award, this potentially results in the plaintiff paying more in taxes on the award than would have been paid while employed. Forensic economists and attorneys have argued that this additional tax burden thwarts the purpose of the award under the "make whole" standard—the plaintiff is paying more taxes than would have been paid had the alleged violations not occurred. Hence, the tax gross-up award represents the amount of money that "neutralizes" the tax effect to the extent that the plaintiff pays no more taxes than would have been paid in the normal course of employment. This practice results in a windfall to both federal and state tax agencies, since the tax neutralization award considers not only the higher taxes the plaintiff will pay due to the lump-sum award, but that any payment to the plaintiff for these higher taxes is also taxable. Both tax components benefit the tax agencies at the cost of the defendant.

The history of tax treatments of litigation awards is inconsistent and the legal precedent not straightforward. The finders of fact are generally empowered to grant tax neutralization awards, but in practice many are reluctant to do so, and can avoid them with thin rationales. Federal Courts in the Ninth Circuit have rejected tax neutralization awards [*Hutchins v. DirecTV Customer Service, Inc., et al.* (2014) and *Dashnaw v. Pena* (1994)], while other courts have found in favor of such awards [*Sears v. Atchison, Topeka & Santa Fe Railway Co.* (1984) and *O'Neill v. Sears Roebuck & Company* (2000)]. Taxes on contingent attorney fees paid out of a judgment or settlement in actions involving certain claims, such as unlawful discrimination, may be reduced by an above-the-line deduction for attorney fees and court costs.

In any case, adjustments for tax neutralizations, if considered, should be presented with the expert economist's report, as such calculations are rarely considered after a verdict is reached. If the plaintiff does not include a tax neutralization amount in the demand for damages it is unlikely to be granted in many jurisdictions, but in some jurisdictions other types of adjustments may be made. For example, the expert may provide a separate letter to retaining counsel showing him or her the gross-up calculation for consideration. Judges in New Jersey have the right to "mold" the jury verdict for collateral source income and to provide an addition to the award for gross-up purposes. The judge usually consults with attorneys for both sides to arrive at an amicable set of adjustments. The tax neutralization calculation need not always be presented to the jury or judge during the trial, but should be calculated by the expert for the retaining attorney.

11.7   WORKER CHARACTERISTICS: AGE

As noted by Ostrofe et al. (2012), certain worker characteristics appear significant in determining either how long displaced or discharged workers sought alternative work, and/or how large the difference was between their lost and their post-discharge earnings. The authors note that these characteristics fell into two categories, as follows:

> They were either variables that described the individual characteristics of the worker, or they were variables that described the macroeconomic environment in which the worker sought a job following termination. Worker characteristics found to influence the duration and magnitude of post-termination economic loss were: age, sex, education, tenure at pre-termination job, receipt of unemployment benefits, and duration of post-termination unemployment. Environmental factors found to be similarly influential were: industry within which the job search was conducted (and whether the worker had to switch industries to find alternate employment) and the macroeconomic conditions under which the worker sought a job. (p. 65)

Age is found to be a prime determinant of the magnitude of loss in employment cases, depending on the stage of the worker's career, the earnings level and growth that can be expected, and the ease with which the worker can find alternative employment. Younger workers, ages 19 to 34, are often assumed to have little to lose from job displacement, yet young workers experience rapid earnings growth from human capital acquisition (on-the-job training). Kletzer and Fairlie (1999) found that displaced young men lost 8.4 % and displaced young women 13.0 % in average annual earnings, relative to their non-displaced peers. Their loss came from loss of the rapid earnings growth young workers often experience while establishing their careers. These losses are magnified for college-educated workers.

Workers of prime working age, 35–55, may be the best positioned to mitigate their losses by finding comparable alternative employment, but these workers can still experience significant losses from discharge. For example, Couch, and Placzek (2010) estimated that average earnings losses were 32–33 % for the quarter following displacement, and an average earnings deficit of 7–9 % persisted six years after termination.

Older workers, age 55 and above, are more vulnerable to job displacement because they have developed highly remunerated human capital in a specific job and industry and are unlikely to recapture this return in alternative employment. Couch (1998) found that those who experienced job displacement late in their careers and later became reemployed experienced an average 30 % wage loss across all occupations and industries surveyed. Employers may feel that the truncated worklife of older workers is too short to recover any investment required to hire and train them. See also Couch et al. (2009) for an analysis of older workers using administrative data.

11.8   Conclusion

As this chapter demonstrates, the economic loss calculation in employment cases is similar in many respects to that of a typical personal injury case. However, there are unique issues that arise in employment cases that demonstrate a need for additional research regarding the duration of unemployment and the magnitude of earnings loss for those individuals who have been wrongfully terminated or discriminated against and pursue litigation against a former employer.

Notes

1. There can be exceptions if a claim is made for loss of lifetime earning capacity, extending beyond the tenure with defendant employer.
2. U.S. Department of Labor, Bureau of Labor Statistics (2014).
3. Gibbons and Katz (1991).
4. Nicholson and North (2004).
5. See Ben-Zion, p. 233.

REFERENCES

Baum II, C. L. (2013). Employee tenure and economic losses in wrongful termination cases. *Journal of Forensic Economics, 24*(1), 41–66.

Baum II, C. L. (2015). Employee tenure and economic losses in wrongful termination cases: A reply to Nicholas Coleman. *Journal of Forensic Economics, 26*(1), 95–97.

Ben-Zion, B. (2000). Neutralizing the adverse tax consequences of a Lump-Sum Award in employment cases. *Journal of Forensic Economics, 13*(3), 233–244.

Bowles, T. J., & Chris Lewis, W. (1996). Taxation of damage awards: Current law and implications. *Litigation Economics Digest, 2*(1), 73–78.

Coleman, N. (2015). A comment on 'Employee tenure and economic losses in wrongful termination cases'. *Journal of Forensic Economics, 26*(1), 85–93.

Couch, K. A. (1998). Late life job displacement. *The Gerontologist, 38*(1), 7–17.

Couch, K. A., & Placzek, D. W. (2010). Earnings losses of displaced workers revisited. *American Economic Review, 100*(1), 572–589.

Couch, K. A., Jolly, N. A., & Placzek, D. W. (2009). Earnings losses of older displaced workers: A detailed analysis with administrative data. *Research on Aging, 31*(1), 17–40.

Fleming, J. G. (1983). The collateral source rule and contract damages. *California Law Review, 71*, 56–86.

Gibbons, R., & Katz, L. F. (1991). Layoffs and lemons. *Journal of Labor Economics, 9*(4), 351–380.

Ireland, T. R. (2010). Tax consequences of lump sum awards in wrongful termination cases. *Journal of Legal Economics, 17*(1), 51–73.

Ireland, T. R. (2012). Possible damage elements in wrongful termination litigation: Back pay, front pay, and lost earning capacity. *Journal of Legal Economics, 18*(2), 93–105.

Kletzer, Lori G., & Robert W. Fairlie. (1999). The long-term costs of job displacement among young workers. Department of Economics, University of California Santa Cruz, July 1997, Revised January 1999. [Funded under contract no. 41USC252C3 from the U.S. Department of Labor].

Nicholson, Kristin A., & Charles M. North. (2004). Unemployment duration under wrongful discharge law. Baylor University, Working Paper #055, 1–32.

Ostrofe, N., Roney, T., & Kirwin, D. (2012). Factors to consider when estimating economic damages from a wrongful termination. *The Earnings Analyst, 12*, 63–88.

Rodgers, J. D. (2003). Handling taxes in employment law cases. *Journal of Forensic Economics, 16*(2), 225–256.

Roney, T. (2012). Estimating duration of economic damages in wrongful termination cases; recent literature on duration and magnitude of earnings losses from job loss. *Journal of Legal Economics, 18*(2), 107–127.

U.S. Department of Labor, Bureau of Labor Statistics. (2014). Economic news release 8/26/2014, Displaced workers technical note.

CASES

Alfredo Villacorta, Plaintiff and Respondent, v. Cemex Cement, Inc., Defendant and Appellant, 221 Cal. App. 4th 1425; 165 Cal. Rptr. 3d 441. (2013).

Commissioner of Internal Revenue Service v. Schleier, 515 U.S. 323, 132 L.Ed.2d 294, 115 S.Ct. 2159. (1995).

Dashnaw v. Pena, 304 U.S. App. D.C. 247; 12 F.3d 1112. (1994).

Hutchins v. DirecTV Customer Service, Inc., et al, 0:14-cv-35733, 9th Cir. (2014).

O'Neill v. Sears, Roebuck and Company, 108 F. Supp. 443, E.D. Pa. (2000).

Sears v. The Atchison, Topeka & Santa Fe Railway Company, 749 F.2d 1451, 10th Cir. (1984).

Williams v. Pharmacia, Inc., 137 F.3d 944, 7th Cir. (1998).

CHAPTER 12

Differences Among State Court Jurisdictions in Damages Calculations

David I. Rosenbaum and David Schap

12.1 INTRODUCTION

In this chapter, we look at similarities and differences in the practice of forensic economics among the 50 states. In particular, we address the methods that forensic economists use as determined by statute, case law and customary practice given legal dictates.

Our research has been guided by a variety of resources. Chief among them is the series of articles begun in 2002 that has appeared in the *Journal of Forensic Economics*, each article of which bears a first portion title of "Assessing Economic Damages in Personal Injury and Wrongful Death Litigation in," followed by a particular state designation (including an entry for Puerto Rico). By the close of 2015, a total of 30 articles had appeared in the series. We have also benefitted from the detailed information available at three websites that concern the laws affecting the practice of forensic economics, namely Thomas R. Ireland's website (http://www.umsl.edu/~irelandt/), Denison University's Forensic

D.I. Rosenbaum (✉)
Department of Economics, University of Nebraska,
USA

D. Schap
Department of Economics and Accounting, College of the Holy Cross,
USA

© The Author(s) 2016   191
F.D. Tinari (ed.), *Forensic Economics*,
DOI 10.1057/978-1-137-56392-7_12

Economics Database (https://forensicsdb.denison.edu/) and a website sponsored by the National Association of Forensic Economics (the State Laws Project, member access only via, http://www.nafe.net). Finally, to clarify subtle aspects, especially related to case law, LexisNexis Academic Universe (http://www.lexisnexis.com/hottopics/lnacademic/?) proved to be useful.

Across the states, the right to sue for losses in the case of a wrongful death originates as established by statute. In contrast, the right to sue for personal injury evolved from common law (i.e., judicial construct) and not initially via specific statute (though many common law norms have subsequently been codified in the statutes of various states). Although not a primary focus herein, we do touch on laws governing medical malpractice litigation. Employment law and commercial damages law fall outside the scope of our discussion.

12.2   The Court System and Basic Legal Structure

All state court systems are structured as hierarchies. The names of the courts at the various levels differ somewhat across the states, but their purposes are nevertheless quite similar. The lowest courts (typically called civil or district courts) hear cases of such limited pecuniary magnitude as to preclude participation by forensic economists as a practical matter. Here occur trials at which there is a presiding judge or magistrate and no separate jury (a "bench trial"), so the presiding official is the legal expert (as always) and also the "finder of fact" in the case at trial.

The next level of courts (often termed superior courts) is where forensic economic testimony would be heard. Cases appear in that venue based on a loss claim exceeding some minimum amount (not infrequently $5,000) or a request by either party for a jury trial. Trial outcomes are subject to review in appellate courts. Each state has a unique highest court, also convened to hear appeals of lower court decisions. The name of the highest court varies across states. Perhaps the oddest terminology appears in New York, where the highest court is called the Court of Appeals and the courts below it consist of the Supreme Court, County Court and a group of specialized courts.

In the trial courts, various testimonies, rulings on motions, formal objections and the verdict are all recorded, which permits review by appellate courts, where written decisions espousing legal reasoning appear. Lower courts are bound by such written decisions in subsequent cases at trial. Written appellate decisions and underlying statutory law assist forensic economists in knowing how to present loss estimates, identifying which elements may be included, and sometimes specifying which elements may not be included no matter how worthy the argument for inclusion from a purely economic perspective. The law trumps economic theory when the two are in conflict.

12.3   WRONGFUL DEATH AND SURVIVAL ACTIONS

States vary with respect to who may recover in a wrongful death action. Three of the more restrictive states are Kentucky, Texas and Pennsylvania, where suit in a wrongful death case can be brought only for the benefit of the surviving spouse, children or parents. Mississippi allows recover of services to the decedent's spouse, children, parents or siblings. Nebraska allows recovery for the spouse and next of kin. States with the broader potential pools of beneficiaries include Florida, West Virginia and Missouri. Section 768.18 of the Florida Wrongful Death Act allows recovery of lost support to "the decedent's spouse, children, parents, and when partly or wholly dependent for support (or services), any blood relatives and adoptive brothers and sisters." West Virginia's code provides for recovery to survivors that include the spouse; children, including adopted children and stepchildren; brothers; sisters; parents; and any other persons who were financially dependent upon the alleged victim. Missouri case law has loosened the financial dependence clause. In *Domijan v. Harp, Mo.* (340 S.W.2d 728, 1960), the Missouri Supreme Court wrote "[t]he test of the right of recovery ... is the reasonable probability of pecuniary benefit from the continued life of the deceased ... and not that of strict legal dependency."

In wrongful death cases, almost all of the states allow recovery for lost support that the deceased would have provided. The only exception is Alabama where recovery is for punitive damages only. Among the other states, it then becomes an issue of what constitutes support. Generally, statutes and case law make it possible to divide support into two separate categories. The first category is financial support, which is thought of as loss of income or earnings that the deceased can no longer provide to the survivors. The other category is composed of lost services.

With respect to financial support, the vast majority of states have case law that creates two important requirements related to recovery: (1) the compensation to the survivors must be supported by the evidence and appropriate to the claim; and (2) the survivors should be compensated for the financial contribution that the decedent would have made to them. This second requirement looks at the financial contribution that would have flowed to the survivors. However, there are three states that take exception to the latter condition. In Georgia, recovery is for the losses suffered by the *decedent*, not the survivors; Georgia code calls for recovery of the "[f]ull value of the life of the decedent (Georgia Code §51-4-1, 2015)." In Kentucky, recoverable damages are "such sum as will fairly and reasonably compensate the decedent's earning power (*Louisville and N.R. Co. v. Eakins' Adm'r*, 103 Ky. 465, 45 S.W. 529, 530, 1898)." In West Virginia, damages shall include "compensation for reasonably expected loss of...income of the decedent (W.V.C. §55-7-6(c)(1)(B))." These three states—by code or by interpretation—change the focus from what was lost by the survivors to what was lost by the decedent.

Most states focus on the financial loss suffered by the decedent's survivor(s). This loss is typically calculated as the income the decedent would have provided less some measure of the amount of that income that the decedent would have used for his or her own purposes. As a consequence, case law and forensic practice have evolved around the deduction for self-consumption from the decedent's earnings. For a more in-depth discussion of types of self-consumption deductions by jurisdiction (state or District of Columbia, Puerto Rico or Virgin Islands), including excerpts from statutory and case law, see Schap (2016). Of course in the three states with a focus on loss to the decedent, there is no deduction for decedent's own consumption. In the other states, with the possible exception of Vermont, there is an adjustment made for what would have been the portion of income consumed by the decedent absent the death event (personal consumption) or what amount of consumption would be minimally required in order for the decedent to have continued to live and work absent the death event (personal maintenance). Table 12.1 presents summary results based on a survey of the law in each of the 50 states, plus District of Columbia, Puerto Rico and Virgin Islands.

In Vermont, the wrongful death statute (14 V.S.A. §1492, 2015) contains the following vague description of pecuniary loss assessment: "The court or jury before whom the issue is tried may give such damages as are just, with reference to the pecuniary injuries resulting from such death, to the wife and next of kin or husband and next of kin, as the case may be." Moreover, no Vermont written case law as of mid-2015 was found to have addressed the issue of whether a reduction for the self-consumption of the decedent absent the death event is appropriate. Among the remaining

Table 12.1 Type of reduction for self-consumption by decedent in wrongful death or survival actions, by jurisdiction (states plus District of Columbia, Puerto Rico and US Virgin Islands)

Type	State
Personal consumption (43 jurisdictions)	AL[a], AK, AZ, AR, CA, CO, DC, FL, ID, IL, IN, IA, KS, LA, ME, MD, MA, MI, MN, MS, MO, MT, NE, NV, NH, NJ, NY, NC, ND, OH, OK, OR, PR, RI, SC, SD, TX, UT, VA, VI, WI, WY, WA
Personal maintenance (6 jurisdictions)	CT, DE, HI[b], NM, PA[b], TN[b]
No deduction (3 jurisdictions)	GA, KY, WV
Unknown classification (1 jurisdiction)	VT

Note:

[a]Personal consumption in Alabama only when federal courts have concurrent jurisdiction; otherwise, punitive damages only apply.

[b]Personal maintenance in Hawaii, Pennsylvania and Tennessee only in survival actions, but personal consumption applies to wrongful death in those states. The Hawaii classification here differs from that in Schap (2016) based on Hawaii Revised Statutes (§§663-7 and 663-8, 2015).

jurisdictions, a deduction for decedent's self-consumption is rarely specified explicitly in the wrongful death statute (Carney and Schap 2008, p. 7; Schap and Thompson 2016, p. 152); examples only include Rhode Island ("Deduct ... the estimated personal expenses that the decedent probably would have incurred") and the US Virgin Islands (which similarly addresses "deducting the decedent's personal expenses").

Far more commonly, a reduction for what would have been decedent's self-consumption is merely implied by statutory language, jury instructions or case law describing the loss to survivors. Examples of such language include "financial support decedent would have contributed" (California Civil Jury Instruction 3921) or "reasonable probability of pecuniary benefit from the continued life of the deceased" (*Domijan v. Harp, Mo.*, 340 S.W.2d 728, 1960). Other states refer to the loss as the net income of the decedent, where net income implies a deduction for decedent's own consumption (and perhaps income taxes, as discussed in Chap. 7 of this volume).

The specific method to be used to account for decedent's consumption absent the death event is typically not dictated by either statute or case law. There are, however, some exceptions. Connecticut, Delaware, New Mexico, Pennsylvania and Tennessee have a personal maintenance rather than personal consumption standard. In Puerto Rico, the Supreme Court guidelines call for reducing income by one-third for personal consumption. No state with a personal consumption deduction specifies whether the deduction is based on decedent or household income, with the possible exception of California. In that state, the Court of Appeals upheld a lower court ruling that "the pecuniary loss suffered...is not to be reduced or enlarged by reason of the financial condition of the heirs (*Johnson v. Western Air Express Corp.*, 45 Cal.App.2d 614, 114 Cal.2d 688, 1941)." Some California-based forensic economists interpret this to mean that a surviving spouse's income is irrelevant in determining the personal consumption deduction. However, there appears to be no case law that explicitly addresses the issue. We understand that in California practicing forensic economists (and apparently the trial courts that entertain their arguments) are divided as to how or whether a restriction on considering household income exists relative to the calculation of the personal consumption deduction.

States vary in their treatment of potential losses of accumulation to an estate occasioned by a wrongful death. This is a loss that occurs because the deceased is no longer able to increase the value of the estate that he or she would have left absent the death event. Three states, Florida, Iowa and Ohio, have statutes that specifically allow for lost accumulation to an estate. Twelve other states have jury instructions, annotations or legal interpretations that may allow for recovery of loss of accumulation to an estate. They are California, Colorado, Delaware, District of Columbia, Hawaii, Louisiana, Michigan, Montana, New York, Texas, Utah and Washington. Four states, Alabama, Alaska, Idaho and Virginia, explicitly disallow such recovery. The rest of the states have no specific statute or case law addressing this issue. For a more complete discussion, see Rosenbaum and Cushing (2016).

There are other financial losses that are considered part of damages as well. Almost universally, and typically by case law, states consider non-cash or fringe benefits provided by employers as part of earned income. In wrongful death cases, states uniformly allow recovery for medical and funeral expenses.

The various jurisdictions commonly recognize lost household services as part of economic damages in either a wrongful death or personal injury case. The sole exception known to us is Puerto Rico, which does not include household services in economic damages. Recognition of household services as an element of damages occurs typically through case law interpreting language related to loss of support of things such as "services, protection, care and assistance." However, there is very little guidance as to how the value of services is to be calculated. The other components in this type of language—care, companionship, protection, assistance, love, community, attention—may or may not be treated as economic losses. Some economists will testify to the value of selected components. Additionally, the courts appear willing to allow juries to assign a value to the loss without specific economic testimony. This is particularly true in cases where a child has died. New Jersey appears to be unique in allowing economic testimony on the dollar value of the child's future companionship, and advice and guidance services.

Two other components of non-economic damages include pain and suffering of the survivors and loss of enjoyment of life of the injured or deceased (termed hedonic losses). Almost half the states allow recovery for survivor pain and suffering (although statutes refer to this loss in different forms across the states, referencing it, e.g., as bereavement). In Massachusetts, special damages are applicable if a spouse has actually witnessed the demise of his or her partner. Generally, testimony by economic experts on the extent of pain/suffering-type losses is considered inadmissible. In contrast, whether economists can testify about hedonic damages is an interesting issue. Presently, only two states, Nevada and New Mexico, permit economic testimony on hedonic loss. In some states, loss to the decedent is not considered; hence, there is no avenue for hedonic damages in those jurisdictions. Other states recognize potential loss of enjoyment of life to decedent, but most commonly a jury assesses the loss without accompanying testimony from an economist on this particular aspect of damages. In other words, in these jurisdictions hedonic loss is regarded as a non-pecuniary element of damages. (For a more detailed treatment, see Chap. 14 on hedonic valuation.)

At a fundamental level, states differ as to whether they have permitted recovery through a survival action for the benefit of an estate, or through a wrongful death proceeding with designated statutory beneficiaries, or through both. The term "survival action" is a bit confusing at first encounter inasmuch as it seems to suggest something about survivors, but that is not the case; it is the cause of action that survives, perhaps best thought of as an action that would be a personal injury-type case if the incident of focus had not been lethal (Ireland 2016). In a survival action, the loss to the decedent that would have flowed to an estate is the relevant loss. Of course, the proceeds of the estate may then be divided up among decedent's survivors, but it will be so divided according to the way the decedent arranged in a will (assuming the decedent did not pass intestate). Contrast that arrangement with a wrongful death proceeding in which there are statutorily designated beneficiaries that recover directly and not through an estate, and recover in respective portions according to the dictates of statutes. As mentioned, there are even some states that blend the two very different kinds of actions. Regardless of the mix, and no matter the number of possible persons that may recover some portion either directly or through an estate, we know of no exception to the rule that coordinates the claims of the various parties into a single death case proceeding.

Given the complexities described in loss to an estate versus individuals (and still others not previously mentioned, like the function of a "personal representative" when one is designated in a death proceeding), the subject matter is too detailed to do it justice here. Instead, we direct the reader's attention to the fact that there is a set of related papers addressing these matters published as a symposium on forensic economics and wrongful death in a special issue of the *Journal of Legal Economics* (22[2], 2016).

12.4   PERSONAL INJURY

In personal injury cases, almost all states use some concept of earning capacity as the standard for future economic losses. Alabama calls it an impairment of ability to earn. Kentucky uses the phrase "power to earn money." In 1986, the Alaska legislature adopted the language "could have expected to earn," which is still under interpretation. Some states, such as Connecticut, New Jersey and Virginia allow a loss of earnings or earning capacity, but draw little meaningful distinction between the two. Only Puerto Rico limits future losses to forgone future expected earnings rather than earning capacity. The states are not as uniform in their standards for past personal injury losses, that is, those from the date of injury to the date of trial. Some use earnings; others use earning capacity; still others use either earnings or earning capacity. The notion of earning capacity itself is the subject of Chap. 2 of this volume.

Most states require that future damages be discounted to their present value. However, as with most topics, there are a few exceptions. In Missouri, a jury instruction that damages be expressed at their present value is not allowed. The plaintiff need not present evidence on discounting; however, the defendant may offer such evidence. New York has quite unique and detailed rules related to when discounting should occur. Interested readers are referred to Spizman and Tinari (2011). Kentucky is another state where statute, jury instructions and case law make it unclear as to when or if discounting is required (Slesnick and Mulliken 2004). In Georgia, only earnings are discounted. Benefits, household services and intangibles are not. In Oregon, it is the responsibility of the trier of fact to discount future damages. Either side may present evidence on the topic, but it is not required. Similar rules apply in Virginia.

Among the states that require discounting, instructions related to growth and interest rates, inflation, and use of net or real discount rates can be quite varied. Some states have no specifications at all. Florida is an interesting example. In the *Delta* case, the Court wrote "we decline to adopt a particular method .... [I]f economists are unable to agree on the subject, we doubt that this Court has the expertise to select one method over another (*Delta Air Lines v. Ageloff*, 552 So.2d1089, 1989)." Many courts have written generally about interest rates. In Alaska, discounting is done using a risk free, long-term interest rate. In California, it is the rate available on "prudent investments." In Mississippi, it is a "fair and reasonable" rate of interest. Other states (like Wyoming) make no specifications, but allow the evidence to account for economic conditions including present and future inflation when discounting.

A few states are more prescriptive in discounting. Georgia had required that earnings be discounted at a 5 % interest rate, changed effective July 2013 to 5% "or any other discount rate as the trier of fact may deem appropriate" (Georgia Code §51-12-13, 2015). Michigan, which had required discounting at 5 % simple interest, changed in 2014 to compound interest at 5 %. Puerto Rico uses a 6 % interest rate. In *Kaczkowski v. Bolubasz* (Pa. 421 A.2d 855, 1971), the Pennsylvania Supreme Court endorsed using a variant of the "total offset method." The court wrote "as a matter of law ... inflation shall be presumed equal to future interest rates with these factors offsetting" (pp. 1038–39). However, Pennsylvania does allow consideration for productivity increases. Consequently, "in many—if not most—cases in Pennsylvania today, economic experts simply add on additional productivity growth factors" (Rogers and Thornton 2002). Different rules apply in Pennsylvania medical malpractice suits.

12.5   MISCELLANEOUS ISSUES

Chapter 7 of this book addresses state treatment of income taxes in personal injury and wrongful death cases. Interested readers are referred to that chapter.

Most states have explicitly recognized as appropriate the accounting for future inflation in reaching suitable lump-sum awards. According to the information compiled at the State Laws Project (mentioned previously), most commonly the recognition exists in case law, but in a few states the issue of inflation is addressed by statute or is simply noted as common practice without supporting case or statute citation in a small number of the *Journal of Forensic Economics* state series articles (mentioned previously).

The collateral source rule is a common law rule that limits the range of what may be considered as evidence before a jury in a court proceeding. In particular, information concerning payments to a plaintiff from sources other than the defendant may be deemed inadmissible; indeed mere mention of such payments may constitute grounds for declaring a mistrial. Collateral source payments to a plaintiff, depending on the trial circumstances and venue, may be those from an insurer, a government entity (e.g., Workers Compensation Fund or state unemployment payments), an employer, family, friends or a charitable organization. Across time and jurisdictions, certain exceptions to the collateral source rule have been introduced, frequently as part of a tort reform movement, most often (but not exclusively) having to do with medical malpractice cases; subsequent to legislated exceptions to the rule, exceptions to the exceptions have also found their way into the law in various jurisdictions. To give a sense of the variety of changes that have been made to the collateral source rule across jurisdictions (the states plus the District of Columbia, Puerto Rico and Virgin Islands), we briefly summarize here a mere portion of the information contained in Schap and Feeley (2008, esp. p. 89), which categorizes changes as being either exceptions to the original rule or partial restorations given an existing exception.

As of August 8, 2005, the collateral source rule had been modified in 38 jurisdictions and eliminated in two. Modifications perceived as exceptions to the rule include consideration of insurance payments (38 instances), an explicit limitation to the effect that a plaintiff may recover only once for the same medical expenses (40), and evidence of collateral source benefits introduced in cases of medical malpractice (22) or only in cases of medical malpractice (17). Exceptions to existing collateral source rule exceptions include allowing evidence of the cost of acquisition of the general collateral source payment (29) or specifically *life* insurance payments (23), and excluding evidence of insurance that was personally acquired or family provided (14) or employer provided (4), or excluding any gratuitous benefit made to plaintiff (5). Additional details concerning treatment of award reductions, subrogation and liens, and public-sector collateral sources appear in Schap and Feeley (2008, esp. pp. 90–91).

Variation in the ordinary practice of taking of deposition testimony will be of interest to forensic economists who practice in more than one specific venue. The range of variation includes venues where there exists a right to depose experts designated by opposing counsel (as in New Hampshire), venues where in practice opposing counsels agree to have each other's experts deposed (as in Massachusetts), and venues where depositions of experts are not taken (as in Pennsylvania). Retaining counsel can inform the forensic economist of the custom or law in the relevant jurisdiction.

12.6 Conclusion

There are some rules and practices that are invariant with respect to jurisdiction (e.g., victims of personal injury may recover pecuniary losses), but far more that differ across and sometimes even within state jurisdictions (e.g., whether it is permissible to bring a cellular phone onto the premises of the local courthouse). Practicing forensic economists need to be aware of such rules and practices, but no one source of information could ever be sufficient.

The laws affecting how forensic economic appraisals are conducted differ across state jurisdictions in complex ways hinted at in the overview presented in this chapter. Besides giving the flavor of both the similarities and differences that exist, we have described the variety of sources available to forensic economists to assist those who may have occasion to undertake casework in what would be for them a new legal jurisdiction. The checklist provided by Thomas R. Ireland in Chap. 16 of this volume would serve as yet another resource.

Besides formal legal rules, there are customary or consensus practices that are also of importance. Here as well, our summary gives merely a sense of the more salient aspects and how they can vary by jurisdiction, but much more exists than can be covered in detail in a single chapter. The journals and listservs (online discussion groups) sponsored by the National Association of Forensic Economics and the American Academy of Economic and Financial Experts are good resources for learning from other practicing forensic economists in an ongoing way.

REFERENCES

Carney, C., & Schap, D. (2008). Recoverable damages for wrongful death in the states: A decennial view. *Journal of Business Valuation and Economic Loss Analysis, 3*(1), 1–9.

Ireland, T. R. (2016). Damage standards for wrongful death/survival actions: Loss to survivors, loss to an estate, loss of accumulations to an estate, and investment accumulations. *Journal of Legal Economics, 22*(2), 5–23.

Rodgers, J. D., & Thornton, R. (2002). Assessing economic damages in personal injury and wrongful death litigation: The state of Pennsylvania. *Journal of Forensic Economics, 15*(3), 335–355.

Rosenbaum, D. I., & Cushing, M. J. (2016). Loss of accumulation of estate in wrongful death: A state-by-state analysis. *Journal of Legal Economics, 22*(2), 65–106.

Schap, D. (2016). The reduction for decedent self-consumption: Jurisdictional mandates for personal consumption or personal maintenance. *Journal of Legal Economics, 22*(2), 107–142.

Schap, D., & Feeley, A. (2008). The collateral source rule: Statutory reform and special interests. *Cato Journal, 28*(1), 83–99 http://object.cato.org/sites/cato.org/files/serials/files/cato-journal/2008/1/cj28n1-6.pdf.

Schap, D., & Thompson, A. (2016). Recoverable damages for wrongful death in the states: A 2015 review of statutory law. *Journal of Legal Economics, 22*(2), 143–153.

Slesnick, F., & Mulliken, C. (2004). Assessing economic damages in personal injury and wrongful death litigation: The state of Kentucky, *Journal of Forensic Economics , 17*(2), 255–274.

Special issue: Symposium on wrongful death. (2016). *Journal of Legal Economics, 22*(2), 1–153.

Spizman, L. M., & Tinari, F. D. (2011). Assessing economic damages in personal injury and wrongful death litigation: The state of New York. *Journal of Forensic Economics, 22*(1), 75–100.

CASES

Delta Air Lines v. Ageloff, 552 So.2d1089, 1989.
Domijan v. Harp, Mo., 340 S.W.2d 728, 1960.
Johnson v. Western Air Express Corp., 45 Cal.App.2d 614, 114 Cal.2d 688, 1941.
Kaczkowski v. Bolubasz, Pa. 421 A.2d 855, 1971.
Louisville and N.R. Co. v. Eakins' Adm'r, 103 Ky. 465, 45 S.W. 529, 1898.

STATUTES AND JURY INSTRUCTIONS

California Civil Jury Instructions (CSCI), 3921.
Florida Wrongful Death Act, §768.18.
Georgia Code, §§51-4-1 and 51-12-13, 2015.
Rhode Island Statute §10-7-1.1.
Vermont Statute, 14 V.S.A. §1492, 2015.
Virgin Islands Code, 5 V.I.C §76(b)(5).
West Virginia Code, §55-7-6(c)(1)(B).

CHAPTER 13

Forensic Economists and Their Changing Viewpoints Over Time

Michael L. Brookshire and Frank L. Slesnick

13.1 INTRODUCTION

In 1990, the authors administered and published the first of 11 survey studies of members of the National Association of Forensic Economics (NAFE), with the last in the longitudinal series administered early in 2015.[1] This chapter represents a summary of survey results over this quarter of a century. We will briefly discuss what we have learned about forensic economists, themselves; concentrate upon substantive results on appropriate methodology in calculation issues; review opinions on issues of forensic practice; and end with viewpoints regarding ethics, for example, which were important to practicing forensic economists and to the NAFE organization, itself.

There is little doubt that the series of surveys has had a major impact on the forensic economics profession. The fact that NAFE has accepted for publication each of the surveys conducted speaks for itself. The surveys are cited in numerous articles when the views of forensic economists are needed. There is also a significant amount of informal evidence based

M.L. Brookshire (✉)
Brookshire Barrett & Associates, USA

F.L. Slesnick
Sun City Center, USA

© The Author(s) 2016
F.D. Tinari (ed.), *Forensic Economics*,
DOI 10.1057/978-1-137-56392-7_13

upon the comments made in the survey and obtained informally at professional meetings. Finally, the results of the survey are cited in court testimony. However, at the beginning of each survey is a disclaimer indicating that the views expressed in the surveys do not represent the views of the NAFE nor all the members of NAFE.

Space limitations prevent a discussion of survey methods and issues for these surveys generally occurring every three years.[2] However, the quality of each survey was significantly enhanced by ten-or-so colleagues who served as "beta testers" in turning survey drafts into a final product. The 2003 move to an electronic survey enhanced an already solid response rate, so that a one-third response rate of NAFE members is the norm.

The series of surveys told us who forensic economists are, at least as represented by NAFE respondents. For example, approximately two-thirds of responding forensic economists have doctoral degrees and another one-fourth have master's-level training. Economics is the major field of study for 65%, finance for another 10%, and smaller percentages for accounting and other business fields. Interestingly, practicing forensic economists believe that forensic experience is more important to effective performance than is degree level or field of study.

The relatively new development of the field of forensic economics is also reflected in survey responses regarding the number of years of forensic experience. In 1990, the average years of reported forensic experience were 11; by the 2015 survey, this average had increased to 26 years. A dramatic change also occurred in this period regarding the size of typical practices and the relative importance of income from forensic work. In 1990, 51% of total earned income of forensic economists came from faculty salary or academic administration salary, 34 % from forensic economic consulting, and 10 % from other consulting work. The typical professional was a fulltime faculty member, practicing alone, with forensic income as a significant supplement to academic pay.[3] By 2015, forensic consulting income was, on average, 73 % of total earned income, with 14 % from academic salaries and 11 % from other consulting income. While some of this change reflected economists retiring from academia and increasing their forensic work, the practice of forensic economics was clearly transitioning to a fulltime effort. Slightly less than half of forensic economists practiced alone; the majority, practicing with others, had an average of 6.2 others working with them.

In terms of the focus of their practices, plaintiff-side work has always outweighed defense-side work as a source of forensic income. In 1990, 67 % of forensic earnings were from plaintiff-side work and 33 % from defense-side work. This defense share had likely grown rapidly over the preceding two decades, as defense trial counsel increasingly hired their own forensic economist as a consultant or testifying witness. By 2015, on average, 59 % of forensic income was plaintiff-side versus 40 % defense-side, so that the relative defense share continued a slow increase. Survey data showed that a significant majority of forensic economists has a reasonable balance between plaintiff and defense work; for almost 30 %, however, 80 % or more of their practice was for either the plaintiff side or the defense side of a case.

The geographical focus of a typical forensic practice also changed little over the 25-year period. Approximately 80 % of forensic income comes from work in the home state of the forensic economist, and 95 % comes from work in either the home state or a contiguous state. Whatever the relative effect of economists' preferences versus hiring attorney preferences, a statewide market is the norm. Forensic economists with national practices or practices over a large collection of states are rare.

Similarly, the type of case upon which a forensic economist works has been very consistent over the quarter of a century. Approximately 70 % of income from forensic consulting involves personal injury and wrongful death damages, 15 % involves antitrust or commercial cases, and 10 % comes from employment cases.

13.2   Basic Variables in Projecting Economic Loss

Since the first survey, questions have been posed concerning three basic variables—the expected rate of inflation (P), the expected rate of increase in compensation (Y), and the expected interest rate (N). These three variables are key for forensic economists when calculating the present value of economic damages.

It is important to note that forensic economists have discounted future values using three approaches. One approach uses nominal values, a second approach uses real values where nominal values are adjusted for inflation, and a third approach uses the so-called net discount rate (NDR). The NDR is defined as the interest (discount) rate minus the rate of increase in compensation. For example, if P is 3 %, Y is 5 %, and N is 7 %, then using the Fisher equation, the forensic economist may use the nominal values of 5 and 7 % to inflate and discount future estimates but also may use the (approximate) real values of 2 and 4 %.[4] In addition, some forensic economists take a simplifying approach by using the (approximate) NDR of 2 %. In this example, future values would be inflated by 0 % and discounted by the NDR equal to 2 %. It is important to note that if these values are calculated correctly, the present value of future loss is unaffected by the approach taken.[5] A forensic economist may choose one particular approach either because it is easier to explain to a jury or perhaps a jurisdiction does not permit any discussion of inflation, which would imply that calculations must relate to real variables.

The rate of inflation is an important variable since many forensic economists utilize that value to assist in determining nominal values (by adding it to a forecast of real values) or in determining real values (by subtracting it from a forecast of nominal values). The question concerning inflation was relatively unchanged from the first survey in 1990 through the most recent survey in 2015 and asked the respondent to forecast inflation as measured by the CPI over the next 30 years. The question asked that the respondent provide a constant value for the expected rate of inflation for all 30 years even though this may not be their usual practice. The survey frequently requested that the respondent "suspend" their usual practice in answering questions.

The average expected values for the rate of inflation fell from 5 % in the 1990 survey to 3.1 % in the 2006 survey and 2.6 % in the 2015 survey. For all of the surveys, the distribution was fairly tight with the interquartile range less than 1 %. Needless to say, forecasting 30 years into the future is not an easy task. Each question requests comments from respondents and they frequently indicate data sources for their information. Sources for forecasting inflation include the Social Security Annual Report, the forecast of the Congressional Budget Office, the forecast of the Philadelphia Federal Reserve, and extrapolating from historical data.

Variables related to the rate of increase in earnings and interest rates will be discussed together since in some of the surveys their values were combined to calculate the NDR. The discussion highlights some of the difficulties obtaining the desired survey information. What transpired through the many surveys was that survey questions related to the increase in compensation, interest rates, and the NDR changed several times, which, unlike the question related to the rate of inflation, make it difficult to compare these values from one survey to the next.

Because forensic economists use different methods for calculating the present value of future losses, surveying their opinions is a challenging task. In the first survey published in 1990, a question was asked concerning the rate of inflation, the growth in real earnings, and the level of real interest rates for all future years. The values, respectively, were 5.01, 1.54, and 2.55 %. These values implied a NDR of approximately 1 %. There was also a question, which asked the respondent to calculate the difference between the interest rate and the rate of increase in earnings. This question related to the NDR and was put in largely as a control given that the respondent should have simply taken his or her answers to the previous questions concerning the interest rate and the increase in earnings to calculate the NDR. Unfortunately, some individuals apparently answered the question in reverse by subtracting the interest rate from the rate of increase from earnings. Although this type of error was usually obvious, it was decided not to tabulate answers to that question. This began a rather long and difficult process of sorting out how to properly ask the question about the NDR.

For the next six surveys, which occurred from 1993 through 2009, the authors tried a number of different combinations with regard to these variables. Some of the surveys examined just the NDRs, some only the variables related to the increase in compensation and interest rates using nominal values, and some where the variables were expressed in real terms. In looking at the surveys over time, there appeared to be a disconnect between the NDR expressed as a direct question and the NDR calculated as the difference between the interest rate and the rate of increase in compensation. The one consistency was that asking for an estimate of the NDR as a direct question produced a higher value than calculating it indirectly as the difference between the interest rate and the rate of increase in compensation.

For the 2013 survey, it was decided to try a set of questions posed back in 1990—namely, as a direct question concerning the NDR but also separate questions about the rate of increase in earnings and the level of interest rates. Values were expressed in nominal terms and an attempt was made to define all words as clearly as possible including the definition of NDR. The hope was that survey responses would be consistent. For the 2013 survey, the average values for the NDR, the nominal increase in total compensation, and the nominal interest rate were 1.61, 3.26, and 4.37 %. Using the indirect method, the NDR is equal to approximately 1.11 % compared to the direct method of 1.61 %. This clearly was an inconsistency. A number of analyses were undertaken to determine why this occurred, including reducing the focus on just those respondents who provided answers to all three variable questions. This, however, did not change the result significantly. One answer may have been provided in the Comments section. Some individuals misinterpreted the meaning of the NDR and, instead, provided a value equal to the real interest rate. That rate is usually higher than the NDR.

The same sequence of questions given in the 2013 survey was also utilized in the most recent 2015 survey. The average values for the NDR, nominal rate of increase in total compensation, and nominal interest rate were 1.36, 2.9, and 4.03 %, respectively. The values for this survey by themselves were consistent with other surveys. The NDR had steadily dropped from 2.13 % in the 1999 survey to 1.36 % in the current survey. Similarly, the nominal rates of increase in total compensation and the nominal interest rate had steadily declined in the 2006, 2012, and 2015 surveys. All of this occurred in an environment of generally falling interest rates. Nevertheless, the 2015 survey showed the same inconsistency in the estimate of the NDR. The value was 1.36 % when asked directly and 1.04 % when asked indirectly. Despite the careful wording of the question and providing a definition of NDR, there still seems to be an unexplained reason why these two methods of calculation do not match up.

13.3   Interest Rate and Portfolio Issues

One of the questions asked since the 1993 survey was the preferred maturity of securities over a 30-year time horizon regardless of the riskiness of the proposed portfolio. In the 1993 survey, 40 % of the respondents favored a short-term or intermediate-term portfolio while 50 % favored a long-term or mixed portfolio. In the most recent 2015 survey, only 23 % indicated a maturity of short-term or intermediate term and 63 % indicated long-term or mixed-term.

Another interest rate question concerns what information the forensic economist utilizes to forecast interest rates. The two primary options are some historical average and current rates as indicated by, perhaps, the yield curve. Two other options provided are an explicit forecast as a function of certain economic variables or some "other" or "mixed" technique. Most questions, in fact, included an option such as "other" that could be explained in the Comments section. This question has remained in fixed form since the first survey in 1990. The general results have been that 24.6 % of the respondents favored using current interest rates as the basis for forecasting future rates in 1990, but this figure increased to 38.1 % by the 2015 survey. Those favoring utilizing historical rates fell from 57.6 to 39.8 % during the same time period. About 20 % indicated they favored either an explicit forecast or some other method. It is clear that there is little consensus among forensic economists concerning this issue.

A third interest rate issue relates to whether the forensic economist utilizes Treasury Inflation Protected Securities (TIPS) in developing an estimate of their interest or NDR. The reason this question was posed was that there is some literature (Chu et al. 2011) indicating that TIPS can provide an estimate of the real interest rate. If so, they would provide a handy, government-sanctioned number that could be used in calculating the present value of future loss. The question was first posed in the 2003 survey, but only 21 % of the respondents indicated that they used TIPS. The question continued through the 2012 survey and the percentage saying they used TIPS actually declined each survey, finally reaching only 14.4 %. The reasons provided varied from the newness of the market to annual tax payments due on interest earned.

13.4 SELF-CONSUMPTION

In most states, self-consumption must be deducted from the income of the deceased. In the earlier surveys, there were several questions asking what percentage the respondent deducted for an adult in a typical family and what percentage was deducted if the person was single. There were also questions concerning data sources utilized. The percentages were, as expected, based upon the major data sources, which were either the direct use of government tables such as the *Consumer Expenditure Survey* or tables published using government data sources (Ruble et al. 2007).

A major issue is whether the base for this self-consumption should be the income of the entire family or the income of the deceased. The issue was first addressed in the 2006 survey, but the question evolved through several surveys. In 2006, the survey question simply asked, "Given no legal constraints, do you deduct consumption from the decedent's income or total family income?" The results were that 53 % indicated decedent's income and 47 % total family income.

In the 2009 survey, the question was changed giving the party's specific incomes. Now, the deceased earned $70,000 and the surviving spouse earned $50,000, and the options were whether the base for self-consumption should be the total family income of $120,000 or the income of the deceased equal to $70,000. 61.7 % indicated total family income and 38.3 % indicated the decedent's income. This represented a significant change in results, which was due either to a change in the wording of the question or to a change in attitude between surveys. It should be noted that the 2009 survey question emphasized that self-consumption was mandated and that the reference should be self-consumption and not maintenance consumption.

This again brings up an issue that has been important throughout all the surveys. Forensic economists work in different states which, in turn, have different legal rules concerning economic guidelines for estimating economic loss. For example, some states will, in fact, dictate that loss must be based only on the decedent. Others, such as the Commonwealth of Kentucky, do not allow any deduction for self-consumption. Still others allow for self-consumption but only an amount related to a "maintenance" level of necessary spending. In order to maximize the number of answers, respondents were asked to ignore any legal parameters they may normally consider. This was evident in the question concerning self-consumption which specified that such consumption must be considered and that it was not based on a maintenance level of spending.

In the 2013 survey, the question evolved once again. This time the income of the decedent was $20,000 and the income of the surviving spouse was $100,000. This change made it likely that self-consumption based upon family income would produce a figure greater than the income of the deceased. Such a result would be difficult to explain to a jury. Nevertheless, even fewer respondents indicated they would use the decedent's income as the base for self-consumption (34.1 %). The identical question was asked in the 2015 survey, and virtually identical results were obtained. The percentage indicating self-consumption based on the income of the deceased was 34.8 % while the percentage based on total family income was 65.2 %.[6]

13.5   Household Services

There were several questions concerning household services. In the last two surveys, a question was asked concerning the general method used in determining the value of household services. In both the 2013 and 2015 surveys, the cost of hiring one or more individuals to replace particular services that were lost was indicated by about 50 % of the respondents while the cost of hiring a general housekeeper or "other" method was favored by 32 %. It should be noted that the opportunity cost method in which the value of household services is assumed to be equivalent to the wage earned in the labor market was specified by less than 3 % of the respondents. The primary data sources indicated were from *Occupational Employment Statistics* and *Dollar Value of a Day*, a publication based upon the BLS's American Time Use Study (Expectancy Data 2013). As a final point concerning this particular question, since the answers were virtually identical from one survey to the next, it is the general practice not to repeat a question a third time unless it is designated as a "Continuity" question.

There were two other areas concerning household services that showed up in recent surveys. In the 2006 and 2009 surveys, a question was asked whether in a death case, self-consumption was deducted from the household services solely for the benefit of the deceased. To take an extreme example, assume the deceased spent a great deal of time washing his sports car on the weekend and that constituted the majority of his "contribution" to the household services. In the 2006 survey, 54 % of the respondents said that a deduction should be made while only 45 % said that was the case in the 2009 survey. It was obvious that this was an unsettled question and was therefore dropped from future surveys, at least for the time being.[7]

Another question was whether an agency cost should be added to the estimate of household services based on the assumption that such services would normally be hired through the marketplace. 81.3 % stated that they never add agency costs, 11.5 % said they only add such a cost "where it is reasonably certain it must be hired through an agency" and only 1.2 % indicated they add an agency cost for all household services estimated. Given the overwhelming result for not adding an agency cost, the question was not repeated.

13.6 WORKLIFE

As explained in Chap. 3 of this volume, worklife issues are critical in determining economic loss. One of the questions that must be addressed is the general technique used in arriving at an estimate of worklife. The options are to use the original BLS Tables (Smith 1982), tables published in economic journals (Skoog et al. 2011), using the mean or median years to final labor force separation, employing the so-called LPE or life-participation-employment technique (Richards and Donaldson 2010), ending worklife at some standard year such as the time when full Social Security benefits are received, and a combination of the above techniques.

This question was first asked in 1991 with the BLS Tables favored by over 71 % of the respondents—no doubt because it was "the only game in town". Now, in the latest survey, these tables, which are no longer published, are used by less than 2 % of the respondents. On the other hand, tables published in economic journals are chosen by nearly two-thirds of the respondents. The options of "A combination of the above techniques" and "Other" are favored by 23 %. This question is an example where a new entry, the worklife tables in economic journals, was added to the options. Although this disrupted the longitudinal analysis, it was necessary to incorporate the information given that the entry became the dominant source for worklife estimates.

Another question asked whether the respondent adjusted worklife in any manner if the case involved a self-employed individual. The reasoning might be that the self-employed have control over the number of years they may work and standard worklife tables generally cover individuals who are employees with relatively fixed work schedules. In the 2013 survey, a question addressing this issue found that 81.5 % of the respondents made no special adjustment when the individual was self-employed. Part of the reason given by some respondents was there were no credible studies showing that the self-employed do, in fact, work longer than the average worker and thus projecting a longer worklife would be speculative. Given the overwhelming percentage that provided a specific answer, it was decided not to repeat this question even though it was not given before. That rarely happens, but when it does a decision is made that asking the question again will likely not add new information.

13.7   THE COST OF LIFE CARE PLANS

Besides forecasting lost earnings, fringe benefits, and household services, forensic economists are also asked to estimate the cost of life care plans. Of course, they do not determine what inputs are required for the plan itself. Rather, they forecast the future rate of increase in the components of medical costs required to care for the plaintiff, usually as part of a life care plan. In the earlier surveys, the focus was on general medical costs as represented by the Medical Care Price Index (MCPI). In the first survey, the 30-year forecast was an annual 7.6 % increase, but the rate of increase dropped by the 2004 survey to 5.1 %. There was also feedback from respondents that the MCPI was not indicative of the costs in most life care plans since that part of the CPI was dominated by hospital and physician costs. Life care plans, though, generally contain a high percentage of costs related to attendant care or costs in some institutional facility. Thus, starting in 2004, a question was asked concerning the respondent's forecast of attendant care costs and starting in 2009 a forecast of nursing home costs. The general result was that respondents felt that attendant care costs rose about the same as wages in general—3.39 % annually in the 2012 survey. In fact, based upon comments provided, many respondents utilized a wage index such as the Employment Cost Index as a measure for the increase in attendant care costs. The growth rate reported for institutional care is higher than for attendant care. In the 2012 survey, the rate was 4.21 %, and that differential was consistent in other surveys. Although attendant care is a major cost in a nursing home facility, respondents felt that other costs would rise more rapidly. Neither of these questions was asked in the 2015 survey but given the impact of the Affordable Care Act on the economy, there is no doubt that medical costs will be a major issue for forensic economists to consider in the future.[8]

13.8   OTHER DAMAGES CATEGORIES

One of the most contentious issues in the forensic economics literature is whether hedonic damages, or the lost enjoyment of life, have a legitimate role in the court system. Put differently, can such damages be accurately measured with regard to a specific individual?[9] The 1999, 2003, and 2009 surveys asked whether the respondent would be willing to calculate damages for the lost enjoyment of life if asked by the hiring attorney. The 1999 survey showed 23.6 % responded "Yes" and 76.4 % responded "No". The results for the 2003 survey were similar, with slightly lower "Yes" responses. In 2009, the results were 16.2 % "Yes" and 83.8 % "No". Thus, there was a steady decline in the percentage who were willing to calculate hedonic damages in a report.

There was a similar question in the same survey that asked whether the respondent would be willing to critique a report by another economist, which contained a section on hedonic damages. The results were consistent with the previous question. In the 2009 survey, 82.8 % indicated that they would write such a critique and 17.8 % said they would not. The results of this question imply that those who stated they would not write a report calculating hedonic damages as expressed in the first question did not do so due to a lack of familiarity with the literature, so the generally negative response to forensic economic estimates in this area was clear.

Responding forensic economists also expressed strong, negative opinions about work by forensic economists in attempting to estimate other categories of possible damages, such as companionship, pain and suffering, and advice and guidance services. They also expressed various opinions about vocational rehabilitation experts, believing their typical role involved a determination of post-injury earnings levels in personal injury cases; privately published tables by some vocational experts, dealing with worklife expectancy of the disabled, were strongly rejected as unreliable.

13.9   OTHER PRACTICE AND INDUSTRY ISSUES

Forensic economists were periodically asked about needed research in their field. The three topics of worklife expectancy, personal consumption, and household services were repeatedly suggested as areas for further research. Specific questions on forensic practice revealed, for example, that policies varied widely on whether retainers were required before beginning work on a new case, partially depending on the characteristics of the attorney client. A slight majority had a minimum charge for discovery depositions, and slightly less than half had a minimum charge for trial testimony. Moreover, out of total new cases received in a year, for example, a written report was prepared in 90 %, a discovery deposition occurred in 30 % of the cases, and the forensic economist testified at trial in only 10 % of the cases. In typical trial testimonies, direct examination was 45 minutes in length and cross-examination averaged 30 minutes.

The series of surveys regularly dealt with issues of ethical conduct and related issues of interest to the general membership and the Board of Directors of NAFE. Practicing forensic economists expressed strong opinions about what is, or is not, unethical conduct. Accepting fee arrangements contingent upon the outcome of a case is considered to be unethical conduct, as is remaining silent when aware of an (undiscovered) error in a loss estimate. Forensic economists would not object to hypothetical calculations performed at the request of a hiring attorney, provided their hypothetical nature is disclosed. They disagree about when all source material behind a calculation should be disclosed—when a report is issued or at a discovery deposition if asked. They agree, on the other hand, that advertisement is ethical conduct, as is charging the highest fee that the market will bear.[10]

Survey responses may have helped prompt the NAFE Board toward developing a code of ethical conduct for forensic economists. Since 2004, members pledge to adhere to the NAFE Statement of Ethical Principles and Principles of Professional Practice; these are eight principles ranging from compensation to disclosure to consistency to knowledge. The 2015 survey indicated continuing strong support for this statement of ethical principles. However, forensic economists have clearly rejected the notion that the NAFE organization should attempt to enforce compliance with these ethical principles.

Similarly, practicing forensic economists have clearly indicated their desire that the Association be significantly involved in a range of continuing education activities. On the other hand, they do not believe that NAFE (or any other organization) should be involved in establishing qualification standards, or a certification process, for courtroom testimony.

13.10   CONCLUSION

The 11 NAFE surveys cover a period of 25 years. Like most surveys conducted within professional organizations, the responses cannot be characterized as a random sample since respondents could decline filling out the electronic survey form. Although a random selection process is theoretically preferred since the sample better represents the targeted population and it is possible to develop confidence intervals, a nonprobability sample is often all that is feasible in surveys of organizations such as NAFE. Not all forensic economists belong to NAFE (although evidence indicates the most experienced economists are members), and it would be necessary to examine the characteristics of those who did not respond to the survey compared to those who did respond. Nevertheless, it is clear from this chapter that a great deal of useful information has been developed over this quarter century for the members of NAFE concerning the methodology used by forensic economists, issues of forensic practice, ethics governing how forensic economists deal with the legal system, and finally the role NAFE should play in governing the behavior of its members. It is hoped that future surveys will continue to serve NAFE and the forensic economics community.

NOTES

1. Dr. Michael Luthy, a survey expert, joined our survey team with the 2003 survey, and economists Dr. David Schap and Dr. David Rosenbaum joined the 2015 survey to replace the two of us for future surveys.
2. Survey methodology is discussed in Daniel (2012) and Weathington et al. (2010).

3. A survey conducted in 2001 by Tinari revealed that 61.5 % of the 234 survey respondents were sole proprietors in their forensic economics practice, a finding consistent with earlier surveys reported in this chapter (Grivoyannis and Tinari 2005, pp. 140 and 143).

4. In the text example, the rate of inflation, P, equals 3 %, the rate of increase in compensation, Y, equals 5 %, and the level of interest rates equals 7 %. The variables Y and N are in nominal terms. Using the Fisher equation, the real variables are calculated as follows:

   N_r = Real Rate of Interest = N – P = 7 % – 3 % = 4 % and

   Y_r = Real Rate of Increase in Compensation = Y – P = 5 % – 3 %.

   However, a more precise formulation is the following:

   N_r = Real Rate of Interest = N – P – (N*P) = 7 % – 3 % – 0.21 % = 3.79 %

   Y_r = Real Rate of Increase in Compensation = Y – P – (Y*P) = 5 % – 3 % – 0.15 % = 1.85%.

   Two items should be noted. First, when P and N are small, then the approximations are very close to the more precise equations since the last term is small. Second, the Fisher equation may not be an accurate reflection of reality. For example, a rise in inflation may not have an equivalent impact on interest rates or especially on the rate of increase in compensation.

5. The discount rate is explored in more detail in Chap. 8 of this volume.

6. Readers may want to read Chap. 4 in this volume dealing with the personal consumption topic.

7. For an examination of this issue, readers are referred to Chap. 10 on household services.

8. For a detailed discussion, see Chap. 9 in this volume on the topic of the Affordable Care Act.

9. For a thorough discussion of this issue, readers are referred to Chap. 14 on hedonic damages in this volume.

10. Ethical aspects of the practice of forensic economics are explored in Chap. 15 of this book.

References

Chu, Q. C., Pittman, D. N., & Yu, L. Q. (2011). When do tips price adjust to inflation information? *Financial Analysts Journal, 67*(2), 59–73.

Daniel, J. (2012). *Sampling essentials: Practical guidelines for making sampling choices.* Los Angeles: Sage Publishing.

Expectancy Data. (2013). *The dollar value of a day.* Shawnee Mission: Time Diary Analysis.

Grivoyannis, E. C., & Tinari, F. D. (2005). Estimates of labor productivity of economic damages experts. *Journal of Forensic Economics, 18*(2–3), 139–153.

Luthy, M., Brookshire, M., Rosenbaum, D., Schap, D., & Slesnick, F. L. (1990 in review). A 2015 survey of forensic economists: Their methods, estimates, and perspectives, submitted to the *Journal of Forensic Economics.*

Richards, H., & Donaldson, M. (2010). The life, participation, employment method. In *Life and worklife expectancies* (2nd ed.). Tucson: Lawyers & Judges Publishing Co.

Ruble, M., Patton, R. T., & Nelson, D. M. (2007). Patton-Nelson personal consumption tables, 2005–06. *Journal of Forensic Economics, 20*(31), 217–225.

Skoog, G., Ciecka, J., & Krueger, K. (2011). The markov process model of labor force activity: Extended tables of general tendency, shape, percentile points, and otstrap standard errors. *Journal of Forensic Economics, 22*(2), 165–229.

Smith, S. J. (1982). *Tables of working life, the increment-decrement model, Bulletin 2135.* Washington, DC: U.S. Department of Labor, Bureau of Labor Statistics.

Weathington, B., Cunningham, C., & Pittenger, D. (2010). *Research methods for the behavioral and social sciences.* Hoboken: John Wiley & Sons.

CHAPTER 14

Hedonic Valuation Issues

Gary R. Skoog

14.1   What Is the Value of a Statistical Life?

We make choices all the time which implicitly reveal how we value health and mortality risks: we get on airplanes to attend conferences, or we drive an automobile, or we eat a cheeseburger, or simply too much. We may purchase hazardous products or work on risky or stressful jobs. There are benefits (attending conferences, arriving more quickly, eating things we like) associated with these costs (increasing death risks). The value of a statistical life (VSL) literature within economics studies this tradeoff. It uses this kind of indirect evidence on market choices that involve subtle tradeoffs between risk and money. The seminal papers are by Dreze (1962) and by Schelling (1968), and important early work was done by Mishan (1971, 1982).

In any model in which economic agents face a tradeoff between consuming more and incurring a larger risk of death, there is implicitly a VSL. It is the slope of an indifference curve generally induced by an indirect utility function, the result of an optimization. Time may be continuous or discrete. There may be one or many periods. There may be labor–leisure choices or not.

G.R. Skoog (✉)
De Paul University, Chicago, IL, USA, and Legal Econometrics, Inc., Glenview, IL, USA

© The Author(s) 2016
F.D. Tinari (ed.), *Forensic Economics*,
DOI 10.1057/978-1-137-56392-7_14

The fundamental objects are the willingness-to-pay (WTP) for small reductions, and the willingness-to-accept (WTA) small increases in mortality risk. These core concepts remain, but from the beginning there were doubts. Consider Zeckhauser's view (1975):

> The accumulating evidence suggests that life valuation should not be approached as a search for an elusive number. Even if we divine which marginal curves to cross, or if we conduct an income survey of motorcyclists, or if we see how much is spent to replace a heart valve, no irresistible answers can be expected. (p. 419)
>
> ... the context in which lives are being sacrificed or saved will affect both the procedures by which lives should be valued, and the valuations themselves. (p. 420)
>
> Most analysts would agree that the appropriate value to be placed on a life depends on who is making the decision about the life, who would be paying to save it, and who would benefit if it were saved. (p. 422)

14.2   Theoretical Exposition of VSL: Three Simple Models

We first consider two models from Rosen (1981, 1988). In the first a person has wealth W and a probability of survival of p. There is one good c, and his utility function if he lives is $u(c)$, so that his expected utility is $pu(c)$. If he does not survive, his wealth is worthless to him, and others are like him. If there are N such people, pN will survive, and their wealth is NW, so that each survivor gets to consume NW/pN or W/p, which is therefore the budget constraint: $c = W/p$. There are two parameters, p and W. Optimization is trivial: consume everything, so that, pedantically, $c(p, W) = W/p$.

Now form the indirect utility function, optimized utility incorporating optimal choices:

$$V(p, W) = pu\big(c(p, W)\big) \tag{14.1}$$

Now the VSL is by definition the negative of the slope of this indirect utility function at the optimally chosen values. We compute it as:

$$dV(p,W) = \frac{\partial V}{\partial p}dp + \frac{\partial V}{\partial W}dW = 0, \text{ or } VSL \equiv -\frac{dW}{dp} = \frac{\dfrac{\partial V}{\partial p}}{\dfrac{\partial V}{\partial W}} \tag{14.2}$$

We need to compute the numerator and denominator of the right-hand side of (14.2), by using (14.1) and the constraint. Hence:

$$\frac{\partial V}{\partial p} = u(c) + pu'(c)\frac{dc}{dp} = u(c) + pu'(c)\left[-\frac{W}{p^2}\right] \text{ and } \frac{\partial V}{\partial W} = pu'(c(p,W))\frac{1}{p} = u'$$

Therefore, $VSL \equiv -\dfrac{dW}{dp} = \dfrac{\dfrac{\partial V}{\partial p}}{\dfrac{\partial V}{\partial W}} = \dfrac{u - cu'}{u'}$. Now define the elasticity of utility with respect to consumption as $\varepsilon \equiv \dfrac{c\dfrac{du}{dc}}{u} = \dfrac{\dfrac{du}{u}}{\dfrac{dc}{c}} = \dfrac{d\log(u)}{d\log(c)}$. Then

$\dfrac{1}{\varepsilon} = \dfrac{u}{cu'}$ so $\dfrac{c}{\varepsilon} = \dfrac{u}{u'}$ and we have

$$VSL = \frac{u - cu'}{u'} = \frac{c}{\varepsilon} - c = \left(\frac{1}{\varepsilon} - \frac{\varepsilon}{\varepsilon}\right)c = \frac{1-\varepsilon}{\varepsilon}c = \frac{1-\varepsilon}{\varepsilon}\frac{W}{p} \qquad (14.3)$$

To say more, one needs a specific utility function, but since ε is the ratio of marginal utility to average utility, it must be positive. If it exceeds one, Rosen gives a clever convexification argument which drives it down to 1. With $u(c) = c^\alpha, \log u(c) = \alpha \log c, \varepsilon \equiv \dfrac{d\log u(c)}{d\log c} = \alpha$. From absolute risk aversion, $A(c) = -\dfrac{u''}{u'} = -\dfrac{\alpha(\alpha-1)c^{\alpha-2}}{\alpha c^{\alpha-1}} = \dfrac{(1-\alpha)}{c}$, we must have $\alpha = \varepsilon < 1$,

and we conclude that with Cobb–Douglas utility,

$$VSL = \frac{1-\alpha}{\alpha}\frac{W}{p} \qquad (14.4)$$

This result implies that, in this special case, there is much VSL heterogeneity in the population, because:

1. VSL is linear in wealth, W, that is, one VSL does not fit all; the wealthier the person, the higher the VSL.
2. VSL grows infinitely large the lower the chance of survival, that is, for large changes in p, that is, as p approaches 0.

3. At $\alpha = 1$, one is not risk averse, $A(c) = 0$, and VSL=0, while as $\alpha \downarrow 0$, $A(c) \uparrow \frac{1}{c}$ and VSL$\uparrow \infty$, that is, the VSL in population is highest among the most risk averse.

In the next model, Rosen (1981, 1988) adds labor supply, which entails an explicit optimization, and permits us to investigate whether the VSL necessarily theoretically exceeds labor earnings, the common empirical result.

The utility function is now $u(c, l)$ where c remains consumption and l is now leisure. Choose the units so that all possible time is 1, so that $1 - l$ is time spent earning income, at wage rate w. The budget constraint says that one may consume the sum of one's unearned income, $\frac{W}{p}$, as before plus one's labor earnings, $w(1 - l)$. The optimization problem is to maximize expected utility $pu(c, l)$ over c, l subject to $c = \frac{W}{p} + w(1 - l)$. The parameters are now W, p, w and we let the optimized values be denoted by $c(W, p, w)$ and $l(W, p, w)$. The indirect utility function is then

$$V(W,p,w) = pu\big(c(W,p,w), l(W,p,w)\big) \tag{14.5}$$

As before, $VSL \equiv -\dfrac{dW}{dp} = \dfrac{\dfrac{\partial V}{\partial p}}{\dfrac{\partial V}{\partial W}}$. Computing the numerator and denominators now requires some real work; Rosen appeals to the envelope theorem to assert that

$$VSL \equiv -\frac{dW}{dp} = \frac{\dfrac{\partial V}{\partial p}}{\dfrac{\partial V}{\partial W}} = \frac{1 - \varepsilon}{\varepsilon} c + w(1 - l) \tag{14.6}$$

I will offer proof of the result directly. Let the Lagrangian for the problem be $L(c, l, \lambda) = pu(c, l) + \lambda \left[c - \dfrac{W}{p} - w(1 - l) \right]$, differentiate with respect to the arguments and set to 0, to obtain:

$$pu_c(c,l) + \lambda = 0, \tag{14.7a}$$

$$pu_l(c,l) + \lambda w = 0, \tag{14.7b}$$

$$c - \frac{W}{p} - w(1-l) = 0. \tag{14.7c}$$

Eliminate λ in (14.7a) and (14.7b) and cancel p, to obtain

$$u_l(c,l) = wu_c(c,l), \tag{14.8}$$

traditional labor supply; I am assuming an interior solution. We now have (14.7c) and (14.8), two equations in two unknowns.

We write the budget constraint, which holds identically in the parameters, as

$c(W,p,w) + wl(W,p,w) = \dfrac{W}{p} + w$. Differentiating this equation gives

$$\frac{\partial c}{\partial p} + w\frac{\partial l}{\partial p} = -\frac{W}{p^2} \tag{14.9a}$$

and

$$\frac{\partial c}{\partial W} + w\frac{\partial l}{\partial W} = \frac{1}{p}. \tag{14.9b}$$

Next we calculate the numerator in (14.6) as

$$\frac{\partial V}{\partial p} = \frac{\partial pu\big(c(W,p,w),l(W,p,w)\big)}{\partial p} = u + pu_c\frac{\partial c}{\partial p} + pu_l\frac{\partial l}{\partial p}$$

and use (14.7a), (14.7b) and (14.9a), to conclude

$$\frac{\partial V}{\partial p} = u - \lambda\frac{\partial c}{\partial p} - \lambda w\frac{\partial l}{\partial p} \overset{(9a)}{=} u - \lambda\left(-\frac{W}{p^2}\right) \tag{14.10a}$$

Similarly

$$\frac{\partial V}{\partial W} = \frac{\partial pu\big(c(W,p,w),l(W,p,w)\big)}{\partial W}$$

$$= pu_c \frac{\partial c}{\partial W} + pu_l \frac{\partial l}{\partial W} \overset{(7a),(7b)}{=} -\lambda \frac{\partial c}{\partial W} - \lambda w \frac{\partial l}{\partial W} \overset{(9b)}{=} -\lambda \frac{1}{p} \quad (14.10b)$$

Finally we establish (14.6):

$$VSL \equiv -\frac{dW}{dp} = \frac{\frac{\partial V}{\partial p}}{\frac{\partial V}{\partial W}} = \frac{u - \lambda\left(-\dfrac{W}{p^2}\right)}{-\lambda \dfrac{1}{p}} = \frac{pu}{pu_c} - \frac{W}{p} = \frac{u}{u_c} - \big(c - w(1-l)\big)$$

$$= \left(\frac{\dfrac{u}{c}}{u_c} - 1\right)c + w(1-l)$$

Recalling $\varepsilon \equiv \dfrac{cu_c}{u}$, $VSL = \left(\dfrac{1}{\varepsilon} - 1\right)c + w(1-l)$, the desired result.

The first term is exactly the VSL without labor supply, as before. Note that the VSL equals $= \left(\dfrac{1}{\varepsilon} - 1\right)c$ plus labor earnings, proving that VSL decomposes into a "pure hedonics" term and "human capital" term, additively. However, the "pure hedonics" component, $\left(\dfrac{1}{\varepsilon} - 1\right)c$ will be negative if $\varepsilon > 1$; this is possible, as long as the sum $\left(\dfrac{1}{\varepsilon} - 1\right)c + w(1-l)$ is non-negative. For $\varepsilon \approx 1$, $VSL \approx$ wage earnings.

The next example, taken from Viscusi and Aldy (2003), describes the supply of labor side of the market in wages and job safety which motivates much of the empirical work in the VSL literature.

A worker becomes injured or dies with probability p, and so escapes injury with probability $1-p$. His wage is w, which varies with the riskiness of the job, that is, $w = w(p), w' > 0$. If he is injured, his utility function, reflecting the workers compensation he will receive, and any personal injury proceeds, is $V(w(p))$, while if he is healthy, his utility function is a different function, $U(w(p))$. His expected utility is thus

$$EU(p) = (1-p)U\big(w(p)\big) + pV\big(w(p)\big).$$

The worker chooses p, *the level of risk he will face*, optimally, that is, he maximizes $EU(p)$ over p given $U(\cdot)$, $V(\cdot)$ and $w(p)$. Notice that p here is risk of the bad event, injury or death, whereas in the previous models, it represented the complement with respect to 1, namely survival.

Further, assume that the worker has higher utility when healthy than injured, $U(\cdot) \geq V(\cdot)$, and that marginal utility is higher when not injured, so that $U'(w(p))$ exceeds $V'(w(p))$ and both are positive.

His first-order condition comes from setting $EU'(p)=0$. This computation is then:

$$EU'(p) = (1-p)U'\big(w(p)\big)\frac{dw}{dp} - U\big(w(p)\big) + pV'\big(w(p)\big)\frac{dw}{dp} + V\big(w(p)\big) = 0,$$

resulting in

$$WTP = \frac{dw}{dp} = \frac{U\big(w(p)\big) - V\big(w(p)\big)}{(1-p)U'\big(w(p)\big) + pV'\big(w(p)\big)} > 0 \qquad (14.11)$$

Equation (14.11) gives the worker's marginal rate of substitution along his highest indifference curve attainable along a set of jobs characterized by the wage offer function $w(p)$. Other workers will have different tastes, meaning attitudes toward risk, and so will have different $U(\cdot)$, $V(\cdot)$ pairs, depicted by EU_1 and EU_2 in Fig. 14.1. The market labor supply function, labeled $w(p)$ will be the lower envelope of these (p, w) pairs of all workers.

Firms on the other hand, given their technology, will be able to offer wages w at each level of risk p, and there will, in Fig. 14.1 be a continuum of different firms, with different and intersecting (p, w) isoprofit loci; OC_1 and OC_2 are shown for two of them. The upper envelope of these curves will depict those finding labor at each risk level. In this way, the curve $w(p)$ represents both the supply and demand sides of the market. This notion of equilibrium appears in the seminal paper of Rosen (1974) which studied general characteristics of goods. Viscusi and Aldy (2003) applied this notion to labor and its characteristic, risk of injury or death, and contains Fig. 14.1's graphical depiction of equilibrium.

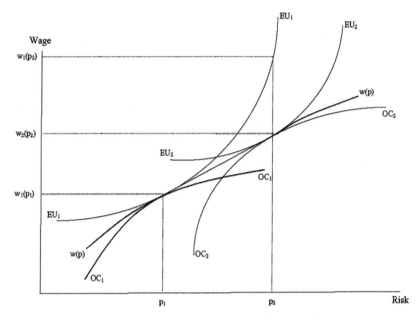

Fig. 14.1 Market process for determining compensating differentials

The insight that labor markets reflect characteristics other than time spent forgoing leisure goes back to the beginnings of economics, to Adam Smith (1776) in *The Wealth of Nations*, Chapter 10, Part 1: "the wages of labor vary with the ease or hardship, the cleanliness or dirtiness, the honorableness or dishonorableness of the employment." (p. 100)

Interestingly, the analogous notion that products' characteristics determine their prices goes back at least to Griliches (1971) where these models were called hedonic econometric models, in which independent aspects of a good are related to price.

14.3   Measurement of VSL

Broadly there have been two approaches to estimating a VSL. The first, and the one most favored by economists, uses market studies, namely, data from actual decisions about wage or income tradeoffs and risks of life and injury. Most of these have involved wages [employing "compensating differentials" from labor economics, sometimes called "hedonic wage" (HW) studies], but goods (safety detectors and homes) and environmental outcomes have been used as well. The second broad approach has been to ask people about their preferences; these are known as stated preference (SP) surveys or contingent valuation.

From our theoretical discussion, because the indirect utility function's indifference curves are smooth, it would make no difference whether the slope were measured from the left or right in Fig. 14.1: WTP for a small risk reduction would equal the WTA a small risk increase, both from a baseline. Labor market studies find this equality generally, per Kniesner et al. (2014), who contrast this with factors of WTA/WTP ratios of 7.2 to 1 in the SP literature.

Returning to Fig. 14.1, econometric models based on labor market outcomes may specify either $w(p)$ as linear in p or as a non-linear curve. The single coefficient, if linear, or several if non-linear, may be constant across various worker characteristics, or they may vary with worker characteristics (i.e., the equation below possesses interaction terms).

Clearly the estimated wage-risk tradeoff curve $w(p)$ for the entire labor market does *not* imply how a particular worker must be compensated for non-marginal changes in risk. Comparing workers 1 and 2, the latter has revealed a willingness to accept risk p_2 at wage $w_2(p_2)$ along EU_2. A change in the risk exposure to worker 1 from p_1 to p_2 would require a much higher wage compensation to keep worker 1 on the expected utility curve EU_1: $w_1(p_2) > w_2(p_2)$.

With large changes in risk, a worker's wage-risk tradeoff will *not* be captured by the slope of the wage function $w(p)$, which some other worker accepts in equilibrium. The linear approximation deteriorates rapidly as risk increases. The tradeoff for an individual worker must be on that worker's expected utility curve, not the estimated market wage-risk tradeoff. These p values in empirical work are on the order of magnitude of $\frac{1}{10,000}$. In the case of a sure death, extrapolating this slope out to 1 is clearly inappropriate, since the indifference curve EU_1 may not even extend to 1. The latter case involves the invaluable goods in Arrow (1997) and supra-monetary values in Ireland and Gilbert (1998).

14.3.1 *Econometric Specification*

Using the notation of Viscusi and Aldy (2003), an econometric equation such as the following is used to estimate the wage-risk relationship in labor markets:

$$w_i = \alpha + H_i'\beta_1 + X_i'\beta_2 + p_i\gamma_1 + q_i\gamma_2 + WC_iq_i\gamma_3 + p_iH_i'\beta_3 + \varepsilon_i \quad (14.12)$$

where the variables are as follows:

w_i is the worker i's wage rate,

H_i' is a row vector of personal characteristic variables for worker i,

X_i' is a vector of job characteristic variables for worker i

p_i is the fatality risk associated with worker i's job,

q_i is the nonfatal injury risk associated with worker i's job

WC_i is the workers compensation benefits payable if a job injury occurs to worker i

ε_i is the random error reflecting unmeasured factors which influence worker i's wage rate.

The coefficients $\alpha, \beta_1, \beta_2, \gamma_1, \gamma_2, \gamma_3, \beta_3$ are parameters to be estimated, often by regression. The authors state:

The personal characteristic variables represented by H_i' often include a variety of human capital measures, such as education and job experience, as well as other individual measures, such as age and union status. They may also include sex, race, wealth, and possibly other variables. The job characteristic variables represented by X_i' typically include indicators for blue-collar jobs, white-collar jobs, management positions, the worker's industry, and measures of physical exertion associated with the job. These two sets of variables reflect both workers' preferences over jobs as well as firms' offer curves for labor. Some studies interact personal characteristics H_i' with the fatality risk p_i to capture how the returns to risk may vary with these characteristics, such as age and union status. (p. 9)

The workhorse statistical model is regression by ordinary least squares. For such estimation to be justified, ε_i must be exogenous, that is, $E\left(\varepsilon_i | H_i', X_i', p_i, q_i, WC_i\right) = 0$ which, in practice, requires that ε_i be uncorrelated with each of H_i', X_i', p_i, q_i and WC_i.

If ε_i is not exogenous, that is, if it is correlated with any regressor, or if *bona fide* determinants are left out of the regressors H_i', X_i', p_i, q_i and WC_i, or if any of the H_i', X_i', p_i, q_i is measured with error, or if the right-hand side of the equation has not adopted the correct (linear) functional form specified for the conditional expectation $E\left(w_i | H_i', X_i', p_i, q_i, WC_i\right) = \alpha + H_i'\beta_1 + X_i'\beta_2 + p_i\gamma_1 + q_i\gamma_2 + WC_iq_i\gamma_3 + H_i'\beta_3 p_i$ because, say, quadratic, higher-order terms of some other non-linear function are needed, or if w_i should be measured as $\ln(w_i)$ or as its Box–Cox transformation $\dfrac{w_i^\lambda - 1}{\lambda}$, then the key coefficient γ_1, the scaled value of life, will be inconsistently estimated.[1] It is common today, among adherents to the value of life literature who may disagree on applicability grounds, to gloss over the econometric points.

14.3.2   VSL Results

From an equation like (14.12) where wage w_i is the dependent variable, so that with the average wage ($\bar{w}$) in the sample, the average fatality risk is $\bar{p}$, average hours worked in a year are $\bar{H}$, and $\hat{\gamma}_1$ is the estimated mortality coefficient, we have $VSL = \hat{\gamma}_1 \dfrac{\bar{H}}{\bar{p}}$. For example, if $\bar{H} = 2000$ and $\bar{p} = \dfrac{6.541}{100,000}$, then $\hat{\gamma}_1 = .03$ would imply a VSL of \$9.353 million. If the dependent variable were measured as the log of wage, then since the estimated equation gives us $\dfrac{d\ln(w)}{dp} = \hat{\gamma}_1$ we have $\hat{\gamma}_1 = \dfrac{d\ln w}{dw}\dfrac{dw}{dp} = \dfrac{1}{w}\dfrac{dw}{dp}$ so that $\dfrac{dw}{dp}$ now equals $\bar{w}\hat{\gamma}_1$ at the sample average; applying the scaling factor of $\dfrac{\bar{H}}{\bar{p}}$ as before produces $VSL = \hat{\gamma}_1 \bar{w} \dfrac{\bar{H}}{\bar{p}}$.

There are hundreds of studies which have appeared over the last 40 years. A potential user must select a study or studies in order to arrive at a VSL value, or a range. Many studies, called meta-studies, have analyzed the results of sets of other studies. These have included Miller (1990, 2000), Viscusi (1993), Mrozek and Taylor (2002), Viscusi and Aldy (2003), Kochi et al. (2006) and Bellavance et al. (2009), in the private sector.

When more than \$100 million are spent within a year, US government agencies are required to perform a cost–benefit analysis. The US Environmental Protection Agency (2016) (USEPA) has recently produced its own meta-study which considered both HW and SP studies. Its current measure of VSL is \$4.8 million in \$1990, which it has increased for inflation and income growth to \$9.7 million in \$2013 (p. 2). It proposes updating this to \$10.3 million in \$2013 by assuming an income elasticity of 0.7.

This study, in its Table 4, lists nine papers which it used in providing the HW estimates, seven of which are from papers by Kip Viscusi, a long-time EPA consultant and the leading academic figure in the field. A recent private sector view of VSL (Kniesner et al. 2012) notes an "extremely wide range of labor market VSL estimates" (p. 74), $0–$20 million (p. 85) and "a series of prominent econometric controversies reviewed by Viscusi and Aldy (2003)" on p. 74, including problems from unmeasured skill differentials among workers and measurement error in the risk variable. This 2012 study controls for a "host of econometric problems" missed in earlier research, mainly latent, time-invariant heterogeneity, and it "reduces the estimated VSL by as much as two-thirds and narrows greatly the VSL range to about $4 million to $10 million."

In addition to a $4–$10 million range, and the fact that the VSL is known to vary with personal characteristics, our theoretical models earlier showed income variation, something that has been established empirically, with a wide range of plausible income elasticity values. The EPA's 2010 Guidelines (cited in USEPA 2016, p. 3) listed 0.08, 0.4 and 1.0, and is using 0.4. Viscusi and Aldy (2003) suggested 0.5 to 0.6. Their Table 4 showed a $7.0 million estimate ($2000) in the USA and much lower VSLs for poorer countries, confirming international evidence. Miller (2000) found income elasticities from 0.85 to 0.96, while Mrozek and Taylor (2002) placed the income elasticity at 0.46 to 0.49.

Aldy and Viscusi (2007) found that estimated VSL varies by age, and that it does not fall with age for all ages, as would be the result if there were a constant VSL in each year. Instead, a graph with the VSL on the vertical axis and age on the horizontal axis exhibits an inverted U-shaped pattern, reflecting the paths of income, consumption and accumulated wealth over the life cycle. Smokers and lower paid workers exhibit lower VSLs, as do immigrants. Explanations may include behavior toward risk and access to less favorable labor markets.

14.3.3   Value of a Statistical Injury

Equation (14.12) has a coefficient for injury as well as for death, and the same methodology generating a VSL generates a value of a statistical injury (VSI). This has received much less attention. Viscusi and Aldy (2003) found a wide range of estimates, $20,000–$70,000 per injury. As with the VSL, there is considerable heterogeneity, with smokers and those not using seatbelts exhibiting lower VSIs. The same pattern of income elasticity appears, with lower VSIs reported for Canada and India versus the USA.

14.4 VSL AND LAW AND ECONOMICS CONSIDERATIONS: COMPENSATION AND EFFICIENCY

There are, as pointed out by Viscusi (1990b), two distinct legal concepts in tort law: appropriate compensation to victims, and efficient incentives for safety for deterrence and accident prevention (amounts of care).

Regarding appropriate compensation, from the work of Kenneth Arrow (1964), (1971), (1974), and extended by Shavell (1987) and others, a property of expected utility maximizations of individuals facing risky situations, who can purchase actuarially fair insurance, is that they use insurance to transfer wealth from the "no accident" to the "accident" state so that they have the same marginal utility of income across states of the world. This result holds when the utility function is not altered by the state of the world—accident or no accident. One chooses to fully insure against property damage, and the law properly allows a full recovery. The law also allows full recovery of a wage income stream or life care costs whether or not the tort alters one's utility function—it provides "free" insurance. In both cases, the legal remedy is economically efficient: it provides recovery to the extent that individuals would value it with the purchase of insurance. If the injury is catastrophic or mortal, however, it directly affects the marginal utility of income. It is diminished if alive, and zero or at a bequest level if dead. One would not choose in this circumstance to fully insure, or to insure at all, for general damages such as pain and suffering or for hedonic damages, and compensation should, on welfare economics grounds, *not* be set above the level at which one would choose to insure. Viscusi (2000a, b, 2008) has made these points repeatedly.

The VSL measure as we have seen has nothing to do with optimal (insurance) compensation, since the individuals in VSL studies are revealing small money-risk exposure tradeoffs, and not certain death or catastrophic injury tradeoffs. Rather, VSL is an efficiency measure: it expresses the idea that deterrence should be undertaken as long as the costs expended yield a positive net payoff when the VSL is used to evaluate the payoff.

Two law professors, E. Posner and Sunstein (2005), proposed to award or add VSL damages in wrongful death cases. There is no economic rationale for this proposal, and, if enacted, would result in large awards against those defendants who could be paying out the much larger amounts. The result would be price increases in associated products and services, including insurance. Viscusi (2008 and elsewhere) argues that such a proposal would be inefficient because it would add unwanted insurance costs to the costs of goods and services.

It is sometimes argued that, since the US government uses the VSL in a regulatory context, that the same measure should be used as guides to compensation by courts. In fact, Viscusi (2007), the US Department of Justice, defending the government, makes the proper distinction between regulation and compensation.

14.5   MISLEADING NAME

From the beginning, Thomas Schelling (1968) was clear that what was being valued were anonymous statistical lives, and not the value of any particular person's life. The amounts were totals of amounts people were willing to pay to achieve small risk reductions, and not the amount that anyone was willing to receive in exchange for giving up their life.

Unfortunately the words "value of life" evoke philosophical and moral meanings which differ drastically from the technical economic VSL concept. Cameron (2008) offers many examples, including a press release by Senator Barbara Boxer excoriating the EPA in 2008 for demeaning human life, when it announced its intention to decrease its VSL from $8.1 million to $7.8 million. The term has created confusion and controversy in politics, in courtrooms and in the public at large. For some, "life is priceless" so that any positive value is meaningless and sacrilegious. Undoubtedly, the fact that governments were using something called a "value of life" helped make it acceptable to use that term and the associated values elsewhere, including in the courtroom.

The USEPA (2016) has announced its intention to scrap the "value of life" name, but has not chosen an alternative; two candidates are "value of mortality risk" and "value of risk reductions."

14.6   VSL APPLICABILITY IN FORENSIC ECONOMICS

Despite the lack of connection between VSL and optimal compensation, a few courts have permitted economic testimony about the VSL to their jurors.[2] Most forensic economists believe that, even if permitted, they have nothing to offer as economists to help jurors make an appropriate award for any of the items among the jury instructions that might conceivably be related to "hedonic damages" or VSL, such as pain and suffering or the loss of some aspects of a normal life.[3]

As Viscusi (2000a, b) has pointed out, there are two appropriate uses of the VSL in the courtroom. One is in products liability cases, where the issue is: did the manufacturer take proper precautions in designing the product. In this case, the VSL is being used for the same purposes that the government uses it, namely, to properly conduct a cost–benefit analysis. A second use may be regarding punitive damages, where the jury hears evidence about whether the defendant's conduct was reasonable, that is, whether proper (efficient) precautions were undertaken.

Regarding the use of VSL in personal injury and wrongful death cases for compensation purposes, it is in the former, and almost exclusively by plaintiffs, where it is offered. I know of no state's Wrongful Death Act where hedonic losses that would have been experienced after the date of death by the deceased plaintiff are permitted. What is sometimes attempted is that a VSL, perhaps net of support, is suggested, along with a percentage loss, to reflect the loss of relationship of the decedent to the survivors.

The problem with such an application of a percentage to a VSL to reflect a loss of relationship in a death case is that there is absolutely no basis for doing so in the construction of the VSL, which only measures the decedent's marginal tradeoffs involving his *own* life.

There are two approaches employed in personal injury cases. In the first, one or a few VSL values are offered to the jury, along with the statement that they come from the US government or professional literature. In the second approach, a VSL net of income and related pecuniary damages is offered, along with an invitation to apply a personal injury percentage (PIP) of the total, reflecting the injuries of the plaintiff.

Regarding the selection of a PIP in a personal injury case, Jones (1994) points out that there is absolutely no basis on which anyone can say that an injury renders one 20 % dead or 40 % dead. There is simply no scale on which measurements between being dead and being alive can be meaningfully measured: the attributes are incommensurable. The VSL number, as we have seen, comes from a death probability tradeoff. However, if an economic expert wanted to apply the methodology of Eq. (14.12), the proper measure would be the VSI. As noted earlier, the VSI ranges from $20,000 to $70,000. This is never done, for obvious reasons.

If one were nevertheless to employ a PIP, one would need to explain why the VSI, the best direct evidence, was being ignored, and the completely *ad hoc* PIP procedure was substituted. In addition, since the application is to an individual, one would need to utilize a far more sophisticated procedure than a "one size fits all" VSL number; rather, as discussed above, the expert should tailor the results to the individual. Ignoring income, age and other personal characteristics is inconsistent with the findings in the VSL literature being relied upon.

Conclusion

The VSL literature is well entrenched in labor economics and in public policy analysis. The measure was designed for a purpose completely different from providing a measure of compensation to personal injury or wrongful death victims or estates. Instead, it measures not a "make whole" amount but a small *ex ante* tradeoff of anonymous persons. The tradeoff cannot be extrapolated from the very small probabilities on which it is estimated to an *ex post* 100 % probability of injury or death to a specific person. Ignoring these problems, which alone are dispositive, it is theoretically inappropriate to apply *ad hoc* PIPs to the VSLs in studies involving death probabilities, especially when VSI numbers are readily available.

Notes

1. It would be of interest to test the null hypothesis that $\beta_3 = 0$, especially since this is maintained both in many studies and in the FE work with which I am familiar.
2. Chapter 16 of this volume offers details about states and legal aspects.
3. This latter point is discussed in Chap. 13 of this volume.

References

Albrecht, G. R. (1994). The application of the hedonic damages concept to wrongful death and personal injury litigation. *Journal of Forensic Economics,* 7(Spring/Summer), 143–150.

Aldy, J. E., & Viscusi, W. K. (2007). Age differences in the value of statistical life: Revealed preference evidence. *Review of Environmental Economics and Policy,* 1(2), 241–260.

Aldy, J. E., & Viscusi, W. K. (2008). Adjusting the value of a statistical life for age and cohort effects. *The Review of Economics and Statistics, 90*(3), 573–581.

Arrow, K. J. (1964, April). Optimal allocation of risk bearing, *Review of Economic Studies, 3.* 91–96.

Arrow, K. J. (1971). *Essays in the theory of risk bearing.* Chicago: Markham.

Arrow, K. J. (1974). Optimal insurance and generalized deductibles. *Scandinavian Actuarial Journal,* 1–42. Reprinted in collected papers of Kenneth J. Arrow,

Vol. 3: Individual choice under certainty and uncertainty. Cambridge: Harvard University Press, 1984, 212–260.

Arrow, K. J. (1997). Invaluable goods. *Journal of Economics Literature, 35*(2), 757–765.

Ashenfelter, O. (2006). Measuring the value of a statistical life: Problems and prospects. *Economic Journal, 116,* C10–C23.

Bellavance, F., Dionne, G., & Lebeau, M. (2009). The value of a statistical life: A meta-analysis with a mixed effects regression model. *Journal of Health Economics, 28,* 444–464.

Berlá, E. P., Brookshire, M. L., & Smith, S. V. (1990). Hedonic damages and personal injury: A conceptual approach. *Journal of Forensic Economics, 3*(1), 1–8.

Black, D. A., & Kniesner, T. J. (2003). On the measurement of job risk in hedonic wage models. *Journal of Risk and Uncertainty, 27,* 205–220.

Blomquist, G. C. (1979). Value of life saving: Implications of consumption activity. *Journal of Political Economy, 87*(3), 540–558.

Blomquist, G. C., Miller, T. R., & Levy, D. T. (1996). Values of risk reduction implied by motorist use of protection equipment. *Journal of Transport Economics and Policy, 30*(1), 55–66.

Blomquist, G. C., Dickie, M. & O'Conor, R. M. (2010). Willingness to pay for improving fatality risks and asthma symptoms: Values for children and adults of all ages. *Resource and Energy Economics, 33*(2), 410–425 [or O'Connor—spelling?].

Brookshire, M. L., & Ireland, T. R. (1994). Converting from a present value lump sum to a future payment stream. *Journal of Forensic Economics, 4*(2), 151–158.

Brookshire, M. L., & Smith, S. V. (1990). *Economic/hedonic damages: The practice book for plaintiff and defense attorneys.* Chapter 9, 161–175. Cincinnati: Anderson Publishing Company.

Brookshire, M. L., Luthy, M. R., & Slesnick, F. L. (2004). Forensic economists, their methods and estimates of forecast variables: A 2003 survey study. *Litigation Economics Review, 6*(2), 28–44.

Bruce, C. (2001). Hedonic damages as deterrent: A reply to Viscusi. *Journal of Forensic Economics, 14*(2, Spring/Summer), 167–173.

Cameron, T. A. (2008). The value of a statistical life: [They] do not think it means what [we] think it means. *AERE Newsletter, 28.* An expanded version is available at: http://pages.uoregon.edu/cameron/vita/REEP_VSL_102509.pdf

Caragonne, P. (1993). The use of the Berla scale in quantifying hedonic damages: A case management perspective. *The Journal of Forensic Economics, 7*(1), 47–68.

Chestnut, L. G., & Violette, D. M. (1990). The relevance of willingess-to-pay estimates of the value of a statistical life in determining wrongful death awards. *Journal of Forensic Economics, 3*(3), 75–89.

Ciecka, J. E. (1992). Why hedonic measures are irrelevant to wrongful death litigation: Comment. *Journal of Legal Economics, 2*(2), 51–53.

Ciecka, J. E., & Epstein, S. (1995a). A comment on the use of value of life estimates in wrongful death litigation. *Journal of Legal Economics, 5*(1), 75–80.

Ciecka, J. E., & Epstein, S. (1995b). The use of value of life estimates in wrongful death matters: A rejoinder. *Journal of Legal Economics, 5*(3), 81–84.

Cohen, M. A., & Miller, T. R. (2003). Willingness to award non-monetary damages and the implied value of life from Jury awards. *International Review of Law and Economics, 23,* 165–181.

Dickens, W. T. (1990). Assuming the can opener: Wage estimates and the value of life. *Journal of Forensic Economics, 3*(3), 51–60.

Dillingham, A. E. (1985). The influence of risk variable definition on value-of-life estimates. *Economic Inquiry, 23*(2), 277–294.

Dillingham, A. E., Miller, T., & Levy, D. T. (1996). A more general and unified measure for valuing labour market risk. *Applied Economics, 28,* 537–542.

Doucouliagos, C., Stanley, T. D., & Giles, M. (2012). Are estimates of the value of a statistical life exaggerated? *Journal of Health Economics, 31,* 197–206.

Doucouliagos, H., Stanley, T. D., & Viscusi, W. K. (2014). Publication selection and the income elasticity of the value of a statistical life. *Journal of Health Economics, 33,* 67–75.

Dreze, J. (1962). L'utilite sociale d'une vie humaine. *Revue Francaise de Recherche Operationalle, 6,* 93–118.

Frankel, M., & Linke, C. M. (1992). The value of life and hedonic damages: Some unresolved issues. *Journal of Forensic Economics, 5*(3), 233–247.

Frederick, S., & Lowenstein, G. (1999). Hedonic adaptation, Chapter 16. In D. Kahneman, E. Diener & N. Schwartz (Eds.), *Well being: The foundations of hedonic psychology.* New York: The Russell Sage Foundation.

Gilbert, R. F. (1995a). A review of the Monte Carlo evidence concerning hedonic value of life estimates. *Journal of Forensic Economics, 8*(2, Spring/Summer), 125–130.

Gilbert, R. F. (1995b). In defense of the application of hedonic models to wrongful death and personal injury litigation. *Journal of Forensic Economics, 8*(1, Winter), 25–35.

Gilbert, R. F. (1995c). The alleged persistent misapplication of economics vs. the economic value of life: A comment [on Havrilesky 1995]. *Journal of Forensic Economics, 8*(3, Fall), 279–286.

Griliches, Z. (Ed.) (1971). *Price indexes and quality change.* Cambridge: Harvard University Press.

Hakes, J. K., & Viscusi, W. K. (2007). Automobile seatbelt usage and the value of statistical life. *Southern Economic Journal, 73,* 659–676.

Hammitt, J. K., & Liu, J. (2004). Effects of disease type and latency on the value of mortality risk. *Journal of Risk and Uncertainty, 28,* 73–95.

Hammitt, J. K., & Robinson, L. A. (2011). The income elasticity of the value per statistical life: Transferring estimates between high and low income populations. *Journal of Benefit-Cost Analysis, 2*, 1–27.

Hammitt, J. K., & Treich, N. (2007). Statistical vs. identified lives in benefit-cost analysis. *Journal of Risk and Uncertainty, 35*, 45–66.

Havrilesky, T. (1990). Valuing life in the courts: An overview. *Journal of Forensic Economics, 3*(3), 71–74.

Havrilesky, T. (1995). The persistent misapplication of the 'hedonic damages' concept to wrongful death and personal injury litigation, [Reply to Albrecht 1994]. *Journal of Forensic Economics, 8*(1), 49–54.

Hersch, J. (1998). Compensating differentials for gender-specific job injury risks. *American Economic Review, 88*(3), 598–627.

Hersch, J., & Pickton, T. S. (1995). Risk-taking activities and heterogeneity of job-risk tradeoffs. *Journal of Risk and Uncertainty, 11*(3), 205–217.

Hersch, J., & Viscusi, W. K. (1990). Cigarette smoking, seatbelt use, and differences in wage-risk tradeoffs. *Journal of Human Resources, 25*(2), 202–227.

Hersch, J., & Viscusi, W. K. (2010). Immigrant status and the value of statistical life. *Journal of Human Resources, 45*(3), 749–771.

Ioannidis, J. P. A. (2005). Why most published research findings are false. *PLOS Medicine, 2*(8), 0696–0701.

Ireland, T. R. (1995). Application of the hedonic damages concept to wrongful death and personal injury litigation: A comment. *The Journal of Forensic Economics, 8*(1), 93–94.

Ireland, T. R. (1996). Hedonic estimates in personal injury analysis: Differences from wrongful death analysis. *The Journal of Forensic Economics, 9*(2), 113–118.

Ireland, T. R. (2010). Different methods used to derive hedonic damages in litigation. *Forensic Rehabilitation and Economics, 3*(2), 67–78.

Ireland, T. R., & Gilbert, R. (1998). Supramonetary values, the value of life, and the utility theory meanings of tort damages. *Journal of Forensic Economics, 11*(3), 189–201.

Ireland, T. R., & Marks, P. (2000). Hedonic damages ten years later: A symposium. *Journal of Forensic Economics, 13*(2), 105–110.

Ireland, T. R., & Marks, P. (2007). Hedonic damages—one more time: A symposium. *Journal of Forensic Economics, 20*(2), 103–112.

Ireland, T. R., & Rodgers, J. D. (1993). Hedonic damages in wrongful death/survival actions: Equitable compensation or optimal life protection? *Journal of Legal Economics, 3*(3), 43–56.

Ireland, T. R., & Ward, J. O. (1996). *The new hedonics primer for economists and attorneys.* Tucson: Lawyers and Judges Publishing Company.

Ireland, T. R., Johnson, W. D., & Rodgers, J. D. (1992). Why hedonic damages are irrelevant to wrongful death litigation. *Journal of Legal Economics, 2*(1), 49–54.

Ireland, T. R., Horner, S. M., & Rodgers, J. D. (1998). *Module I: Reference guide for valuing economic loss in personal injury, wrongful death and survival actions, part three: Hedonic damages. Expert economic testimony.* Tucson: Lawyers & Judges Publishing Company.

Johansson, P. O. (2002). On the definition and age-dependency of the vale of statistical life. *Journal of Risk and Uncertainty, 25*, 251–263.

Jones, D. D. (1994). Hedonic damages and the index problem. *Journal of Forensic Economics, 7*(2, Spring/Summer), 193–196.

Jones-Lee, M. W. (1976). *The value of life: An economic analysis.* Chicago: University of Chicago Press.

Jones-Lee, M. W. (1989). *The economics of safety and physical risk.* Oxford: Basil Blackwell.

Kahneman, D., Diener, E., & Schwartz, N. (Eds.) (1999). *Well being: The foundations of hedonic psychology.* New York: The Russell Sage Foundation.

Kaplow, L. (2005). The value of statistical life and the coefficient of relative risk aversion. *Journal of Risk and Uncertainty, 31*, 23–34.

Kniesner, T. J., & Leeth, J. (1991). Compensating wage differentials for fatal injury risk in Australia, Japan, and the United States. *Journal of Risk and Uncertainty, 4*, 75–90.

Kniesner, T. J., Viscusi, W. K., & Ziliak, J. P. (2006). Life-cycle consumption and the age-adjusted value of life. *Contributions in Economic Analysis & Policy, 5*(1), Article 4.

Kniesner, T. J., Viscusi, W. K., & Ziliak, J. P. (2010). Policy relevant heterogeneity in the value of statistical life: New evidence from panel data quantile regressions. *Journal of Risk and Uncertainty, 40*, 15–31.

Kniesner, T. J., Viscusi, W. K., Woock, C., & Ziliak, J. P. (2012). The value of a statistical life: Evidence from panel data. *Review of Economics and Statistics, 94*(1), 74–87.

Kniesner, T. J., Viscusi, W. K., & Ziliak, J. P. (2014). Willingness to accept equals willingness to pay for labor market estimates of the value of statistical life. *Journal of Risk and Uncertainty, 48*(3), 187–205.

Kochi, I., Hubbell, B., & Kramer, R. (2006). An empirical Bayes approach to combining and comparing estimates of the value of a statistical life for environmental policy analysis. *Environmental and Resource Economics, 34*, 385–406.

Krupnick, A. (2002). Commentary on: What determines the value of life? A meta-analysis. *Journal of Policy Analysis and Management, 21*(2), 275–282.

Linnerooth, J. (1979, January). The value of human life: A review of models, *Economic Inquiry, 17*(1): 52–74.

Loh, K., & Richardson, S. (2004). Foreign-born workers: Trends in fatal occupational injuries, 1996–2001. *Monthly Labor Review, 127*, 42–53.

Miller, T. R. (1989). Willingness to pay comes of age: Will the system survive? *Northwestern Law Review, 83*(4), 876–907.

Miller, T. R. (1990). The plausible range for the value of life–red herrings among the Mackerel. *Journal of Forensic Economics, 3*(3), 17–39.

Miller, T. R. (2000). Variations between countries in values of statistical life. *Journal of Transport Economics and Policy, 34*(2), 169–188.

Miller, T. R. (2007). Hedonic damages: Were the crippling blows to the golden goose well-founded? *Journal of Forensic Economics, 20*(2), 137–153.

Mishan, E. J. (1971, July/August). Evaluation of life and limb: A theoretical approach. *Journal of Political Economy, 79*, 687–705.

Mishan, E. J. (1982). *Cost-benefit analysis: An informal introduction* (3rd ed.). London: George Allen & Unwin, Chapters 45 and 46.

Moore, M. J., & Viscusi, W. K. (1988a). Doubling the estimated value of life: Results using new occupational fatality data. *Journal of Policy Analysis and Management, 7*(3), 476–490.

Moore, M. J., & Viscusi, W. K. (1988b). The quantity-adjusted value of life. *Economic Inquiry, 26*, 369–388.

Mrozek, J. R., & Taylor, L. O. (2002). What determines the value of life? A meta-analysis. *Journal of Policy Analysis and Management, 21*(2), 253–270.

Murphy, K. M., & Topel, R. H. (2006). The value of life and longevity. *Journal of Political Economy, 114*, 811–904.

Posner, R. A. (1995). *Aging and old age.* Chicago: University of Chicago Press.

Posner, E. A., & Sunstein, C. R. (2005). Dollars and death. *University of Chicago Law Review, 72*(2), 537–598.

Rosen, S. (1974). Hedonic prices and implicit markets: Product differentiation in pure competition. *Journal of Political Economy, 82*, 34–55.

Rosen, S. (1981, May). Valuing health risk. *American Economic Review*, Papers and Proceedings, *71*, 241–245.

Rosen, S. (1986). The theory of equalizing differences. In O. Ashenfelter & R. Layard (Eds.), *Handbook of labor economics* (pp. 641–692). Amsterdam: North-Holland.

Rosen, S. (1988). The value of changes in life expectancy. *Journal of Risk and Uncertainty, 1*, 285–304.

Rubin, P. H., & Calfee, J. E. (1992). Consequences of damage awards for hedonic and other nonpecuniary losses. *Journal of Forensic Economics, 5*(3, Fall), 249–260.

Schelling, T. C. (1968). The life you save may be your own. In S. B. Chase (Ed.), *Problems in public expenditure and analysis* (pp. 127–162). Washington, DC: Brookings Institution.

Shavell, S. M. (1987). *Economic analysis of accident law.* Cambridge, MA: Harvard University Press.

Shepard, D. S., & Zeckhauser, R. J. (1982). Life-cycle consumption and willingness-to-pay for increased survival. In M. W. Jones-Lee (Ed.), *The value of life and safety.* Amsterdam: North Holland.

Shepard, D., & Zeckhauser, R. (1984). Survival versus consumption. *Management Science, 30*, 423–439.

Smith, A. (1776). *The wealth of nations.* Chicago: University of Chicago Press. Modern Library Cannan Edition.

Smith, S. V. (1990). Hedonic damages in the courtroom setting—A bridge over troubled waters. *Journal of Forensic Economics, 3*(3), 41–50.

Smith, S. V. (1996). The value of life to close family members: Calculating the loss of society and companionship, Reading 31. In *The new hedonics primer for economists and attorneys.* Tucson: Lawyers & Judges Publishing Company.

Smith, V. K., Evans, M. F., Kim, H., & Taylor Jr., D. H. (2004). Do the near-elderly value mortality risks differently? *Review of Economics and Statistics, 86*, 423–429.

Tengs, T. O., Adams, M. E., Pliskin, J. S., Safran, D. G., Siegel, J. E., Weinstein, M. C., et al. (1995). Five-hundred life-saving interventions and their cost-effectiveness. *Risk Analysis, 15*(3), 369–390.

Terman, S. A. (1996). A psychiatrist's comment on 'a better alternative to hedonic damages' and a suggestion for a meta-analysis. *Journal of Forensic Economics, 9*(2, Spring/Summer), 211–221.

Thaler, R., & Rosen, S. (1975). The value of saving a life: Evidence from the labor market. In N. E. Terleckyj (Ed.), *Household production and consumption* (pp. 265–300). New York: Columbia University Press.

U.S. Department of Transportation. (2013). *Revised departmental guidance 2013:Treatment of the value of preventing fatalities and injuries in preparing economic analysis.* Available at: http://www.dot.gov/office-policy/transportation-policy/guidance-treatment-economic-value-statistical-life.

U.S. Environmental Protection Agency. (1999). *The benefits and costs of the Clean Air Act 1990 to 2010.* Report 410-R-99-001. Washington, DC: Office of Air and Radiation, USEPA. Internet: http://www.epa.gov/oar/sect812/copy99.html

U.S. Environmental Protection Agency. (2000a). *Guidelines for preparing economic analyses.* Report 240-R-00003. Washington, DC: Office of the Administrator, USEPA. Internet: http://yosemite1.epa.gov/ee/epa/eed.nsf/pages/guidelines

U.S. Environmental Protection Agency. (2000b). *Regulatory impact analysis: Heavy-duty engine and vehicle standards and highway diesel fuel sulfur control requirements.* Report 420-R-00-026. Washington, DC: Office of Air and Radiation, USEPA.

U.S. Environmental Protection Agency. (2016, February). *Valuing mortality risk reductions for policy: A meta-analytic approach prepared by the USEPA's Office of Policy, National Center for Environmental Economics, for review by the EPA's Science Advisory Board, Environmental Economics Advisory Committee.* Accessed 26 Mar 2016 at https://yosemite.epa.gov/sab/sabproduct.nsf/0/0CA9E92 5C9A702F285257F380050C842/$File/VSL%20white%20paper_final_020516.pdf

U.S. Federal Aviation Administration. (1998, June). *Economic values for evaluation of federal aviation administration investment and regulatory program.* Report no. FAA-APO-98-8. Washington, DC: Department of Transportation. Internet: http://www.api.faa.gov/economic/TOC.PDF.

U.S. Office of Management and Budget. (1992). *Guidelines and discount rates for benefit-cost analysis of Federal programs.* Circular A-94. Washington, DC: The White House. Internet: http://www.whitehouse.gov/omb/circulars/a094/a094.pdf.

U.S. Office of Management and Budget. (1996). *Economic analysis of federal regulations under executive order 12866.* Washington, DC: The White House. Internet: http://www.whitehouse.gov/omb/inforeg/riaguide.html.

U.S. Office of Management and Budget. (2001) *Making sense of regulation: 2001 report to congress on the costs and benefits of regulations and unfunded mandates on state, local, and tribal entities.* Washington, DC: The White House. Internet: http://www.whitehouse.gov/omb/inforeg/costbenefitreport.pdf.

Viscusi, W. K. (1978a). Labor market valuations of life and limb: Empirical evidence and policy implications. *Public Policy, 26*(3), 359–386.

Viscusi, W. K. (1978b). Wealth effects and earnings premiums for job hazards. *Review of Economics and Statistics, 60*(3), 408–416.

Viscusi, W. K. (1980). Union, labor market structure, and the welfare implications of the quality of work. *Journal of Labor Research, 1*(1), 175–192.

Viscusi, W. K. (1981). Occupational safety and health regulation: Its impact and policy alternatives. In J. P. Crecine (Ed.), *Research in public policy analysis and management* (Vol. 2, pp. 281–299). Greenwich: JAI Press.

Viscusi, W. K. (1990a). The econometric basis for estimates of the value of life. *Journal of Forensic Economics, 3*(3), 61–70.

Viscusi, W. K. (1990b). The value of life: Has Voodoo economics come to the courts? *Journal of Forensic Economics, 3*(3), 1–15.

Viscusi, W. K. (1993). The value of risks to life and health. *Journal of Economic Literature, 31*, 1912–1946.

Viscusi, W. K. (2000a). The value of life in legal contexts: Survey and critique. *American Law and Economics Review, 2*(1), 195–222.

Viscusi, W. K. (2000b). Misuses and proper uses of the values of life in legal contexts. *Journal of Forensic Economics, 13*(2), 111–125.

Viscusi, W. K. (2003). Racial differences in labor market values of a statistical life. *Journal of Risk and Uncertainty, 27*(3), 239–256.

Viscusi, W. K. (2004). The value of life: Estimates with risks by occupation and industry. *Economic Inquiry, 42*(1), 29–48.

Viscusi, W. K. (2007). The flawed hedonic damages measure of compensation for wrongful death and personal injury. *Journal of Forensic Economics, 20*(2), 113–135.

Viscusi, W. K. (2008). The value of life. In S. N. Durlauf & L. E. Blume (Eds.), *The new Palgrave dictionary of economics* (2nd ed.). London: Macmillan.

Viscusi, W. K. (2009a). Valuing risks of death from terrorism and natural disasters. *Journal of Risk and Uncertainty, 38*, 191–213.

Viscusi, W. K. (2009b). The devaluation of life. *Regulation and Governance, 3*, 103–127.

Viscusi, W. K. (2010). Policy challenges of the heterogeneity of the value of statistical life. *Foundations and Trends in Microeconomics, 6*, 99–172.

Viscusi, W. K. (2013, October). Using data from the census of fatal occupational injuries to estimate the 'value of a statistical life'. *Monthly Labor Review, 31*, 99–172.

Viscusi, W. K. (2014). Using data from the census of fatal occupational injuries to estimate the 'value of a statistical life. In M. J. Machina & W. Kip Viscusi (Eds.), *The value of individual and societal risks to life and health* (pp. 385–452). Amsterdam: Elsevier.

Viscusi, W. K., & Aldy, J. E. (2003). The value of a statistical life: A critical review of market estimates throughout the world. *Journal of Risk and Uncertainty, 27*(1), 5–76.

Viscusi, W. K., & Aldy, J. E. (2007). Labor market estimates of the senior discount for the value of statistical life. *Journal of Environmental Economics and Management, 53*(3), 377–392.

Viscusi, W. K., & Evans, W. (1990). Utility functions that are dependent on one's health status: Estimates and economic implications. *American Economic Review, 80*, 353–374 .

Viscusi, W. K., & Gentry, E. P. (2015). The value of a statistical life for transportation regulations: A test of the benefits transfer methodology. *Journal of Risk and Uncertainty, 51*(1), 53–77.

Viscusi, W. K., & Hersch, J. (2001). Cigarette smokers as job risk takers. *Review of Economics and Statistics, 83*(2), 269–280.

Viscusi, W. K., & Moore, M. J. (1989). Rates of time preference and valuations of the duration of life. *Journal of Public Economics, 38*, 297–317.

Viscusi, W. K., & Zeckhauser, R. J. (1994). The fatality and injury costs of expenditures. *Journal of Risk and Uncertainty, 8*(1), 19–41.

Viscusi, W. K., Huber, J., & Bell, J. (2014). Assessing whether there is a cancer premium for the value of a statistical life. *Health Economics, 23*, 384–396.

Zeckhauser, R. (1975). Procedures for valuing lives. *Public Policy, 23*(4, Fall), 419–464.

CHAPTER 15

Ethical Dimensions of Forensic Economics

Frank D. Tinari

"There are unavoidable ethical dilemmas in every profession and industry, of course, but the dilemmas entrepreneurs face are more formidable and more difficult to manage. ... entrepreneurs have little time or focus for monitoring their own behavior" (Hanson 2015). Economic experts embody both academic knowledge and practitioners' knowledge and experience. So Hanson's observation would appear to apply to forensic economists whose practice may be characterized as small business or even entrepreneurship. But do economic experts have little time or focus to monitor their ethics-laden behavior? Or, more broadly, what is the nature of the ethical dilemmas facing forensic economists, and how successfully are they able to deal with the pressures that tempt them to act unethically?

Nearly all aspects of human life involve decision-making, and nearly all decisions have some moral or ethical component. Most people want to do the "right thing" in their daily lives including their working lives, but the fact of the matter is that incentives and disincentives are usually present that push people's decisions in one direction or the other. But what possible ethical concerns do forensic economists face, economists who want to apply their knowledge in the most professional way possible for the attorneys who hire them?

F.D. Tinari (✉)
Professor Emeritus, Seton Hall University, USA

© The Author(s) 2016   245
F.D. Tinari (ed.), *Forensic Economics*,
DOI 10.1057/978-1-137-56392-7_15

15.1   Pressures to Act Unethically

State and federal courts all share at least one universal proscription for experts, namely, that experts shall provide their best, impartial, professional opinion within their fields, and that any form of compensation tied to the results of their work for the courts is strictly forbidden. In other words, contingency fees for work done by experts engaged in litigated matters are not permitted.

In a wide-ranging article on ethical issues faced by applied economists, DeMartino (2013) sets out three categories of pressures to act unethically: pressures to generate biased work, market pressures, and time constraints.[1] The first category, pressure to generate biased work, refers to client expectations of the expert "to produce evidence that justifies decisions that are already reached prior to the execution of the economic research." (p. 9) DeMartino identifies a related bias, namely, the pressure to avoid certain kinds of research. For forensic economists, this might mean not wanting to publish certain findings if such findings were to adversely affect how the economist calculates economic damages. It could also include choosing not to do research that might have a similar effect.

Regarding the second category, market pressures "sometimes push the economist in the direction of providing the client with the result that best serves its interest rather than that which is best supported by the evidence." (DeMartino 2013, p. 11) Given that there is a fair amount of room for forensic economists to make judgments regarding a number of elements in the calculation of damages, the pressure to shade one's analysis toward the viewpoint of the client is very real, indeed. A related pressure not mentioned by DeMartino is competitive market pressure that comes into play when damages experts, in order to attract additional clients, do or say things that cross the ethical line. Such unethical decisions are self-imposed and in the complete control of the expert.

Finally, in forensic economics work, it is not unusual to face court deadlines for submission of an economic loss report. If the time constraint is too severe to do a thorough and complete appraisal of economic damages, the expert could turn down the assignment or, if the assignment is taken, the time pressure may cause the expert to cut corners in order to meet the deadline, thereby creating an ethical problem.[2]

To promote ethical decision-making among forensic economics experts, both the American Academy of Economic and Financial Experts (AAEFE) and the National Association of Forensic Economics (NAFE,

2004) developed statements of ethical standards to help guide their members (see Appendix A and B for the respective statements).

> Although these ethical statements do not have the same force as legally recognized standards in other professions such as accounting or engineering, they do make explicit what is expected of their members. In the case of NAFE, moreover, members are required to attest to their adherence to the Statement of Ethical Principles and Practice. (Tinari 2010, p. 400)

Given the similarity between the statements of the two organizations, we examine the NAFE statement to determine the types of ethical issues of concern that are implied by the standards they set forth.[3]

Regarding the pressures exerted by clients to have the expert provide output favorable to their side, the NAFE Statement of Ethical Principles and Principles of Professional Practice (SEP) contains statements regarding engagement (decline assignments if asked to assume invalid facts), compensation (reject contingency fee arrangements) and consistency (apply the same methodology regardless of client). The time-constraint issue is not addressed directly in the SEP, but it does contain a number of principles that set forth minimum standards of work that may preclude accepting assignments with limited time allowance. The SEP statements of diligence (employ sound methods), disclosure (be prepared to disclose all methodology and sources), and knowledge (stay current in one's discipline) set out standards that should not be short-circuited due to time constraints or any other reason.

The SEP contains two principles that are not encompassed within DeMartino's categories, but are ethically important nonetheless. The first is a discourse principle that seeks to preserve open and academic discussion of professional matters by prohibiting use or citation of oral remarks made at educational conferences without the permission of the person who made the remarks. The other is a responsibility principle that encourages members to promote the SEP in their litigation work, and to offer criticisms of members who violate the principles.[4]

15.2   Unethical Behavior and Its Motivations

Given this background, what do we mean by the unethical behavior of forensic economists? Unethical behavior includes, but may not be limited to, any of the following:

(a) Assuming invalid facts or assumptions
(b) Slanting or changing methods and sources for different clients
(c) Accepting contingency fee arrangements
(d) Doing less than professional work to meet deadlines
(e) Using out-of-date or unreliable methods and/or insufficient data
(f) Failing to supply information sufficient for others to replicate one's findings
(g) Lying about one's background or experience
(h) Using oral statements of others made at professional conferences without permission

But why would any testifying expert act in one or more of these ways? Forensic economists operate within an adversarial legal process. As documented in a survey of attorneys who made use of economic experts (Colella, Johnson and Tinari 1995), attorneys strive to do everything they can to put the best light on their client's position. Correspondingly, attorneys will name witnesses and hire experts who will assist them in mounting a successful case. The adversarial mindset can easily spill over into pressure placed on witnesses and experts by the attorney who engages them to make assumptions, select facts, apply methods and give testimony that would generate results most favorable to their side. So, in the first instance, we may say that the motivation to act unethically comes from some attorneys who overstep the legal and professional bounds of their own profession. Thankfully, in this writer's experience, many litigating attorneys understand their own profession's ethical guidelines and allow experts to provide professional and unbiased opinions. Nevertheless, it would be helpful if attorneys were to adopt an ethical code in relation to the experts they engage. Such a code might read as follows:

15.2.1   Lawyers' Relations with Expert Witnesses

1. Experts should be treated with respect and professional courtesy and be addressed with civility. A lawyer must always be aware that experts are involved as integral parts of the justice system.
2. To experts, a lawyer owes full disclosure of relevant facts. Lines of communication must be kept open.
3. A lawyer should respect an expert's schedule and procedures, and should provide requests well ahead of the time services are needed.
4. A lawyer should not exert undue influence on experts that would compromise the integrity, principles, ethical rules or standards of the

expert. Experts should never be asked to assume invalid representations of fact or to alter their methodologies without foundation or compelling reason.

5. A lawyer should ensure that retained experts be prepared to provide sufficient disclosure of sources of information and assumptions underlying their opinions.

6. Payment practices should be fully explained to an expert at the time the engagement is undertaken. An expert must never be exposed to contingency arrangements since they would undermine the expert's credibility or objectivity.

Alternatively, motivation can originate in the mind and practice of the testifying expert. Consulting as an expert often generates substantial monetary rewards and serves to boost the ego and reputation of the expert. Thus, some experts may make decisions that violate ethical standards in order to generate additional revenue for their practice, or for other personal reasons (such as slanting their analysis for a friend or relative in a litigated matter).

In a recent discussion regarding ethical problems on one of the electronic forensic economics lists, a member relayed that in an initial meeting with the plaintiff and plaintiff's attorney to explain the case, the plaintiff, alleging permanent inability to work, discussed a good job offer he had received. The plaintiff's attorney told the plaintiff in the presence of the expert not to take the job until after the present litigation was completed. At that juncture, the expert had a decision to make: Should he take the assignment, adding to his revenue stream, or turn down the assignment because he would be asked to assume false information? The expert reported that he made excuses and bowed out of the case before being retained. However, had the expert learned of this information after being named in the case as the plaintiff's expert, the ethical issues would be more complicated. If the expert were to decide to drop the assignment in the face of possible pending deposition or trial testimony, his action might endanger the entire case and would expose him to legal action by the plaintiff. Alternatively, if the expert decided to remain in the case until its conclusion, there would still be a chance that he would be asked about the plaintiff at trial and, under oath, would have to tell the truth. If so, again there would be the possibility of litigation against him, although it is likely the expert would prevail. Many forensic economists who regularly work on cases and testify at trial pay for professional errors and omissions insurance in order to have resources available to them in the event of involvement in a personal or professional law suit against them.

A more obvious example of unethical behavior in the calculation of economic damages is the expert who uses a higher earnings growth rate when engaged by a plaintiff attorney, and uses a lower growth rate when engaged by a defendant attorney in a similar case. And there are other opportunities for forensic economists to alter their opinion of economic damages. An exercise was carried out by a colleague, Kurt Krueger, which demonstrates that variations in any of a number of the expert's selected values can cause substantial differences in the final value of loss, as outlined in Table 15.1.

Table 15.1 demonstrates that a base earnings figure for a decedent could vary as well as the age-earnings profile selected, the length of the individual's assumed worklife expectancy, the unemployment probability adjustment, the extent of personal consumption being deducted from earnings, the selected earnings growth rate, and the interest rate used for discounting future values. The ultimate present values that were calculated under alternative input values ranged from $315,000 to $1,750,000, reflecting the substantial impact that variations in assumptions can make.

The ethical principle in this example is not that picking a different assumption can alter the valuation outcome. Rather, it is that an expert should determine assumptions with great care, ensuring that there is methodological consistency from one assignment to the next, and between plaintiff and defense work.

15.3   Ethics-Enhancing Mechanisms in Tort Litigation

Having reviewed the potential ethical violations faced by economic damages experts, we now turn to the environment in which forensic economics is carried out. Do forensic economists, in their work as experts in tort litigation, encounter mechanisms sufficient to allay the temptations to act unethically?

In his analysis of applied economic work in litigation, DeMartino (2013) recognizes that forensic economists operate within a unique environment characterized by substantial counterbalancing forces that serve to reduce the ethical pressures felt by experts. These forces are embedded in the adversarial process of tort litigation. The adversarial nature of law suits creates real constraints on the behavior of experts at three potential

Table 15.1 Two sets of assumptions and corresponding estimates of the present value of lost financial support for deceased 25-year-old married female

Variable	Plaintiff-favoring assumptions	Defendant-favoring assumptions
1. Base earnings	$35,000 (earnings at time of death)	$30,000 (average over last three years)
2. Age-earnings profile (future wage adjustments based on age)[a]	Average age-earnings profile for males with bachelor's degree	Average (median) age-earnings profile for females with bachelor's degree
3. Length of work life	To age 67 (current social security retirement age) adjusted by risk of death	Expected work life of females with Bachelor's degree (33.2 years to age 58.2, reduced again by husband's survival probability)
4. Unemployment	3 % (historical average for Bachelor's degree holders, 25+ years old)	Historical population average of 6 %
5. Personal consumption (decedent's consumption of earnings)	25 % of own earnings	30 % of the average of the last three years of family earnings of $60,000 which equals $18,000 (60 % of the decedent's average earnings)
6. Net discount rate (discount rate minus earnings growth rate)	0.0 %	2.50 %
7. Present value of earnings	$2,342,738	$788,521
8. Present value of personal consumption	($585,685)	($473,113)
9. Net earnings loss (line 7 minus line 8)	$1,757,054	$315,408

[a]The US Department of Labor publishes earnings data by age, gender, education, and race. These cross-sectional age-earnings profiles capture the earnings trend associated with increased age at a given point of time. Using such data allows the earnings loss projection to capture the life-cycle of earnings growth associated with age alone. Some forensic economists justify using age-earnings profiles for *men* in evaluating the lost earnings of women by arguing that doing so eliminates the effects of past discrimination still reflected in tables for women

stages, depending on the state venue and its rules (see Tinari 1993, 2014, pp. 94–5):

(1) Report Stage. The first level of constraint occurs after submission of a written economic loss report. The opinions contained in the expert report may be subject to written rebuttal by an economist hired by the adversary attorney in a case. Such scrutiny is all the more likely when substantial financial interests are at stake. As DeMartino (2013) states: "[T]he economist's work may very well undergo a more rigorous test than it would under the review process of a prestigious journal" (p. 12).

(2) Discovery Deposition Stage. The second level is that of deposition cross-examination wherein, under oath, the forensic economist must explain his or her methods, sources, communications, research and opinions. This is often preceded by a comprehensive request for all documents and communications on which the expert relied in developing an opinion of economic losses. The adversarial pressure will vary, depending as it does on the personality and strategy of the examining attorney. Other things equal, the more biased or exaggerated the expert opinion being offered, the more likely it is that opposing scrutiny will be triggered. At professional and social gatherings, experienced forensic economists often relate stories of deposition cross-examination that would make anyone's palms clammy.

(3) Trial Stage. While it is a fact that most litigation settles before ever getting to trial, the first two levels of potential challenge and examination still serve as strong incentives to minimize bias and unprofessional conduct. Also, since attorneys representing their clients do not know for sure whether or not there will be settlement before trial commences, they need to make sure that their experts are credible and prepared to give trial testimony. At this stage, experts must be ready to clearly explain their analysis and conclusions, again under oath, and be able to hold to their opinions in the face of cross-examination.

At all three stages, it is the professional obligation of the expert to answer questions fully and truthfully, irrespective of the implications of one's answers for the parties' positions. Over all, therefore, the adversarial process poses threats to forensic economic consultants who do biased or otherwise unethical work. Most other applied economists do not face this tri-level gauntlet that is part and parcel of working on litigated matters.

This is why DeMartino (2013) believes that there is a lower level of unethical behavior among forensic economists than among other applied economists: "The adversarial process ensures that tainted or otherwise inadequate work will fail to advance the client's interests; hence, clients will rationally come to demand expertise rather than opinion." (p. 12)

Ward and Thornton (2013) tabulated the views of NAFE members who responded to an ethics survey. A common theme among respondents was that problems in reports issued by economic damages experts seem to stem from incompetence, a lack of knowledge of the literature in the field, and a lack of background facts to make proper calculations, rather than outright ethical violations.

Related to adversarial constraints is the fact that an expert's reputation is, perhaps, his or her most valuable asset. Therefore, forensic economists have a strong incentive to maintain as much objectivity and consistency as possible. The fear of losing credibility is acknowledged as one of the most powerful incentives for forensic economists to perform professionally and ethically (Sattler 1991, pp. 264–66).[5] And credibility can be lost outside of the adversarial, cross-examination process. The ubiquity of the internet in accessing information serves to reinforce adversarial pressures inasmuch as, in our experience, attorneys have ready access to their colleagues at meetings, on discussion lists, blogs and the like, and can obtain copies of an expert's reports and testimony transcripts from other cases. The existence of a record of past depositions and trial testimony helps to enforce consistency in methods. Experts who ignore such potential access do so at their own peril.

At present, courts in the USA have settled on well-developed requirements for accepting or rejecting expert testimony. In federal cases, opposing counsel may file a motion requesting a Daubert hearing to challenge the admissibility of an expert's testimony.[6] Similarly, in many state courts, a challenge to an expert can be made by means of a motion *in limine*. In these actions, the judge holds the hearing and acts as the court's "gatekeeper" to determine who, if anyone, would or would not be permitted to testify before the jury.[7]

Another factor serving to minimize biased work is the policy, widely used by forensic experts, of providing one's services to either side of a litigated matter. With rare exceptions, such availability forces the forensic economist to maintain consistent and defensible methods of analysis: "Providing services to clients of divergent interests is consistent with the conception of the work as objective and unbiased. At the same time ... it enhances the consultant's professional reputation" (DeMartino 2013, p. 13). A colleague has related that in personal injury matters a retention rate for plaintiff of over 70 % is normal, and few economists testify at trial for the defense. So, balance may be less important than consistency and unbiasedness in the methodologies used by the expert.

15.4   CONCLUSION

While there remains a certain degree of concern, both within and outside the profession of forensic economics, over the potential for unethical behavior, the general consensus seems to be that ethical violations are the exception to the norm. As explained in this chapter, the countervailing forces embedded in civil litigation go a long way toward uncovering, exposing and preventing various forms of unethical and unprofessional work by experts. In part, this is the result of the efforts of experienced attorneys and, in part, the efforts made by forensic economists in their adherence to high ethical standards.

In addition, our field has seen more than 25 years of published research that has led to the development and acceptance of better measurements and sounder methodologies that set the standard for acceptable work as experts. This, too, constrains individuals from producing uninformed evaluations of loss that make use of sloppy methods, out-of-date statistics, and unacceptable sources. To this point, in response to a question in a NAFE survey asking whether or not higher ethical standards are more common today, one member wrote:

> The availability today of a substantial literature about practically every topic in forensic economics is the primary reason for the more ethical behavior. It is no longer as easy for maverick experts to design unusual models on their own and exaggerate the economic damages in one direction or another. (cited in Ward and Thornton 2013, p. 38)

One other common observation by forensic economists is that many errors and problems stem not from unethical behavior as much as incompetence on the part of some experts. A lack of knowledge of the literature, or current data sources, or newer methodologies, is often encountered by economists who are asked to examine and rebut the opposing side's economic expert. Ward and Thornton (2013) observe that "what is perceived as a problem of unethical behavior may instead be the result of incompetence in certain cases. Others, though, would argue that incompetence itself is a form of unethical behavior" (p. 39). This criticism, of course, harkens back to the Knowledge standard in the NAFE SEP: "Practitioners of forensic economics should strive to maintain a current knowledge base of their discipline." Not doing so, therefore, would be viewed as a breach of professional ethical standards.

Appendix A: American Academy of Economic and Financial Experts

Ethics Statement

As a practicing forensic economist and a member of the American Academy of Economic and Financial Experts, I pledge to provide unbiased and accurate economic analysis for all litigation related engagements, to strive to improve the science of forensic economics, and to protect the integrity of the profession through adherence to the following tenets of ethical practice:

1. Employment

While all forensic economists have the discretionary right to accept retention for any case or proceeding within their expertise, they should decline involvement in any litigation when asked to take or support a predetermined position, when having ethical concerns about the nature of the requested assignment, or when compensation is contingent upon the outcome.

2. Honesty and Candor

Forensic economists shall be honest, thorough and open in their analyses and shall not provide the retaining or opposing attorney or the court, any information, through commission or omission that they know to be false or misleading. They shall exert due diligence, and at all times strive to use competent judgment to avoid the use of invalid or unreliable information.

3. Disclosure

Forensic economists shall clearly state the sources of information and material assumptions leading to their opinions. Such disclosure should be in sufficient detail to allow identification of specific sources relied upon, and replication of the analytical conclusions by a competent economist with reasonable effort.

4. Neutrality

Forensic economists shall at all times attempt to operate from a position of neutrality with respect to their calculations and analyses. Whether retained by the plaintiff or the defense, the approach, methodology and conclusions should be essentially the same.

5. Knowledge

Forensic economists shall at all times attempt to maintain a current knowledge base of the discipline and shall provide the retaining attorney with the full benefit of this knowledge regardless of how it may affect the outcome of the case.

6. Responsibility

Forensic economists shall at all times strive to practice within the boundaries of professional and disciplinary honesty and fairness. To this end, they must assume the responsibility of holding their colleagues in the profession accountable to the ethical principles promulgated herein.

Appendix B: Statement of Ethical Principles and Principles of Professional Practice National Association of Forensic Economics (NAFE) (Effective July 1, 2014)

Forensic economics is the scientific discipline that applies economic theories and methods to matters within a legal framework. Forensic economics covers, but is not limited to:

- The calculation of pecuniary damages in personal and commercial litigation.
- The analysis of liability, such as the statistical analysis of discrimination, the analysis of market power in antitrust disputes, and fraud detection.
- Other matters subject to legal review, such as public policy analysis, and business, property, and asset valuation.

When providing expert opinion for use as evidence by the trier of fact, a NAFE member pledges, as a condition of membership, adherence to the following:

1. Engagement

Practitioners of forensic economics should decline involvement in any litigation when they are asked to assume invalid representations of fact or alter their methodologies without foundation or compelling analytical reason.

2. Compensation

Practitioners of forensic economics should not accept contingency fee arrangements, or fee amounts associated with the size of a court award or out-of-court settlement.

3. Diligence

Practitioners of forensic economics should employ generally accepted and/or theoretically sound economic methodologies based on reliable economic data. Practitioners of forensic economics should attempt to provide accurate, fair and reasonable expert opinions, recognizing that it is not the responsibility of the practitioner to verify the accuracy or completeness of the case-specific information that has been provided.

4. Disclosure

Practitioners of forensic economics should stand ready to provide sufficient detail to allow replication of all numerical calculations, with reasonable effort, by other competent forensic economics experts, and be prepared to provide sufficient disclosure of sources of information and assumptions underpinning their opinions to make them understandable to others.

5. Consistency

While it is recognized that practitioners of forensic economics may be given a different assignment when engaged on behalf of the plaintiff than when engaged on behalf of the defense, for any given assignment, the basic assumptions, sources, and methods should not change regardless of the party who engages the expert to perform the assignment. There should be no change in methodology for purposes of favoring any party's claim.

This requirement of consistency is not meant to preclude methodological changes as new knowledge evolves, nor is it meant to preclude performing requested calculations based upon a hypothetical--as long as its hypothetical nature is clearly disclosed in the expert's report and testimony.

6. Knowledge

Practitioners of forensic economics should strive to maintain a current knowledge base of their discipline.

7. Discourse

Open, uninhibited discussion is a desired educational feature of academic and professional forensic economic conferences. Therefore, to preserve and protect the educational environment, practitioners of forensic economics will refrain from the citation of oral remarks made in an educational environment, without permission from the speaker.

8. Responsibility

Practitioners of forensic economics are encouraged to make known the existence of, and their adherence to, these principles to those retaining them to perform economic analyses and to other participants in litigation. In addition, it is appropriate for practitioners of forensic economics to offer criticisms of breaches of these principles.

NOTES

1. Some of these arguments were made earlier in his book (DeMartino, 2011).
2. In our experience, the blame sits squarely on the shoulders of the retaining attorney who, for one reason or another, delays engaging an economic expert until the very last minute. More often than not, the plaintiff's attorney is hoping to settle the case without the need to hire many experts. Also, since proving liability and causation take precedence over proving damages in the early stages of a case, attorneys tend to put off hiring economic damages experts until absolutely necessary.
3. More details regarding NAFE and its ethics statement are given in Thornton and Brookshire (2013).
4. A small minority of NAFE members argue that the absence of an ethics enforcement mechanism renders the SEP useless in curtailing unethical behavior among its members.

5. The Sattler article (1991) was one of several published in a special symposium issue on ethics in the Journal of Forensic Economics, Fall 1991. The symposium editor was Walter Johnson (1991) whose article addressed the ethical and professional responsibilities of forensic economic experts.
6. In recent years, Daubert challenges seem to have become more common. The expert whose testimony is being challenged is typically not present at the hearing, and may not even be aware that such a hearing is being held.
7. A very helpful website, created and managed by Thomas Ireland, contains listings and brief descriptions of court rulings including one section entitled "Legal Decisions Involving Admission of Expert Economic Testimony."

REFERENCES

Colella, F., Johnson, W. D., & Tinari, F. D. (1995). Attorney perspectives on the use of economic experts: survey results. *Journal of Forensic Economics, 8*(1), 13–23.

DeMartino, G. (2011). *The economist's oath: On the need for and content of professional economic ethics.* New York: Oxford University Press.

DeMartino, G. (2013). Professional economic ethics: The Posnerian and Naïve perspectives. *Journal of Forensic Economics, 24*(1), 3–18.

Hanson, K. (2015, November). The ethical challenges facing entrepreneurs. *Wall Street Journal, 23*, R1–R2.

Ireland, Thomas R. University of Missouri-St.Louis web page: http://www.umsl.edu/divisions/artscience/economics/ForensicEconomics/useful.html.

Johnson, W. D. (1991). Qualifications, ethics and professional responsibility in forensic economics. *Journal of Forensic Economics, 4*(3), 277–285.

National Association of Forensic Economics. (2004, October 1). *Statement of ethical principles and principles of professional practice.* Available at www.nafe.net.

Sattler, E. L. (1991). Economists, ethics and the marketplace. *Journal of Forensic Economics, 4*(3), 263–268.

Thornton, R. J., & Brookshire, M. L. (2013). NAFE and the ethics question. *Journal of Forensic Economics, 24*(1), 19–23.

Tinari, F. D. (1993). Competition for forensic economists and their ethical behavior. *Journal of Forensic Economics, 6*(3), 263–269.

Tinari, F. D. (2010). The practice of forensic economics: An introduction. *Eastern Economic Journal, 36*(3), 398–406.

Tinari, F. D. (2014, April). A comment on George DeMartino's "professional economic ethics: The Posnerian and Naïve perspectives". *Journal of Forensic Economics, 25*(1), 91–97.

Ward, J. O., & Thornton, R. J. (2013). Can statements of ethical principles and codes of practice make a difference? The results of a NAFE survey. *Journal of Forensic Economics, 24*(1), 25–39.

CHAPTER 16

Understanding Law as a Part of Forensic Economic Practice

Thomas R. Ireland

16.1   INTRODUCTION

A key defining characteristic of a forensic economist is knowledge about the special requirements of law that relate to how economic questions must be answered in the context of litigation. The economic questions that must be answered usually relate to the amount of pecuniary damages that have been caused by some type of harm, though some forensic economists are also called upon to answer questions regarding whether or not liability exists. Both statutory and case law have more impact on how forensic economists, compared with experts in other fields, must answer questions. Thus, although most economists are not trained in law, they need to know more about law than experts in other fields who may also be called upon to testify. For a basic example, forensic economists understand that "present value" has a different meaning in legal contexts than in other types of work that economists do. This is because most legal venues in most circumstances do not allow economists to add past interest to losses that have occurred in the past. Thus, what forensic economists usually calculate is the sum of actual past losses plus the present value of future losses. Even this, however, can become more complicated, depending on the venue, as will be discussed below.

T.R. Ireland (✉)
Department of Economics, University of Missouri—St. Louis, USA

© The Author(s) 2016
F.D. Tinari (ed.), *Forensic Economics*,
DOI 10.1057/978-1-137-56392-7_16

Knowing which special rules and which legal distinctions apply to cases in which an economic expert has been employed is a very important part of forensic economic practice. Some experts pointedly limit their practices to one state, but even work in one state would require an expert to follow a number of legal rules and be aware of a number of legal distinctions. The special legal rules and distinctions of the state would be one of the sets that the expert would need to understand, but that expert would still need to know how to comply with the special rules and distinctions that apply to federal statutes. Depending on the federal statute involved, cases under federal statutes can be brought in both state courts and federal courts, and state cases may be brought in federal court. A case under a federal statute in a state court may be subject to different requirements than a federal case in a federal court in that same state. To avoid mistakes, an economic expert has to develop an understanding of the possible differences. However, unless one has also attended law school, much of this understanding will be developed on a largely self-study and experiential basis.

No one chapter could provide a full development about how law impacts on the practice of forensic economics, but this chapter deals with several aspects of such impacts that many forensic economists are likely to confront.

16.2   Why Law Restricts Economic Expertise

In civil actions, monetary damages represent the only way that defendants can be required to compensate successful plaintiffs. From that standpoint, the amount of monetary damages is the ultimate endpoint of most civil litigation. To get to that endpoint, most civil trials go through a liability phase in which it is determined whether the defendant has any responsibility for the harm allegedly or actually suffered by the plaintiff. If no liability is found, the litigation results in a defense verdict and any opinion of damages experts become irrelevant. If liability is found, a jury turns its attention to the question of the amount of monetary damages to be awarded. Since monetary damages are the only tool a court has for resolving the harms being litigated in civil litigation, courts have retained more control on how monetary damages are calculated than with respect to how most types of expertise are provided in court. It is because economic experts are calculating monetary damages that economic experts are more restricted than experts in other areas. There is some tendency for economic experts to conclude that legal restrictions are based on bad economics. That is probably true in some instances, but an economic expert would be wise to make sure that he or she understands why the law imposes some of the restrictions that the law imposes on damage calculations before reaching that conclusion.

The most obvious example is that economic experts calculate what both financial experts and mathematicians would regard as incorrect versions of present value. What economists typically calculate is the sum of past actual losses plus the present value of future expected losses. Interest on past losses is a tool that judges can use to deal with delays of one side or the other that would have the effect of impacting damages. This instance will be discussed further later in this chapter in the section dealing with "footnote 22 of the Pfeifer" decision. However, even this requirement can sometimes create complications. Some economic experts, for example, have assumed that they can convert past damage amounts into current dollar values. Even though this does not directly add interest in terms of the time value of money, it effectively adds the part of past interest that compensates for expected future changes in the price level. As such, converting past losses into current dollar values has been ruled in at least one important federal case to be a violation of the restriction against adding interest to past losses (Sandstrom v. Principi 2004).

Legal reasons for the collateral source rule and the complex exceptions to that rule that exist in many states, on the nature of periodic payment provisions and many other aspects of how economists ordinarily calculate economic damages are complex and, in some instances, probably require having attended law school for a full understanding. However, economic experts should understand that what they don't understand can be significant and not take the attitude that all that is involved is bad economic analysis.

16.3   QUESTIONS TO ASK WHEN WORKING IN A NEW STATE

If an economic expert is called upon to develop damages projections in a new state or an unfamiliar legal venue, he or she is going to need answers to a number of questions about how law applies to the calculation of damages in the new state or unfamiliar legal venue. The specific questions will depend on the type of litigation involved and perhaps on the nature of the assignment of the economic expert. The person who should be asked is the retaining attorney. The questions posed here are only a sample of the questions that may be of concern. It is important to keep in mind that different types of cases may have different requirements. That is especially true of medical malpractice cases, which often have special rules and requirements that would not apply to other types of cases. The questions that immediately follow are general questions that an economic expert may want to ask while keeping in mind that the retaining attorney may not immediately know the answers. These general questions are followed by a set of questions that are more specific to particular types of cases.

A. General Questions

1. Are written reports of damages required? Not all states require experts to prepare reports. If reports are required, what must be included in the report? (Some economic experts are unwilling to testify without providing a report even if a report is not required by law.) If expert reports are required, by what date are they required and what is the date of the closing of discovery after which further information from the other side cannot be obtained?

2. Are depositions usually held? In some states, including Pennsylvania, depositions are almost never held.

3. Are depositions routinely required of experts, and, if so, must expert reports, if required, be provided before an expert's deposition?

4. What information must experts keep in their files that is discoverable by the other side in the litigation? Most states require that the expert must keep hard copies of e-mailed messages and draft reports that may have been prepared before issuing a final report. However, the most recent version of the Federal Rules of Civil Procedure prevents discovery of such e-mail transmissions and draft reports. A few states have adopted the new federal rules, which apply generally to all cases in federal court. It is important for the expert to know what materials are required to be kept and make available to the other side upon request from the other side. An older rule under the Federal Rules of Civil Procedure is a requirement since December of 1993 that an expert provides a list of all testimonies at deposition and trial over the previous four years. Since such lists of testimonies are required in federal cases, attorneys in state cases frequently ask for an expert's "Rule 26 list of testimonies" even though such

a list is not required in that state. The retaining attorney may request that a copy of the expert's Rule 26 list be provided to the other side even though it is not required.

5. What are experts required to divulge about their incomes? Can an expert be required to provide tax returns or specific tax forms, and under what circumstances? In general, if the expert provides general information about earnings from economic consulting, the expert will not be required to provide tax returns, but may be required to provide 1099s that document payments to the expert in previous years by the retaining law firm. It is important to keep in mind that the attorney who retains an expert is his client's attorney and not the expert's attorney. It is conceivable that the expert may need to retain his or her own legal representation to preserve the expert's own privacy.

6. Are opposing experts permitted to be present at depositions or during trial testimonies, and under what circumstances?

7. Are income taxes subtracted or not subtracted when calculating lost earnings for personal injury cases?

8. Are income taxes subtracted or not subtracted when calculating either financial support or lost earnings in a wrongful death action? (Income taxation for purposes of litigation, as noted in this and the preceding question, is a topic that is covered in greater detail in Chap. 7 of this volume.)

9. Is the state one in which the standards for admission of expert testimony are based on Daubert v. Merrell Dow Pharmaceuticals (1993), Frye v. United States (1923), or some other decision within that state that defines those standards? The expert may wish to ask the retaining attorney what decision in that state is considered the ruling decision in regard to this question. Reading a copy of that decision may be helpful in the expert's work on the case.

10. What past decisions have been made in the state regarding admission of economic testimony? If there are decisions excluding economic testimony, on what basis was economic testimony excluded?

11. Are there any special requirements about discount rates the expert should or may use in his or her calculations? Two states, Michigan and Georgia, mandate use of 5.0 % gross discount rates when calculating present value in those states. In state

cases other than medical malpractice cases in Pennsylvania, a real net interest rate of 0 % must be used. (In Pennsylvania, some experts add real growth, which results in a negative net discount rate.) In Kentucky, use of a 0 % net discount rate is allowed, but not required. Other states may have other special discount rate treatments that the expert needs to be aware of.

12. What are the state's Pattern Jury Instructions (PJI) for the type of case in which the expert has been retained? Can the retaining attorney provide you with a copy of the state's PJI? Using wording found in the PJI in an expert's report can be helpful.

13. Are there special features in the state's collateral source rule that the expert needs to be aware of? In general, benefits from insurance and government programs that have been available to the plaintiff after an injury, death or wrongful termination cannot be considered in determining the economic losses suffered by plaintiffs, but some states have special rules for how specific collateral sources can be considered. In New Jersey, for example, there are special rules for how disability benefits from Social Security must be treated when determining lost earnings. Many states have special rules about collateral sources that apply only to medical malpractice litigation.

14. Are rebuttal experts permitted to discuss the opinions of experts on the other side of a case? In general, the answer is yes, but the expert may need to be sure that the retaining attorney can answer this question effectively because some judges may not be aware of the state's rules in this regard. In some states, there are different dates by which "primary" reports and "rebuttal reports" must be submitted. In a "rebuttal report," an expert is limited to "rebutting" a portion of the other side's expert's report or testimony, but cannot introduce new material not considered by the opposing expert.

15. Are there key cases with respect to damages of the sort that will be claimed in the particular case assignment that the expert could read and consider?

16. Are there tables that have been deemed authoritative for use in calculating economic loss. If so, are they outdated and ignored as a practical matter?

B. A Sample of Questions for Particular Types of Cases

17. What special rules exist for medical malpractice cases? Tort reform movements in many states have resulted in special rules for cases when the cause of action is alleged medical malpractice.

18. What is the state's approach to "lost chance of survival and/or recovery" litigation? Cases of this sort arise when a missed diagnosis by a medical doctor or a hospital has resulted in an individual having either a smaller chance of surviving a medical condition or recovering from that condition with less loss of capacity to earn income or provide household services. Not all states allow such claims to be brought and special rules may apply if such claims can be brought.

19. Does the state allow "wrongful birth" or "wrongful pregnancy" litigation? Some states allow claims of damages to be made for either "wrongful birth" or "wrongful pregnancy," some do not.

20. What special rules, if any, exist for valuing loss of household services in a wrongful death action? In Illinois, for example, claims can be brought in a wrongful death case for the entirety of the period during which a decedent spouse would have provided financial support, regardless of remarriage of the surviving spouse. However, loss of household services is treated as part of loss of consortium and claims for loss of household services terminate on the date of remarriage.

21. How does a surviving spouse's remarriage affect her claims for losses resulting from the death of the decedent spouse? In most states, the surviving spouse's remarriage cannot be mentioned, but in a few states remarriage can be mentioned and taken into account in awarding wrongful death damages. There is even case law on the very narrow question of whether a surviving widow who has remarried can use her previous married name in a wrongful death action to avoid revealing her remarriage to the jury. Of states that have ruled on this narrow question, most, but not all, have said that the widow must use her legal name during trial deliberations.

22. If the state has a wrongful death act such that survivors can recover their own losses, but not losses suffered by the decedent,

should expenditures by a surviving spouse on a decedent spouse be taken into account when calculating losses of the surviving spouse? If both spouses were earning incomes, a portion of the surviving spouse's income would have been spent on the decedent spouse. Should those expenditures be subtracted from losses of financial support the decedent would have provided to the surviving spouse? What the law should be on this question is a source of controversy among forensic economists, but what the law of a state is, if any, a legal question.

23. How are cases involving parental losses resulting from the death of a child handled in the state?

24. In personal injury actions, how have legal decisions interpreted the concept of "earning capacity" for purposes of determining loss of income?

25. How are "survival actions" handled in the state? A survival action is any legal action in which the estate of a decedent is entitled to recover damages after the death of a decedent (the legal action "survives" the death of the decedent), which may or may not involve claims based on the death of the decedent. In a death case, should the expert consider losses falling under the survival action and, if so, how?

26. What is the language of the damages section of the state's wrongful death act? Reading the statute may suggest good wording for an expert's report.

27. In a state in which losses are recovered by the estate of the decedent rather than survivors of the decedent and personal maintenance is to be subtracted from earnings losses, how have legal decisions refined the meaning of which consumption expenditures of the decedent should be considered as part of personal maintenance? Personal maintenance usually means something less than the total amount a decedent would have spent on his or her own consumption. In general, personal maintenance refers to expenditures necessary for the decedent to have maintained himself or herself in the commercial labor market. However, the language used can sometimes be hard to interpret. "Personal consumption" in New Mexico, for example, means largely the same thing as "personal maintenance" in Connecticut.

28. Is the provision of household services considered equivalent to earning capacity in the commercial labor market or as provision of ordinary life care services required for an individual or family to function adequately? The "earning capacity" concept is based on the assumption that time spent providing household services could have been used as time employed in the commercial labor market and thus should be valued as a part of earning capacity. The "ordinary life care concept" is that household services are necessary services that must be provided for a family to function normally, and that must be replaced if an individual who was providing household services no longer can do so. Both concepts lead to a conclusion that "loss of household services" is a compensable loss, but there are implications for how those losses should be measured and for whether past loss of household services should be recoverable.

29. What provisions for "periodic payments" of damages exist within a state? Periodic payment provisions require defendants to make periodic payments rather than lump-sum payments of damages. Some states allow defendants to seek periodic payments of damages rather than having to pay a single lump-sum amount, but such provisions sometimes contain complex requirements. It is helpful for an economic expert to be aware of such provisions and the special requirements that are involved.

30. Are tax "gross-ups" permissible in employment cases? If a worker recovers back pay, front pay and/or loss of earning capacity in an employment discrimination case, the worker will have to pay taxes on amounts recovered. Under tax law, taxes must be paid in the year income is received, including a legal award that may incorporate multiple years of earnings. Under a graduated (progressive) income tax, this will result in a higher tax rate being paid than if those amounts had been paid during years of alleged discriminatory loss. A tax "gross-up" calculates the size of an increase needed so that the worker will pay the same amount of tax that the worker would have paid if lost earnings were received when they should have been received. Such calculations are allowed in some legal venues, but not others. (Readers are referred to Chap. 11 of this volume for a discussion of gross-up calculations.)

31. Are economic experts permitted to calculate dollar values for family relationship values such as advice, counsel and companionship? In New Jersey, in particular, economists may be able to calculate dollar values for lost advice and counsel and for lost companionship in addition to other types of household services of a decedent that are lost in wrongful death cases.

16.4   CONFRONTING LEGAL CITATIONS IN THE REPORTS OF OPPOSING ECONOMIC EXPERTS

Reports of forensic economic experts often contain citations of legal decisions that an expert may believe support the types of calculations he or she has made in a given case. This can be dangerous in that citing legal decisions can appear to be claiming legal expertise that a person who is not trained in law would not have. If done cautiously, however, citing legal decisions that are directly on point can strengthen an economic expert's report. When an economic expert on the other side of a case makes legal claims and cites specific legal decisions in support, the opposing expert can have less concern about being accused of claiming legal expertise, but it is still wise to be cautious in offering interpretations of legal decisions.

When an opposing economic expert cites a legal decision, it is useful to read that decision. In many cases, the decision has been cited to give the impression that the expert knows something about the law under which the expert's calculations are being offered. Thus, the citations are there for decorative purposes that are not particularly important for an expert's own calculations. In a recent case, this author found citations to a decision that allegedly defined "earning capacity," but did not provide a definition relevant to the case at hand. "Earning capacity" was defined as "the ability to earn money" even if an injured person was not currently earning income. This was not an issue between the parties. Another citation was to a decision that held that damages were to be reduced to present value, which was relevant to the case at hand, but did not involve any issue in contention between the parties. Still another reference to a statute was provided that held that medical costs related to an injury are a recognized economic damage, which was also not an issue between the parties in that case. The report provided two citations that the report claimed associated the inability to perform household services with the loss of earning capacity, which was also not an issue between the parties in that case. The citations themselves were not quite correctly reported in that some periods were missing after letters in the "addresses" in the decisions being cited. However, the citations were sufficiently close to correct legal citations to give a reader the impression that the expert knew something about law, even if none of the citations related to any issue in contention. This author did not feel that anything needed to be said about these citations, but it is always useful to be sure that nothing needs to be said when citations appear.

Sometimes such citations may be relevant, as when the legal decision is being cited as authority for legal interpretations that are relevant to a consideration of damages. One particular area of some importance has been with respect to the recoverability of economic losses for the lost "advice and counsel" and lost "companionship" of decedents in wrongful death actions in New Jersey. Frank Tinari has argued that these areas are appropriate damage areas in New Jersey cases bases upon the 1980 decision of the New Jersey Supreme Court in *Green v. Bittner* and subsequent decisions interpreting that case (Tinari 1998, 2004). For reports in the state of New Jersey, it is common to see citations to the *Green v. Bittner* decision both in support of and in opposition to the manner in which Tinari described his calculations for "advice and counsel" and "companionship" in his 1998 paper. The back and forth literature on that matter is covered in Tinari's 2004 note.

The most extensive use of citations, however, has been in the area of hedonic damages, which is covered in the next section.

16.5   LEGAL DECISIONS IN REPORTS INVOLVING HEDONIC DAMAGES

Cases involving hedonic damages involve economic citations more often than not. This is because most courts in most states and most federal venues have ruled that hedonic damages testimony is not admissible. The two states that are exceptions to that rule are New Mexico and Nevada, both of whose supreme courts have accepted hedonic damages testimony at the discretion of trial court judges (Ireland 2009, 2012). In all other states, and in those states as well, the major battles are over the admissibility of hedonic damages testimony. As such, reports of plaintiff experts proffering hedonic damages calculations often contain extensive discussion of specific legal cases. Brian McDonald's paper on "Loss of Enjoyment of Life Damages in New Mexico" (McDonald 2007) has a discussion of New Mexico legal decisions that is similar to the coverage contained in his reports for attorneys in New Mexico. Significant portions of his reports read more like legal briefs than reports of economic experts. As a result reports by economic experts for the defense sometimes consider the same legal decisions in New Mexico cases.

Similarly, Stan Smith, who functions as an expert willing to provide calculations of loss of enjoyment of life damages (hedonic damages) on a national level, includes appendices that are intended to defend their admissibility. In one of those appendices, Stan Smith tries to argue that his loss of enjoyment of life calculations meet the standards of both *Daubert v. Merrell Dow Pharmaceuticals* (1993) and *Frye v. United States* (1923). All federal courts rely upon "*Daubert* and progeny," meaning the *Daubert* decision itself and decisions subsequent to Daubert that were based in significant part on *Daubert*. A number of states have also adopted *Daubert* as their standards for admission of expert testimony. Other states apply the old *Frye* standard for admission of expert testimony, which means "generally accepted within the relevant scientific community." Still other states have their own versions of rules for admission of expert testimony or legal decisions holding that those standards are somewhat different from either *Daubert* or *Frye*. In cases involving hedonic damages, the most important damages battle between the parties is often over whether or not loss of enjoyment of life testimony by Stan Smith will be admitted or not. It is often the case that plaintiffs withdraw hedonic damages experts on the eve of a motion *in limine* hearing on whether or not the trial court judge will allow hedonic damages testimony.

This is because hedonic damages testimony, as typically presented by an economic expert, involves discussion of millions of dollars in damages, sometimes far in excess of earnings loss and household service loss damages. Having an economic expert, with sanction from the court, testify to those large sums of money, is generally thought to be an enormous advantage for a plaintiff case. As such, defendants will fight as hard as they can to prevent having such testimony presented to juries. Thus, the legal issue of whether such testimony will be allowed is central to the interests of both plaintiffs and defendants. One result has been that Stan Smith, who is the most frequently used hedonic damages expert in the USA as a whole, provides extended arguments that his hedonic damages testimony meets the four tests of the *Daubert* decision, one of which is the general acceptance standard that is the *Frye* standard. In other words, while it is a simplified generalization, *Daubert* can be characterized as increasing the number of criteria to be considered from one to four criteria. Stan Smith correctly identifies those four criteria as:

1. Testing of the theory and science
2. Peer review
3. Known or potential rate of error
4. Generally accepted

Stan Smith then spends several pages arguing that his hedonic damages calculations meet *each* of those standards. This author responds to Stan Smith's arguments by spending several pages arguing that Stan Smith's hedonic damages calculations fail to meet *any* of the four standards. In his reports, Smith also cites a number of publications that he argues supports his calculations and this author's response reports consider and reject most of Smith's arguments. This author is often asked to provide affidavits that state arguments in opposition to Smith's calculations. Law obviously plays an important role in such cases.

16.6   THE IMPORTANCE OF READING AND RE-READING THE *PFEIFER* DECISION

It is this author's strong opinion that *Jones & Laughlin Steel Corp. v. Pfeifer* (1983) is essential reading for any forensic economist. This US Supreme Court decision sets out the framework for evaluating earnings loss damages for a personal injury lawsuit under federal maritime law, which also applies to injuries at work to railroad workers under the Federal Employers Liability Act. It also provides a basic understanding of the role of economic testimony. This short chapter is not the place for a full expansion of all that is said in the *Pfeifer* decision, but there are several statements in that decision that deserve the full attention of a forensic economic expert who is trying to understand the impact of law on how that expert prepares reports and testifies in court. The *Pfeifer* decision provides a "how to" guide for preparing a personal injury lost earnings analysis. It talks at great length about requests from both plaintiff and defense organizations that filed *amicus* briefs for the Supreme Court to dictate exactly how discount rates must be considered. The *Pfeifer* decision was explicitly not to dictate any one approach to discount rates, reversing a decision of the Pennsylvania Supreme Court to do so in a federal maritime action.

Those discussions, including footnote 22, which is discussed in the next section, are well worth reading and re-reading from year to year. The *Pfeifer* decision is like a textbook on how to perform such an evaluation.

The focus of this section on *Pfeifer*, however, is for a different purpose. *Pfeifer* is also important because it explains what is possible and not possible for an economic evaluation to accomplish. Three sections are particularly clear. In the first passage, Justice Stevens explained the intent of the Court, saying:

> The litigants and the *amici* in this case urge us to select one of the many rules that have been proposed and establish it for all time as the exclusive method in all federal trials for calculating an award for lost earnings in an inflationary economy. We are not persuaded, however, that such an approach is warranted. For our review of the foregoing cases leads us to draw three conclusions. First, by its very nature the calculation of an award for lost earnings must be a rough approximation. Because the lost stream can never be predicted with complete confidence, any lump sum represents only a "rough and ready" effort to put the plaintiff in the position he would have been in had he not been injured. Second, sustained price inflation can make the award substantially less precise. Inflation's current magnitude and unpredictability create a substantial risk that the damages award will prove to have little relation to the lost wages it purports to replace. Third, the question of lost earnings can arise in many different contexts. In some sectors of the economy, it is far easier to assemble evidence of an individual's most likely career path than in others.

In the second passage, Justice Stevens explained that an economic analysis of damages should not become a graduate seminar, saying:

> In calculating an award for a longshoreman's lost earnings caused by the negligence of a vessel, the discount rate should be chosen on the basis of the factors that are used to estimate the lost stream of future earnings. If the trier of fact relies on a specific forecast of the future rate of price inflation, and if the estimated lost stream of future earnings is calculated to include price inflation along with individual factors and other societal factors, then the proper discount rate would be the after-tax market interest rate. But since specific forecasts of future price inflation remain too unreliable to be useful in many cases, it will normally be a costly and ultimately unproductive waste of longshoremen's resources to make such forecasts the centerpiece of litigation under § 5(b). As Judge Newman has warned: "The average accident trial should not be converted into a graduate seminar on economic forecasting." (Citations removed)

In the third passage, Justice Stevens warned that judges should avoid allowing economic calculations for an uncertain future than it is possible for such calculations to be, saying:

> We do not suggest that the trial judge should embark on a search for "delusive exactness." It is perfectly obvious that the most detailed inquiry can at best produce an approximate result. And one cannot ignore the fact that in many instances the award for impaired earning capacity may be overshadowed by a highly impressionistic award for pain and suffering. But we are satisfied that whatever rate the District Court may choose to discount the estimated stream of future earnings, it must make a deliberate choice, rather than assuming that it is bound by a rule of state law. (Citations removed)

All three of these passages suggest that economic experts should use caution when worrying about the minutia of economic calculations when preparing reports and testifying. The role of an economic expert is to assist a jury in making the decision a jury wants to make, not educating a jury to make the decision the expert would like it to make.

16.7 FOOTNOTE 22 OF THE *PFEIFER* DECISION

This chapter ends with a discussion of footnote 22 of the *Pfeifer* decision, which states:

> At one time it was thought appropriate to distinguish between compensating a plaintiff "for the loss of time from his work which has actually occurred up to the time of trial" and compensating him "for the time which he will lose in [the] future." This suggested that estimated future earning capacity should be discounted to the date of trial, and a separate calculation should be performed for the estimated loss of earnings between injury and trial. It is both easier and more precise to discount the entire lost stream of earnings back to the date of injury – the moment from which earning capacity was impaired. The plaintiff may then be awarded interest on that discounted sum for the period between injury and judgment, in order to ensure that the award when invested will still be able to replicate the lost stream. (Citations removed)

In this footnote, Justice Stevens began by describing what most forensic economists still do, not what forensic economists did at one time. He then said that the "easier and more precise" way for such calculations to be made is to determine the present value of losses as of the date of injury, not as of the date of trial. The plaintiff is then to be awarded interest on that present value from the date of the injury to the date of trial. This leaves unanswered who will add interest to the present value (presumably the trial court judge) and how the interest rate that is to be used will be determined. Using this "easier and more precise" method would have a major impact on how damages were to be calculated. At the moment of injury, an economic expert would have to use both a life expectancy and worklife expectancy that existed at the moment of injury, regardless of what might have happened later (such as the death of the plaintiff for unrelated reasons). If and only if the interest rate was determined in the same way that the present value was determined and applied in the same way the interest rate was applied in calculating the present value, Justice Stevens would be correct that this method would be more precise. It is questionable, however, whether those conditions could be "easily" met.

Paul Taylor, a retired economic expert from Alaska, spoke about his use of footnote 22 in his practice in presentations at meetings of the American Academy of Economic and Financial Experts. When confronted with a plaintiff economic expert report that made calculations of present value at the time of trial, Taylor would ask his retaining attorney to enter a motion to recalculate to force the opposing expert to calculate present values at the moment of injury rather than the date of trial. His logic was that the language of footnote 22 is clear and would give the judge the impression that the opposing expert did not know what the opposing expert was supposed to do to calculate present values for damages. Taylor recommended this approach to other forensic economists and it probably worked for Taylor at least some of the time. This author has not heard of the same approach working for anyone else, but this seemed like a good closing story for a chapter on "Understanding Law as a Part of Forensic Economic Practice." What you don't know can hurt you.

REFERENCES

Ireland, T. R. (2009). The last of hedonic damages: Nevada, New Mexico and Running a Bluff. *Journal of Legal Economics, 16*(2), 91–110.

Ireland, T. R. (2012). Trends in legal decisions involving hedonic damages from 2000 to 2012. *Journal of Legal Economics, 19*(1), 61–88.

McDonald, M. B. (2007). Loss of enjoyment of life damages in New Mexico. *Journal of Forensic Economics, 20*(2), 171–186.

Tinari, F. D. (1998). Household services: Toward a more comprehensive measure. *Journal of Forensic Economics, 11*(3), 253–265.

Tinari, F. D. (2004). A note on 'household services: Toward a more comprehensive measure'. *Journal of Forensic Economics, 17*(3), 383–385.

CASES CITED

Daubert v. Merrell Dow Pharmaceuticals, 113 S. Ct. 2786 (U.S. 1993).

Frye v. United States, 54 App. 46; 293 F. 1013 (D.C. Cir. 1923).

Green v. Bittner, 85 N.J. 1; 424 A.2d 210 (N.J. 1980).

Jones & Laughlin Steel Corp. v. Pfeifer, 103 S.Ct. 2541 (1983).

Sandstrom v. Principi, 358 F.3d 1376 (D.C. Cir. 2004).

CHAPTER 17

Effective Communications as a Forensic Economist

Frank D. Tinari

17.1 Introduction

A chapter devoted to communications issues would, at first, seem a bit odd in a volume of otherwise substantive economics content. Yet, because forensic economics involves relationships between experts and clients, and between experts and the courts, effective communications is an integral part of any expert's professional practice. In this regard, one might think that normal telephone, letter, fax and email communications, conducted in a professional manner, would take care of things. While that is true, to some extent, much more can be done to maintain a credible and thriving forensic economic practice. Of course, there are numerous styles of speaking, writing and teaching as well as substantial differences in personality types. But the guidelines and general principles offered in this chapter should serve a great many individuals whose practice involves the calculation of economic damages in litigated matters.

The first section of this chapter addresses communications issues between experts and clients. The subsequent section discusses written communications in an expert's economic damages report. That is followed

F.D. Tinari (✉)
Professor Emeritus, Seton Hall University, USA

© The Author(s) 2016
F.D. Tinari (ed.), *Forensic Economics*,
DOI 10.1057/978-1-137-56392-7_17

by a section on effective communications at deposition. The last section addresses effective communication with the jury at trial.

17.2   COMMUNICATING WITH ATTORNEY/CLIENTS

Experienced experts understand that when there is an inquiry regarding the expert's services, nearly always from a litigation attorney, there is no guarantee that an actual engagement will follow. Of course, if the expert has an established practice, then inquiries may be perfunctory from those attorneys who already know their experts and want to continue to use their services. In representing their clients, attorneys may make inquiries of the expert about a number of important facts, the answers to which help determine whether or not they are interested in engaging the expert to evaluate economic damages.

An inquiry may come in the form of a letter or email message, but most commonly via telephone. After briefly describing the case at hand, an attorney may ask the expert a number of questions, including: Have you had any experience in the type of case I have just explained? With which attorneys have you worked? Have you ever testified at trial or at deposition? Can you provide me with references? May I obtain a copy of your C.V.? How quickly can you provide me with your report? What are the fees that you charge?

At this initial stage of communications, it is important for the expert to demonstrate professionalism by providing full and complete responses to the questions, and to do so in a timely fashion. It is strongly recommended that notes be taken during the telephone discussion and that accurate contact information be obtained for follow-up communications. Since the expert cannot rely solely on the facts provided either orally or in writing by the attorney, limited as they are in scope and completeness, the expert should request complete information on all facts needed to prepare an evaluation of economic damages. Many forensic economists regularly make use of a questionnaire or form letter that specifies all of the facts that should be provided to the expert. In today's world of electronic communication, it has been the practice of this author to send a timely response via an email letter explaining the expert's services and expectations, with various attachments including a C.V., questionnaire, and fee schedule. Further, a record should be maintained of each inquiry, date, name of attorney and name of the case. Some time may elapse, even many months, between the initial inquiry and actual engagement, so good records will help to ensure proper management of the case assignment.

It often occurs that follow-up communication with the attorney is required. This may be due to questions that arise during the expert's review of facts and documents provided. For example, if the earnings record of a decedent exhibits variation from year to year, the expert would want to know the reason. Were there periodic opportunities for overtime earnings? Were there periods of unemployment?

Or, the information provided may be incomplete in some way. Again, the follow-up communication can be made by telephone or by written means. It may even be necessary to speak directly with the clients represented by the attorney. This can sometimes be a bit touchy, especially in cases of severe injury or death wherein clients carry heavy emotional burdens. And since it is likely that the information obtained may likely be used by the expert in the evaluation of economic loss, it is necessary for the expert to take notes to document the discussion. Such notes become part of the expert's file that may be open to scrutiny later in the case.

Another potential opportunity for communicating with the retaining attorney occurs when the expert uncovers and unusual or unexpected finding. For example, the expert's calculations may reveal that the economic damages are substantially lower than perhaps alluded to by the attorney in the initial conversation. Or some fact is uncovered by the expert that changes the nature of the case, e.g., that a sole proprietor client's claim of high past income loss is inaccurate because the client was referring to gross income, not net income after expenses. In such instances, the expert may serve in the role of consultant and advisor to the attorney in explaining the implications of the particular findings. In rare instances, the expert may discover that the retaining attorney unwisely withheld some critical fact that changes the entire case. Such a discovery must be quickly and honestly discussed with retaining counsel. This author recalls one such assignment in which the plaintiff's past criminal conviction and incarceration was not revealed by the attorney and only came to light at the deposition by opposing counsel, thereby undermining nearly all of the loss calculations that had been made.

17.3   COMMUNICATING BY MEANS OF A WRITTEN REPORT

The purpose of an economic damages report is to lay out the facts relied upon, the assumptions, method, calculations and concluding opinion of the expert. Sometimes the "report" from the expert may comprise only a spreadsheet of calculations and a brief narrative. Nevertheless, a report should, at a minimum, state the assumptions and basic factual foundation of the calculations. As explained in the chapter on ethics, The National Association of Forensic Economics (NAFE) and the American Academy of Economic and Financial Experts (AAEFE) have established standards that identify the minimum needed for a report to pass muster. In the practice of this author, who believes providing more information is better than less, each source from which facts are taken and used in the report is fully identified in the report, down to its page number.

Whichever form it takes, a report is meant initially for the eyes of the retaining attorney who, in turn, may share it with his or her client. This is a good reason for writing a report that is not only accurate but also clear and understandable to an educated reader. This author has found that his fully documented reports are often exchanged with the other side as a way of both demonstrating the seriousness of the claims and encouraging settlement discussions.

Most economic reports contain one or more spreadsheets that lay out the calculations made by the expert. But, generally speaking, retaining attorneys and their clients are not likely to understand large spreadsheets. One of this author's colleagues argues that he writes his reports and includes spreadsheets so that an opposing expert, and not his retaining attorney, can understand the calculations he has made. But even with the use of complex spreadsheets, a clear narrative explanation would serve to educate attorneys and their clients about the procedure used as well as the ultimate opinion of economic damages. In other words, the economist's report is a means of communicating the methods and bases of findings presented by the expert.

With respect to potential opposing experts, the NAFE ethics statement and that of AAEFE specify that an expert's work should be structured such that another expert could replicate and confirm the first expert's findings and opinion. The NAFE statement is a bit weaker in that it requires that members "stand ready to provide sufficient detail to all replication of all numerical calculations" rather than AAEFE's requirement that experts should provide the information in their reports.

Some states (e.g., New York) do not require an attorney to share the expert's report, if there is one, with opposing counsel. Instead, only a brief (and, sometimes, cryptic) description of the expert's background, method, data sources and opinion is provided. Even in these situations, a clearly written report would help retaining counsel in drafting a correct description of the expert's intended testimony.

17.4   COMMUNICATIONS DURING A DISCOVERY DEPOSITION

When an oral deposition of an expert takes place, it offers the expert the first opportunity to respond to questions posed by adverse counsel. Compared to the calculations and opinion expressed in a written report, the communications that take place in a deposition are oral, and are structured in a question/answer format. A deposition held by opposing counsel is designed to find out many things such as:

- Is there anything in the expert's background or experience that might undermine his or her opinion? Are the expert's credentials accurately presented and verifiable?
- Can an aggressive series of questions cause the expert to become nervous and unsure, or answer questions in such a way as to help undermine the expert's own opinions?
- How well versed is the expert in his or her field of knowledge?
- When did the expert receive such-and-such information? From whom?
- Can the expert defend each and every assumption made in the analysis?
- How competent and clear is the expert in explaining the basis and mechanics of his or her calculations?
- How does the expert react to the introduction of new or contrary evidence?
- Is the expert acting in a biased way compared to his or her work in other cases?
- Is the expert offering opinions outside of his or her area of expertise?
- Are there any documents in the expert's case folder that would raise doubts about the expert's methods or conclusions?

The preceding list is by no means comprehensive. But it should be apparent that an oral deposition can be unnerving to an expert. All the more so since responses are made under legal oath to tell the entire truth. This is why many retaining attorneys choose to schedule a pre-deposition discussion with the expert during which advice may be proffered regarding the expert's demeanor, the questioning style of the opposing attorney, and a review of the expert's case file documents. In some states, certain documents, such as communications between counsel and expert, are exempt from discovery. If so, those documents should be kept in a separate folder, and identified for opposing counsel in general terms as to their contents.

This author has found that a deposition can run more smoothly when (1) case file contents are organized, and (2) written reports contain full reference to the sources relied upon. File contents can be organized, of course, in a number of ways. This author prefers to maintain everything in reverse chronological order, with the most recent communication at the top followed by preceding documents and communications. Often, the very last item in the sequence contains the notes taken during the inquiry telephone discussion of the case. This system has been enormously helpful in those times when an initial report had been drafted and, then later, additional information was received that required recalculation of some aspect of economic damages. With a clearly organized document file, the sequence can be clearly explained and readily documented.

The expert's written report itself can serve an important supporting role in a discovery deposition. If the expert's report cites the source of each and every fact and statistic used, and the basis for every assumption, then answering questions about the bases of the expert's calculations and opinions is that much easier by simple reference to the expert's report.

A final observation regarding depositions is in order. An expert's retaining counsel also learns quite a bit about the expert and his or her work. The answers that the expert gives also aid retaining counsel in making decisions regarding the strength of the case, the credibility of the expert, and whether or not pre-trial settlement would be the better course of action. This is true even when one of the attorneys is not physically present but is participating via telephone, something that is allowed in a number of states. A written transcription of an oral deposition is nearly always requested by the participating attorneys so that they can review the expert's precise wording of responses to questions posed during the deposition.

17.5   TRIAL TESTIMONY COMMUNICATIONS

Trial testimony marks a significant departure from the various modes of communication we have described thus far. One reason for the big difference is the structure of the court protocols. Plaintiff presents the expert's findings in a series of questions and, when the expert has completed his or her testimony, then opposing counsel proceeds with cross-examination that is limited to the subject matter of the expert's direct testimony. So one key difference is that trial testimony is oral. The jury never gets to see the expert's report.

But a more fundamental reason is that the audience is quite different from those encountered by the expert up to this point in the process of a litigated matter. In civil trial actions, the term *trier of fact* refers most often to a jury of one's peers. But it could be an individual judge in what is called a "bench trial". In the latter instance, trial testimony is more in line with what has occurred before. That's because the "audience" is an individual educated in the law and likely knowledgeable about the calculation of economic damages. But the vast majority of civil trials involve a jury, which is the focus of the remainder of this section.

Given that the recipient of the expert's oral trial testimony is a jury of individuals with varied backgrounds and educational attainments, the language and delivery of the expert's testimony should be tailored to the average juror. Of course, the composition of a jury varies from case to case, so it is helpful to the expert when retaining counsel can advise the expert as to the educational background and employment of the members of the jury. But it is safe to say that very often the average educational background would be high school, sometimes more, sometimes less. Thus, experts are faced with the prospect of orally communicating their calculations, statistical sources, assumptions, methods and conclusions in terms that would be understandable to the average juror.

Expert reports come in all shapes and sizes. But a jury does not see or read the report. Rather, jurors listen to the oral testimony of the expert, supported by whatever charts, slides or other evidence that is presented by the expert. It takes some thought and preparation to transition from the expert's report to demonstrative evidence that will aid the jury in understanding the expert's methods, assumptions and calculations. The expert's oral testimony, not his or her report, becomes the evidence provided to the jury. The task is to have the expert "translate" complex and busy spreadsheet calculations of lost earnings and services into an understandable story—clear, concise and engaging. The expert in the witness box is watched, listened to, and sized up by jurors who judge not only the content of what is being said but the expert's credibility and competence. Making sure that what they hear and what they see are clearly communicated can only enhance the expert's effectiveness.

Most economic experts recognize that visual aids are needed to communicate lengthy and often complex data. In preparing visual aids, the expert must adopt the perspective of typical jurors. One guiding principle is to keep things simple. Complexity must be broken down into simpler steps. And technical language must be minimized, "translating" key terms into words and ideas understandable by the average juror. One study found that jurors "were suspicious of experts who appeared to be obfuscating". Clarity, simplicity and logical order must guide the preparation of the expert's testimony and exhibits.

It is known that effective testimony engages several senses. Experienced experts have learned that visual aids are not only helpful, they are often a necessity in attempting to convey lengthy and often complex data. Supporting exhibits should be designed to clarify and support the oral testimony of the economic damages expert. In short, the job of the testifying expert is to connect with the jury and help them understand the analysis by means of visual information. But how can that be accomplished?

One way is to have enlarged charts made up ahead of time. These are typically charts and tables excerpted from the expert's report. Then, during the economic expert's testimony, the charts are placed before jurors to illustrate and help them understand what is being said. For effective communication, it may be necessary to make changes in various respects to the charts, formulas and tables contained in the expert's report. (See Tinari, 2016 for an explanation of exhibit simplification.)

Many attorneys like blown-up poster boards because they can be used by them in closing arguments to drive home the value of losses in the case. But it may take several days to have them made up. So if any foundational testimony differs from what the expert assumed, or if a ruling by the judge limits what the expert may testify to, then there may very well occur a scramble to substitute other charts or to use another method to present the expert's testimony.

Some economic experts use a laptop computer and projector. But that could get complicated due to technology glitches. Also, with a laptop computer in the hands of the expert, opposing counsel could ask the expert to make new calculations based on hypothetical assumptions. This puts the expert in an unplanned and often uncomfortable position. In effect, the other attorney is using the expert to achieve his or her own goals without the necessity of bringing in an opposing economic expert.

In making use of demonstrative charts, it is important to ensure that all charts and tables are absolutely clear to the lay reader. Terminology should be simplified. For example, instead of using "dob" or "date of birth", it may be better to use "born". Change technical jargon to everyday language. Instead of "annual growth rate" it is better to use "yearly increase". The same applies to mathematical formulae or expressions: it is better to use percentages instead of decimals. For example, suppose in the written report an expert uses 2010.5 to represent half a year in 2010. This may not be clear to the average person. So a helpful change could be to express the year as 2010 (50 %). If an expert's report contains a birth date in standard statistical form, i.e., 03/27/51, it may be better for jury understanding to have the exhibits show March 27, 1951, instead.

The amount of information presented in any given slide or chart should be relatively modest. A busy or crowded chart could easily make the jury's eyes glaze over. Small font size could be a killer if the jury cannot see clearly what is being presented. Clear and bold headers are also important in delivering targeted information to the jury.

Since the objective is to have jurors focus on the content of the exhibits, any extraneous "noise" could reduce their retention of the information. So, for example, it may be helpful to de-emphasize the use of color, logos, background images and the like. The available fancy design tools available to almost anyone with a computer should not be used simply because they are available. Rather, the purpose of the communication should drive the design.

Finally, exact hard copies of the demonstrative exhibits should be made. Retaining counsel may, in turn, want to share them with opposing attorneys and the judge. The hard copy can also be marked as an exhibit for subsequent reference in the case.

17.6   Conclusion

In a litigated matter, the various stages of work by a forensic economist encompass numerous opportunities for communication—with retaining counsel, possibly with counsel's clients, with opposing counsel and, ultimately, with jurors. Each opportunity, be it in written or oral form, has its own target audience and level of sophistication. Therefore, it is wise for an economic expert to be sensitive to the differences in the various audiences who will receive the work product of the expert, and to tailor the means of communication accordingly.

The most significant difference occurs between the writing of an economic damages report, and giving oral testimony at trial. The purpose of this chapter has been to elaborate on these differences and to make recommendations on effective means to communicate with the intended audiences.

REFERENCE

Tinari, F. D. (2016). Demonstrating Lost Earnings: Algebraic vs. Spreadsheet Method. *The Earnings Analyst*, 15, 21–32.

CHAPTER 18

Reflections on the 9/11 Victim Compensation Fund

Frank D. Tinari and John O. Ward

18.1 Background

This chapter deals with a significant step taken soon after the terrorist attacks of September 11, 2001 (9/11), namely, the creation by Congress of a federally funded September 11th Victim Compensation Fund (VCF), authorized under a quickly enacted Air Transportation Safety and System Stabilization Act (the Act). As the name of the Act implies, its main goal was to minimize potentially harmful effects on the air transport industry resulting from both a crisis in passenger confidence in airline use in the wake of the terrorist attacks, and litigation that would likely ensue.[1]

Congress set aside federal funds to deal with both effects, thereby restoring some sense of normalcy in the industry. The focus of this paper is Title IV of the Act dealing with "Victim Compensation," i.e., issues of compensating individuals who were injured or the personal representative of those who were killed as a result of the aircraft crashes in the 9/11 attacks. The VCF was designed to provide a no-fault alternative to tort litigation that could involve up to 15,000 individuals.[2]

F.D. Tinari (✉)
Professor Emeritus, Seton Hall University, USA

J.O. Ward
John Ward Economics, USA

© The Author(s) 2016
F.D. Tinari (ed.), *Forensic Economics*,
DOI 10.1057/978-1-137-56392-7_18

In order to implement the VCF, regulations and guidelines had to be written to achieve the stated goals and in a way that would be viewed by the public as fair and just. A well-respected private-sector attorney specializing in mediation, arbitration, and negotiation, Kenneth Feinberg, was asked to serve as Special Master to administer the "Fund" (as he termed it). The Special Master established guidelines for determining the amount of monetary compensation, and stated that award amounts would be equal to the sum of economic losses plus non-economic losses, less collateral offsets, such as life insurance.

On December 20, 2001, after receiving numerous comments and suggestions from attorneys and other members of the public, the Special Master of the Fund publicly announced the completion of Interim Final Regulations and unveiled several charts illustrating in a general way presumptive, non-binding estimated awards available for those eligible claimants filing on behalf of certain deceased victims. At that time, Mr. Feinberg announced that the regulations had three primary objectives.

First, "fairness and consistency ... in the treatment of individual claims." This was an attempt at achieving horizontal equity in assessing award amounts, since all individuals in specific age-income categories would presumably receive the same award.

Second, "speed and efficiency in getting these awards out to eligible claimants." The standardized tables made implementation efficient since economic award calculations could be made in a straightforward way, thereby avoiding the lengthy and complicated process of tort litigation. Claimants who chose to file for compensation from the Fund had to waive any right to file a civil action in any federal or state court for their sustained damages.

Third, "consistent with the statute, to minimize award disparity from the upper end to the lower end ... to try to make the gap between higher-end claimant awards and lower-end claimant awards narrower." This was an effort to achieve vertical equity (i.e., reducing the disparity between the upper and lower ends of the income distribution) by truncating award amounts for individuals with yearly incomes higher than $250,000.

The US Department of Justice also solicited further comments from the public on the Interim Final Regulations for a 30-day period, and received thousands of comments during the 30-day period, helping the Special Master further adjust the Interim Final Regulations.

18.2   THE ROLE OF THE NATIONAL ASSOCIATION OF FORENSIC ECONOMICS (NAFE)

Members of NAFE quickly responded to the events of September 2001. The organization president's message in the "NAFE Member News" for November 2001 included a web address where comments could be submitted about the proposed VCF damage rules and another for those wishing to volunteer their services to compute damages. (Later in 2002 the NAFE Board would discuss the ethical pros and cons of such *pro bono* work.) There was considerable discussion about 9/11 on the group's electronic list (NAFE-L) and some members reported that some of their scheduled case trials were being postponed due to the events of 9/11.[3]

NAFE's 2002 annual conference, held each January in conjunction with the Allied Social Sciences Associations annual conference, was the only time in its history (before or since) at which a record five sessions were scheduled; an extra session was added that focused on analysis of the VCF damages compensation scheme.[4]

Co-author Ward recalls that he and forensic economist Michael Piette (now deceased) chaired a session at the meeting that generated numerous comments and questions. Issues discussed included the soundness of the interim proposed VCF methodology with an emphasis on its omission of guidelines for the recovery of lost services. Subsequent to the meeting, NAFE members submitted recommendations for changes in the rules to the Justice Department (as did attorneys and others), all of which were posted on the VCF webpage.[5] The authors believe that some of these comments were fruitful since Special Master Feinberg made some modifications prior to issuing final guidelines.[6]

In early January 2002, the co-authors were invited to address the families of 9/11 victims at the Park Avenue Armory, New York, along with Governor Pataki, Mayor Bloomberg, and various members of Congress. It was apparent that public pressure was being garnered to foster changes to the VCF guidelines.

18.3   ECONOMIC CALCULATIONS UNDER VCF RULES

VCF rules ultimately were modified to permit inclusion of valuation of lost household services.[7] Where specific information on the claimant was unavailable, the publication *Dollar Value of a Day* (Expectancy Data various) was used. In addition, in response to a large volume of suggestions submitted by the public, the Interim Final Regulations were amended to allow the Special Master discretion to consider on a prorated basis a victim's income from 2001 (instead solely of 1998–2000) as well as published salary scales from government or military employees. Additional amendments were introduced at this stage to take into account valid criticisms. The Department of Justice and the Special Master concluded that no single perspective would dictate the economic compensation of the victims under the Fund.

Within the Special Master's framework, a series of tables set forth presumed awards based on age, income, and household size. The award amounts, derived using standard growth rates and discount rates, were intended to measure the lost income that victims would have likely received over their lifetime had they not been killed or injured in the 9/11 attacks (adjusted downward by the decedent's self-consumption in death cases). Of significance is that service losses were not incorporated in the VCF presumed award tables, so use of an economist was an important part of quantifying claimants' total losses. In most death cases the economist would quantify three components of loss: lost earnings, pension loss (if any), and loss of services. Services included any loss of household services, companionship services to both spouse and children, and advice and counsel services to both spouse and children. In injury cases, the economist would evaluate lost earnings and pension benefits and, depending on the case, a partial loss of ability to perform household services.

The vast majority of the thousands of families and beneficiaries of those killed, along with individuals who suffered physical injuries, chose to file a Compensation Form with the Victim Compensation Fund. The Compensation Form solicited information to (i) identify the victim and establish eligibility requirements, (ii) identify and acquire documentation with relevant information for the calculation and distribution of the economic award, and (iii) acquire a certification that the provided information was true, accurate, and complete, and the authority to release this information to appropriate third parties. A checklist with all supporting documents was to be submitted with the Compensation Form.

Applicants had to choose one of two tracks to adjudicate (process) their claim. Track A had two steps. In Step 1, the claim was reviewed and a presumed award was calculated. In an optional Step 2, applicants could request a hearing and have the presumed award reviewed. At a hearing they could present additional information and witnesses to justify a higher award than the one calculated by the Office of the Special Master.

Track B had one step. The Special Master acknowledged the importance of individual circumstances and allowed claimants to present their case in prescheduled hearings.[8] The claim was presented at a hearing after which the Office of the Special Master calculated the award. The applicant had to submit all information before the hearing was held and could offer witnesses, like an economic expert, to testify at the hearing.[9] Hearing officers were appointed by Feinberg to assist him in handling numerous hearings, and they oftentimes listened to emotional testimony from victims' family members as well as testimony from experts, such as forensic economists.

In a news conference on December 20, 2001, the Special Master explained that his office would follow three steps for determining the amount of the monetary awards for each claim:

1. Compute the economic loss, "the lost income, looking forward, as a result of the death or the serious injury."
2. Compute the "non-economic loss – pain and suffering, emotional distress, loss of consortium – listed in the statute."
3. Deduct "collateral offsets … such as life insurance" to derive the final amount of the award to be paid to the claimant.

Regarding non-economic loss, the VCF did not make distinctions among claimants on the basis of pain and suffering, consortium and emotional distress. The only variation in non-economic loss was the number of dependents. The award for non-economic loss was fixed at $250,000 per family in death cases, plus an additional amount of $100,000 for each dependent. Unlike civil litigation where "pain and suffering" types of claims cause substantial variation from case to case, the VCF rule on non-economic loss served the cause of horizontal equity in limiting the variation of award totals based on non-economic elements.[10]

As for the economic loss component, the following steps were followed in death claims:

1. Establish the victim's age and compensable income by considering the past three years of income data.
2. Determine after-tax compensable income by applying an average effective combined federal, state, and local income tax rate for the victim's income bracket.
3. Add the value of employer-provided benefits.
4. Determine a measure of the victim's worklife expectancy.

5. Use an earnings growth rate and calculate projected compensable income and benefits through the victim's expected work-life.
6. Adjust future earnings for the probability of unemployment.
7. Adjust future earnings for the victim's personal consumption.
8. Calculate the present value of projected compensable income and benefits using an appropriate discount factor.[11]

At least two aspects of this procedure must be noted. The first is that income taxes were to be subtracted from estimated earnings. As readers have learned (see Chap. 7 of this volume), very few state courts permit the subtraction of income taxes in determining economic loss, whereas federal courts do require their subtraction in federal employment liability, Jones Act, and federal tort claims. From a purely economic perspective, and barring other considerations, making whole a plaintiff, or claimants on behalf of a deceased family member, would require income tax subtraction inasmuch as, while living, the person would have been liable for such taxes. Thus, given that the VCF was a federal government program, federal rules were applied with respect to the calculation of economic damages.

The second aspect is something we have already mentioned, namely, that there was no direct provision for inclusion of lost services. However, the Special Master permitted such calculations (and testimony) at the discretion of each applicant to the Fund. From all appearances, claimants who chose to use Track A (i.e., filing paperwork to receive the listed award shown on the VCF tables) relinquished, willingly or otherwise, any potential claims for lost services. The authors were told by attorneys that some of their clients wanted to "put the tragedy behind them" by expediting the claim via Track A, without a hearing.

A complication arose in the process early in 2002 when attorneys in New Jersey, representing victims who had resided in the state, began discussing their cases with co-author Tinari. It had been customary in death cases in New Jersey for economists to include calculations for the loss of various services including companionship services, and advice and counsel services. (These are explained in detail in Chap. 10 of this volume.) However, such loss claims are not allowed under New York court rules. It was reported that New York attorneys argued to Feinberg that this was putting their client claimants at a disadvantage vis-à-vis comparable claimants residing in New Jersey. As a result, Feinberg permitted claims for calculations of the value of the two services for all claimants. Inasmuch as the vast majority of victims resided in the two states, the decision by Feinberg evened the playing field for most applicants. The authors do not know if forensic economists included these specific losses for claimants residing in other states.

Harking back to the overall guidelines issued by the Special Master, we note that the face value of life insurance policies was treated as a collateral offset to the calculated awards. Since this type of offset is not permitted in either state or federal tort claims, many attorneys objected to its inclusion. But, the Special Master did not change the regulations despite the complaints. The decision very likely reflects Feinberg's desire to strive for vertical equity, i.e., to reduce the awards to high-earning individuals by the larger life insurance coverage they most likely had, either through their employers or individually. In standard torts, the argument against including life insurance proceeds is that doing so would serve as a disincentive to individuals deciding to obtain life insurance or not. However, for the VCF, which was an unusual and one-time program, no such disincentive was created.

Finally, the VCF was established to replace standard tort litigation. As such, attorneys' contingency fees that can represent 20–35 % of civil awards were substantially reduced or eliminated for claimants to the Fund. Because of the unexpected and tragic results of the terrorist attacks, trial attorneys worked *pro bono* or at substantially reduced fees (10 % comes to mind) on VCF claims. Thus, claimants retained nearly all of the monies awarded by the Fund. This policy served as an incentive for potential claimants to file an application to the Fund, and likely served to help achieve some vertical equity because those receiving proportionately lower awards were most likely able to keep all of their awarded funds.

A question thus arises: should a VCF-type system be used in other litigation contexts, especially mass torts? We address this question in the next section.

18.4   THE VIABILITY OF A VCF SYSTEM FOR OTHER MASS TORTS

By mass torts, we refer to not only natural or man-made disasters, but industrial harm such as asbestosis claims. While we do not pretend to provide a thorough-going analysis of mass torts here, it is instructive to consider the differences and similarities among possible claims.

Civil litigation often takes years, with awards varying greatly from one claimant to another, particularly where the incomes of the victims vary. Indeed, under the tort system, while some claimants receive extremely large awards, many others walk away empty-handed due to the requirement that plaintiffs prove fault. In contrast, the Fund was a no-fault alternative to civil litigation designed to provide compensation in a matter of months.

The United States likely has the most costly tort resolution system in the world. Contributing to those high costs are plaintiff contingency fee contracts, protracted court costs over often long periods of time, high defense costs, and costs of various experts used to establish liability and damages. Such costs can be a bar to seeking to recover compensation for damages or coercion to settle otherwise weak cases. The achievement of either vertical or horizontal equity in verdicts and awards is adversely affected by such high transaction costs and by the facts that state laws can differ greatly in rules defining and determining damages, including treatments of collateral sources, taxes, and caps on non-economic damages. Such high transaction costs and variations in US tort laws have resulted in frequent attempts to improve the system through tort reform. As discussed in this book's Chap. 19 on the topic of determining economic damages in an international setting, tort reform advocates in the USA have proposed:

1. Elimination of the jury system
2. Enforcement of a loser-pays-all legal fees system
3. Elimination of plaintiff's contingency fee arrangements
4. Imposition of caps on nonpecuniary damages
5. Curtailment of "expert" testimony through judicial screening and scheduled damages
6. Admission of collateral income/payment sources for plaintiffs

Others have urged the adoption of a system of administrative-driven damages for personal injury torts, much like Workers Compensation or Social Security or the use of actuarial formulas, such as the Ogden Tables used in Great Britain.[12] The VCF format has some of the features of the British system.

The use of "Schedules of Damages" systems, often coupled with periodic payments, has been proposed for the awarding of damages in large class cases such as asbestosis, lead poisoning, or the Vioxx litigation. The VCF model has been offered as a potential model for such compensation schemes. Robert Minnehan has provided a description of a variety of "Schedule of Damages" compensation plans used in such cases as the Barcelona bombing compensation plan and compares those plans to the VCF mechanism.[13] The major difference between the various EU tort compensation plans and the U.S. tort system is the fact that state law generally controls damages and there are 50 individual states compared to one State system. Also, the VCF plan's successes rested on attorneys largely waiving fees, the waiving of rules on a number of collateral sources of compensation, and the reduction of awards for taxes, which is generally absent in state tort laws.

So, while the VCF was a success by most standards, its application to general personal injury/death torts or special class actions will likely be very limited.

18.5   A Note on the 2013 Boston Marathon Bombings

After the terrorist bombings during the 2013 Boston Marathon, neither Massachusetts nor the federal government created a special victim compensation fund for those affected. Because the attacks were apparently carried out by two lone individuals, regular tort litigation would not have been feasible. This made the situation critically different from the 9/11 attacks in which airlines and other parties potentially could be sued as responsible parties to the harm done.

However, there were two sources of aid that were created and/ or activated soon after the bombings: the One Fund, and the state Victims of Crime Compensation Fund (VCCF), administered through the Massachusetts Attorney General's Office (AGO). "Hours after the attack, Boston's Mayor Menino and State Governor Patrick decided to establish the One Fund, a charity to which donations could be made to help those affected by the bombings. The One Fund was established as a separate s. 501(c)(3) organization ..." (Hunter 2015). In addition, the state VCCF was activated to provide financial assistance to eligible victims of violent crime, including those who were affected by the marathon bombings, to cover costs such as medical care, mental health counseling, and lost wages, up to $50,000 for those suffering from "catastrophic injuries."

In retrospect, the majority of financial assistance came from the One Fund.[14] Without it, the severely impaired could have faced significant financial hardship had their only support come from the VCCF. Table 18.1 summarizes the One Fund distributions that occurred over two fund distribution rounds.

Table 18.1   One fund distributions: summary of first and second rounds

Amount	Recipient
$2,195,000	Each of the four families of those killed in the blasts, for the two individuals who lost multiple limbs, plus
$100,000	For "loss of life" for each of the four families of those killed
$1,195,000	Each of the 14 people who lost a single limb
$125,000	Injured persons, depending on the length of their hospital stay, plus to $948,300
$150,000	35 awards to each amputee and to those who may become amputees in the future to $1,095,000
$8,000	Those treated as an emergency outpatient, plus
$75,000	Each of 6 persons whose extremity injury resulted in 12 or more nights in the hospital
$25,000	Each of 37 individuals whose injury resulted in 1–11 nights in hospital
$12,500	Each of 125 persons who experienced outpatient treatment (including 10 people who had not received any money in the first distribution)

Source: Hunter (2015)

It is evident that even when litigation is not a possibility, various public and private groups can step in to assist victims of violent actions. Other similar terrorist acts, such as the one that occurred in San Bernardino, California, in December 2015, will likely generate comparable outpouring of support even in the absence of a federal-type compensation fund.

18.6   REACTIVATION OF THE VCF

On January 2, 2011, President Obama signed the James Zadroga 9/11 Health and Compensation Act of 2010 (P.L. 111–347). On December 18, 2015, a bill reauthorizing the act included Title II that reactivated through the year 2090 the September 11th Victim Compensation Fund of 2001 to compensate individuals (or survivors of deceased individuals) harmed or killed as first responders to the 9/11 attacks. In addition to first responders, other eligible recipients include financial district workers and residents, students, and tourists near the World Trade Center when the airliners struck. The Special Master appointed to manage the task is attorney Sheila Birnbaum (September 11th Victim Compensation Fund 2015).

Although the rules and guidelines are similar to the original VCF, restrictions were enacted that placed a maximum on the amount that could be paid to attorneys, experts, and for other expenses. In order to receive payment, a person must have been present at one of the three attack sites, and the application must provide evidence that the attack killed, sickened, or injured the applicant. By the end of 2015, 9131 applicants had received a total of $1.815 billion, with the highest award being $4.1 million, and having a mean amount of $199,658 (see September 11th Victim Compensation Fund 2016, p. 6, Table 5a). Of the total amount distributed, 7730 first responders from New York received a total of $1.6 billion (September 11th Victim Compensation Fund 2016, p. 6, Table 5b).

So, the VCF was continued and the potential application of the VCF continues as well.

18.7 Concluding Observations

Was the original VCF a success? Did it meet the objectives set for the plan at its inception? Most believe it did. Certainly the Act saved the airline industry. As to Special Master Feinberg's stated goals regarding victim compensation, the horizontal equity goal of treating equals equally was, for the most part, achieved. However, as explained in Tinari et al. (2006), applicants who used Track B hearings tended to receive more than the VCF tables listed as appropriate awards. But, given that the majority of applicants used Track A, and that additional individuals such as first responders have been included in the extension of the original VCF, it may be concluded that the VCF process by and large attained horizontal equity in assessing award amounts.

The second goal of quickly granting awards also appears to have been achieved, given the alternative of a potentially lengthy process involved in standard tort litigation. The Special Master made determinations on 7,403 claims and completed the work by the statutory deadline in June 2004.[15] The third goal, that of minimizing award disparities, is arguably the most controversial. Stockbrokers with high incomes did receive substantially higher awards than moderate-income claimants. Standardizing the Fund awards for non-economic losses did serve somewhat to reduce award disparities. However, a number of families continued to object that the families of fire department and police department "heroes" received much lower awards than a number of highly paid employees in the twin towers. This was a dilemma that was not, and could not be, resolved by Feinberg, and may be the reason that, upon completion of his assignment, he recommended giving all claimants the same award amount.

The Families of 9/11, an organization representing the victims, prepared a final report outlining their experience with the VCF, a portion of which is attached as the Appendix. It contains results of a 2004 Rand survey of awardees as well as a breakdown of award recipients. The group's report urges Congress to think pro-actively about designing standing legislation that would "ensure that victims of future terrorist attacks and their families are made whole" (Goodrich and Roger 2004, Executive Summary, p. iii). But the report also indicated that many of the goals of the Fund were, in fact, achieved.

NOTES

1. The Act did not prevent litigation against other parties such as foreign countries and terrorist organizations including Iran, Saudi Arabia, and al Qaeda. Indeed, as of mid-2016, class action and individual litigation has continued in New York's U.S. District Court involving several thousand individuals and multiple law firms.
2. This chapter relies a good deal on Tinari et al. (2006). That paper examines how economists' calculations affected the Special Master's final award decisions.
3. Rodgers and Weinstein (2014), pp. 176–77.
4. Ibid.
5. In the spring of 2002, the NAFE Board discussed certain disparaging comments about NAFE posted by a Joseph Scarbrough on the VCF website. A letter was sent to him, and a copy was published in the August 2002 NAFE Member News (Rodgers and Weinstein 2014, p. 177).
6. Co-author Ward was publicly thanked by pro-bono attorneys "for his critical assessment of the methodologies and assumptions imbedded in the presumed economic loss awards and his efforts, many successful, to effect changes" (Goodrich and Roger 2014). Co-author Tinari received a recognition award for his work with Trial Lawyers' Care on the 9/11 Victim Compensation Fund (Trial Lawyers for Public Justice 2004).
7. Detailed analysis of the valuation of services is presented in Chap. 10 of this volume.
8. Co-author Tinari worked on over 150 VCF cases, including more than 50 that were processed through special hearings. The Special Master scheduled thousands of such hearings. One day on which Tinari was scheduled to testify at three hearings, he learned that the Special Master had begun hearings at 7:30 am, and had them scheduled each half hour for the entire day.
9. About 53 % of claimants for deceased victims and 11 % of physical injury victims chose Track B.

10. While unusual, this rule is not without precedent in civil courts. Several states have legislated caps or limits on the non-economic losses that could be claimed, especially in medical malpractice tort cases.

11. Readers will recognize the importance of each of these components in analyzing pecuniary losses as explained in the chapters of this volume.

12. See Ward and Thornton (2009) for a discussion of such alternatives to U.S. torts used in E.U. countries.

13. The Minnehan paper is found in Ward and Thornton (2009), pp. 291–309.

14. Kenneth Feinberg, the federal 9/11 VCF Special Master, was asked for assistance in determining how the One Fund donations should be distributed.

15. Goodrich and Roger (2004), Executive Summary, p. ii.

Appendix

The Report of the Families: The Introduction

FOS11 Report: Executive Summary
September 11th Victim Compensation Fund of 2001
pp. i–iii
Prepared by Donald W. Goodrich, Esq. Thomas Rogér

In many respects, the Fund was a success. Much of this success was due to the efforts of the Special Master and his staff in meeting with individual family members, demonstrating flexibility where possible in making determinations of awards, and expressing compassion for family members in the process. But, the Special Master's view, expressed in the introduction to his Final Report, that "the Fund was an unqualified success" is not shared by many who participated in the Fund and most of those who did not. The options available to the victims and families of September 11 were substantially impaired by the Victim Compensation Act and subsequent legislation. Lawsuits were confined to a narrow population of potentially responsible parties whose liability exposure was limited to available and inadequate insurance (e.g., the airlines). Evidence for use in litigation was sure to be (has been) compromised by government intervention (e.g., assertions of national security and criminal prosecution grounds for non-disclosure). Families were, thus, faced with a Hobson's choice and for most the Fund was the better one.

In December 2004, Families of September 11 conducted a Web-based survey of its members consisting of 14 questions and an opportunity to make narrative comments designed to elicit information that might be helpful in assessing whether there should be a compensation mechanism in place before another terrorist attack occurs. One hundred forty four (144) members responded. Though not designed to conform with scientifically reliable protocols, the results are of interest and are included in our Report. Much of the Special Master's report is devoted to efforts made by him and his staff to assure that families could obtain detailed information about their likely recovery from the Fund and assist families in the process. Although our Report applauds him for these efforts, it points out that had there been pre-existing comprehensive legislation in place, the Special Master's extraordinary efforts to educate potential participants about and assist them with the Fund would not have been necessary and the enormous anxiety created by the uncertainties surrounding the Fund would have been avoided. The regulations Congress passed [as] the September 11th Victim Compensation Fund of 2001 [occurred] within a fortnight of the most catastrophic terrorist attack of modern times. Since then the executive branch, acting through the Attorney General and his designee, the Special Master, issued implementing regulations and additional guidelines, and made determinations on 7,403 claims completing its work by the statutory deadline in June 2004. Congress now has the benefit of more than 11,000 comments made to the Justice Department during the rule making process; the comments of the Special Master; the opinions of lawyers, economists, academics, the mental health community, victims and survivors of the attacks; and the developing history of terrorism and its effects on our society. Families of September 11 is submitting our Final Report to encourage Congress and the Administration to:

1. use the perspectives of time and experience in implementation of the Victim Compensation Fund to consider carefully issues it was forced to address hastily in the immediate aftermath of the terrorist attacks of September 11, 2001;
2. assess how well the rules adopted in 2002 to implement the legislation met Congressional intent;
3. consider the incentives and disincentives to reducing the risks of terrorist attacks implicit in the legislation; and
4. fashion legislation that will reduce those risks and ensure that victims of future terrorist attacks and their families are made whole.

REFERENCES

Expectancy Data. (various). *The dollar value of a day*. Shawnee Mission, Kansas: Expectancy Data.

Goodrich, D. W., & Roger, T. (2004). *Final report of families of September 11 on the September 11th Victim Compensation Fund of 2001*. Privately-published. http://www.familiesofseptember11.org/docs/FOS11_VCF_FINAL_REPORT.pdf

Hunter, J. (2015, February 3). *Blood on the streets of Boston: Medical care and financial support*. Action on Armed Violence (AOAV) report. https://aoav.org.uk/2015/blood-on-the-streets-of-boston-medical-care-and-financial-support/

Rodgers, J. D., & Weinstein, M. A. (2014, December). An updated history of the National Association of Forensic Economics: 2002–2014. *Journal of Forensic Economics, 25*(2), 175–202.

September 11th Victim Compensation Fund. (2015). https://www.vcf.gov

September 11th Victim Compensation Fund. (2016, February). *Fourth annual status report*. S. L. Birnbaum, Special Master. http://www.vcf.gov/pdf/VCFStatusReportFeb2016.pdf

Tinari, F. D., Cahill, K. E., & Grivoyannis, E. (2006, January). Did the 9/11 Victim Compensation Fund accurately assess economic losses? *Topics in Economic Analysis and Policy, 6*(1), 1–42.

Trial Lawyers for Public Justice. (2004). *Trial lawyers doing public justice 2004*. Privately-published.

Ward, J. O., & Thornton, R. (Eds.) (2009). *Personal injury and wrongful death damages calculations: Transatlantic dialogue*. London: Emerald Books.

CHAPTER 19

Differences Among Nations in Measuring Economic Damages

John O. Ward

19.1 Introduction

In 2003, the National Association of Forensic Economics (NAFE) initiated an annual international meeting for the purposes of expanding members' knowledge of the differences among nations in measuring and awarding economic damages in torts, and introducing European economists to the work of NAFE. Participants in those meetings have included attorneys and law school faculty from six European Union (EU) members, the head of the Irish High Court, economics and actuarial faculty from Ireland, England, Italy and Hungary and members from NAFE from the United States. In 2009, the results of the first five of these meetings were published by Emerald Books (London) in a book titled *Personal Injury and Wrongful Death Damages Calculations: Transatlantic Dialogue* edited by John O. Ward and Robert Thornton. Chapters in that book, written by EU and US authors, outlined many of the commonalities and differences in tort actions between the US and EU nations, and described the methodologies, rules and procedures used in those nations in calculating and awarding damages in personal injury and death actions. European participants in the NAFE international programs

J.O. Ward (✉)
John Ward Economics, USA

© The Author(s) 2016
F.D. Tinari (ed.), *Forensic Economics*,
DOI 10.1057/978-1-137-56392-7_19

have also participated in NAFE national meetings over the years, sharing their research on the measurement of damages in torts in the EU with forensic economists in the USA.

In practical terms the need to understand the differences among nations in measuring economic damages arises from three situations that a forensic economist (FE) may encounter in his or her practice. First, as FEs, we may become involved in cases that are tried in the USA. involving the injury or death of a foreign national that occurred in the USA. Such cases would typically be tried in a state or federal court using specific state laws as the foundation for calculating damages consisting of wages, wage growth, costs, interest rates and actuarial data specific to the plaintiff's or decedent's residence.

Locating such information can be time consuming, and converting it to a form useful in a damages model can be difficult. Wage and employment data sources are easily accessible in the USA. but the same is not true in many other nations. Occasionally, a case may be tried in the USA. using elements of law drawn from the plaintiff's home nation. Recently this author worked on a case involving a Norwegian national injured in Missouri in which it was agreed that Norwegian law of damages would apply to the calculation of damages. This involved incorporating collateral sources of income and national health care support in Norway as offsets against loss. Given the fact that Norway has a free National Health Care system, future life care costs were significantly reduced. Unlike in the USA, such collateral sources of payment are commonly considered in torts in the EU.

Second, an FE may be retained in a case where a US national is injured or dies in a foreign nation and that nation's rules for recovery of damages may apply in that country's courts, with actuarial data drawn from the USA. In such cases the FE may be asked to provide support to an actuary, economist or attorney in that nation. If the plaintiff or decedent was a visitor to the foreign country, economic damages may consist of earnings capacity in the USA, with fringe benefits applicable to that employment. Where the US citizen was a worker in the foreign country, different standards of calculating economic damages may apply. In the next section, we discuss sources of information available to FEs involved in such cases described above, and give literature citations that may be helpful in addressing the issues presented by them.

A third reason for studying the differences among nations in measuring economic damages is to learn how such differences impact tort damage determination and resolution in terms of economic efficiency, predictability and equity. While forensic economics, as an applied discipline, focuses on the measurement of damages in the context of laws, the analysis of the predictability, efficiency and equity of laws is an important extension of our discipline into the field of law and economics. Predictability, it is argued, allows industry to more efficiently allocate resources and produce optimal quantities of products and services. Similarly, legal rules can impact efficiency, the lesson of the "Coase Theorem." Finally, equity is impacted by rules covering the admissibility of collateral sources in calculating damages—the "make whole" and deterrence functions of tort laws.

19.2 Sources of Data for International Damages Claims

In the section above, we outlined three reasons for studying damages recovery in other countries. The first two reasons result from the potential use of foreign data or tort damages rules in calculating a loss report. An FE in the USA might need access to information about economic damages laws in other nations or information about wages, wage growth, cost, inflation, interest rates and other economic data in other nations. One source for such information is Piette and Williams (2009). Ward and Thornton (2007) provide a list of statistical sources of information on wages, costs and benefits in other nations including the following:

- For information on the treatment of foreign nationals in torts see the 2002 New York decision permitting recovery of damages using data specific to wages in the country of origin at: www.insurancejournal.com/news/east/2005/01/06/49283.htm.
- A California brief to bar illegal aliens from recovering future damages based on US earnings is at: www.wlf.org.
- A good review of recent case law, particularly in Texas, on the treatment of damages in wrongful injury and death cases involving illegal immigrants can be found at: www.abrahamwatkins.com/CM/Articles/Alien-Paper.asp.
- For data sources and methodologies appropriate for valuing losses to Canadians see Bruce (1999). Also, for data on wages and employment in Canada see: www.canadianeconomy.gc.ca/english/economy/index.cfm.
- For data sources and methodologies appropriate for valuing losses to Mexicans see: www.inegi.gob.mx/inegi.default.asp, www.geoinves-

tor.com/statistics/mexico/economicdata.htm, and www.banxico. org.mx/sitiongles/polmoneinflacion/estadisticas/cpi/cpi.htm.

- Piette and Williams (2006) describe the availability of data sources for calculating economic losses of foreign nationals.

In recent years, one common example of using such resources is in cases involving Mexican and Central American nationals wrongfully injured or killed in the USA. The calculation of economic damages becomes an issue resting on whether lost earnings capacity, household service losses, benefits or life care costs should be based on the premise that the plaintiff would have lived in the USA or in the country of origin.

The treatment of foreign nationals with no legal immigration status may be significantly different than such nationals with green card status. Some states require calculations to be made based on living conditions in the plaintiff's home country and other states allow calculations to be based on plaintiff's continuing to live in the USA. Another source of such information is the archives of NAFE-L or AAEFE-L on the internet. A simple search on "illegal aliens" or "international wage comparison" provides numerous state citations for data and court rulings.

This author has been retained to make loss calculations based both on US wage data and international data sources. Several years ago, I had a number of Bridgestone tire blowout cases in Mexico. The trials were in Nashville, the home of Bridgestone, and the economic data were drawn for Mexico where the blowouts occurred, involving Mexican nationals. Given the expansion of world markets, such cases will likely expand in the future.

Finally, an important issue faced by FEs in calculating damages for a foreign national with an award to be made in the USA is the appropriate currency exchange rate to use in converting estimates of wages, services and health care costs to US dollars to be awarded. Using the official exchange rate can create biases. International exchange rates may not reflect true living costs in another country. The preferred method is to use purchasing-power parity exchange rates. Adjusting exchange rates for purchasing power parity is complex and is discussed by Weisskoff (1998) and Salazar-Carrillo (1998).

19.3   ISSUES OF EFFICIENCY, PREDICTABILITY AND EQUITY

The third reason given for the study of tort systems in other nations is to learn something about the strengths and weaknesses of the US tort system. As evidenced by the *Journal of Forensic Economics* (JFE) State series, in the USA there are numerous differences in measuring damages among the states as well as various types of legal actions (FELA, Federal Tort Claims Act, etc.). Tort reform advocates suggest that these differences create excessive unpredictability in the tort system. It is also argued that such differences in tort rules between states promote inequity as measured by a lack of uniformity of awards between states. Also, plaintiffs generally have the right to a jury trial (unless trial by judge is selected) and typically, each side of the litigation is represented by legal counsel. Such contests carry high transaction costs in legal fees and court costs, and damages awarded and the resolution process can be lengthy.

Critics of the ligation tort system frequently point to the Workers Compensation system in which an administrative judge allocates awards, as a preferable model for resolving torts. Proponents of tort reform in the USA frequently point to specific features of tort rules of Western European countries in terms of enhanced efficiency, predictability and equity to support their positions on proposals that include:

- Elimination of the jury system
- Enforcement of a loser-pays-all legal fees system
- Elimination of plaintiff's contingency fee arrangements
- Imposing of caps on nonpecuniary damages
- The curtailing of "expert" testimony through judicial screening and scheduled damages
- Admission of collateral income/payment sources for plaintiffs

Such proposals, of course, may run counter to the common law principles of making the person whole and placing full cost of the injury on the defendant. In the USA and the EU, the objective of damages awards in personal injury and death litigation is to make the plaintiff "whole," that is, to restore the plaintiff to the position her or she would have enjoyed but for the tort. However, in the USA additional objectives of damages awards may be deterrence and the assignment of all damages to the defendant. Punitive damages for deterrence are not uncommon in such torts in the USA.

Curtailing expert testimony on damages may come at the expense of greater exactness in measuring such damages by downplaying or ignoring circumstances unique to the plaintiff. In addition, taking into account offsets of loss for collateral income from Social Security or payments from Medicare or Medicaid would certainly shift damages from a defendant to society unless subrogated. For torts in which damages have been awarded and past Workers Compensation awards have been made, awards might be subrogated by the Workers Compensation Board. So, allowing a jury to consider Workers Compensation awards as a source of income to reduce the loss could result in an under-compensation if such awards were then reduced by Workers Compensation subrogation.

The barring of contingency payments to plaintiff's attorneys might mean that deserving claims would never be litigated. Similarly, "loser pays all" rules would sufficiently increase the "cost" of losing that only a well-funded plaintiff could risk litigation. Caps on general damages would distort the "make whole" principle; such caps already exist in many states. Some of those state-imposed limits on general damages have been declared unconstitutional but they remain prevalent among the states, especially for medical malpractice torts.

Most of the tort reform proposals noted above are already features of torts in the EU. Tort reform advocates in the USA suggest that their adoption would substantially reduce the transaction costs of providing compensation to deserving plaintiffs, improve the efficiency of the tort system, and provide manufacturers and service providers greater predictability and "fairness" or equity in potential tort damages in the USA (Ward 2009). One example of such a comparison of the USA with other western tort systems is provided by Bernstein (1996). He begins by stating:

> By all reasonable measures, the American tort system is a disaster. It resembles a wealth-redistribution lottery more than an efficient system designed to compensate those injured by the wrongful actions of others. Modern product liability litigation is particularly problematic. As has been well documented elsewhere, product liability lawsuits have made a few plaintiffs' attorneys and their clients rich. (p. 1)

Bernstein summarizes his position on tort reform by stating:

Perhaps the most radical and important measure that legislatures can take to eliminate the pernicious States effects of civil juries is to remove the issue of damages from the jury and put it in the hands of judges. Judges are repeat players with a stake in the coherence of the system, and have some idea of what the going rate for certain injuries is. (p. 3)

19.4 Jury Trials, Contingency Fees and Collateral Sources

Trial by jury was a central feature of tort law in common law nations until the 1960s. Civil law nations do not allow trials in torts. The UK and Wales basically eliminated trial by jury for civil actions in the late 1960s, and Ireland and Northern Ireland eliminated trial by jury in torts in 1988. Outside of the USA, only Scotland and Canada (in most provinces) continue to allow jury trial for torts (most common law countries allow jury trial for criminal cases). In the rest of the EU, civil (Napoleonic) law prevails and torts are heard before a judge or judges. In the USA trial by jury in torts remains an option in virtually all jurisdictions. However, mediation and arbitration have reduced the number of trials elected in favor of settlement. Some countries have replaced trial by judge with judgment by a panel where attorneys are not present. Ireland has such a system (not mandatory) and New Zealand has had such a system since 1974.

Since the passage of the New Zealand Accident Compensation Act in 1974 it has been virtually impossible to bring a tort action to the courts. The Accident Compensation Commission (ACC) operates much like a Workers Compensation system in a no-fault support system for personal injury/death actions. Firms and individuals pay insurance premiums into the system to fund distributions. In his 20-year review (1974–1994) of the operation of the ACC, Sir Geoffrey Palmer concluded that, in general, the system provided better compensation to the majority of claimants than the tort system it replaced. Moreover, the transaction costs of the system were far less than the prior system of tort advocacy (Palmer 1994).

In Ireland, the Personal Injury Assessment Board was established in 2004. According to Shane Whelan, the Board was established to provide a quicker and less expensive alternative to the assessment of compensation for personal injuries arising either in the workplace, as a result of a motor accident, or due to a public liability accident. Claimants are required to first take their case to the Injuries Board, which applies a document-based system (rather than the court's adversarial system) to arrive at an assessment of fair compensation. The principles on which compensation for future loss are computed are the same as those on which the courts operate and, if necessary, an actuarial report will be commissioned. Claimants or defendants are, of course, not obliged to accept the assessment of the Board, being free to appeal their case to the courts, but in practice the award recommended by the Board is accepted in the majority of cases (Whelan 2009).

A Manhattan Institute study argues that the US system relies too heavily on litigation to compensate injured parties (Presser 2002). In the EU, compensation for injured parties incorporates both social welfare programs and awards from the litigation process, and greater concern is given to a consistent regulation of the safety of products and services. Presser states that:

> Even though the European Community recently altered its tort doctrines from a pure fault-based system to strict products liability, there are features of the European legal system that lessen the effects of even strict liability. Consequently, European courts are much less likely to hand out unpredictable and disproportionate damage judgments—unlike American courts, where ruinous States verdicts are a potential in too many laws, Europe has escaped an American style litigation explosion by erecting barriers to excessive litigation. Such barriers include
>
> * Absence of contingent fees
> * Loser pays winner's attorney fees
> * Discouragement of massive discovery filings
> * Lower damage judgments
> * Absence of punitive damages
> * Non-use of juries in civil cases
> * Lower expectations of damages
>
> Unless similar barriers to excessive litigation are created in the United States, American companies face an ongoing competitive disadvantage relative to European manufacturers who operate in a more predictable, less costly, and less litigious States legal environment.

The opinions of Stephen Presser and David Bernstein are shared by a substantial number of policymakers in the USA. The accuracy of their opinions is greatly contested, but the process of tort reform in the USA will likely continue, with or without evidence of need. While the elimination of the jury system in civil cases is unlikely in the near future, alternative dispute resolution methods are effectively replacing jury trial in a growing number of personal injury and death cases. Other adoptions of Western European civil tort procedures and rules will likely occur. Punitive damages caps, the admissibility of collateral source payments to plaintiffs as offsets against economic damages, limits on class action suits, and/or lowered expectations of damages through caps on noneconomic damages, such as pain and suffering, have been adopted in a growing number of states. To the degree that FEs in the USA are part of the tort system, we have a professional and vested interest in the future direction of tort reform.

19.5 SCHEDULED DAMAGES AND MULTIPLIERS IN LIEU OF AN EXPERT WITNESS

One aspect of damages determination in European torts of direct importance to forensic economists has been the replacement of expert-driven damages calculations with systems of scheduled damages using multipliers and schedules (Ward and Thornton 2009). Matthias Kelly, a former Chair of the Council of Barristers in the UK and a leading proponent of the Ogden Tables of scheduled damages in the UK, provides a detailed history of the evolution of the scheduled damages system in the UK (Kelly 2009). It is common for judges in EU countries to rely on scheduled damages in making awards and some in the USA have suggested that a similar system would promote equity, uniformity and predictability of awards in the USA Rather than having a jury consider evidence of pecuniary losses of earnings, benefits, and services provided by an economic, financial, or actuarial expert (loosely designated as "forensic economists"), the judge in the US court would direct a loss award on the basis of statutory damages schedules and multipliers that would be consistent across similar cases.

Such systems already exist in awarding compensation in Workers Compensation actions, Social Security disability hearings, Veterans Administration disability compensation hearings, and some class action torts. Among the suggested benefits of such a system would be simplicity and uniformity of awards, predictability of awards, diminished potential for unreasonable jury awards, and lower litigation costs by reducing or eliminating the use of competing expert witnesses in the damages calculation. The 9/11 VCF Fund (described in Chap. 18 of this book) was a successful alternative to traditional torts in resolving a large number of torts at minimal transaction costs.

The Ogden tables used in the UK are one example of a system of scheduled damages. In the UK, actuaries, economists, barristers, and legislatures have successfully adopted the use of actuarially based damages multipliers in the courts through legislation and the precedent of *Wells v. Wells* in 1999. The methodologies underlying those multipliers are similar to the methodologies used by damages experts in the 50 state jurisdictions in the USA. The Ogden tables consist of actuarially derived numbers that, when multiplied by the base earnings of the individual at time of death or injury, given the individual's age and gender, yield a present value of loss. This number can then be adjusted by the judge for industry- and case-specific factors. This process is a simplified version of what an FE might do in calculating lost earnings capacity in the USA, but the process of applying the methodologies in the courts is much different.

In the UK there is effectively one court system rather than the federal and 50 state tort systems of the USA. In the UK one set of multipliers (and qualifiers) is directly available to judges as a starting point for calculating damages, while in the USA a presentation of economic damages by a forensic economist is unique to each personal injury or death case, and is also unique to each jurisdiction. In the UK the House of Lords mandates a net discount rate (currently at 2 %) for the use of multipliers, although judges have some flexibility in using those rates.

The Ogden Tables are the subject of considerable debate by actuaries and economists in the UK. Matthias Kelly, Richard Lewis, Victoria Wass, Robert McNabb, Zoltan Butt, Steven Haberman, Richard Verrall and Richard Cropper have provided a concise history of the evolution of the Ogden Multipliers and specific criticisms of the multipliers. (See their chapters in Ward and Thornton 2009.) Lewis, McNabb and Wass (2002) are advocates of adopting a damages model similar to that used in the USA Criticisms boil down to the question of whether the simplicity offered by the tables is at the cost of fairness of an award. Robert Minnehan (2009) provides an overview of the uses of schedules for both general damages and economic damages used in EU countries and for specific situations in the USA. In the USA, the Victim Compensation Fund, created after the September 11, 2001, World Trade Center/Pentagon attacks, was an attempt to provide a uniform set of formulas to calculate both economic and general damages (see Chap. 18 in this volume). A similar effort was made in adjudicating Vioxx claims.

The methods used in resolving tort claims in other countries may inevitably impact methods used in resolving torts in the USA as tort reform in the USA progresses. The roles of FEs in US courts may be impacted by an adoption of EU-type multiplier systems. Knowing the strengths and weaknesses of such systems becomes important as we respond to potential reform proposals.

19.6   Conclusion

Most nations provide for recovery of wrongful personal injury and death damages on a fault basis with many using a strict liability standard. Methodologies used in calculating such damages, both economic and general, have a number of common features with the objective of making whole the injured person or survivors. Economic damage awards are based on actuarial calculations, but typically rely on predetermined multipliers rather than expert testimony as in the USA. Some EU nations (Denmark, Iceland and Norway) rely on state health care systems to compensate for past and future health care costs with no recovery from defendants, and some (the UK, Germany and the Netherlands) rely on national health care to pay for medical costs, but then recover such costs from the defendant. Some nations (New Zealand) have moved to no-fault damages panels based on insurance payments (taxes) paid by industries, individuals and institutions.

The most significant differences among nations in awarding damages in torts are differences of structure and rules. The absence of jury trials, contingency fees by attorneys, and punitive damages are the rule in the EU and most other nations. The supposed efficiency, equity and predictability resulting from EU tort rules and structures are often used to promote tort reform proposals in the USA. Interestingly, in the UK, economists such as Richard Lewis, Robert McNabb and Victoria Wass (2002) have urged the adoption of methodologies used by FEs in the USA. to enhance the fairness of damages awards in the UK.

Inevitably, a US FE will encounter a case with an international component. Most commonly such cases involve Mexican and Central American nationals injured in the USA. Finding appropriate wage, employment and cost data and interest rates for the foreign country of origin for the plaintiff can be time consuming. Hopefully, the sources of such information contained in this paper will be useful.

REFERENCES

Bernstein, D. (1996). Procedural tort reform: Lessons from other nations. *Regulation, 19*(1), 1–14.

Brookshire, M., Slesnick, F., & Ward, J. (Eds.). (2007). *The plaintiff and defense Attorney's guide to understanding economic damages.* Tucson: Lawyers and Judges Publishing Co.

Bruce, C. (1999). *Assessment of personal injury damages.* Toronto: Butterworths.

Butt, Z., Haberman, S., Verrall, R., & Wass, V. (2009). Estimating and using work life expectancy in the United Kingdom. In Ward & Thornton, pp. 35–72.

Kelly, M. (2009). The development of an actuarial approach to the calculation of future loss in the UK. In Ward & Thornton, pp. 11–34.

Lewis, R., McNabb, R., & Wass, V. (2002). Methods of calculating damages for loss of future earnings. *Journal of Personal Injury Law, 2,* 151–165.

Minnehan, R. (2009). Examples of schedules of damages used in Europe and the United States. In Ward & Thornton, pp. 291–308.

Palmer, G. (1994). New Zealand's accident compensation scheme: Twenty years on. *University of Toronto Law Journal, 44,* 1–52.

Piette, M. J., & Williams, D. R. (2006). A guide to international data sources. *Journal of Forensic Economics, 19*(2), 207–215.

Piette, M. J., & Williams, D. R. (2009). International data and forensic economists: A guide to sources and uses. In Ward &Thornton, pp. 309–320.

Presser, S. (2002, April). *How should the law of products liability be harmonized? What Americans can learn from the Europeans* (Global liability issues, pp. 1–11). New York: Manhattan Institute.

Salazar-Carrillo, J. (1998). The forensic economist in the international setting: A comment. *Journal of Forensic Economics, 11*(1), 55–56.

Ward, J. (2009). Economic damages and tort reform: A comparative analysis of the calculation of economic damages in personal injury and death litigation in the United States and the United Kingdom. In Ward & Thornton.

Ward, J. O., & Thornton, R. J. (2007). International issues in economic damages. In Brookshire, Slesnick & Ward, pp. 175–179.

Ward, J. O., & Thornton, R. J. (Eds.). (2009). *Personal injury and wrongful death damages calculations: Transatlantic dialogue* (Contemporary studies in economics and financial analysis, Vol. 91). London: Emerald Press.

Weisskoff, R. (1998). The forensic economist in the international setting: A reply and new findings. *Journal of Forensic Economics, 11*(1), 57–65.

Whelan, S. (2009). Principles of compensation for injury and death in Ireland. In Ward & Thornton, pp. 233–254.

CASES

Wells v. Wells. (1999). 1 AC 345 at p. 383F (UK).

INDEX

Note: Page numbers followed by 'n' denote notes

© The Author(s) 2016
F.D. Tinari (ed.), *Forensic Economics*,
DOI 10.1057/978-1-137-56392-7

Printed by Printforce, the Netherlands